Studies in Social Policy and Welfare XXVIII

AGEING AND SOCIAL POLICY

A critical assessment

To
Jane and Carol

Studies in Social Policy and Welfare

AGEING AND SOCIAL POLICY

A Critical Assessment

Edited by

Chris Phillipson
and
Alan Walker

Gower

Published by

Gower Publishing Company Limited
Gower House
Croft Road
Aldershot
Hants GU11 3HR
England

Gower Publishing Company
Old Post Road
Brookfield
Vermont 05036
U.S.A.

British Library Cataloguing in Publication Data
Ageing and social policy: a critical
    assessment.——(Studies in social policy
and welfare; 28)
  1. Aged——Care and hygiene
  I. Phillipson, Chris II. Walker, Alan,
  1949– III. Series
  362.6   HV1451

Library of Congress Cataloging-in-Publication Data
  Ageing and social policy.
  (Studies in social policy and welfare = 28)
  Bibliography: p.
  Includes index.
  1. Gerontology. 2. Gerontology – Great
Britain. 3. Social Policy. 4. Great Britain –
social policy.
I. Phillipson, Chris. II. Walker, Alan. III.
Series.
HQ1061.A427   1986   305.2′6   86–14245

ISBN: 0 566 05218 0
      0 566 00902 1 (Pbk)

Printed and bound in Great Britain by
Biddles Ltd, Guildford and King's Lynn

Contents

Tables and Figure

Contributors

Ric Bowl is Lecturer in Social Administration in the Department of Extra-Mural Studies at Birmingham University. He has been engaged in teaching social workers and in research into the personal social services, particularly for old people, for twelve years and continues to be involved with groups campaigning for wider recognition of the needs of old people. His recent publications include *Changing the Nature of Masculinity: A Task for Social Workers?* (1985) and, with others, *Social Work in Context* (1983).

Toni Calasanti is an Instructor in Sociology at the University of Kentucky. She is presently engaged in a study of the structural determinants of retirement satisfaction among women. In addition to co-authoring *The Social Creation of Dependence Among the Elderly*, Ms. Calasanti has published in the area of dual economy and retirement and is continuing her work on the political economy of ageing.

Shirley Dex is Lecturer in Economics at the University of Keele. Her previous posts include Lecturer in Economics at the University of Aston, Birmingham and Tutor in Sociology at Exeter University. She is the author of *The Sexual Division of Work: Conceptual Revolutions in the Social Sciences* (1985) and she has done considerable research on women's work histories in Britain. She is co-author with Lois Shaw of *Do Equal Opportunities Policies Work?: A Comparison of British and American Women* (1985).

Anne-Marie Guillemard is Professor of Sociology at the Centre d'Etude des Mouvements Sociaux in the Centre Nationale de la Recherche Scientifique, Paris and teaches in the Department of Sociology, University of Paris VII. She has researched and written extensively on the subject of old age. Her previous publications include *La Vieillesse et l'Etat* (1980) and *Old Age and the Welfare State* (ed.) (1983). She is president of the International Sociological Association's Research Committee on Ageing.

Jon Hendricks is Professor of Sociology at the University of Kentucky. Co-author of *Ageing in Mass Society*, now in its third edition, he is also the associate editor of *The International Journal of Ageing and Human Development*. In addition, Dr Hendricks serves as the Senior Editor of the Little, Brown and Company series on Gerontology. Together with Toni Calasanti, he has just finished a volume entitled *The Social Creation of Dependence Among the Elderly: A Critical Perspective*.

Beverley Hughes is a Lecturer in the Department of Social Administration at the University of Manchester. After working as a probation officer, she conducted post-graduate research concerned with services for the mentally ill. She subsequently worked with David Wilkin on a study of residential care for the elderly, before taking up her current post. She has published various articles concerned with aspects of health and social services provision for the elderly. Current research interests include an evaluation of a case conference model for families with young children, and the needs of carers looking after old people.

Robin Means is a Research Associate at the School for Advanced Urban Studies, University of Bristol. In 1976 he obtained a PhD from the University of Birmingham for his research on local authority community work. From 1976–79, he was employed as a social worker by Birmingham City Council. Since joining SAUS, he has been involved in a range of research projects including work on services for elderly people, the Youth Training Scheme, and the evaluation of an alcohol education programme. He is author of *Social Work and the 'Undeserving Poor'* (1977), *The Development of Welfare Services for Elderly People* (with Randall Smith, 1985), and *Ethnic Minorities and The Youth Training Scheme* (with Steve Fenton, Tom Davies and Paul Burton, 1985).

Sheila Peace is a Research Fellow and founder member of the Centre for Environmental and Social Studies in Ageing at PNL. A social geographer by discipline, she obtained her PhD (concerning the spatial behaviour of old people within an urban environment) from the University of Wales in 1977; and was then Research Officer at the Polytechnic of North London from 1977 to 1979, working on early studies of the quality of life of the elderly in residential care. She spent a year with the International Federation on Ageing in Washington D.C. as their first British international intern. She returned to PNL in 1981 to work with the National Consumer Study in Local Authority Residential Care. She has written widely on a broad range of gerontological topics.

Chris Phillipson is Lecturer in Social Gerontology in the Department of Adult and Continuing Education, University of Keele. His current research concerns the training of paid carers involved with older people. His publications include *Capitalism and the Construction of Old Age* (1982), *The Impact of Pre-Retirement Education* (with Patricia Strang, 1983), *Older Learners: The Challenge to Adult Education* (ed. with Susanna Johnston, 1983), and *A Manifesto for Old Age* (with Joanna Bornat and Sue Ward, 1985).

Hazel Qureshi is Research Fellow in the Hester Adrian Research Centre, University of Manchester. She previously worked on the Sheffield Family Care of the Elderly Project with Alan Walker. She has also been a Research Associate at the University of Kent, undertaking research on helpers working for the Kent Community Care Project. A number of articles and books have been published or are forthcoming from this research work.

Peter Townsend is Professor of Social Policy at the University of Bristol and former Professor of Sociology at the University of Essex. He is Chair of the Child Poverty Action Group and the Disability Alliance. His books include *The Family Life of Old People* (1957), *The Last Refuge* (1962), *The Aged in the Welfare State* (with Dorothy Wedderburn, 1965), *Sociology and Social Policy* (1965) and *Poverty in the United Kingdom* (1979). He is currently conducting research on inequalities and poverty in London.

Alan Walker is Professor of Social Policy at the University of Sheffield. His publications include *Disability in Britain* (ed. with Peter Townsend, 1981), *Unqualified and Underemployed* (1982), *Community Care* (ed., 1982), *Public Expenditure and Social Policy* (ed., 1982) and *Social Planning* (1984). He has published numerous articles on retirement and old age. He is currently conducting research on the family care of the elderly and evaluating the Elderly Person's Support Units innovation in Sheffield.

Rose Wheeler is a Research Fellow in the Institute for Research in the Social Sciences at the University of York. Formerly a lecturer in Social Policy at Leeds Polytechnic. She has recently completed an evaluation of the 'Staying Put' project which assists older homeowners with repairs or improvements to their homes. As well as having written numerous articles on this subject, she has now completed a book to be published by the Institute of Housing. She is currently engaged in research on the use of home equity in old age, the role of housing advice, and the development of 'Staying Put'. She is a member of Shelter's Policy and Projects, and Research Committees.

David Wilkin is a Senior Research Fellow in the Department of General Practice at the University of Manchester. He is a sociologist who has specialised in research on the provision of health and social services. Previous work includes studies of family caring for a mentally handicapped child, residential care for the elderly and services provided for elderly people referred to health and social services. He is currently working on studies of urban primary health care with particular emphasis on the measurement of outcomes of care.

Dianne Willcocks is a Research Associate and founder member of CESSA, the Centre for Environmental and Social Studies in Ageing, based at the Polytechnic of North London. She began a market research career in 1966 studying aspects of general practice in the context of the pharmaceutical industry. In 1973 she transferred to academic research in social policy issues. She has been at the Polytechnic of North London since 1979. She was responsible for managing the National Consumer Study of Residential Care, and has been involved in the dissemination and implementation of the research findings from this study. She recently completed a survey of Homes in the private sector.

Abbreviations

CSO	Central Statistical Office
DE	Department of Employment
DHSS	Department of Health and Social Security
DOE	Department of the Environment
EOC	Equal Opportunities Commission
ERISA	Employee Retirement Income Security Act (USA)
IRA	Individual Retirement Accounts (USA)
OPCS	Office of Population Censuses and Surveys
NSF	National Solidarity Fund (France)
PRO	Public Records Office
PSI	Policy Studies Institute
SBC	Supplementary Benefits Commission
SERPS	State Earnings Related Pension Scheme
SSAC	Social Security Advisory Committee

Preface

This book represents the meeting-point of two related disciplines: social policy and social gerontology. It also reflects two parallel trends in these disciplines: the recent development of both a critical social policy and a critical social gerontology. We have brought together some of the leading researchers in the field of social gerontology in order to illuminate the relationship between old age and social policy and thereby, it is hoped, promote more informed policy. We hope also that this collection will contribute to the continued cross-fertilisation of the fields of social policy and social gerontology.

Underlying this endeavour is our shared commitment both to challenge the present situation in which old age is too often associated with poverty, deprivation and dependency, and to combat the age segregation, or ageism, that is endemic in Britain and other western societies. The social structures and processes that create dependency and ageism have a deep, sometimes devastating, impact on the individual person's experience of old age but they also diminish the worth of the whole society in which they take place. In the words of Maggie Kuhn – founder and national convenor of the Gray Panthers in the USA, which has a membership of over 60,000:

> Ageism permeates our Western culture and institutions. It infects us, the ageing and the aged, when we reject ourselves and despise our powerlessness, wrinkled skin, and physical limitations. It's revealed when we succumb to apathy and complacent acceptance of the things that society does to diminish us. . . . Our image of ourselves reflects the image society has of us. Our self-image is affected by a society that considers old people superfluous because they are not productive and useful.

We are extremely grateful to Sue Allingham, Christine Bell and Margaret Jaram for their help in preparing the manuscript for publication with great efficiency and goodwill. Special thanks are due to

Jane, Carol, Alison and Christopher for bearing all of the domestic costs that this enterprise entailed.

Chris Phillipson
Alan Walker
October 1985

1 Introduction

Alan Walker and Chris Phillipson

There is a very close connection between old age and social policy. Elderly people have always been one of the primary subject groups of social policy. In most advanced industrial societies insurance provision for pensioners preceded other welfare state measures. Today, elderly people are the main recipients of welfare state resources, with over half of expenditure on social security, health and the personal social services being directed towards them. Current and future generations of pensioners are the main target of the recent expansion in private welfare.

Yet recognition of the primacy of elderly people as recipients and users of welfare benefits and services has occurred only recently. The main focus of attention – in some cases, alarm – has been the rising numbers of elderly, especially very elderly, people and the projections for further increases into the next century. It is only since the recent rapid increase in the numbers of people aged 75 and over that policy-makers, policy analysts and the general public have started to examine the link between elderly people and the welfare state. But demographic trends are only one among many secondary influences on the level of social spending. The major determinant is ideology, and it is the irresistible combination of increases in the demand for benefits and services, caused mainly by demographic changes, and ideological opposition to increasing expenditure on the welfare state that lies behind the current cost-effectiveness imperative which dominates public policy. This has produced cuts in public expenditure, a search for greater efficiency in the distribution of resources, and the promotion of alternatives to public benefits and services. As one of the main recipients of these benefits and services, the 'crisis' experienced by the welfare state in recent years has had an immediate and, in some cases, pernicious impact on older people, resulting in thousands of privately endured crises.

Despite both the longstanding association between elderly people and the welfare state and these new challenges, analyses of old age within the field of social policy have tended to concentrate on the 'burden of dependency' that old age is said to entail or, alternatively, the changing volume of services or standards of care available to elderly people. Although the actual *experience* of old age on the part of individual elderly people is inextricably bound up with social policy, whether in the public or private sectors, very little attention has been paid by policy analysts to the fundamental role of social policies in shaping the lives of older people and in, effectively, producing many of the characteristics associated with old age.

The aim of this volume is to contribute to a critical assessment of both the social and economic status of elderly people and the role that social policy plays in structuring their lives. This is the unifying feature of all the contributions to this book: the endeavour to evaluate critically the relationship between social policy and old age and, therefore, to promote more informed discussion and better policy. It represents the meeting-point of two similar developments in different disciplines. In the field of social policy there has been a shift in recent years from the traditional description and assessment of the administrative organisations of the welfare state towards a more critical appreciation of the social, economic and political functions of both public and private sectors in the production and distribution of welfare (Gough, 1979; Walker, 1981c; Wilding, 1983).

This development of a political economy of welfare has been mirrored, in social gerontology, by the growth in the USA (Dowd, 1980; Estes, Swan and Gerard, 1982; Minkler and Estes, 1984) and Britain (Walker, 1980, 1981b; Townsend, 1981; Phillipson, 1982) of a similarly critical perspective on ageing. The political economy of old age has very quickly moved beyond a critique of conventional gerontology – in which elderly people are treated as a homogeneous group distinct from the major structures and processes of society – towards an understanding of the relationship between ageing and economic life, the differential experience of ageing according to social class and the role that social policy plays in producing the dependent status of elderly people. The central assumption of this approach – and therefore of this volume – is that the process of ageing and the experience of old age cannot be understood without reference to the elderly person's location in the social structure and their relationship to the economy (Walker, 1981b).

Themes of the book

The book is divided into three parts. Part I establishes the theoretical foundation for the rest of the volume. The four chapters in this Part examine the construction of dependent social and economic status in old age. Chapter 2 shows that the main social policies that affect older people – retirement, pensionable status, residential and 'community' care – have been developed in ways which have created and reinforced the social dependency of the elderly. This 'structured' dependency has arisen not by unhappy accident but through conscious thought and action. Of particular importance are the management of modern economies, including the degree of access granted to older people to the labour market, and the distribution of power and status in such economies. The thesis that the dependent state of the elderly has been socially manufactured entails a prescription as well as an explanation. It suggests that the processes can be modified and the severity of the dependency reduced. It is within this analytical and policy-oriented framework that the other contributions to this book should be read.

Further attention is paid, in Chapter 3, to the crucial role of employment and the labour market in structuring the lives of older people. It is the social process of exclusion based on the labour market which determines the age barrier between working life and retirement. This is followed by a discussion of the especially depressed social status of elderly women, a subject long neglected in studies of both ageing and social policy. Through a combination of discrimination over the whole course of the life-cycle and dependency associated with old age elderly women are often acutely disadvantaged.

The final chapter in Part I traces the post-war growth of the personal social services and illustrates clearly the paradox which is reflected in each of the sectors of welfare analysed in Part II. The benefits and services of the welfare state have contributed to the well-being of elderly people and, to a considerable extent, have enhanced their standards of living and freedom compared with previous generations of elderly. Yet many of those same benefits and services have been organised and delivered in ways which have restricted freedom and increased dependency. The resolution of this paradox is one of the major challenges facing social policy and social planning over the next decade and we hope that this volume will be one contribution towards that end.

Part II subjects each of the main sectors of welfare provision to critical evaluation. It opens with a discussion of the relationship between the family and the welfare state in order to emphasise the fact that the caring activities of the informal sector, especially female kin, far outweigh the total contribution of all of the formal services put together. This chapter shows that there is a complex relationship between the family and the state whereby the latter seeks to *maintain* the primacy of the former in caring for elderly and other people with disabilities. Other chapters also consider the role of services in structuring the lives of elderly and, to a considerable extent, in determining the elderly person's experience of old age. There is one important omission from this section – we were unable to secure, in time for publication, a chapter on education. Some discussion of the growing importance of education in old age is contained in the concluding chapter.

Part III includes two contributions from leading gerontologists from France and the United States. These are presented partly to represent the world-wide field of social gerontology (which appears to be expanding fast in every country in the world other than Britain). British social policy and, to a lesser extent, social gerontology have remained insulated from comparative studies with other countries for too long. In addition, however, recent developments in policy on ageing in these two countries, under apparently contrasting political regimes, have considerable relevance for the progress of policy in this country.

The concluding chapter provides some constructive answers to much of the critical commentary on existing policies and practice in previous chapters and proposes an alternative path. The central intention of these proposals is to help elderly people themselves to overcome dependency and ageism and to play a leading role in defining need, determining priorities and management within what should be *their* social services. Elderly people may be the main users of welfare services, but they never occupy positions of authority in those services. One of the main prescriptions of critical social policy and social gerontology is a redistribution of power from service providers to service users.

Before proceeding, a few preliminary comments are required on two issues that are central to the analyses of ageing and social policy contained in the rest of this volume: the scale of the challenge to social policy posed by the demographic changes that British society is undergoing and the nature of the dependency experienced by many elderly people.

An Ageing Population
In common with other advanced industrial societies Britain is undergoing a major transformation in the age structure of its population. The main causes have been declining mortality among all age groups (Ermisch, 1983, p. 11), coupled with a long-term downward trend in fertility, which has reduced the proportion of children in the population to an all-time low. Together, these demographic changes have produced this unique late twentieth-century phenomenon: an ageing population.

As Table 1.1 shows, in a remarkably short space of time (1931–81) the numbers of people aged 65 and over more than doubled, while those aged 75 and over nearly quadrupled. This means that in 1931, 1 person in 14 was over the age of 64 whereas today it is 1 in 7. In 1931 the chances of encountering a citizen aged 75 and over were, on average, 1 in every 49; now it is 1 in 16. The main growth in the population has taken place among women, who, in the 75 and over age group, outnumber men by 2 to 1 (see Chapter 4).

Table 1.1 Numbers of elderly people in Great Britain, 1901–2021 (000s)

Year	65+	per cent (a)	75+	per cent (a)	85+	per cent (a)
			Past trends:1901–81			
1901	1734	4.7	507	1.4	57	0.15
1931	3316	7.4	920	2.1	108	0.24
1951	5332	10.9	1731	3.5	218	0.45
1971	7140	13.2	2536	4.7	462	0.86
1981	7985	15.0	3052	5.7	552	1.03
			Current situation: 1983–88			
1983	8246	15.1	3377	6.2	620	1.1
1988	8697	15.8	3736	6.8	757	1.4
			Future trends: 1983–2021			
1983	8246	15.1	3377	6.2	620	1.1
1991	8795	15.9	3844	6.9	757	1.4
2001	8656	15.3	4082	7.2	1047	1.9
2011	8911	15.7	4053	7.1	1187	2.1
2021	9956	17.2	4401	7.6	1230	2.1

Note:
(a) per cent of total population of Great Britain.

Source: Population projections by the Government Actuary. Mid-1981 based principal projection 1981–2021: and OPCS Census data 1901–81. From Henwood and Wicks (1984, p. 4).

Table 1.1 also shows that the increase in the numbers of elderly people is continuing. During the period 1983–88 (the expected lifetime of the present government) the numbers of people aged 65 and over are expected to increase by 5.5 per cent, while the numbers aged 75 and over and 85 and over will rise at twice and four times that rate, respectively. By 1988 those aged 75 and over will comprise 1 in 15 of the population.

Table 1.1 shows, finally, the projected future path of this major population change. Although it is important to bear in mind Abrams' (1978b, p. 5) warning – 'predictions and projections based on demographic data are, of all types of social prediction, the ones most likely to go wrong' – on current projections the population aged 65 and over is set to increase steadily, apart from a slight decline between 1991 and 2001, until well into the next century. However, the largest rises and are expected in the numbers aged 75 and over and 85 and over: 30 per cent and 98 per cent, respectively. By the end of this period women will outnumber men in the 85 and over age group by around 2.5 to 1.

Ageing and Disability

The significance to social policy of the ageing of the population – and particularly increasing longevity – lies mainly in the rising incidence of disability in successively older age groups (Townsend, 1979, p. 706). As age increases beyond about 50 there is a marked rise in the incidence of disability – particularly at the lower levels of severity – in successively older age groups. Then there is a rapid increase in severe incapacity beyond the age of 70. Thus the concept and measurement of disablement are crucial not only in developing any policy of income and social service support for the elderly but also in understanding the nature of old age itself.

In the first place, poverty and deprivation are greater among disabled than non-disabled elderly people. The last official survey of people with disabilities found that they had lower incomes and other resources compared with the non-disabled (Harris *et al.*, 1972, pp. 8, 13). Secondly, people with disabilities require higher personal incomes and more support from the social services than non-disabled people. These needs result from the special costs associated with disability. There are direct, easily identifiable, costs of disablement – drugs, spectacles, wheelchairs, special diets, transport, large-print books, non-slip mats and handrails – some of which are provided free of charge through the health and personal social services or subsidised through social security. Then there are indirect costs – for example, the inability to shop in cut-price supermarkets because of limited mobility, and the need for extra heating to offset pain or discomfort (Walker, 1976). Thirdly, as a general rule, the need for income and services increases with severity of disability (Townsend, 1979, p. 706). This means that priorities for policy can be established partly on the basis of discriminating between different degrees of severity of disability.

Although there is no up-to-date official information on the numbers of people with different degrees of disability – a deficiency that should be rectified by the survey currently being carried out by the OPCS – reliable national data are provided by the 'Elderly at Home Survey' carried out in 1976 and the annual *General Household Survey*.

The application of the proportions of the population found to be disabled in the 'Elderly at Home Survey' to the current (1983) population suggests that there are some 900,000 severely disabled elderly people living in their own homes. Another 1,900,000 are moderately disabled (Walker, 1985c, p. 7). To these must be added the estimated 200,000 elderly people in institutions who are bedfast or severely disabled, and a further 100,000 moderately disabled. Altogether, therefore, there are approximately 1,100,000 severely disabled elderly people – more than 1 in 8 of the population aged 65 and over. This represents an increase of more than 100,000 since

1976. In addition there are approximately 2 million moderately disabled people over 65.

Table 1.2 Changes in indicators of need among the elderly, 1971–2021 (Great Britain)

	1971	1981	Change 1971–81	2001	Change 1981–2001	2021	Change 1981–2021
Total elderly persons							
65–74	4604	5100	+496	4574	−526	5555	+455
75–84	2074	2615	+541	3035	+420	3171	+556
85+	462	584	+122	1047	+463	1230	+646
Total 65+	7140	8299	+1159	8656	+357	9956	+1657
Unable to bath/shower or wash all over alone							
65–74	244	270	+26	242	−28	294	+24
75–84	228	288	+60	334	+46	349	+61
85+	157	199	+42	356	+157	418	+219
Total 65+	629	757	+128	932	+175	1061	+304
Unable to go outside and walk down road unaided							
65–74	290	321	+31	288	−33	350	+29
75–84	361	455	+94	528	+73	552	+97
85+	221	280	+59	503	+223	590	+310
Total 65+	872	1056	+184	1319	+263	1492	+436
Unable to get in/out of bed unaided							
65–74	64	71	+7	64	−7	78	+7
75–84	48	60	+12	70	+10	73	+13
85+	46	58	+12	105	+47	123	+65
Total 65+	158	189	+31	239	+50	274	+85
Unable to go up and down stairs unaided							
65–74	198	219	+21	197	−22	239	+20
75–84	234	295	+64	343	+48	358	+63
85+	143	181	+38	325	+144	381	+200
Total 65+	575	695	+120	865	+170	978	+283
Living alone							
65–74	1243	1377	+134	1235	−142	1500	+123
75–84	933	1177	+244	1366	+189	1427	+250
85+	221	280	+59	503	+223	590	+310
Total 65+	2397	2834	+437	3104	+270	3517	+883

Elderly people (000s)

Note:
Totals derived by applying proportion in each age group with above characteristics in 1980 General Household Survey to projected population figures. These projections may slightly overestimate the numbers involved (see Table 1.1).

Source: Henwood and Wicks (1984, p. 16), with addition of 1971 data.

Table 1.2 is derived from the second source of national information about the needs of the over-65s: the *General Household Survey*. It shows that the needs of the elderly have grown considerably since 1971 and will continue to grow, though not uniformly, over the next three decades. Although based on a method of estimation which is admittedly 'unsophisticated', these figures do indicate the broad order of magnitude that social care policy must address. At the same time it is important to stress the point made in Chapter 6: although the measurement of disability in old age is a necessary prerequisite for the effective allocation of social care resources, it demonstrates, paradoxically, that the vast majority are *not* in need of care and are able to look after themselves without help from either relatives or the social services. More than a half of those over 65 have no disabilities and a further 20 per cent have only slight ones. Even among those aged 75 and over nearly half experience no or only slight disablement.

This gives some indication of the scale of the challenge facing social policy and social planning over the next 40 years or so. On the basis of the analyses in this volume of the failure of successive governments over the *previous* 40 years to meet the needs of the rising numbers of elderly people, the welfare state is inadequately prepared to respond to this continuing challenge. A crucial factor in this failure, though by no means the only one, has been the longstanding shortfall between rising needs and the resources allocated to meet them. Thus increases in a population in need do not necessarily result in increased public resources. As Ermisch (1983, p. 283) has shown, expenditure on the health and personal social services has not been sensitive in the past to increases in the need for care but, instead, has been determined by what the government has decided to spend. So, whatever pressures derive from rising numbers of elderly people in the future, the deciding factors in the allocation of resources to services and benefits for the elderly will be political. It is important for social policy analysts and social gerontologists to propose constructive alternatives to existing inadequacies in policies but unless there is change at a political level there is little chance of reforms being instituted (Chapter 14). The role that elderly people themselves occupy in the battle for resources may well develop in future years towards a more concerted and overtly political one, as in the USA (see Chapter 12), and thereby contribute to the change in social and economic priorities necessary if the needs of older people are to be met adequately.

Dependency and Old Age
While the statistics in Tables 1.1 and 1.2 reveal the extent of the urgent challenge facing social policy-makers in Britain and other similar societies, the tendency – in the UK at least – has been for them to respond with descriptions of the ageing population in terms

of alarm and crisis rather than with the busied construction of responsible plans of action. Descriptions such as 'the growing burden of dependency', 'social disaster', 'flood' and 'rising tide' create the impression that we are being swamped by multiplying hordes of frail elderly people (see, for example, Health Advisory Service, 1983). True, the present government has gone much further in this than any previous one by its repeated references to elderly people as a burden on the economy and the suggestion that the future financial commitments to elderly people – the pensions 'time-bomb' – are a threat to Britain's economic recovery (Treasury, 1984; DHSS, 1985), but elements of this 'burden of dependency' thesis can be found in the policies of successive administrations (see Chapter 10). The increasing proselytisation of this thesis over the last 20 years has had a considerable negative impact not only on the quest for a better understanding of the relationship between ageing and social policy and the construction of social policies to meet the needs of elderly people which do not increase dependency, but also, both directly and indirectly, on the quality of life experienced by elderly people themselves.

There are four main points to be considered.

First, it has helped to foster and legitimate a caricature of elderly people, which is at best limited and at worst downright degrading, as a burden on the community. Although unwarranted, this view of old age helps to sustain the strong element of ageism in British society (see Chapters 2 and 3). We have already seen that the majority of elderly people are fit and healthy and keen to lead independent lives. Only a minority of even those in need receive a social service. Today's state pensioners contributed, in one way or another, to the pensions received by previous generations. However, the fact that elderly people are *not* a burden on the economy or society (as is shown further in Chapters 2, 6 and 10) is difficult to establish in the face of official amplification.

Secondly, the primary motivation behind changes in policy to-wards the elderly has been purposefully obscured. The main factor in determining the nature of policy on ageing or any other subject is *not* demographic but ideological. The rising needs of elderly people described above have coincided with a period of enforced financial stringency in the public sector. Elderly people are one among many groups to suffer recently from cuts in their living standards *because* they are heavily reliant on the welfare state.

The recent history may be summarised: the evolution of the liberal welfare state was based on post-war economic prosperity – the twin policies of economic growth and relatively full employment. Sustained growth and near full employment during the 1950s and 1960s delivered a welfare surplus which, although it did not create equality of conditions, did finance rising real levels of benefits and services with resulting reductions in economic insecurity, and so provided for the massive expansion in social expenditure over the post-war period. Thus the proportion of total public expenditure going to the welfare state nearly doubled between 1950 and 1984 and currently stands at 60 per cent of the total. This era of unparalleled growth in the welfare state was abruptly halted in the mid-1970s by a combination of events – the rise in world oil prices, a slowdown in economic growth, the simultaneous rise in unemployment and inflation, and a growing resistance to taxation (for a fuller discussion of these factors, see Walker, 1982f, pp. 7–9) – which together created the fiscal crisis of the state. In the wake of economic crises and upheaval came political and ideological change; the rise of monetarism in response to the economic problems of the 1970s echoed the adoption of Keynesian policies in response to those of the 1930s. Attention has turned from the problem of how to divide the extra annual increment of public expenditure to viewing this expenditure itself as one of the main *causes* of economic failure. As the first Thatcher government put it in the first sentence of its first White Paper on public expenditure: 'public expenditure is at the heart of Britain's present economic difficulties' (Treasury, 1979, p. 1).

Despite blanket condemnations of public expenditure such as this, expenditure on some programmes has been increased while that on others has been cut back. For example, some £7000 million was cut from the social security budget between 1979 and 1984 while, at the same time, defence expenditure was increased by £9500 million. Thus, linked with the desire to control the overall growth of public expenditure, is a specific ideological aversion to the welfare state. Briefly, this encompasses the belief that public services stifle initiative and individual responsibility. In the words of the former Secretary of State for Social Services, 'our statutory services should be a safety-net, not a blanket that smothers initiative and self-help' (House of Commons, 1981, col. 136). Secondly, it is assumed that the private sector is necessarily more efficient than the public sector. Thirdly, the 'non-productive' public sector is held to be a costly burden on the 'productive' private sector. For these reasons it is argued that the frontiers of the welfare state should be rolled back.

The essential precondition for the current policy of privatisation and cuts in welfare spending is the belief that the welfare state is wasteful, inefficient and unproductive. This 'public burden' model of welfare therefore characterises expenditure on public social services as a burden on the economy (Titmuss, 1968, pp. 124–5). It is underpinned by the crude division between economic policy and social policy and the presumption of supremacy of the former over the latter (Walker, 1984c, pp. 45–68). Narrowly defined 'economic' objectives such as profit-maximisation, economic growth and cost-efficiency are considered without question to be legitimate, while 'social' objectives such as good health and community care must secure legitimacy in the policy system, and are believed to rest ultimately on economic policy for their achievement (Pinker, 1974, p. 9). Thus the subordination of the equity concerns of social policy to the efficiency concerns which dominate economics and economic policy follows from and reinforces the assumption of the superiority of the market, and paves the way for the adoption of policies aimed at reducing the size of the welfare state when economic growth no longer provides a sufficient surplus for welfare.

The primary motivation behind current economic and social policies, then, is ideological. It is, of course, impossible to regard expenditure on the welfare state as a public burden without implying that the *recipients* of public welfare benefits and services are themselves a public burden (see Chapter 10). Thus there is a danger not only that public opinion will be influenced to regard elderly people and others in a similar position as the problem, rather than the specific policies pursued by governments; but also that elderly people internalise this thesis and end up blaming themselves – the victims of economic and social policies – for being a burden on the economy. This process of scapegoating the elderly has also been observed in the United States (Minkler and Estes, 1984, p. 17).

Thirdly, there is the paradox that Titmuss (1963, p. 56) illustrated more that 20 years ago. To conceive of increases in the numbers of elderly as a threat or burden is vastly to undervalue the social progress that British society has made, and particularly the achievements of public welfare, in putting an end to many of the causes of premature death that prevented earlier generations reaching advanced old age. This paradox has reached acute proportions recently by the official juxtaposition of the ageing of the British population and the worsening of the ratio of contributors to pensioners, with the conclusion that the state earnings-related pension scheme (SERPS) is 'burdened by the threat of people staying alive' (Reddin, 1984, p. 11; DHSS, 1985, p. 15). The prospect of a fundamental conflict between social progress and economic fortune has rarely been posed so sharply.

Fourthly, the burden of dependency thesis has hindered an understanding of the true nature of dependency in old age. We are encouraged to believe that the social problem of dependency exists just because the numbers in a particular age group are increasing, by the simple but mistaken translation of demographic projections into social realities. But dependency is a socially rather than a biologically constructed status. It is primarily the product of a particular social division of labour and structure of inequality rather than a natural concomitant of the ageing process (Walker, 1980, 1981b; Townsend, 1981; Chapter 2 this volume). So, the description of ageing by means of demographic statistics has largely substituted for social analysis of the changing meaning and experience of old age. As a result, the extent to which we have *created* a dependent status in old age has been obscured. This is not to say that people do not grow old and suffer from disabilities, some of which might entail dependency, but rather, what we regard as old age is manufactured socially and not a function of the biological ageing process.

This alternative 'social construction of dependency' thesis is discussed at length in the following chapter. The practical implication of the structural analysis we are proposing here is that, since age and dependency are social institutions, they can be altered as they have been in the past, through social and economic policies such as those affecting the age of retirement (Chapters 3 and 10). In the social services there is a wide range of powerful groups and interests that may unwittingly encourage the myth that old age and dependency are synonymous. Staff of domiciliary services and residential homes alike, health and social services unions, social services managers and directors, local politicians, the medical profession and DHSS officials and ministers have all stressed, from time to time, the worrying implications of the rising numbers of elderly people in their wholly honourable pursuit of better benefits and services, conditions of service or more resources for the social services (Walker, 1982c, pp. 124–5). But in doing so they have helped to spread and legitimate an inaccurate picture of elderly people and the true nature and origins of their needs.

There is a continuing danger, therefore, that policy will be formulated in a climate of alarmist speculation, following the familiar path of least resistance, rather than on the basis of a careful analysis of actual needs among the elderly. We hope that this book will contribute to the long overdue process of reassessing the relationship between ageing and social policy, in order to formulate alternative policies that meet the needs felt by elderly people themselves without creating or enhancing dependency. We believe that this is one of the major challenges confronting social policy and social planning over the next two decades.

Part I
Social Policy and the Construction of Old Age

2 Ageism and Social Policy

Peter Townsend

The infirmity, isolation, loneliness, poverty, dependence and social need of many if not all elderly people in the late twentieth century has been described with varying degrees of force in different rich countries. But how are those conditions conceived and measured, and how are they explained? Too many studies of ageing are carried out in a theoretical vacuum, rather as if the abstract and impractical business of explanation could be left to scientific outsiders, and the assumptions, observations and generalisations of unscientific insiders did not have to be submitted to any kind of theoretical test. There is a growing volume of writing about elderly people, little of which is scientifically grounded and much of which defers to an insufficient and unsubstantiated intellectual tradition.

This chapter develops the thesis that the dependency of the elderly has been 'structured' by long-term economic and social policies: elderly people are perceived and treated as more dependent than they are or need to be by the state, and this outcome has been fostered by the rapidly developing institutions of retirement, income maintenance, residential and domiciliary care, which comprise a subordinate but necessary part of the overall management of state policy. In short, ageism has been and is being institutionalised in modern society. There are forms of discrimination against the elderly which are as deep as forms of discrimination against women and ethnic minorities.

Theories of Ageing

One starting point in analysing the conditions of elderly people in society is the influence exerted by scientific theory. Ultimately, those who interpret the problems of ageing, or construct, administer and service those institutions which are designed to cater for the elderly, depend on scientific and moral authority for their beliefs and actions. Thus, the principal economic policies of the Thatcher government are known to draw inspiration from the edicts of monetarism, just as the consensus about economic management on the part of successive previous governments drew their inspiration from Keynesianism. We must begin, therefore, by recognising that attitudes towards the elderly and specialized acts to understand their problems and meet their needs are shaped by cultural and scientific beliefs which reflect the dominance of what might be called the 'liberal–pluralist' tradition. This tradition is represented by a kind of 'family' of theories which share much in common and tend to complement each other. Theories in the social sciences – like neoclassical economics, democratic pluralism, sociological functionalism, and most theoretical social psychology – have tended to reflect and approve developments in the capitalist democracies, reinforce individualistic rather than social values, and accept the changing structural inequalities of a competitive market.

There are alternative theories in each of the social sciences, of course, but in historical and contemporary terms the numbers of their adherents are many fewer than of the more orthodox or predominant theories. The continuities of economic individualism within classical economic theory, neoclassical theory, monetarism and even Keynesianism have to be recognised just as the complex and sometimes half-understood ways in which their ideas or findings are taken up by influential social interests have to be traced. Neither is the influence only in one direction. Just as we need to explore how theory comes to influence politics and policy so we have to understand how scientists can be motivated by political aspirations and indeed by financial sponsorship. None of this attracts much systematic enquiry in our present culture. It would be possible to take the more dominant theories in the social sciences and trace what implications they hold for explanations of enforced retirement, or poverty, or admission to an institution in old age. Fortunately, there are a number of examples of general theorists who have applied their ideas to ageing or where social scientists within a particular school of thought have specialised on the problems of ageing.

What can we say, therefore, about the implications of the literature on ageing for social policy? The debt to the liberal–pluralist tradition can be illustrated from all the compendia of social gerontology (for example, Donahue and Tibbitts, 1957; Tibbitts, 1960; Atchley, 1977; Stearns, 1977; Clark and Spengler, 1980; Ward, 1984).

As applied to the elderly, neoclassical economic theories have fostered the idea that the retirement of the elderly is a natural and inevitable phenomenon by virtue of the division of labour, the exclusion of groups outside the labour market to the periphery of interest, and the attribution of the low pay of older workers and the low pensions of retired workers to individual characteristics. The operation of preferences or prejudices by social institutions is excluded from attention as are functional capacities and potentialities for learning new skills on the part of people attaining some arbitrary chronological age of retirement or entitlement to pension. And while Marxian theory has done much to contradict individualistic theories of unemployment, such theory has as yet done little to contradict a too facile approach to interpretations of retirement. So the problems of ageing are viewed very much as 'natural' by most economists because they are believed to arise largely from inevitable differences between individuals or as an inevitable consequence of desirable industrial and technological change.

An even better example is provided from within sociology by functionalism, or in its more sophisticated version of 'structural differentiation', as advocated by Neil Smelser (1959) and his successors. Talcott Parsons was the most influential theorist of functionalism. He argued that class divisions, and the relative isolation or domestic independence of the nuclear or immediate family of the two youngest generations, were inevitable and necessary outcomes of industrialisation (for example, Parsons, 1942). And he went on to argue that as a consequence of the loss of economic, educational and welfare functions by the family, the elderly were structurally isolated 'from kinship, occupational and community ties'. This, he believed, helped to explain agitation to develop social services to help old people (Parsons, 1964). However, he did not confront a major theoretical issue in his work. There are two alternative and contradictory interpretations of the development he describes. One is that the state benevolently makes good any gaps in social support left by industry's deliberate aim to break up the extended family so that labour will be sufficiently mobile to move to the new centres of production. The other is that the state connives with industry to bring about a sufficient break-up of the extended family to permit the mobility of labour.

The theories of Cumming and Henry (1961; and Cumming, 1963) provide a more specific example of the influence of functionalism. They enlarged upon common observations of the fact that as people move into old age, their activities tend to shrink in number and range. They did not ask whether that is attributable in part to the institutions of retirement, cultural expectations of limited activity and impoverishment as well as greater risk of ill-health and disability. They argued that *independent of ill-health and poverty* 'normal ageing is a mutual withdrawal or "disengagement" between the ageing person and others in the social system to which he belongs – a withdrawal initiated by the individual himself, or by others in the system' (Cumming, 1963, p. 377).

This theory seemed to fit in very well with contemporary attitudes towards the elderly. According to the theory, individual development and senescence pursued a linear course during the lifespan, with activity reaching a high point in early middle life and then declining, first because children married and left home, and then because people retired from work and became widowed. In old age the individual prepared for death and tended to disengage, a motivation which coincided with a reduction of the pressure on the individual to maintain an active part in community and society. This disengagement theory suggested an 'ultimate biological basis for a reduction of interest or involvement in the environment' (ibid., p. 379). Whether steps towards this disengagement were initiated by society or by the ageing person, the effect was that he or she played fewer roles and his or her relationships changed in quality. People were believed to be more content with this disengaged position. 'Disengagement is a triple withdrawal: a loss of roles, a contraction of contact and a decline in the commitment to norms and values.'

Criticisms of this disengagement theory were made from a number of standpoints, including that from those occupying a general theoretical position in the social sciences or a particular moral or social policy position rather than on the basis of offering an alternative – specifically gerontological – theory. The theory was attacked for implicitly reflecting the middle-class values of middle America (the work for the thesis was carried out in Kansas) instead of the diverse values of all industrial countries, and for failing to take account of the structural values of capitalism (see Talmon, 1961 and 1963, in particular). Its implications for policy made people particularly uneasy. The empirical grounds for the theory were also found wanting. Thus, a major survey in three countries failed to provide much statistical evidence that the activities of the oldest people declined in range or number if they maintained both health and a reasonable income (Shanas *et al.*, 1968). The approach logically led to the adoption of policies which leave old people alone rather than policies which improve the quality of later life. If the theory were true why should people be encouraged to join clubs, or to maintain their relationships with others or engage in alternative activities? If ageing were an inevitable period of contraction and disengagement, why intervene in the process of withdrawal? The implication was that policies of non-interference would be a greater kindness. Reactions of these kinds have led to a search for better developed alternative theoretical standpoints.

Acquiescent Functionalism

Within a dominant national social scientific approach to theory which I have described as 'liberal–pluralism' there has been an approach to the study of ageing and the elderly which might be characterised as that of 'acquiescent functionalism'. It is a body of thought about ageing which attributes the causes of most of the problems of old people to the natural consequences of physical decrescence and mental inflexibility or to the failures of individual adjustment to ageing and retirement, instead of to contemporary developments of the state, the economy and social inequality. These latter developments are not themselves regarded as possible causal culprits. They have tended to be treated variously as commonly sanctioned, inevitable and unalterable – as the necessary accompaniments of market forces, technological change and democratic process. And if this is correct, the true interests of the elderly will have been poorly represented or even recognised over many years. Public and state perceptions of the functions and capacities of the elderly population may now be completely at variance with properly independent scientific evidence about those functions and capacities. The problem is in distinguishing uncontaminated from contaminated evidence. At the very least, the extent to which institutionalised ageism may be becoming a major feature of modern social structure deserves close investigation. Because of the growth in numbers of the elderly population, and the accompanying increase in costs and provisions for that population, the dispositions towards them of the rich and powerful have been 'institutionalised' in a form which could be said to represent a new type of schism in society, namely ageism. At the time of writing this does not yet attract as much disquiet publicly as sexism and racism.

The set of theories which I have described as 'acquiescent functionalism' legitimates ageism in practice in contemporary society. The 'functionalism' legitimates the exclusion of elderly people from the labour market and from significant alternative social roles. It also legitimates incomes for the elderly at levels well below the employment incomes of the low paid. The epithet 'acquiescent' is intended to suggest the passive rather than active role played by intellectuals who have concerned themselves with issues affecting elderly people and tend to advocate 'minimalist' solutions to their problems. Either they have not questioned larger institutional developments and have not linked them with events in which the elderly have been concerned, or they have accepted them without fuss or protest. Often this is because they have worked within an individualistic theoretical tradition, and often because they avow their concern with 'practice' and do not appreciate that practice can never be divorced from theory, nor from the institutional ideologies governing practice which are legitimated by and reflect theory.

The power of this tradition must not be underestimated. It deserves to be examined in a number of ways. It could be examined, as I have suggested, as a by-product of the evolution of different theories within the social sciences – as part of the historiography of knowledge. It could be examined extensively as a facet of contemporary social structure – looking at the many different types of relationship between old and young, representative organisations, party politics, professional practice, and media characterisation. It could be handled in terms of individual chronological experience. Or it could be examined in relation to the major institutions established for elderly people in the twentieth century – retirement, pensions, residential inmate status, and community care. Elsewhere in this book some of these themes will be illuminated and developed. In this chapter I shall adopt the last of these possible forms of exposition, and will first express an alternative theoretical standpoint to that of 'acquiescent functionalism'.

Structured Dependency
A more radical interpretation of the needs of the elderly could be said to have deep historical roots. Those who wrote impassioned analyses of the plight of the aged within the workhouse, especially after the Poor Law Amendment Act of 1834, showed all too clearly how needs could be over-borne by implacable authority. From the nineteenth century onwards there has been a tradition of literature critical of the institutionalisation of the elderly (for example, Minority Report of the Royal Commission on the Poor Laws, 1909; Webb and Webb, 1929; Townsend, 1962; Henry, 1965; Roth and Eddy, 1967). Sympathetic survey reports of the conditions of the elderly in the community also provided a basis for questioning the complacent assumptions of 'acquiescent functionalism'. (One of the earliest post-war surveys, for example, was that of Sheldon, 1948.) The report of a major survey of the elderly in the United States, Denmark and Britain drew a major distinction between the private and publicly institutionalised aspects of the lives of old people.

> First, persons aged 65 and over are more strongly integrated into industrial society than is often assumed either by the general public or by sociological theorists . . . by their general health or, more specifically, the personal and household functions they perform, in the services they receive from their families, and in the frequency of their contacts with children and other relatives, most old people are fairly securely knitted into the social structure . . . integration with the family and the local community is maintained by the immediate network of personal, or 'privatised', relationships, based on reciprocity, common interests, inculcated loyalties, and affection. . . . Second, major problems are none the less to be found. . . . Many of their problems, though by no means all, arise as the consequence of formal actions on the part of mass society that confirm their separate retired status. Political actions are taken to introduce social security legislation, permit cheaper travel on public transport, and build special types of housing. Public services, private corporations

and large firms adopt fixed ages of retirement ... this dual relationship of the elderly to the rest of industrial society ... can be represented as a balance between the integrative impulses of informal primary relationships and the segregative impulses of formal industrial society or, more crudely, as a balance between the private and public aspects of the life of the elderly in modern society. (Shanas *et al.*, 1968, pp. 425–6)

In the early 1970s Harris put forward a thesis that ageing is a process of deprivation: 'In terms of both income and employment, the old are deprived relative both to the rest of society and relative to their previous life experiences, but that this deprivation is mediated by the class structure, magnifying it at the bottom and minimising it at the top' (Harris, 1975; but see also Harris, 1972 and 1977). In recent years such critical themes have been elaborated from within alternative theoretical approaches (see for example, Talmon, 1968, 1972; Guillemard, 1972, 1980, 1983; Townsend, 1976, 1979, 1981; Estes, 1979; Walker, 1980, 1983; Phillipson, 1982).

The condition of dependency of the elderly is not the inevitable outcome of a natural process of ageing, but is socially structured, and hence potentially open to change. In this process the state plays a large part, by determining the events in the latter half of life which result in the dependence, poverty or isolation experienced by many elderly people. By the state is meant not just the elected government of the day, but that ruling complex of central administrative, legal, economic and political institutions which have become established over a long period of time, and which govern the scope and, in large measure, the nature of everyday social activities. Some such concept as 'structured dependency' is required to understand current developments. Otherwise some recent policies are liable to misinterpretation as contributing to an enhancement of welfare when real change is more complex. Thus it is possible on the one hand, to interpret the improvements in cash and services to the elderly against historical benchmarks, but those self-same levels of cash and services may have deteriorated relative to other groups in the population. Again, changes in legislation and administrative arrangements may be interpreted on the one hand, as having improved the quality of life of some or all elderly people, but they have to be interpreted, on the other hand, in relationship to the enlargement of dependency and the deepening of deprivation by virtue of increased unemployment and redundancy, earlier retirement, and increased isolation from the mainstream of social development. Forms of professionalisation and technological innovation and mass production can inhibit control over some aspects of personal and family life and obstruct reciprocal social relationships.

Retirement, poverty, institutionalisation and restriction of domestic and community roles are the experiences which help to explain the structured dependency of the elderly. They are discussed in turn below. The approach is one whereby society is held to create the framework of institutions and rules within which the general problems of the elderly emerge or, indeed, are 'manufactured'. In the everyday management of the economy and the administration and development of social institutions the position of the elderly is subtly shaped and changed. The policies which determine the conditions and welfare of the elderly are not just the reactive policies represented by the statutory social services but the much more generalised and institutionalised policies of the state which maintain or change social structure. Social policy itself has to be conceived not as that limited set of measures designed to alleviate and meet what are conceived to be the problems which arise from a natural individual senescence, but as the principal initiatives and forms of management of societies as a whole conditioning public attitudes to the elderly, shaping public expectations of behaviour and status, and fashioning the opportunities which individuals actually find are open to them in particular situations and places.

Retirement as a basis for dependency

I shall first review the various factors inflating the dependency of the elderly. During the twentieth century retirement has become a universal social institution. Statistics published by the International Labour Office show the dramatic decline in all societies in the percentage of the older age groups who remain economically active. In some industrial countries with buoyant economies covering a large span of years, like Japan, the rate of decline has been smaller than in other countries, but is still pronounced. In Britain, according to one review (Johnson, 1985), 73 per cent of the male population of 65 and over in 1881 were occupied, but by 1981 the percentage had shrunk to less than 11 per cent (see Figure 2.1).

A change of this magnitude cannot be explained by changes in the prevalence of ill-health or disability, or the masking of disability in the period before substitute pensions were available. It is true that we lack good historical evidence about the health of the elderly over long periods of time, but there are now local and national surveys spanning periods of more than 30 years (see for example, Sheldon, 1948; Shanas *et al.*, 1968; Hunt, 1978; Abrams, 1978, 1980) which fail to provide evidence of a marked decline in standards of health and levels of disability among the different age groups over 65. There is, however, some evidence of an increase in self-reported chronic illness and disability during the last ten years, because there may have been a shift in the pattern of ill-health towards the more disabling diseases, and the prolongation of life of some people already disabled, including some saved from death by new forms of surgery and medical treatment, or because disabling conditions are

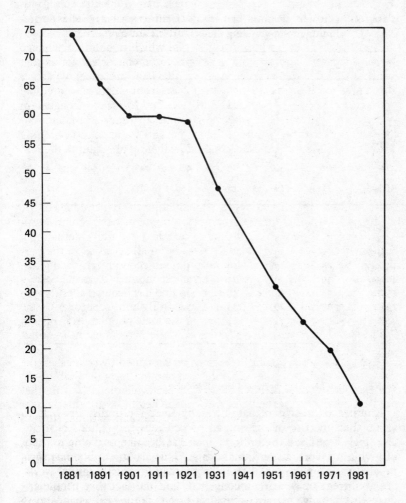

Figure 2.1: Per cent of male population aged 65+ who were occupied (England and Wales)

Source: Based on Census Reports; Johnson (1985).

now being reported when formerly they were not recognised or admitted. The data are presented in Table 2.1. But the increase in the percentage reporting disability accounts for only a fraction of the decline in the percentage remaining in paid employment, even if that increase could be said to apply only to those who were formerly in paid employment, which in any event would be hazardous to assume.

Table 2.1 Chronic sickness and disablement: prevalence of reported limiting long-standing illness, by sex and age

Sex & age	1972	1974	1976	1979	1980	1981	1982
Males:							
0–4	2	3	2	2	3	3	3
5–15[a]	5	5	6	7	8	8	7
16–44[a]	7	8	9	10	12	10	10
45–64	19	23	25	26	28	26	26
65–74	34	33	38	37	39	35	41
75+	34	39	48	45	45	44	43
All ages	11	13	15	16	18	16	17
Females:							
0–4	2	2	2	2	3	3	3
5–15[a]	3	3	5	5	5	6	6
16–44[a]	6	8	9	10	12	11	12
45–64	19	20	23	24	26	26	26
65–74	32	38	40	38	42	41	39
75+	42	49	53	54	54	56	54
All ages	13	15	17	18	20	19	19

Note:
a.   5–14 and 15–44 in 1974 and 1976.

Source: Annual Reports of the General Household Survey.

Another path of explanation, along liberal–pluralist lines, is to argue that because of the spread of pensions individuals have increasingly exercised the option which has become available to them of giving up work at pensionable age. This argument is *prima facie* persuasive. Some types of work, especially low-paid manual work, are abhorrent or at least uncongenial, and the fact that people endeavour to change certain occupations, to take time off work, and to give up work when the means at least of a minimum livelihood are available, is unsurprising. But the argument takes little account of the vast array of evidence that the mass of the population obtains considerable satisfaction from work, and many, in the early stages of retirement at least, actively dislike or oppose retirement. The array of evidence is not unambiguous, and certainly invites a much more sophisticated model of explanation than the rather simple models afforded by neoclassical economics and liberal–pluralism more generally, which concentrate on the themes of individual choice. What poses the central challenge to the simple model is, however, the evidence from national as well as local studies that millions of people in retirement, particularly men in the early years, dislike or deplore the termination of economic activity (see in particular Shanas *et al.*, 1968; Parker, 1980). Thus a national study in England in 1976 found that as many as 26 per cent of those aged 65 and over had retired before the age of 65. None the less, as many as 40 per cent of those retiring at 65 or over, and 61 per cent of those retiring at 65 or under declared that they would have preferred to go on working. For women giving up work at 65 or over the figure is 55 per cent, for women giving up work at 60–64 the figure is 39 per cent, and for women giving up work in their fifties the figure is 52 per cent. Perhaps surprisingly, the differences between socioeconomic groups were negligible (Hunt, 1978, pp. 62–3). A report of a later survey carried out on behalf of the Departments of Employment and Health and Social Security showed that a majority of both retired and non-retired men and women preferred staged rather than complete retirement (Parker, 1980).

Exploration of evidence about subjective attitudes allows a more three-dimensional picture to be drawn. Those reaching retirement age do not welcome retirement as warmly as they thought they would or others suppose. Many who have retired deeply regret their inactivity or loss of status, and as time goes on many regret the restrictions on their activities imposed by a greatly reduced income. The satisfaction often expressed by many retired people turns out on closer examination to be more an assertion of hope, or what they think is expected of them, than a true representation of what they feel. As in most human situations of change, there are profound reservations and regrets as well as advantages or at least mild compensations.

The diversity of subjective reactions demonstrates the need for a more structured analysis of behaviour and belief. Retirement practices vary widely by culture. Pension ages vary arbitrarily and do not show any demonstrable systematic relationship to the distribution of individual characteristics, skills or preferences. For individual societies neither does the history of the adoption of new retirement or pension schemes show much correspondence with trends in the distribution of individual health, skills and preferences. Such developments are much easier to understand in relation to the interplay of market and political forces. Close historical examination of retirement as a social institution shows that its adoption has also been associated with pressures to shed moral if not contractual obligations to loyal workers and to exclude certain groups of workers from the bargaining process (see Stearns, 1975; Thane, 1978, for example). Gradually the public is encouraged to accept the lessened value to the economy of workers beyond certain ages. At times both of high unemployment and relatively 'full' employment retirement has come to be used as one of the most important strategies for adjusting the numbers and structure of the labour force, with the additional advantage that it is much more acceptable to the unions than some other options. Perhaps for different reasons both management and unions have come to accept the expendability of older workers. The accelerated rate of technological change, and the successive adoption of new forms of training and educational qualifications, have contributed in no small measure to the over-valuation of the productive capacity of younger workers and the under-valuation of the productive capacity of older workers. The evidence down the years from social psychology, that despite some fall in levels of dexterity and speed older workers more than compensate by experience, wisdom and reliability, have been ignored (Welford, 1961). Investigation of individual capacities shows also that older people are not so troubled by heavy work as is commonly assumed and are also better candidates for re-training.

The restructuring of the labour force has been proceeding at an accelerated rate during recent years. The initiatives are coming from institutions, not individuals. The combined effects of industrial, economic and educational reorganisation are leading to a more rigid stratification of the population by age. There have been changes in the organisation of work and in the definition by industrial and political élites of the kind of people expected to do that work. Bigger work organisations, with more pronounced hierarchies, have become established and career promotion through successive tiers of these hierarchies is regarded as normal and to be expected. The objectives of economic growth, productivity and increasingly rapid replacement of skills have been adopted within these organisational settings and, as a direct consequence, more workers at older ages have found themselves displaced. During the 1970s and early 1980s another factor has contributed both to trends in retirement and unemployment. The development of multinational corporations and improvements internationally in transport and communications have led to a relocation of production and workforces in countries where very low wages are paid. The outflow of investment and relocation of production by subsidiaries in the Third World have exacerbated the problem.

There are many examples of the pressures upon the elderly. Early retirement has been adopted as a common practice in a large number

Table 2.2 Economic activity of males and females by age, 1973–84

Age	Percentage economically active[a]				
	1973	*1979*	*1981*	*1983*	*1984*
Males aged 16 and over					
16–17	63	56	47	40	52
18–19	88	87	84	81	79
20–24	92	92	92	93	90
25–34	98	98	97	97	97
35–44	99	98	98	97	97
45–54	98	96	95	94	94
55–59	94	88	90	85	83
60–64	85	75	73	63	57
65+	19	15	11	9	9
16–64	94	92	99	88	88
Total	82	79	77	75	75
Females aged 16 and over					
Non-married women[b]					
16–17	57	53	40	41	40
18–24	84	79	83	81	79
25–34	82	76	76	69	73
35–44	76	70	75	70	73
45–54	74	72	74	67	71
55–59	69	61	61	53	59
60–64	34	23	23	17	18
65+	6	5	4	4	3
16–59	74	70	70	67	68
Total	45	42	44	41	41
Married women					
16–17	(7)	(nil)	(4)	(nil)	(3)
18–24	50	52	57	52	53
25–34	44	55	51	52	54
35–44	64	70	69	69	68
45–54	63	68	69	68	67
55–59	48	55	54	52	53
60–64	25	25	21	20	17
65+	8	6	5	4	3
16–59	55	62	61	60	61
Total	48	52	51	49	49

Notes:
a. Full-time students who were working or unemployed in the reference week are classified as economically inactive.
b. Single, widowed, divorced and separated women.

of occupations and professions. There have been Private Member's Bills in Parliament, reports of the Equal Opportunities Commission, measures like the Job Release Scheme introduced by the government, and resolutions at successive Labour Party Conferences, which favour the lowering of the pension age. Table 2.2 shows how the earlier reduction in the workforce aged 65 and over has now been extended significantly to those aged 60 and over and even those in their late fifties. It would be absurd to separate the discussion of trends in retirement from trends in unemployment. Both are features of the same underlying structural process. For many people in middle life, retirement is becoming a euphemism for unemployment. It is being enforced in a number of industrial countries at increasingly early ages and yet is, paradoxically, being represented as a social achievement in capitalist and state socialist societies alike. In many societies there are millions of people now expecting to live at least ten of their potentially most active years in a situation which is described as one of 'retirement'.

The categorisation affects rich and poor differentially. Some of the rich, especially those in professions like politics, the arts, and the judiciary, can postpone retirement to a time of their choice. There are a number of studies showing greater levels of contentment among those from middle-class than from working-class occupations. People in non-manual jobs often have associations and spare-time responsibilities which can be more easily continued into retirement. They also have greater resources like gardens, cars and other assets which permit substitute occupations to be more fully developed. Like high rates of unemployment, high rates of early retirement represent costs to those who bear them which permit those who remain in employment to obtain higher levels of remuneration and, by virtue of their greater political power, pay lower taxes. The extension of retirement is associated with the growth of social inequality.

Pensions and Dependency

Just as the development of retirement has to be understood as an aspect of labour force and state management, so the institutionalisation of pensions has to be understood as an aspect of market and state management of the distribution of incomes. Against the evidence, the idea that the income needs of elderly people are much smaller than those of people of 'economically active' age, and simultaneously the idea of the 'adequacy' of a low level of 'subsistence pension' has been accepted.

Modern attempts systematically to describe the income conditions of the elderly began with the work of Charles Booth (1894): 'The aged poor who seek parish assistance in the course of a year amount to nearly 30 per cent of the old. The proportion is greatest in

London, where the figure is no less than 38 per cent, and least in those urban unions which have a small rural element, where it is only 25 per cent' (Booth, 1894, p. 48). He pointed out that the rates both of pauperism and poverty among older people were much higher than among young adults. Elsewhere he argued for a pension of 5 shillings a week which 'does not pretend to be "an adequate provision" but is the contribution of the state towards it, being about the sum (and less rather than more) which the bare maintenance of a destitute person actually costs' (Booth, 1892, p. 236; see also Booth, 1899). State pensions were interpreted in much of the ensuing debate as a method of income maintenance which rescued the deserving elderly poor from the stigmatisation of parish relief without adding too greatly to state expenditure.

The irony is that after decades of struggle the percentage of elderly dependent on means-tested social assistance is almost identical to what it was when Booth surveyed the population in the 1890s. Despite the qualifications that have to be entered about the development of occupational pensions, improvements during certain years, and the extension in scope and augmentation of the basic flat-rate universal pension, the fact remains that, on various alternative definitions of poverty, far more of the elderly than of younger adults remain in poverty or on its margins. The risks of poverty in the 1980s are highest among the elderly, especially over the age of 75, next highest in childhood and lowest in late middle age (see for example Townsend, 1979, p. 294). The recent increase in the numbers and percentage of elderly with incomes of less than the supplementary benefit standard is discussed in Chapter 10.

The result of the containment of resources for the elderly is the outcome of different causal elements, those tending to augment their resources being counterbalanced by those tending to diminish them. In most industrial societies state pensions and other cash benefits administered centrally comprise the most important source of income. In most countries the initial rate of state pensions after retirement, and the levels of social assistance, which are paid to the elderly, tend to be low relative to the earnings of younger adults. However, during the last 20 or 30 years the levels of pensions reached in some other countries, such as Denmark, The Netherlands and The Federal Republic of Germany, are much higher, and in some cases nearly twice as high, as in the United Kingdom (Walker, Lawson and Townsend, 1984, p. 54). In Britain, various studies place the net incomes of single or widowed retired people, allowing for dependants, at about a third, and of married couples less than half, of younger non-retired people (Wedderburn, in Shanas *et al.*, 1968; Townsend, 1979). State assistance is granted on condition that people retire from paid employment. The age at which people are entitled to a pension is fixed by the state and industry, and is often accepted by individuals as a social norm. There is a long history legitimating the levels of pension, but, as explicitly formulated by Lord Beveridge, they have been related to the minimum subsistence concept (limited in the main to the physical necessities of food, shelter and clothing) and the levels have been fixed considerably below those of net earnings during the period of paid employment. The initial rates of private or occupational pensions, with some exceptions, are also low relative to the earnings of young adults. Provisions for widows under the terms of such schemes have generally been very poor, and occupational pension fund managers have not responded to ministerial exhortations in recent years. The poor financial prospects of widows, combined with the failure of the occupational pensions schemes to provide for sufficient increases during periods of inflation, help to explain why so many people from non-manual occupations descend, along with their working-class counterparts, into poverty or near poverty after retirement.

During the last 20 years there have been a number of improvements to the levels of income expected by many elderly people. Examples are the additional earnings-related pension (payable to people retiring after 5 April 1979), the introduction of the formula to maintain state pensions at a level commensurate with earnings, the extension of mobility allowance, and the addition of disability benefits. But some of these additions have now been withdrawn or are threatened with withdrawal, and there have been other changes which have contributed to the numbers and percentage of the elderly population with relatively low incomes. Thus, the widening gap between women and men in their expectation of life has tended to increase the proportion of elderly who are widowed women and hence magnified the shortcomings of both state and occupational pension schemes to protect the interests of women. The proportionate shift among the elderly population towards the older age groups has also begun to highlight the deficiencies of both state and occupational pension schemes in maintaining not just the purchasing level of pensions but levels appropriate to the re-capitalisation of the homes of the elderly (repairs, modernisation, equipment, furnishings, linen and carpets) as well as the levels of income comparable with the young elderly. Yet again, the steady diminution of the number of elderly who continue to obtain full-time or part-time earnings has greatly increased the numbers of those dependent on the provisions respectively of state and occupational pension schemes.

Lacking access to many of the positions where sectional interests can be properly represented, the elderly find their position in a rapidly evolving economy getting worse. Their incomes and other resources fail to keep pace in value with the resources of other groups in society; either certain forms of assets held, such as household goods and equipment and certain types of income from savings, and occupational pensions depreciate in value absolutely or relatively to the rise in living standards, with increasing length of retirement, or many do not have, and have not in the past had, an opportunity of obtaining types of resources which are newly becoming available to younger people. Moreover, in some areas, particularly inner-city areas, larger numbers of elderly are exposed to the problems not only of isolation but of the impoverishment of the local economy and of other households around them, so that the possibility of help in times of trouble is reduced and costs may be higher.

There is a gulf between survey evidence about the needs of elderly people and political recognition of those needs in the form of developing proposals for more adequate levels of pension. A particular example is disablement. Liability to disablement restricts access to resources and, in the absence of compensating cash benefits and services for the elderly, leads to additional costs for many older people which outweigh any savings in expenditure which are arguably brought by retirement. Ageism has been institutionalised in the social security system, especially whereby elderly people are denied access to a number of disability benefits, the mobility allowance being perhaps the most striking example. Compulsory or near-compulsory retirement at a fixed age and a level of pension at a level which is wholly inadequate as compensation for lost earnings have combined to impose a form of dependency which is inescapable.

Dependency and Institutional Care

The institutionalisation of retirement and pensions has greatly influenced public views about the dependence of the elderly. But professional and service relationships have also been affected. Confronted with disabled people who are also elderly, social workers do not assume they have the means to overcome their problems themselves and do not resort to the advocacy of self-reliant strategies. And there is a tendency to see admission to an institution as a more desirable step than the evidence would warrant. In the nineteenth century admission to the workhouse was recognised to be a deterrent to those intending to seek relief from the parish or from the Boards of Guardians. It is sometimes forgotten today that unconsciously if not consciously, professionals use admission to a residential institution as a regulator of demand for complex and expensive service. Certainly the point is not lost on many old people themselves, who will often fail to apply for local services for fear that they will be removed from their homes.

This fear is very understandable in relation to the strange division of functions between geriatric and residential care. Some enlightened local authority social service departments have done a great deal to make it possible for old people to be admitted only temporarily to residential care, but few, if any, have gone on to make the restoration of self-dependence and domestic autonomy a key objective in the case of longer-stay as well as short-stay residents. By contrast, those elderly people who are in principle far worse in health are admitted to geriatric hospitals on the assumption that many can be successfully treated and restored quickly to their homes and families. This is a paradox which deserves the closest study.

The contradictory policies towards 'rehabilitation' on the part of health and personal social services can only be understood when it is remembered that both have to regulate demand and minimise the costs of caring for old people as well as show they are meeting socially defined priority needs. In theory hospital costs can be displaced onto the local authority. Local authorities, in their turn, do not have the same opportunities to displace costs onto some other organisation, except in so far as they can argue that the costs should be borne by voluntary agencies and the family. The 'deterrent' features of residential homes for the elderly are therefore greatly underestimated at the present time. Such deterrence has to be interpreted as a complex phenomenon. It is not just a question of the images held by old people and their relatives living in the community. It is the system of working and social relationships embodied within the residential institution itself.

The argument here is that residential homes for the elderly serve functions for the wider society and not only for their inmates. While accommodating only a tiny percentage of the elderly population they symbolise the dependence of the elderly and legitimate their lack of access to equality of status. This argument depends in particular upon evidence about the capacities of the inmates or residents, and evidence about social restriction or authoritarian styles of management. I shall discuss these two in turn.

A law enacted in 1948 placed a duty on local authorities to provide residential homes for those 'in need of care and attention' (Part III of the National Assistance Act 1948). The implications of this duty for the dependent status of the inmates were then translated into administrative and operational form. There are, of course, implications for staff–resident relations, but also for the assumptions that are made about the potentialities or capacities of the residents. In the past 25 years there has been a great deal of research designed to compare the dependent status of residents implied by the legislation with measures of the infirmities or incapacities of the residents according to their mobility, continence or incontinence, capacity to wash and dress, and their lucidity or otherwise. (Among recent reviews see, for example, Hughes and Wilkin, 1980; Davies and

Knapp, 1981; Townsend, 1981, 1982; Bland and Bland, 1983; Wilkin, 1984). There are difficulties in amalgamating criteria to obtain some overall criterion of degree or severity of disablement. There are difficulties too in devising objective measures. Among careful discussions of the meaning of disablement are Bond (1976) and Bond and Carstairs (1979). Thus there might be grounds in principle for doubting the testimony of residents themselves, but there may be grounds for questioning the alternative testimony of staff. Measures of mental capacity are less common than of physical capacity, but have been attempted. In a 1963 national survey, for example, 42 per cent of elderly psychiatric patients were said by staff to be severely mentally impaired and 55 per cent were said to have no incapacity or only slight or moderate incapacity (Townsend, 1972).

During the last three decades much of the research has concentrated on a concept or measure of self-care and associated elements. (For examples see Townsend, 1962; Harris, 1967; Carstairs and Morrison, 1971; Meacher, 1972; Hare, 1977; Wilkin *et al.*, 1978; Plank, 1978; Vaswani *et al.*, 1978; Pattie and Gilliard, 1979; Schiphonst, 1979; Wade, Sawyer and Bell, 1983; DHSS, 1983b; Booth, 1985.) Table 2.3 illustrates some of the findings from the more substantial surveys of the last 25 years. Variations in the findings have to be interpreted with care, since the methods adopted are only broadly, and not exactly, comparable. It seems reasonable to conclude from the evidence:

(i)   a substantial minority (perhaps two-fifths) of elderly residents can undertake most or all self-care tasks; assessments of their capacities contradicting the idea that they are 'in need of care and attention';

(ii) the proportion of elderly residents who are capable of undertaking most or all self-care tasks has diminished in the last 20 years but not as substantially as often supposed by administrators and staff, and does not appear to have shown signs of further diminishing in the last five years, despite the high average age of residents in many homes;

(iii) contrariwise, a minority of residents are very severely disabled. There is little sign of administrative success in placing such severely disabled people, many of whom require medical and nursing or hospital care quickly enough in the geriatric residential or day-care facilities which they need, or that appropriate specialist services are made available where they live.

I will now review some of the principal evidence in relation to these three conclusions. A national survey in 1963 showed that 58 per cent of all residents had only slight or no incapacity (Townsend,

Table 2.3 Evidence of capacity of elderly residents of homes for self-care

Date of study	Scope of study	Percent of residents with capacity for self-care (local authority residents only unless otherwise specified)
i) 1958–59	National sample survey of Homes in England and Wales	72% neither bedfast nor requiring help dressing 59% mobile outside Home without assistance 52% (new residents only) with little or no incapacity for self-care
ii) 1963	National sample survey, Homes in Britain	37% little or no incapacity for self-care 21% little or no incapacity for self-care and household management
iii) 1969	National survey, Homes in Scotland	67% complete capacity for self-care (ie able to wash, dress and use toilet) 45% "fit", ie having complete capacity for self-care plus no impairment or only mild impairment of mobility, mental state and continence
iv) 1970	National census, Homes in England	45% minimally dependent (ie, continent, mobile without assistance, able to eat and drink without assistance, and mentally alert)
v) 1972	Survey of council Homes in eight London Boroughs	55% high or very high capacity for self-care
vi) 1973	64 Homes in Cheshire	63% able to wash, dress, feed and go to toilet unaided 42% no mobility problems, no assistance of any kind required and no behavioural problems
vii) 1981	National sample survey of Homes in England and Wales	25% minimally dependent and a further 36% "limited" dependency
viii) 1982	175 Homes in four local authorities	45% "independent" on self-care scale (42% ranked independent on scales of self-care, continence, social integration and orientation)

Sources: (i) and (ii) Townsend (1962, 1972); (iii) Cairstairs and Morrison (1971); (iv) DHSS (1975); (v) Plank (1977); (vi) Kimbell and Townsend (1974); (vii) Darton in Laming et al (1984); (viii) Booth (1985).

1972). A major survey in Scotland in 1969 showed that 67 per cent of residents of local authority homes were able to wash, dress and use toilets on their own initiative, and 45 per cent were defined as 'fit', that is, have complete capacity for self-care. The authors concluded that 54 per cent could have lived in sheltered housing (Carstairs and Morrison, 1971). In 1970 a DHSS census of England showed that as many as 45 per cent in local authority homes were 'minimally dependent' in the sense that they were 'mobile without assistance, continent, able to feed themselves and mentally alert' (DHSS, 1975, p. 44). In 1981 the DHSS sponsored a postal survey by the Personal Social Services Research Unit at the University of Kent, which found that the percentage of residents of local authority homes whose dependency was classified as 'minimal' was 25, but another 36 per cent were classified as of 'limited' dependency (11 per cent were classified as appreciable and 28 per cent as heavy) (Darton, in Laming *et al.*, 1984, pp. 9–21). Elsewhere from the survey, 71 per cent of the local authority residents were said to be able to wash, 52 per cent to dress, and 45 per cent were stated to be 'mentally alert'. These were all staff assessments.

Recent evidence from other sources produces higher rates of independence. Booth and his colleagues assessed 6947 residents in 175 homes for the elderly in North Yorkshire, Derbyshire, Nottinghamshire and Kirklees, and repeated the exercise for the residents of these homes in 1981 and again in 1982. Thus there were three successive censuses. These produced no evidence that 'dependency' was increasing. Moreover, a very substantial minority (two-fifths) required little or no help. In 1980, 42 per cent were classified as 'independent', with 41 per cent as moderately and 17 per cent severely dependent (Booth, 1985).

Other recent research supports Booth's conclusion. For example, a study of 11 local authority homes in Scotland showed that there had been no increases in the degree of behavioural disabilities in two years: 'Residential homes are no longer absorbing additional numbers of dependent or demented old people' (Masterton *et al.*, 1981). A study of 500 residents in 14 local authority homes in Manchester between 1978 and 1981 also found very little change: 'Fears that the resident population is becoming concentrated in the most dependent categories do not seem to be justified by the evidence' (Charlesworth and Wilkin, 1982).

Booth's study is helpful in bringing out something which is not acknowledged in many studies – that staff must not be treated as disinterested or unbiased witnesses of residents' capacities. Because of the duties laid upon them by management and the tendency to regard residents as passive recipients of care, staff are liable to take an unduly pessimistic view of residents' capacities. To some extent they are conditioned by past experiences. The force of this can be appreciated by references to the literature in Britain of studies of residents' experiences (for example, Barton, 1961; Apte, 1968; Robb, 1968; Meacher, 1972; Burrage and Phillips, 1973; Hare, 1977; Willcocks *et al.*, 1982). While indeed there are a minority of residents who undoubtedly require a great deal of assistance, there are also, possibly the majority, who receive little or no help and yet who, because they reside in such an institution, are understood none the less to be very dependent and who certainly are not expected to play much part in the day-to-day activities of the home. Levels of staffing and the organisation of daily routines do not allow the number of very severely disabled residents to exceed a kind of 'tolerance' level.

Staff are also naturally concerned to maintain a 'manageable' level of care. Pressures to maintain this mixture of very disabled and non-disabled residents are maintained in a variety of ways. Staff can be very protective of some residents entering a terminal phase of life. Some residents seek to stay where they are, irrespective of whether their health has deteriorated or improved. The visible and incontrovertible presence of some very severely disabled residents can serve not only as persuasive justification for the existence of such an institution but of the need for more resources. Such pressures have to be remembered when efforts are made to change policy.

The problem is not just that there are still many elderly residents of Homes who are much less dependent than they are assumed to be, but also that there are a minority at the other end of the continuum who are more disabled than there are facilities in residential homes to provide for them. This 'mismatch' has been documented for many years (Kidd, 1962; Mezey *et al.*, 1968; Carstairs and Morrison, 1971; Townsend, 1972; Wilkin *et al.*, 1978; Wilkin and Jolley, 1979; Wilkin, in Laming *et al.*, 1984). There are elderly residents in geriatric hospitals, psychiatric hospitals and residential homes, and there is evidence of considerable overlap in their conditions and needs. There are glaring contrasts in their facilities and management, as well as ideology. Some have argued that a single form of residence might be provided for the most seriously disabled of present inmates; and that measures should otherwise be taken for less disabled people to live in homes of their own with supporting services (Townsend, 1972). Others have argued for greater rationalisation and inter-linkages between facilities, so that 'a full range of health services is available to people living in residential homes, including assessment, treatment, rehabilitation and care ... the emphasis has to some extent shifted away from sterile arguments about appropriate placement and towards issues of how best to meet people's needs' (Wilkin, in Laming *et al.*, 1984, pp. 26–7).

Two conclusions can be drawn from the array of studies of capacity for self-care. One is that at any particular time there is an enormous range among elderly residents, with some who are unquestionably so severely disabled as to require help with almost every act of life, but a substantial proportion at the other extreme who, even on the testimony of staff themselves, require little or no help to look after their own personal needs and achieve at least a sheltered domestic independence. The other conclusion is no less pregnant with implications for policy. It is that the assumptions made about elderly persons admitted to residential institutions, when translated into organisational form and management practice, contain and inhibit the capacity of elderly residents to undertake a variety of activities on their own behalf and on that of others. In short, the concept of 'dependence' must not be treated as individual or inevitable. Dependence is in part socially created.

A very clear distinction has to be drawn between staff assessments and independent measures of both capacities and potentialities. An excellent example is provided by a study of patients on long-stay geriatric wards (Adams, Davies and Northwood, 1979) the patients were moved temporarily into bungalow accommodation while their permanent accommodation was being renovated. The bungalow units were said to be 'homely', with single or double bedrooms, domestic-style furniture, and fitted carpets. Changes were observed in the patients which were described by the authors as remarkable. Patients moved about more, exercised choice more frequently, abandoned some of the behaviour of 'sick' persons, and began to perform domestic tasks in the kitchen and elsewhere. Rates of incontinence and mental confusion diminished. The literature on such instances and controlled experiments of changes induced is summarised in Wade, Sawyer and Bell (1983).

We have seen that the literature on self-care and dependence cannot be properly appraised independent of the knowledge of social conditions. I shall turn now to consider how social dependence is constructed. The elderly population of institutions is very unrepresentative. According to the 1971 Census relatively four times as many bachelors as married men and three times as many spinsters as married women of 90 years of age or over in Britain were in different types of institution. As many as 37 per cent of bachelors and 44 per cent of spinsters of this age were living in institutions. However, marital status is only a crude indicator of family status. A study in 1963 found that the chance of admission to an institution was correlated closely to the structure of family relationships. The richer the network of family associations, the smaller the chance of admission. Those with rich family associations who are admitted tend to be more severely disabled than others. This has implications for the pattern of likely social association within the institution. Residents are more dependent on what their immediate surroundings have to offer. Proportionately more of them than in the elderly population as a whole are unlikely to be practised in communal activities and associations. Some potentialities may have been dormant for many years. This helps to suggest why some capacities may be unsuspected.

While family background helps to explain the disproportionate representation of unmarried, widowed and childless people it does not easily explain the presence of some people who are active. Only by examining circumstances at admission does it become possible to find explanations. One important causal element is homelessness. This may arise as a consequence of loss of job, failure to pay rent, or eviction from housing provided by an employer or a husband's employer, and dispossession of property during stays in hospital. Then there are people who have gone through severe episodes of bereavement or other instances of social dislocation and become described as 'confused' or 'wandering', 'forgetful', 'a danger to themselves' and whose homes have become thoroughly neglected. Desolation can easily be mistaken for physical or mental incapacity, especially when sharpened by malnourishment. A few weeks of warmth and good food can sometimes work seeming miracles.

If this helps to explain why some residents are found to be physically and mentally active then we must go on to explain why they are not transferred home. One problem is that entry to a residential home is thought to be like that of changing home address, and steps are often taken to transfer a tenancy, sell a home and sell possessions. In some cases physical and mental recovery comes too late, when there is no home to which to return. Another part of the problem lies in the lack of power on the part of the social service department managing residential homes to ensure transfer to new tenancies, even those in 'sheltered' housing. But another part of the problem lies in a kind of severance from former community, family and a whole range of social contacts and relationships. Many homes are miles away from former areas of residence, and some are very difficult to reach by public transport. Relatives often feel discouraged from undertaking small tasks for elderly residents and feel they are not welcomed by staff, often because staff themselves fall into attitudes of blaming relatives for abandoning their elderly members. Visits to home areas are rarely sponsored by staff and there is a general failure to maintain lines of communication so that a return home may be kept open as a viable option.

An even more fundamental problem is the social isolation into which too many residents find themselves thrust. Numerous research studies have revealed the isolation of a high proportion of residents: the lack of even a single friend; the higher rate of severe or frequent loneliness; the discouragement of spontaneous social activity; the inability of visiting relatives and friends to adopt useful roles; the lack of participation in the decisions governing the daily programme; the lack of satisfying, and sociable occupation. For example, a study of a cross-section of 100 local authority homes in England, published in 1982, found that 44 per cent of residents believed that residents 'no longer do anything that is of real use to other people'; that 43 per cent felt lonely; and that 33 per cent felt they 'no longer have anyone to talk to about personal things' (Peace, Kellaher and Willcocks, 1982, p. 9). In representing practice throughout England, the testimony of this study is more significant perhaps than the large number of local studies. The authors pointed out that the new philosophy of care, and the principles on which it is based, which had been advocated in several publications in the 1970s (Hanson, 1972; DHSS, 1976; Personal Social Services Council, 1977) and backed by Age Concern England, was 'still far from being expressed in common practice'. The more that residential care moved towards life in a private household the more acceptable it was to residents. Homes which were organised into small groups, with single rooms, more control over what happened and more opportunity to undertake domestic activities and receive and provide hospitality to visitors, were preferred, providing there was enough space and opportunity for privacy. The authors believed that 'the residential flatlet represents one practical alternative to existing institutional arrangements which would promote a dignified and less dependent style of living for elderly residents' (Peace *et al.*, 1982, p. 52).

For many years it was believed that the gradual abandonment of large institutions and the adoption of more personalised regimes in homes with 30–50 residents would resolve many of the criticisms of residential care. A great deal of research money has been put into the examination of different types of 'regime'. A large number of specialised studies of models of care have been carried out (examples are: King, Raynes and Tizard, 1971; Miller and Gwynne, 1972; Kimbell, Townsend and Bird, 1974; Peace, Kellaher and Willcocks, 1982; and especially Booth, 1985). Booth's study showed that too much importance should not be attached to the possibilities of improving the character of regimes in residential homes. He and his team had come to

> reject the comforting idea that most of the damaging consequences of institutional living could be avoided by improved methods of care and better training for staff. ... Sociologically, the differences between regimes must, in the light of this study, be seen as a veneer that decorates the massive uniformity of institutional life, and catches the eye for precisely that reason. Underneath lies the same crushing panoply of controls over the lives and doings of the residents. Changing the wrapper does not alter the contents. ... The findings of this study suggest that the detrimental effects of residential living cannot be allayed within the bounds of current residential practice. (Booth, 1985, pp. 205–7)

The recent studies by Peace, Kellaher and Willcocks, and of Booth and his colleagues, suggest that the various regimes practised in the residential homes system do not provide a sufficient contrast to provide any kind of solution to the problems of institutional living. The more radical solutions of geriatric nursing home care for a small minority of very disabled elderly and sheltered housing and day-care facilities for the more substantial minority of less severely disabled elderly are the right alternatives. Studies of sheltered housing schemes continue to provide evidence of satisfaction among tenants. One recent study in Scotland concluded that sheltered housing was 'an overwhelming success' (Wirz *et al.*, 1981, p. 94).

At least two criticisms of existing residential institutions for the elderly have to be remembered. One is the disorienting and controlling features of different institutions in the same 'system'. There are three types of long-stay institution: geriatric hospitals, psychiatric hospitals and residential homes. They vary enormously in standards of furnishing and amenities as well as daily routine and management. Their inmate populations overlap in their characteristics, and forms of social control are induced by fears on the part of inmates to transfer. It might be argued that those requiring highly specialised facilities 24 hours a day should be brought to one single type of institution, under the formal authority of a geriatrician and social service director. The three forms of long-stay institution could in time be merged and that type of care provided in very small hospitals or nursing homes with homely management regimes. The majority of the remaining patients and residents of hospitals and residential homes (or, rather, their successors) could live in sheltered or special housing supported in part by domiciliary services, including day-care arrangements.

Internally, the majority of residents are placed in a situation of enforced dependence. The routine of residential homes, made necessary by small staff and economical administration, and committed to an ideology of 'care and attention' rather than the encouragement of self-help and self-management, seems to deprive many residents of the opportunity if not the incentive to occupy themselves and even of the means of communication. A large number of research sources could be quoted in justification (for an interesting example, see DHSS, 1979). The type and level of staff, amenities and resources have been developed not only in relation to the characteristics, including the perceived capacities, of inmates but also the roles staff expect inmates to play. Staff have tended to resist any increase in the number or proportion of inmates requiring a great deal of attention. They become conscious of the value of inmates who perform large and small tasks in the organisation and tend to give excuses rather than rational grounds for the presence in the institution of these inmates. On the other hand, the roles are distinguished from those played by staff by their subordinate and even menial status and the derisory forms of payment which accompany them. Occupational roles are clearly distinguished partly to maintain the lower status and presumed dependency of inmates.

Dependency and Community Care

Artificial dependency is fostered, however, not just in too many of the existing structures of residential care, but in the community services. Elderly people tend to be treated as the passive recipients of services the nature and extent of which are decided by others. Meals and services are 'delivered' – the widening use of the term 'service delivery' is significant and reflects the relationship. People visit, or are transported, to day centres where programmes are often restricted and entirely within the control of social workers, physiotherapists and others to decide and organise. There is a 'take it or leave it' approach to the provision of domiciliary services which recreates the passivity of the recipient which is such a notable observation in many residential homes. What is neglected is the social structure, and psychology of independence and interdependence. One study has reviewed 60 or 70 studies on the domiciliary services (Goldberg and Connelly, 1982). The studies seem to produce more questions than answers, but the authors comment frequently on the tendency to maintain services without frequent review of need, or the possibility of facilitating self-management or management by relatives and neighbours. A substantial proportion of aids were not used. A substantial number of meals delivered were delivered to people who cooked for themselves on other days. Home-help services were sometimes of a character which the recipients could undertake themselves, when they needed alternative kinds of service. In general a picture emerges of a very rough relationship between need and service, and little relationship of service to the initiation or restoration of reciprocal services among neighbours or members of a family, or the participation of an isolated old person in a new social grouping.

The planning documents of successive governments have sought a shift in priorities from residential to community care. Despite powerful expressions of opinion, however, the emergence of a coherent and substantial community care sector cannot be said to have properly materialised. This is not easy to explain. The failure to achieve a shift in priorities has to be explained partly in relation to a failure to conceptualise meaning, both in terms of objectives and in operational terms. Government plans can be shown to be inconsistent, and often unspecific (Townsend, 1981, pp. 105–9). In large measure it must be explained by the powerful vested interests of certain branches of the professions, staff associations and unions, and sections of administration. The great majority of medical, nursing and attendant staff work in hospitals or other residential institutions. Two-thirds of qualified medical practitioners work in hospitals and between 80 and 90 per cent of qualified nursing staff. This helps to preserve the traditional emphasis on residential institutions, which in any case tend to serve wider regulative functions in society. For example, they regulate and confirm inequality in society, by reflecting social class in the nature and quality of provision. They regulate deviation from the central social values of self-help, domestic independence, personal thrift, willingness to work, productive effort and family care. Their functions cannot be properly understood except in relation to external structures, organisations and groups.

The numbers of bedfast, severely incapacitated and infirm elderly people who are living in the community dwarf the numbers in residential care, and there are real dangers in the present situation of concentrating too high a share of available resources on the few at the expense of the much larger numbers living in the community, who require only supplementary supporting services to live independently or with their families (Economist Intelligence Unit, 1973; Booth, 1978; Hunt, 1976; Abrams, 1978, 1980). To redress the imbalance, plans and departments would have to be restructured and priorities of service in the community with associated services clearly defined. In principle it is easier to organise the provision of services varying by nature and quantity in the community than it is in residential settings.

However, the problem of recreating dependency in community care services is very real, as argued above. Not only are domiciliary services frequently converted into 'commodity' services, particularly involving the delivery of meals and aids, but day centres and physiotherapy are sometimes organised in ways which allow little scope for diversity of occupation, self-management and self-development. The duties of home helps and community nurses are often heavily circumscribed and, because they are often rationed severely as well, they become less relevant to personal needs and more the token gestures of a public authority to people who are perceived as passive recipients of services. The organisation of services as 'preventive' services, or as services which involve a great deal of collaboration on the part of family, friends and other members of a local community, and the organisation of programmes which promote recovery of health and morale and the substitution of new for lost activities are still rare examples among the activities of social service departments.

By not addressing this objective the community services fail to complement the much more extensive network of informal – primarily familial – services. In the 1950s a comparative study of statutory and informal services for the elderly concluded: 'The family has the care of a far larger number of the infirm and aged and chronic sick than all our hospitals, welfare homes and domiciliary services put together' (Townsend, 1957, p. 194). 'Extensive services were also found to be undertaken by elderly people for members of their families' (ibid., pp. 45–50). For the 1980s the few research studies which treat the family seriously have come to much the same conclusion. Thus 'what is clear is that there are more elderly providing help of one sort or another than there are receiving help, and where help is given it comes preponderantly from spouse, family or friends and neighbours, while help from formal services is minimal' (Wenger, 1984, p. 134). The 'formal' services turn out to be poorly related both to individual needs and to existing networks of reciprocal services (see also Parker, 1985). The statutory social services are exaggerated by professionals, voluntary bodies and politicians in their importance – relative to family and community. Elderly people are conceived as isolated recipients of service, and the stultifying, restricted and restrictive character of that service is not properly acknowledged. As a consequence the conception and development of community services helps to foster and deepen public images of elderly people as dependent wards of the state.

Conclusion
The argument of this chapter is that twentieth-century processes of retirement, establishment of minimum pensions, residential care and delivery of community services have created forms of social dependency among the elderly which are artificial. Forms of institutionalised ageism have been developed to suit the management of industry and the economy in capitalist and state socialist societies alike, and has come to be reinforced by the shifting social distribution of power. This conclusion is very hard for some people to accept. On the one hand, there has been abundant evidence of strongly motivated concern about retired and particularly infirm people, with many speeches being made about a caring, compassionate society, and a flow of special measures and subsidies for the elderly section of the population. On the other hand, retirement has been imposed on a much higher proportion of people at 60 or 65; substitute incomes have been kept far below average earnings; there is continued pressure to reduce the pensionable ages further; there are continuing tendencies to segregate the frail and even the physically active elderly, and within the community as well as the residential services there are tendencies to reinforce the dependent and non-participative status of the elderly. An artificial dependency is being manufactured for a growing proportion of the population at the same time as measures are being taken to alleviate some of the worst effects of that dependency. This paradox deserves to be understood and argued about more passionately than it is.

There is, of course, a sharp contrast between the low status in which old people are held publicly and the regard in which they are held privately within their families. In the family, age is of secondary importance. People are grandparents, parents, brothers or sisters and friends or neighbours first and foremost. Retirement from familial roles is a much more flexible contingency, dependent primarily on health or disablement. In some respects the family also provides an escape from the psychological and social bruises which can be inflicted externally, and up to a point provide meaningful activity and genuine respect. The positive contribution to the welfare of grandchildren and children of many elderly women is greatly underestimated just as their labour specifically on behalf of their husbands and in general on behalf of the economy throughout adult working life goes largely unrecognised. Capital and state, separately or in combination, may have fostered the dependency of women within the family but, paradoxically, has created an independent reactive system of interdependence, occupation, mutual respect and loyalty. The defensive and restorative mechanisms of the family temper the dependency created by the state.

There is clearly room for an alternative interpretation of the roles to be played by the elderly whereby many more have opportunities to continue in paid employment, to find alternative occupation, to have rights to a larger income, to maintain control over the homes and environment where they would wish to live, and the kind of local community activities and services to which they would wish to contribute as well as to have access.

3 Social Policy and the Older Worker

Shirley Dex and Chris Phillipson

In this chapter we shall examine the position of older workers (men and women aged 50 and over) in the British labour market. Our intention is to provide a review of historical and current trends which have contributed to the displacement of older people from full-time employment. The starting point for our discussion revolves around two major developments: first, the use of retirement as a key element in manpower policy (Phillipson, 1982); secondly, the acceleration of trends favouring early retirement (Jackson, 1984). The *expectation* of retirement is now a prominent feature in the lives of older men and women. Few are likely to have paid work after leaving their full-time occupation; many will be contemplating the possibility of leaving before the state retirement age.

In our discussion we shall provide an assessment of post-war debates about the skills and abilities of older workers. We shall review the current position of older women and older men in the labour market. Finally, there will be a critical review of employment policies aimed at older people.

Population and Productivity

The extent to which older people have been excluded from work has been established in a number of surveys (Casey and Bruche, 1983). Labour statistics reveal a major transformation in work experiences: in 1931 one-half of men aged 65 and over were in the labour force; in 1951 the figure was 31 per cent; and by 1983 it had fallen to just 9 per cent (OPCS, 1984). The situation of women is more complex and is discussed in detail below, but the trend is again downward.

However, the post-war history of the older worker shows remarkable fluctuations in respect of labour and social policies. The statistics cited above fail to do justice to recent labour history. In the 1940s and 1950s there was a vigorous debate on how to assist older people's engagement or re-engagement in the sphere of paid work

(Clark and Spengler, 1980). Indeed, running parallel to the institutionalisation of retirement in the 1950s and 1960s was the emergence of a discipline – industrial gerontology – which was concerned with assisting the retention of older people in the labour force.

The stimulus for this research came from anxieties about a population inbalance between 'productive' and 'non-productive' groups within the economy. Amongst the non-productive, it was the threat of an ageing population which caused most concern. For the Royal Commission on Population (1949), prolonging active working life appeared the best solution to easing the burden of too many elderly people and too few workers. The immediate task, therefore, was to remove the various constraints which prompted people to withdraw from working during their sixties.

Fortunately for the Commission, help was at hand to address precisely this problem. In 1945 the Nuffield Foundation initiated three research projects concerned with investigating the social and medical implications of an ageing population. One of the projects was concerned with the capacities of older people for work, and was 'inspired by the belief that the increased proportion of older people would mean that many would have to continue working beyond normal retiring age if there was not to be a serious shortage of labour' (Welford, 1976, p. 129). The project was supported by a grant given to the Psychological Laboratory of Cambridge University where the Nuffield Unit for Research into Problems of Ageing was formed in 1946.

Additional research units concerned with the problems facing older workers were formed under Murrell at Bristol University, Hearnshaw and Heron at Liverpool University, and Eunice Belbin at London University. The work at Bristol continued the laboratory and industrial work of the Cambridge group. The Liverpool Unit was concerned with the use of standard tests and the assessment of attitudes in industry. Belbin's work at London University examined the question of training and retraining in middle age (Welford, 1976).

The potential of older workers

The mid-1940s to the mid-1950s were, in many respects, a 'golden age' for interest in older workers – men in particular. Key figures were Welford, Heron, the Belbins, Le Gros Clark and Murrell. The range of interests was impressive: the age structure of occupations (Murrell, 1957); performance problems of older workers on conveyor-belt or assembly-line work (Brown, 1957); the difficulties of semi-skilled workers (Heron and Chown, 1960); preparation for retirement (Heron, 1962); and the relationship between skill and human ageing (Welford, 1958).

Most of these topics were discussed in articles appearing in *Occupational Psychology*, a journal which carried, throughout the 1950s and early 1960s, numerous papers on experimental work relating to the position of older people in industry. Despite the limitations of this work (particularly in its bias against women workers) it did reveal serious deficiencies in the way people were treated as they matured in the labour force. Heron and Chown, for example, reported the way in which for older semi-skilled men, 'Alternative work always involves change to a relatively menial occupation – with loss of status and earnings' (Heron and Chown, 1967, p. 46); and Murrell posed questions (in 1959) which remain radical given the present treatment of older workers. Amongst the questions he asked were: 'What avoidable long-term health hazards ... are present in a work situation?'; 'What is the basis for discrimination against older workers in employment policies?'; 'What is the effect of bonus schemes on older men?'; 'What are the determining factors in promotion, and how do they discriminate against the older man?' (Murrell, 1959, p. 126).

As well as raising important questions, research demonstrated the extent to which chronological age was a poor guide to understanding work capacity and ability. Experimental research suggested that individuals could adjust to, and offset, the changes affecting them in middle and later life (Welford, 1958). Such research also stimulated work in areas such as job redesign and retraining (Griew, 1964; Belbin, 1965).

However, we also find, running alongside work concerned with the placement of older workers in industry, a gradual appreciation that long-term trends were making permanent retirement at 65 or 60 increasingly likely. This was the message from the work of, for example, Le Gros Clark. His study *Work, Age and Leisure* was published in 1966, and had as its sub-title: 'Causes and consequences of the shortened working life'. Clark's was a prophetic study, which looked ahead to the emergence of groups of older people existing outside the labour market, with an independent life-style and values and demands of their own. It was realisation of the economic and social changes described by Le Gros Clark, which was to undermine the position of industrial gerontology. According to A. J. Welford, in his review 'Thirty Years of Psychological Research on Age and Work':

> In 1955, revised population estimates made it clear that, as a result of the post-war 'baby bulge' there was unlikely to be a serious imbalance between those of working age and dependents above and below it during the next few decades. At the same time, automation appeared on the scene as a bogey which seemed to threaten many jobs and so to remove the need for older people to go on working – indeed, to make it undesirable

that they should do so. The expected results of automation did not occur, but in Britain there was an immediate collapse of both interest in industrial gerontology and concern for the psychological aspects of ageing which had been largely inspired by it. The Bristol and Liverpool units continued for a few years and then ceased, while Dr Belbin's unit expanded its interests to industrial training in general – a field in which it now plays a leading international role. The psychological studies of ageing that continued were almost entirely by individual members of university teaching staffs. (Welford, 1976, p. 131)

This 'collapse of interest' was highlighted when, in 1958, the Advisory Committee on the Employment of Older Men and Women was terminated (National Advisory Committee, 1953, 1955). The Chairman recalled that wide publicity had been given to the committee's two reports and there was evidence of 'considerable success in breaking down the traditional barriers against the employment of older workers' (Ministry of Labour, 1959, p. 26). It was also emphasised that the winding-up of the committee did not mean that 'the government had lost interest in the employment of older workers' (Ministry of Labour, 1959, p. 27). However, when at the beginning of 1959 the Minister of Labour was asked how many men had been forced into retirement as a consequence of the trade depression over the previous twelve months, the reply came: 'I regret that statistics giving the information are not available' (Hansard, vol. 599, col. 59).

Older men's employment
By the 1960s and early 1970s numerous studies pointed to the employment difficulties of older workers in settings as diverse as mining (Department of Employment, 1970) and car assembly (MacKay, 1972). MacKay's work suggested that redundant car workers beyond their mid-forties stood a much lower chance than younger workers even of being re-engaged by their previous firm. Daniel's (1972) study of redundant workers at Woolwich indicated that the older the worker the greater the likelihood of lower earnings in any subsequent employment. Fogarty's comprehensive review, *40 to 60: how we waste the middle-aged*, found a widespread tendency to bar middle-aged applicants from recruitment to professional and managerial jobs '[a] tendency [which] probably increased from the 1950s to the early 1970s' (Fogarty, 1975, p. 83).

The exclusion of older men from work gathered pace throughout the 1970s and early 1980s (Makeham, 1980). The striking decline in economic activity of men over pensionable age has already been mentioned. Even more remarkable is the trend towards early retirement: the percentage of men aged 60–64 economically active declining from 85 per cent in 1973 to 63 per cent in 1983; amongst men aged 55–59 the figures were 94 per cent to 85 per cent (OPCS, 1984).

These developments have received various forms of support from the state. The Job Release Scheme (JRS) was introduced in 1977. This allows older workers to leave employment before normal retirement age, in return for which they receive a weekly allowance from the state. The scheme also has a 'replacement condition' whereby the retiring person must be replaced, directly or indirectly, by someone on the unemployment register.

In 1983 the scheme was extended to include part-time work. Men aged 62–64, women aged 59 and disabled men aged 60–64 who are willing to give up at least half their standard working week can receive a taxable job-release allowance at half the full-time rate; an unemployed person must, at the same time, be recruited for the other half of the job. The scheme has, however, attracted very few applicants. The Department of Employment estimated that it would provide part-time job opportunities for up to 53,000 persons by March 1985. However, despite an expensive advertising campaign, 11 months after the scheme began only 138 people were receiving a part-time job-release allowance (Laczko, 1985).

In addition to the JRS, a higher long-term rate of supplementary benefit is paid to workers aged 60 and over, on the condition that they no longer actively seek employment. One final factor in reducing the supply of workers is the operation of the Redundancy Payments Act. Payments are related to length of service, a feature which has encouraged a higher proportion of older employees to leave their jobs.

The causes of early retirement
The growth of early retirement is closely linked to the emergence of mass unemployment (Walker 1982e). Indeed, as Jackson points out, early retirement must be seen 'as a response to unemployment rather than as the response to a demand for change on its own merits from any section of industry' (Jackson, 1984, p. 28). We can, of course, list a number of factors which, taken together, reinforce, emphasise or contribute to the pressure for early retirement. Amongst these are: (1) the decline in semi- and unskilled jobs (Bosanquet, 1983); (2) the entry or re-entry into the labour market of women workers (see below), and the willingness of employers to accommodate them at lower wages (Townsend, 1979); (3) the growth – through occupational pension schemes – of financial provision for early retirement on the grounds of ill-health; and (4) the growing number (albeit a minority) who *choose* early retirement as a positive and valued alternative to full-time work (McGoldrick and Cooper, 1980).

Other causative factors exist, but they must be regarded as more speculative. For example, there is some evidence that work disability is *increasing* at the same time as a decline in mortality rates

(Feldman, 1983; Verbrugge, 1984). This may arise through improved survival rates for diseases which in the past were usually fatal. At present, however, the disabled or partially disabled are likely to be regarded by employers as suitable candidates for redundancy; alternatively, they are the least likely to be selected for work by employers choosing from a large pool of unemployed people.

Despite the above points, the context of mass unemployment is crucial for understanding the dynamics of earlier retirement. Thus, as many commentators have pointed out, present conditions may lead people to accept early retirement not because they really want to do so, but because of workplace pressure, or their own view that retirement may lead to a younger person getting a job. Such pressures may be felt most keenly by unskilled and semi-skilled workers, a group who are more likely than white-collar groups to suffer from ill-health and to work in industries experiencing long-term decline and/or technological change. The social implications arising from these trends may be a deepening of class divisions between, on the one hand, high status groups who are able to construct a new and enriched life-style in middle age; and on the other hand, working-class groups for whom early retirement means an extension in the number of years spent in poverty (Altmann, 1981).

Older Women's Employment

So far the bulk of our analysis has concentrated on men's experience in the labour market. Indeed, in the past, it is the male experience of work and non-work which has preoccupied industrial gerontologists. More general discussions about retirement policies have neglected to consider whether the policies are relevant and appropriate for women workers, or what their implications for women might be. Such a neglect is perhaps not so surprising if one starts from the assumption that women are a marginal or trivial proportion of the workforce, or that women are more committed to family life and domestic work than they are to paid employment. It could be argued that the neglect of a marginal workforce is quite reasonable. We find such arguments unacceptable for a number of reasons: first, they fail accurately to reflect women's actual position and experiences; secondly, they treat all women as homogeneous when clearly there are major variations between them; thirdly, the assumption that a marginal workforce is unimportant fails to recognise the inter-relationships between core and peripheral sectors of either labour markets or of industry and that both can be vital to each other. The time is ripe, therefore, for a thorough examination of the implications of retirement policies for women workers in the context of women's actual working experiences and behaviour.

An examination of these issues with respect to women raises a number of problems. On the whole, data collection about employment and economic activity trends has been biased towards men, as the unemployment statistics most clearly illustrate. The regular Department of Employment series of unemployment figures are based on a count of those who register as unemployed and available for work, usually in order to be eligible for unemployment benefit. It is well known that women have often failed to register because they were not eligible for benefits, and the register therefore underestimates women's unemployment (Roberts, 1981). If women's unemployment figures are inaccurate then so too will be their economic activity rates; both will be too low. The annual figures from the *General Household Survey* (GHS) show that as many as 60 per cent of all unemployed women fail to register (Roberts, 1981).

Another complication when examining women's employment arises because many women work part-time. The regular statistics on employment and economic activity rates do not always give a breakdown of part-time and full-time work. In the case of men's employment this omission is not important because the number of men in part-time work is very small.[1] In 1983 however, 43 per cent of all women workers were in part-time jobs (EOC, 1984, p. 77). Even when part-time and full-time jobs are distinguished as in the Census of Employment, part-time work is likely to be under-reported because it often falls outside the PAYE net which is used to collect the data. Surveys of women can make up for some of these deficiencies but only on an *ad hoc* basis.

Having established some of the difficulties in this area, we can now begin to collate the information about the employment of older women which is available from the regular series and from occasional surveys of women's employment in Britain.

Women's economic activity rates can be seen to fluctuate over time according to their age and marital status. For women aged 55–59, the economic activity rates of women who were not married have been on a downward trend since 1971.[2] In 1973, for example, this age group had an economic activity rate of 69 per cent whereas in 1983 the percentage was 53 per cent. A similar trend is visible in the activity rates of married women between the ages of 60–64 and over 65 years old. For example, married women aged 60–64 had an economic activity rate of 25 per cent in 1973 but only 20 per cent in 1983. Although the size in the rate varies, these trends are the same as those for men of the equivalent ages, i.e. 55–59, 60–64 and 65+. The fluctuations in the activity rates of these groups of older women and men are considerably greater than those visible in other age groups over the same periods. Married women aged 55–59 are the exception to these trends since they have economic activity rates which were increasing from 48 per cent in 1973 to 52 per cent in 1983.

Older women and the recession

Women's unemployment has been increasing as the 1970s recession has deepened, but we do not have readily available statistics on women's registered plus their unregistered unemployment by age. An analysis of the registered unemployment flows by the DE illustrates that for both women and men, the likelihood of becoming unemployed decreased with age, the likelihood of ceasing to be unemployed after becoming unemployed also decreased with age; older workers tended to experience much longer spells of unemployment than younger workers and it was harder to cease being unemployed as the duration of unemployment lengthened (*Employment Gazette*, 1984, p. 225). The GHS shows that the proportion of all non-married women who were unemployed increased from 3 per cent in 1973 to 12 per cent in 1983. A large increase in the proportion of married women registered as unemployed took place after 1977 largely because the married women's option was then removed.[3] Older women do not seem to be unemployed disproportionately to other women, as far as we can tell from the published statistics. A recent survey of women confirms this conclusion. The Women and Employment Survey (1980) found that 21 per cent of all women in the survey were aged 50 and over, and 21 per cent of all unemployed women were over 50 years old. Similarly, 11 per cent of all women in the survey were over 55 and 10 per cent of all unemployed women were aged 55 and over (Martin and Roberts, 1984, p. 16).

In a period of rising unemployment, therefore, we find that a number of groups had marked declines in their economic activity rates. The groups with this similar experience were women over the age of statutory retirement, non-married women approaching retirement age who presumably are most like men in their work histories, and men who are on both sides of their statutory retirement age. Married women were the exception and they constitute the vast majority of economically active women: approximately two-thirds of all economically active women are married. The other evidence on women's economic activity from employment levels and unemployment also shows that married women have seen an increase in their employment, and this increase has been in part-time work.[4]

The fact that the employment and economic activity of some groups of older women (and men) appear to feel the effects of the deterioration in labour market conditions to a greater extent than younger (although not very young) workers supports the idea that they constitute part of a reserve army of labour, the latent component (Phillipson, 1982). But it would seem to be the case that not all women workers have this experience. Older (and younger) married women's location in the growth area of part-time work in service industries in the British economy appears to have given them a measure of protection from the effects of the 1970s/1980s recession. This conclusion has been noted by other analyses of women workers. Bruegel (1979) and Dex and Perry (1984) for example, in their studies of women of all ages noted that women could not be regarded as a disposable workforce on the basis of their employment fluctuations over the post-war period up to 1976 and 1981, respectively. Joshi's (1982) analysis of the cyclical elasticity (sensitivity) of certain groups of workers of different ages from 1961 to 1974 found that older women were a very stable group and that the elasticities of women and men were not significantly different. We conclude that the reserve army of labour notion is probably deficient as a description of older married women's role in the British economy of the 1970s and 1980s because of their location in part-time work and in certain sectors of the labour markets. These results also challenge the idea that older married women are a marginal or secondary workforce.

Women and work
Before considering the implications of these results for retirement policies we can document other findings which also challenge the idea that women are marginal workers. The recent Women and Employment Survey (WES) compiled detailed work histories of the women aged 16–59 in the survey. These showed that on average women worked for 65 per cent of their potential working lives, but all the trends suggest that this proportion will increase as the time spent not working because of childbirth has been declining markedly. Women aged 50–54 in 1980 had spent 59 per cent of their time working – 43 per cent in full-time work, and 16 per cent in part-time employment. Women aged 55–59 at this date had also spent 59 per cent of their time working – 42 per cent full-time and 17 per cent part-time. These proportions represented average time spent working of between 22.2 and 25.1 years of which 16.2–17.9 years were spent in full-time work and 6.0–7.2 years were in part-time employment for each age group, respectively (Martin and Roberts, 1984). Women start to work part-time on their first return to work after childbirth. Thereafter they change between full-time and part-time employment, sometimes repeatedly (Dex, 1984). Equivalent figures for men are not available since detailed work histories have not been compiled for men over their whole working lives.[5] We would expect, however, that on average men would have spent longer in employment than women, and longer in full-time work, but that there are variations within both sexes.

The WES data also found that 9 per cent of both 50–54 and 55–59 year age groups had been economically active throughout their working lives; 99 per cent of each age group had had some working experience and 67 per cent and 53 per cent respectively were currently working in 1980 which was higher than the average of 62 per cent for all women (Martin and Roberts, 1984). The WES data are important in showing that work is clearly very important to women. The idea that women work for pin money was shown to be false. The majority of women disagreed with this view of women's employment, and women's earnings, whilst being less than those of men, could contribute as much as 60 per cent of family income. Other data show that this figure can be as high as 75 per cent (EOC, 1984). The main reason women worked was financial although other aspects of working were cearly important to these women. Many women experienced financial stress even though many did not see themselves in a breadwinner's role, and this stress was a large part of why these women worked. Of the women over 50 who were working at the interview, approximately 80 per cent expected to continue working until statutory retirement age. A recent survey of British social attitudes asked people, 'If you received what you would regard as a reasonable living income while unemployed do you think you would still prefer to get a job or wouldn't you bother?': 78 per cent of women approaching retiring age said that they would prefer a job (Jowell and Airey, 1984, p. 54).

These WES findings, combined with the result of studies like Bruegel's (1979) and Joshi's (1982) suggest that we should think of women as permanently attached to the labour force rather than as marginal workers, having once-and-for-all breaks from work over childbirth. The sectors in which women work are clearly important determinants of their 'characteristics' or behaviour as workers, their stability or otherwise, rather than these things being inherent in a particular gender group. These findings are quite different from the assumptions about women's employment which have 'justified' their neglect from retirement policy discussions.

We can now go on to consider the relevance of certain retirement policies in the context of these findings about women's work histories and other findings about retirement behaviour.

Women's and men's responses to retirement
If workers' job histories are important influences on their attitudes and behaviour at retirement, as Parker (1980) suggests that they are, then differences in the work histories of women and men might be expected to produce different responses to retirement. On the other hand, it is not sufficient to expect that the main differences between men and women will be that women will have no problems about retiring from work because they still have their work in the home, or that women never retire for the same reason, that they still work in the home.

Parker's (1980) analysis of workers' approaches to retirement found that there was a large measure of similarity between men's and women's responses to retirement, and between what each group indicated was important about work. For example, 35 per cent of women workers under pension age expected to find that it would be difficult to settle down when retired compared to 27 per cent of men (Parker, 1980, Table A3.13). The types of problem workers expected to have were also very similar for both women and men; financial problems were the most common (ibid., Tables A4.12 and A3.10). Parker's analysis of the work histories of those in his sample also revealed similarities between women and men, but this aspect of the study is less satisfactory. Parker uses the concept of 'main life work' and he provides a classification of the socioeconomic group as well as other relationships with the respondent's 'main life work'. It is far from clear what those interviewed would take this concept to mean, however. Many women are known to experience downward occupational mobility over their life-time (Dex, 1984a), and it is not clear how such an experience would be incorporated into a response about 'main life work'. The concept would appear to be biased towards men's careers, although it may be equally inappropriate for describing both women's and men's work histories. In any case, we cannot derive conclusions about the effects of work histories on retirement behaviour from such vague and possibly inappropriate concepts.

Studies have shown that the availability and size of (occupational) pensions influence individuals' retirement decisions in Britain and in the USA. Most of the studies have been done in the US but one British econometric study has been done on Parker's OPCS data (Zabalza *et al.*, 1980). (The American studies are reviewed in Clark, Kreps and Spengler (1978) and Shaw (1984).) The availability of an occupational pension is related to whether a job is full- or part-time. Since many women are in part-time jobs, or have spent some proportion of their working life in part-time work, their eligibility for an occupational pension will be limited. Statistics on occupational pensions confirm that this is the case, and women are distinguishable from men in this respect (Martin and Roberts, 1984, p. 48; EOC, 1984, p. 93). The lack of occupational pension is likely to act as a disincentive form women to retire, and certainly to retire early.

Zabalza *et al.* (1980) found that women were similar to men in so far as both were more likely to retire early because of ill-health. Women were found to differ from men – perhaps unexpectedly – in being more responsive to economic incentives; at least in Britain women were more likely to continue to work even as they approached or passed retirement age if the rewards from working increased. Men appeared to put more value on leisure.[7]

Given that most women work for financial reasons, that they also enjoy other aspects of working, that they often have no occupational pensions to retire to, and that they are more likely than men to live alone in retirement, it seems reasonable to argue that women are less likely to want to retire than men, and that they may well be less likely to want to retire early than men. Parker's finding that more women than men would like to continue to work after reaching statutory retirement age supports this conclusion (Parker, 1980, Table A5.11). However, the evidence on this is contradictory. To set against Parker's result, there is the support for equalising the pension ages which was demonstrated in a survey carried out in 1983 for the Equal Opportunities Commission (Ritchie and Barrowclough, 1983). A majority of those surveyed stated a preference for equalisation. Amongst women aged 55–59, 61 per cent wanted equalisation at 60, 19 per cent at an age below 60, and 17 per cent at an age above; the equivalent figures for men aged 55–59 were 17, 11 and 18 per cent.

For the majority, it would seem that retirement at 60 is the most desirable option. For women (as well as for some men), however, there is a considerable financial cost. Women experience a sharp drop in personal income on retirement, although total family income will vary substantially, as Parker (1980) has shown. The decision to retire is a serious one, therefore, for both full- and part-time women workers.

Women must have 39 qualifying years between the ages of 16 and 60 if they are to gain a statutory pension in their own right, although this period may be reduced by home responsibility credits. Thirty-nine years is equivalent to 60 per cent of a working life, a figure which is close to the average period which women work (Martin and Roberts, 1984). Many women work less than this amount, however, and if they have been part-time workers for some of their working life, they are likely to have been earning below the level where national insurance contributions are paid, which was £35.50 in April 1985. In addition, few are likely to receive an occupational pension (Ritchie and Barrowclough, 1983). For the foreseeable future, in fact, a considerable number of women will retire without a pension in their own right. The policy implications of this are explored below. Inequalities between the sexes are encouraged by advocating early retirement policies. Women's retirement must be viewed in the context of women's work histories and their reasons for working and their husband's retirement plans.

Alternative Policies

Constructing radical policies for older workers, in the context of the current pressures facing capitalist economies, will be extremely difficult. As the foregoing analysis has made clear, the main thrust of labour policy has been towards the exclusion of older people from work, with the provision of a variety of forms of income support to maintain the individual until the onset of state retirement age. However, the generosity of these schemes is subject to wide variation, with female early retirers and blue-collar workers often receiving lower rates of benefits in comparison to those from white-collar and managerial occupations.

A number of countries have introduced measures to improve the security of older workers. The American age discrimination legislation is probably the best known and most comprehensive. Unfortunately, it has had negative as well as positive consequences. It has increased the job security of those fortunate to be in employment, whilst, at the same time, reducing the options for those already unemployed – the older workers' protected situation making employers reluctant to hire them (Casey and Bruche, 1983).

The case for flexible retirement has been discussed since the early 1950s (Brown, 1950; Mathieson, 1957), and policies for greater flexibility have been pursued with considerable vigour by pressure groups representing older people. Despite the long history of debates in this area, genuine flexibility (allowing workers to retire early or to continue to work beyond normal retirement age) are comparatively rare. Flexibility as Babic (1984) notes, has usually been in one direction only – an exit from the labour force. The Swedish model of gradual retirement is generally regarded as the most advantageous system designed so far. The phasing out of work and phasing in of retirement pensions enables a worker to leave the labour force at a pace that can be described as individualised (Babic, 1984). Under the scheme working hours must be reduced by an average of at least 5 per week, but an average of at least 17 hours per week must be worked after this reduction. The partial pension amounts to 50 per cent of the gross earnings lost (before 1981 the level of compensation was 65 per cent). Comparing phased retirement with full early retirement, Laczko (1985, p. 4) has documented the following changes:

> The growth in the number of new partial pension awards since 1976 has been considerable. Indeed, over the period 1976–1982 more men and women aged 60–64 took partial early retirement (131,910) than full early retirement with a disability pension (120,497), which is the principal form of public support for full early retirement in Sweden. Thus in Sweden, although an increasing number of older workers have been retiring early since the mid-1970s, a large part of this increase has been in partial rather than full early retirement. ... This is reflected in the economic activity rates of men aged 16–64, with a much smaller fall in Sweden: 88.7% to 87.2% between 1977 and 1982, than in Britain during the same period: 81.5% to 69.4%.

A more modest area of work has been in the field of retirement preparation programmes. Originally devised in America in the late 1940s, such schemes cover in Britain just 5 or 6 per cent of people who retire each year (Coleman, 1982). Moreover, in both Britain and America (the countries with the most developed programmes), low-status and low-income workers (particularly women) are least likely to have access to such a programme (Phillipson and Strang, 1983; Beck, 1983). The bulk of employers have, in fact, shown little interest in this limited step of supporting older men and women in the transfer from full-time employment. Despite (or because of) the recession, there has been little growth in retirement education. This pattern is likely to continue into the foreseeable future.

Developing a social policy for the older worker

Given the likelihood of continuing high levels of unemployment, a major initiative is required to assist older employees. Amongst the most urgent of the many issues that must be tackled, the following can be listed:

* Policy initiatives are required for those forced to leave work because of ill-health or disability. To meet the needs of the disabled, a comprehensive disability income scheme should be introduced (Walker, 1982e, 1984). For all workers faced with early retirement, existing wages or salaries should be maintained (and inflation-proofed) up to state retirement age.
* Further reforms must be made to improve the pension received by older women (see Chapters 4 and 10, this volume). In particular, we would recommend the abolition of contribution conditions; instead, all men and women would receive a pension in their own right. In order to acheive independence for women, this pension would need to be paid at the same rate whether or not the person was single or married.
* In the workplace, campaigns must be launched to safeguard the rights of older workers. Attempts to coerce people into retiring must be resisted; rights to retraining must also be secured.
* The problems faced by older workers must be used to develop a broad strategy to remove inequalities in working and safety conditions inside factories and offices. This must be related to the right for people to retire free from work-related injuries and illnesses.
* Extensive retirement preparation schemes should be provided as a right to all workers. These should be organised and run by workers in the firm's own time.
* Opportunity should be provided for greater educational activity amongst those in later middle-age, with free access to college and university courses.

* Domiciliary and home nursing schemes must be expanded to assist those workers (often single or married women) caring for a handicapped person or an elderly relative.
* The dependent status of older people must be challenged (Townsend, 1981; Walker, 1980, 1981b; Bornat *et al.*, 1985). This will require an attack on pension inequalities and social policies which stigmatise older people. Political and community structures must be changed to allow older people to participate on an equal basis with other age and social groups.

Conclusions
The growth of retirement reflects major changes in the distribution of work through the life-cycle. The concern in the 1950s with maintaining people in work is currently shared by few capitalist economies. Most are attempting, albeit with limited success, to redistribute work in favour of the young (Walker, Lawson and Townsend, 1984; Laczko and Walker, 1985); few take seriously the argument concerned with maintaining older people in the labour market (Fogarty, 1982). Part of the reason for this lies in forces of labour supply or demography, rather than of demand. The population of working age is growing rapidly at present and the proportion seeking work, the 'activity rate', has been higher than expected, particularly among women. New jobs have been created primarily within the services sector, a significant proportion of these being part-time jobs filled by women. Although the growth in the size of the working population may start to slow down, the tendency for part-time women's employment to increase is likely to persist.

There are at least three very broad implications arising from these trends. First, given the increased importance of retirement, the pension must be increased to a level which allows older people to participate on an equal basis with other social groups. This level would probably need to be higher than the pensioner movement's current goal set at one-third of the average wage for a pension for a single person. We should find out what a reasonable level of pension is by a programme of discussion, education and research amongst pensioners themselves (Bornat *et al.*, 1985).

Secondly, to remove some of the pressures on working women there must be a major reassessment of the pattern of informal care which leaves women with the major responsibilities for supporting both the very young and the very old (Henwood and Wicks, 1984). This will involve a considerable extension is statutory domiciliary services, together with a realignment in the traditional division of care between men and women.

Thirdly, policies are required to give greater security to people facing the transition from work to retirement. Partial retirement as developed in Sweden may prove of value, but its benefits remain to be tested in the long run. Ultimately, the test will be whether firms, both public and private, are prepared to rethink their approach to older workers. Will they be prepared to establish new rights for people in their fifties, sixties and seventies as workers and as retirees? Alternatively, will they continue, as most do, to treat them as commodities, to be displaced or retained according to market conditions and the scarcity value of the skills of the individuals involved? The evidence at present suggests that the latter situation will continue to weigh heavily in the experience of many older workers.

Notes

1. The figures on the sizes of men's and women's part-time employment can be found in the Census of Employment published in the *Employment Gazette*. The Census of Employment began in 1971 on a yearly basis and it provides a breakdown of full-time and part-time employment by sex. Since 1978, this valuable source appears to have become occasional rather than annual.
2. The figures used here are contained in *Social Trends, 1983* and the *OPCS Monitor*, Ref: GHS 84(1).
3. Prior to 1977, married women could choose to opt out of paying a full national insurance stamp. This meant that they would not be eligible for unemployment benefit if unemployed, and so they were unlikely to register as unemployed. This option is no longer offered and the same benefit conditions now apply to both men and women working full-time.
4. See OPCS (1984, Table 15) for supporting figures. Figures from the Census of Employment also illustrate the same point. It is important not to attach any causal influence to the marital status of women. Published statistics are usually of married women. What makes the difference to women's behaviour, however, is whether or not they have children.
5. The National Training Survey contained details of men's work histories over a ten-year period and these are described in Elias and Main (1982).
6. Jowell and Airey (1984) report a higher proportion of men saying that they would prefer a job, but 78 per cent is a very high figure for older women in view of the expectations which have been held in the past, that women are not particularly committed to working, and only work for pin-money.
7. The review of US studies by Clark *et al.* (1978) suggests that this result does not apply in the USA.

4 The Forgotten Female: Social Policy and Older Women

Sheila Peace

It would appear that in our society old women are all around us and yet invisible – invisible in that their existence is seldom acknowledged; their needs are seldom recognised and their voices seldom heard. Yet amongst the 20 per cent of the population over 60 years of age, women outnumber men by almost two to one, and with increasing age the proportion rises until more than two-thirds of those over 75 years are women. The world of the very old is therefore a woman's world, and it is amongst this group that we find the most frail members of the older population and those most likely to be in need of some form of welfare provision. Yet any discussion of welfare policy for older people in post-war Britain has to acknowledge the piecemeal development of such policies as exist. We have been slow to recognise the implications of an ageing population and whilst post-war legislation saw the development of the pension system and the provision for some of residential accommodation, it was not until the 1960s and 1970s that local authorities were empowered and obliged to provide services for older people within the community. The recent White Paper on the elderly, 'Growing Older', did little more than confirm existing policies. It offered no attempt, however, to develop a coherent strategy for the needs of older people (DHSS, 1981c).

This chapter seeks to examine how being a woman may affect both the range and quality of welfare services received in old age. In doing so it considers the evolution of particular social policies within a patriarchal capitalist society. Given this perspective, attention will be paid to how and why the lives of older women have, until recently, failed to be considered by both the women's movement and feminist writers on social policy, and by gerontologists concerned with the social welfare of old people. Such a discussion leads us to ask how a recognition of the different life experiences of men and women, which do not magically disappear with age, can be incorporated within a framework of welfare provision for older people. In drawing upon the experiences of the older women's movement within the USA and other countries, we can assess the importance of concessions won so far, and question whether they attack the root cause of the problems faced by women in old age.

The characteristics of older women

Older women form a much higher proportion of the very old population than their male counterparts; they also form a much higher proportion of the unmarried (i.e. not currently married and never married) at all ages. Even during the early years of retirement a third of women aged 60–64 years are widowed, single or divorced, as opposed to less than a fifth of men. This difference increases with age so that amongst those over 75 years 80 per cent of women are unmarried (including 64 per cent who are widowed), whereas only 39 per cent of men fall into this category (OPCS, 1983, p. 15). (See Table 4.1.)

Table 4.1 Marital status of older people in Great Britain, 1981 Census

	(%)			
	Single	*Married*	*Widowed*	*Divorced*
Women				
60 years and over	11	44	42	2
75 years and over	14	20	64	1
Men				
60 years and over	8	76	14	2
75 years and over	8	61	30	1

Sources: OPCS, Census 1981, National Report, Great Britain, part 1, HMSO, 1983, p. 15 Table 6. Usually Resident Population: age by marital status by sex.

The differences between men and women reflect a number of factors: first, male life expectancy at birth is currently six years below female. In 1901 life expectancy was 52 years for women and 48 years for men; in 1979, it was 76 years and 70 years, respectively (CSO, 1984). Secondly, women have traditionally married men of a similar age or older than themselves, which, given uneven life expectancy, makes it more likely that women will experience widowhood. Finally, the higher numbers of single women amongst those over 75 years reflects to some extent the experience of living through two world wars when male mortality and morbidity was high. This fact, of course, also has an effect on the figures for older men in general. Patterns of marital status are reflected in household composition. So, although most older people live either with their elderly spouse or on their own, there is a marked difference between the sexes. Women of all ages are more likely to be living alone than men. This tendency increases with age so that amongst women in their late seventies and early eighties over 50 per cent are living alone. However, with increasing age more women than men will be living with other people – members of the family or friends. Data for 1981 show that 17 per cent of women over 65 years and 9 per cent of men live with others. Yet this pattern varies with age: for women of 75–84 years the number living with others rises to 21 per cent and for those 85 years and over to 37 per cent. For men the increase in those living with others is most marked amongst the over 85 years old (CSO, 1982, p. 25).

The increasing tendency to live with others late in life is often associated with the presence of disability. Indeed, those living with others are least likely to be able to manage on their own (Hunt, 1978, p. 69). Yet although ill-health is associated with increasing age and subsequently more likely to affect women than men, this is not the whole picture. Recent studies show that older women of all ages are more likely to experience chronic disability than men, often leading to serious mobility problems. This may be accounted for by the particular prevalence of conditions such as rheumatism and arthritis amongst women (Hunt, 1978). These trends may also account for the fact that, whereas social class is an important determinant of health in old age, the middle-class advantage is less noticeable amongst women over the age of 75–80 years (Taylor and Ford, 1983). Yet despite these difficulties, women may continue, as Hunt observes, 'to live with disabilities that might cause men to go into institutions' (Hunt, 1978, p. 69). The implication is that women in poor health continue to live in the community for longer, often supported by family and friends.

Though less active and more house-bound than men, older women are likely to see relatives and friends more frequently. They are also more likely than men to be visited and visit others, especially within their immediate neighbourhood. This pattern is particularly true of those women who have been or who are married; those living alone who have never been married being far more isolated (OPCS, 1982, pp. 174–5). However, all visiting declines with increasing age, and it is amongst the very old living alone that we find some of the most isolated and lonely old women (Abrams, 1980).

Older women, the family and employment
These demographic characteristics indicate that although the lives of most old men are still firmly rooted within the family, albeit a family of two, for older women life may be more solitary. Yet the family, and women's position within it, still forms the main influence on

their lives both in terms of the personal resources available to them and the informal support offered in old age. Furthermore welfare policy, and specifically that relating to older people, is predominantly 'family' policy (Land, 1978), and because of this the lives of older women remain enmeshed within its web. In trying to untangle the factors that have led to the development of welfare policy concerning older people, we have to consider a number of ideological issues. First, within Britain the inequalities of a patriarchal society, as reflected in women's dependent position within the family as wives and mothers, by far pre-dates the development of industrialisation and the growth of capitalism. Thus, before the separation of 'workplace' and 'home', and the development of a distinction between paid and unpaid labour, women's lives were subjugated to the needs of men.

The importance attached to women's roles as wife and mother cannot be overemphasised, for it has a direct bearing on how the present generation of older women view themselves and their role within the family. Wilson (1977) states:

> In Victorian society women were, for the first time valuable because they did not work. It was her status as a non-worker that gave woman as wife and mother a very special ideological role.

Such a viewpoint, although to a certain degree still espoused today, must have far greater significance for those born at the turn of the century when the influence of Victorian values was still prevalent. Indeed, the centrality of those roles, and the importance that women attach to them, has a major bearing on how many older women cope with the ageing process and old age. Thus, motherhood is seen as a productive period in women's lives and is commonly associated with early and middle adulthood. In contrast, the older woman is seen as non-productive, past her prime, and so in some senses useless (Sontag, 1972; Preston, 1975; Itzin, 1984). It can be argued that this form of non-productivity is qualitatively different from that experienced by older men on retirement. For women, whose sexuality has been commonly linked to reproduction, may feel a sense of personal inferiority internalised as part of being female; rather than an imposed sense of uselessness through being no longer economically active. Of course, as Leonard (1984) has argued, many women now experience both forms of deprivation.

Women's caring role has been an important factor in the development of social policies for older people. This role is one which women usually take on for life; and it is carefully nurtured through social policies which reinforce the ideological position of the woman in supporting a stable family life.

However, in contrast with the Victorian ideal of woman as 'non-worker', the increased separation of workplace and home has served to expose the commonly held dual roles of women, especially married women, as both waged and unwaged workers. Those women currently in their seventies and eighties, born at the turn of the century, have witnessed immense social change; they are the first generation to have experienced these dual roles *and* to have lived to an advanced age. Yet in the twentieth century, the development of capitalism has reinforced the secondary status given to women's non-domestic labour. Although most women below retirement age are now economically active they are still seen as a reserve labour force. Their paid employment is still predominantly low-status and low-paid, and considered secondary to their 'more important' role within the family. Wilson (1977) gives this description of how women's employment was seen in the 'affluent' 1960s:

> The emphasis on the overriding importance of women's role in the home as wife and mother, and the emotional value given this role, masked the backward and therefore peculiar nature of housework and its economical value to the employer as a cheap way of serving the worker. It also masked women's usefulness as a reserve of cheap and docile labour. It was said that women only worked for pin money; this meant that any job the wife and mother might do would be fitted in with her household duties.

Thus, the underlying ideologies of both patriarchy and capitalism with their emphasis on male power and male domination, have culminated in the use of the family and woman's traditional role within it as a controlling vehicle for reproducing the status quo and reinforcing sexual inequalities. Such trends can be seen to underlie successive post-war social policies, which have formed the basis of the welfare state.

To date, however, few writers have shown an interest in older women and the impact on their lives of current welfare policies for older people. Only in the past few years have we seen the publication of an important series of papers on the caring role of women, which question the underlying assumption about community care policies for people in need (Finch and Groves, 1980, 1983; Walker, 1982a). This chapter focuses therefore on two aspects of older women's lives: first, their relationship with the personal social and health services; and secondly, their financial security and economic dependency.

'Till Death Us Do Part': The Personal Social Service

It would appear that this phrase from the marriage vows could be applied equally to all women with regard to their position within the extended family. Such is the construction of the role of women that the task of caring for other members of the family is 'second nature'. Yet caring for women is a twofold process of labour and love – we care about people and we care for them, though not always simultaneously (Ungerson, 1983). It is the instrumental task of caring for people, which Roy Parker has termed 'tending' (Parker, 1981, p. 17), that is common to both the unpaid role of women within the family and to the more recent role of the state in the provision of personal social services for those seen to be in need (see also Chapter 6, this volume). So, in trying to gain an accurate perspective of how the state supports women in old age, we must first consider the development of personal social services for old people and the assumptions on which policies are based. The fact that such services are predominantly supplied by women as paid employees (e.g. home help, district nurse, day-care attendant) indicates the strength of association between women and the caring role.

It seems pertinent that one of the earliest forms of state control, the Poor Law, should still have a strong influence on the attitudes of old people to one of the main forms of current welfare provision – albeit for a minority of elderly – residential care. Yet although the horror stories of the workhouse offered an explicit form of social control which was to be avoided at all costs, so too, residential care is seen today as a last resort by most older people. The undesirability of the Part III home, however well disguised, has reinforced the widespread desire to stay 'at home' for as long as possible; and 'home' with all its connotations of private family life bring us full circle to the domain of caring women.

Care at home is both an ideal and a reality for most older people who are supported either directly or indirectly by their family; indeed, it is a myth that the family do not care (Shanas, 1974). But it is also an ideal which has been encouraged by the state through the formulation of a community care policy for dependent old people. The development of community care policies bears no allegiance to any particular political persuasion, and examples of such initiatives can be found in policy documents spanning the past four decades. Indeed, there is a commonly held belief that care by the community is far more beneficial than care by the state. Such a view has been nurtured by a realisation of the so-called growing financial burden of an ageing population. In recent years, economic recession has placed further emphasis on such apparently costless care. This is clearly demonstrated in the 1981 White Paper 'Growing Older':

> Whatever level of public expenditure proves practicable, and however it is distributed, the primary sources of support and care for elderly people are informal and voluntary. These spring from the personal ties of kinship, friendship and neighbourhood. They are irreplaceable. It is the role

of public authorities to sustain and, where necessary, develop – but never to displace – such support and care. Care in the community must increasingly mean care by the community. (DHSS, 1981c, p. 3)

In the following sections we shall explore the social and economic implications of this policy.

Care by women
'In 1978, an Equal Opportunities Council survey found that three times as many women as men were looking after elderly or handicapped relatives' (EOC, 1982b, p. 2). When we think of women who care for older people it is common to think first of the 'women in the middle', those middle-aged women caught between the generations of young and old, who often have to cope with the competing pressures of paid employment and family care (Brody, 1981). The traditional picture conjures up the unmarried daughter looking after her elderly parents or, more commonly now, the married daughter or daughter-in-law caring for a widowed parent. However, current trends in divorce, re-marriage and life expectancy will increasingly complicate this neat pattern of kinship relationships. In future we may well be asking who will care for the step-grandmothers and grandfathers. And we may find that more widowed daughters will be caring for parents who have outlived their spouse. Recent work by Brody and colleagues at the Philadelphia Geriatric Center has begun to shed some light on what we may expect from future patterns of care. In an important study of three generations of women, their attitudes and preferences concerning the care of elderly parents, findings reveal that a majority from all generations agree that it is better for a working woman to pay someone to care for her elderly parent than to leave her job to do so, and that children should help meet the expenses of care for the elderly parent, if necessary. Old women and those in their middle years felt strongly that the generations should not live together, confirming the view expressed by many older people that they want to live near to but not in the same household as their children. However respondents felt that women should adjust their family schedules in order to carry their caring responsibilities. Only the older women showed reservations about this adjustment, which, as the authors indicate, may reflect the desire of old people not to be a burden on their family. When asked about their preferences concerning a number of areas of service provision and support in old age, a mixture of both informal and formal sources was given. Whereas all age groups looked to children or other relatives for emotional and financial support, younger generations were more receptive to accepting help from formal services for more instrumental tasks. Of particular interest is the fact that all three generations

agreed that personal care was not acceptable from male helpers. Given such attitudes, the authors quite rightly state, 'the findings speak to the increasing involvement of women in care of one or more generations of elderly relatives as they themselves age' (Brody *et al.*, 1983, p. 45). Such findings also highlight the complex nature of the multiple roles of women.

The costs of caring
The effects of caring on the lives of older women can be financial, social or emotional. In terms of financial costs it is easy to see how caring for a dependent spouse or parent/relative can incur extra costs. For example, in terms of heating bills, special dietary require-ments, laundry, the adaptation of accommodation, the provision of special aids and transportation (EOC, 1982a; Willcocks, 1983). Yet such costs may fall on those with limited resources – a two-pensioner household, an unmarried woman, or a family with growing children. In some cases women may have to give up their current employment, in order to look after an elderly relative or spouse (Parker, 1980; Phillipson, 1983).

At present only limited financial support is available. An atten-dance allowance can be claimed by those who are severely disabled, either mentally or physically, and have needed the attention of another person by day or night for at least six months. However, the EOC reports that take-up of this benefit may be artificially low and that many people may be reluctant to apply, as the allowance is determined by a medical examination and the level of disability must require 'frequent attention ... in connection with bodily function i.e. eating, using the toilet, and moving about' (EOC, 1982, p. 16). Such a narrow definition of disability excludes those who need help with tasks such as shopping, and preparing and cooking food, which often form a major part of the caring role.

In the case of financial support for those caring women below retirement age, marital status is all important. The invalid care allowance, introduced in 1975 (a non-contributory cash payment, basic 1985/86 value £23), is available to men and categories of unmarried women who have given up full-time paid employment (or who have never been in paid employment) in order to care for a severely disabled relative or friend (Finch and Groves, 1983).[2] How-ever, to be eligible the dependent relative/friend must be in receipt of the attendance allowance. As we have seen, qualification for this allowance is limited to a particular level of disability, and conse-quently many carers fail to qualify.

Nevertheless, in spite of these difficulties some single women do benefit from this allowance. In contrast married and cohabiting women, who may also have given up work to care for elderly relative/

friend, are excluded from this benefit on the grounds that they are financially dependent on their husband/cohabitee. At present, this ruling may change as a result of a test case currently (1986) before the European Court of Justice.[3] Such a policy serves only to reinforce the present male-dominated structure within the family, which sees the wife as carrying out the major caring role and her economic role outside the home as only a minor contribution to the family income.

Whilst the loss to family income incurred by a wife giving up work to care for a dependent relative may currently be smaller than if the husband gave up a similar level of employment (Ungerson, 1983, p. 38), this fact is used to sustain a vicious circle whereby women's low-paid, low-status employment reinforces the position in which women's place is seen to be in the home. Any financial loss can have a devastating effect on lifestyle, and figures for 1980 show that non-retired wives contributed 20–30 per cent of the family income (DOE, 1982, pp. 108, 109). Furthermore in a small study of 22 households where a handicapped elderly relative was being cared for, Nissel and Bonnerjea calculated that the cost of time spent caring came to £2500 per family per annum (before tax), and that the opportunity incurred through earnings lost by the wife not working is as much as £4500 per annum (Nissel and Bonnerjea, 1982).

In terms of social and emotional costs, those caring alone may also find themselves socially isolated, cut off from social activities and from contact with friends. A further disruption of her paid employment later in life may not only prevent the older woman from finding further employment but also affect her future pension entitlements. Her health may suffer, and tension, mental stress, physical ill-health and acute tiredness are commonly reported symptoms amongst carers, especially those caring for the mentally frail (Levin, 1983; Sanford, 1975; Jones and Vetter, 1984).

Older women – objects of community care
Although a number of studies have focused on gender as a major discriminating factor in the type of support, both formal and informal, received in old age (Shanas *et al.*, 1968; Abrams, 1978; Hunt, 1978), little attempt has been made to understand why and how such support is given, and what effect this has on the life of the older person. Most old people living alone or with their spouse are able to care for themselves without too much difficulty (Hunt, 1978). Yet there are those who need help in order to remain living within the community, and amongst this minority, women, those over 75–80 years, and those living alone predominate.

In a recent study, Abrams has shown that amongst respondents over 75 years, 13 per cent experienced difficulty with a number of self-care tasks, ranging from 31 per cent who had difficulty bathing, to 3 per cent who had difficulty feeding themselves. Although most of the help given was from family members, particularly an elderly spouse, only 27 per cent of those in need received assistance, which means that most needing help had to cope alone (Abrams, 1980).

As with self-care, domestic tasks may also prove difficult. Given their greater mobility, it is not surprising that more old men than women are able to carry out the more physically demanding household chores, e.g. cleaning windows, gardening (Hunt, 1978). Yet in spite of their better health, traditional roles still govern the performance of certain tasks, and old men are less likely to wash small amounts of clothes, cook a main meal or do the shopping (OPCS, 1982). For those receiving assistance with these tasks, the immediate family is again the first port of call; men more commonly assisted by their wives and women by daughters or daughters-in-law (Hunt, 1978).

Such studies highlight the fact that only a small percentage of old people receive support from statutory domiciliary services. The 1981 *General Household Survey* reported that 3 per cent of elderly people had received meals-on-wheels in the month before the study; 3 per cent had attended a lunch club, and 5 per cent had visited a day centre. The most frequently used service was the home help service, which 9 per cent had used frequently. This figure rose to 19 per cent for those living alone, compared to 4 per cent for those living with their spouse, and 5 per cent for those in other types of households (OPCS, 1983).

Yet despite the low level of statutory provision, there is some indication that different criteria are used in the allocation of domiciliary services to men and women, and to male and female carers. Audrey Hunt has shown that older men living alone are more likely to receive the services of a home help than are older women, even though they may be far less disabled and far more mobile (Hunt, 1978). Moreover, in a recent study carried out in Manchester (Charlesworth *et al.*, 1984) male carers were more likely to receive the services of a home help and meals-on-wheels, plus rehabilitation, assessment and long-term care; while female carers received short-term respite in the form of day-care and short-stay care. Such patterns reflect different expectations concerning male and female carers, and an underlying assumption that women are expected to go on caring for a longer period of time than men. The study also revealed that male carers tend to receive support at an earlier stage in the caring process (Charlesworth *et al.*, 1984).

Although the assumptions on which practitioners base their decisions over the provision of services are seldom explicit, there appear to be some grounds for believing that hidden rules concerning role divisions based on gender do exist, even in extreme old age. This is an area where far more research is needed. We know very little about the relationship between older women and service providers, or such influential gatekeepers to services as GPs. How far do the internalised beliefs that women have about their roles throughout life prevent them from accepting or asking for formal support? And how far do these same assumptions prevent service providers from offering it?

The work of Evers, concerning the lives of old women living alone, is beginning to provide some answers to these questions (Evers, 1983). Her study seeks to understand the subjective experience of dependency, support and service provision by both the cared-for and the carer. In work reported in 1983, she discussed how old women do not identify domestic work as 'meaningful activity', and therefore when asked how they spend their time often reply that they have been 'doing nothing much' (Evers, 1983). One explanation given for such apparent modesty again relates to the hidden nature of domestic work. She states: 'such work is essentially private, home-centred, unremarked and unremarkable right across the lifespan of a majority of women' (Evers, 1983, p. 36). Evers goes on to demonstrate how, by accepting the view of 'doing nothing much', service providers may fail to understand fully the heterogeneity of older women's lives and may offer services that do not meet individual requirements. To highlight this point she differentiates between those women she calls *'active initiators'* – those who have invested 'energy in activities over and above their involvement in traditional women's work ... right across the lifespan' and *'passive responders'* – women who 'have engaged in care-work to the exclusion of all else for a substantial proportion of their lives'. She suggests that a different approach is needed in terms of the formal support offered to such women, and that we need to know far more about women's self-perception of their lives in order to make such assessments.

Both the lives of old women living alone and those living with others are seen to be moulded by expectations about family life. For the minority living with children, the older women will have to face the conflicts caused by changing roles within the family – who does the 'mothering' and who is 'mothered'?[4] Where a mother is cared for by a daughter or daughter-in-law, the strengths and weaknesses of their past relationship will be all-important in facilitating role definition. Two problems may commonly arise in such relationships. First, the mother may resent giving up her maternal role and becoming dependent on her daughter/daughter-in-law; and second the daughter/daughter-in-law may treat the mother as a child, resulting in overdependency or conflict, which may be of harm to both carer and cared-for (McKenzie, 1980; Ungerson, 1983). Such a relationship is potentially more complex than that between mother and son, where the woman does not necessarily have to relinquish the maternal or caring role. Indeed the differential support given to male carers may be reinforced by the cared-for. In Wright's study of single carers, mothers living with sons undertook far more domestic activities than those who lived with their daughters. Half of the mothers living with their sons did the main cleaning and almost half cooked a main daily meal compared with only 6 per cent in both cases for those who lived with their daughter (Wright, 1983). The following quotation highlights this domestic role of the cared-for male:

> Mrs Green only managed to cook an evening meal for her son. She was 93 and had been crippled with arthritis for many years. Two years earlier she suffered a stroke which left her with very limited movement on one side of her body. Walking was very slow and with the aid of a zimmer frame. Her son said that it took her an hour to get from the sittingroom to the kitchen which was next to it. A substantial part of her day was spent in preparing and cooking an evening meal for her son. (Wright, 1983, p. 97)

Wright offers two interpretations of this relationship between carer and cared-for. The first concerns sex-role expectations. The daughter is expected to carry out the caring role for aged parents, whereas a mother living with a son will also strive to maintain her female caring role. Secondly, a severely impaired old woman living with her son is more likely to be admitted to a geriatric ward or a residential home than if living with a daughter (Wright, 1983). No doubt one consequence of the possibility of admission to residential care is to encourage the older woman to remain active for as long as possible.

The picture of community care when viewed from a woman's perspective appears very different from that expressed in the rhetoric of most policy documents. For the female carer the costs of caring – financial, social and emotional – can be devastating. Yet the burden often goes unrecognised, hidden behind a sense of 'duty', and only uncovered at times of crisis; when the burden of caring is all too often replaced by the burden of guilt and a sense of failure at having to give up.

> Eventually she will have to go into a home but I won't let them take her yet, as I would feel very guilty indeed. It wasn't a matter of deciding to look after her, it was really a matter of duty. (A married woman looking after her mother; EOC, 1980, p. 13)

Older women – objects of institutional care

Whilst a large proportion of the money available for services for old people is spent on institutional care, such facilities only cater for a minority – 5–6 per cent of those over retirement age, including 2–3 per cent in residential homes (Tinker, 1981). Yet within such settings a majority are women and the proportion increases with age. Figures for 1981 show that 75 per cent of old people in residential accommodation are women (GHS, 1982). Furthermore, a majority of women are over 80 years of age, in contrast to male residents who are more likely to be in their seventies (Willcocks *et al.*, 1982). The institutional world is therefore very much a female environment in old age.

While much has been written about the lives of older people living in institutional settings, focusing on such aspects of institutionalism as depersonalisation, block treatment, poor environment, the lack of trained staff, little has been written about the qualitatively different experiences of men and women within care (Townsend, 1962; Isaacs *et al.*, 1977; Clough, 1981). The work of Willcocks and Adams in residential homes (Adams, 1981; Willcocks, 1983) and Evers (1981) concerning geriatric wards, therefore, provide useful starting points. Willcocks, using material from the National Consumer Study in 100 local authority old people's homes (Willcocks *et al.*, 1982), has shown that men and women living in residential homes have markedly different profiles. Within the homes studied women outnumbered men by 3 to 1, and whilst only a quarter of men (26 per cent) were very old (i.e. 85 and over), this group accounted for nearly half of the women (44 per cent). Men therefore come into residential care at a younger age, and are in better health and are more mobile than their female counterparts (Willcocks, 1983). These characteristics can in the main be explained by the differing circumstances surrounding male and female admission. Whilst the main precipitating factor for both men and women was an inability to cope within their previous domestic setting, often compounded by prolonged ill-health or a sudden accident, bereavement was more commonly seen as a reason for admission amongst men. Males living alone, especially those recently bereaved, were seen by service providers as less likely to be able to look after themselves than females in a similar position, who may remain in the community until a much later state in their lives (Willcocks, 1983, p. 6). Women are more likely to report that a third party such as a GP or social worker had 'managed' their admission, taking control out of their hands.

The combination of both sex-role expectations and the circumstances surrounding admission to care can have a profound effect on how older people adjust to residential living. Although such a move is often frowned upon by both sexes, the transition for a younger, more active male, who may have experienced the routines of communal living at some stage in his life, may be relatively less traumatic than for an older, frailer woman, who has lived a more private, home-centred life. For many men such a move is also accompanied by the replacement of home care by women within the family, by predominantly female care staff within the 'Home'. For women the experience may be far more complex, involving not only the loss of home and community status, but also of their major domestic role. As Phillipson states:

> It is again a source of irony that, whilst the domestic identity of women has been a pervasive theme in social policy (Wilson, 1977), this is apparently cast aside in their commital to and treatment within institutions. (Phillipson, 1981, p. 198)

The old woman currently in care not only suffers from disadvantages of poor health and declining mobility, she is also subjected to a living arrangement in which her traditional domestic skills are no longer needed or recognised, something which may have a major effect on her self-esteem (Adams, 1981). Such feelings may be made worse by a belief that the family, particularly a daughter, whom she thought would care for her has failed her, resulting in anger and frustration (ibid., p. 47). Yet over the past 20 years one of the central aims of policy concerning residential provision has been the creation of old age homes that are 'domestic', as befits its function (DHSS, 1973). Yet it would appear that to date attempts at recreating domesticity within institutional settings have produced little more than tokenism (Willcocks *et al.*, 1982), and although models such as small-group living offer some older women greater potential for maintaining their caring role (Willcocks *et al.*, 1983), in essence such activities that do take place are rarely acknowledged. The role of the old woman within this setting metaphorically called 'home' has been usurped by female care staff.

If community care inevitably means care by women, so too does residential care, and in both cases this commonly means women caring for women. The professionalisation of the caring role within service provision whether this be the home help, the care assistant or geriatric nurse, often brings women into direct conflict with each other. Whilst the old woman continues to live within her own home she still exercises a degree of power and control over her life, but once removed to an institutional setting this power-base crumbles away and dependency takes on the form of subordination. In Evers' (1981) work concerning geriatric wards, this process of depersonalisation is dramatically illustrated. She categorises female patients into three types – the 'Grans', the 'Poor Nellies' and the 'Awkward Alices' – formed on the basis of their relationship with the nursing staff. In so doing she explores how nurses legitimise the professionalisation of the caring role within a public domain, and maintain control over female patients by such strategies as avoidance, ignoring patients' requests, publicly rebuking patients for being demanding, and leaving certain patients until last – tactics often used with naughty children.

Old women should have the right to end their days in an environment which promotes a dignified and less dependent style of living, and which recognises their unique individual history (Peace *et al.*, 1982). Adams suggests a number of ways in which the lives of old women in residential care may be changed, including both improved case work and the idea of support groups for women, especially during the admission period. The possibility of meeting other applicants, as well as current residents, prior to admission and the development of a women's discussion group in the Home were welcomed by respondents in her study (Adams, 1981, p. 1). Given the increasing numbers of frail very old women who may need the supportive care offered by a residential setting, it is time we gave more thought to both the quality of life offered to residents and the quality of working conditions offered to staff.

The Poor Relation
Financial security and income maintenance are two major preoccupations in old age (see Chapter 10, this volume). This is not surprising given that for many, to be old is also to be poor, and that to be female only makes matters worse. In 1979, Townsend found that two-thirds of older people were living in or on the margin of poverty, as indicated by supplementary benefit level, as opposed to just over one-quarter of the population as a whole (Townsend, 1979, p. 788). In the hierarchy of financial security elderly couples fare better than lone men, who fare better than lone women, and amongst older women it is the older widow who fares worst of all (Layard, Piachaud and Stewart, 1978, p. 115). In 1975, 40 per cent of elderly women had incomes at or below the poverty line, compared with one-quarter of men and one-sixth of couples. Over 70 per cent of elderly family units living at or below the supplementary benefit level were unmarried women, and 60 per cent were widows (Ermisch, 1982, p. 46).

Both social class and age are major factors in determining financial security amongst older people. Thus the young–old (60–74 years) are more secure than the old-old (75 years and over), and those from middle class backgrounds are better off than those from the working class (Townsend, 1979; Taylor and Ford, 1983).[6] Given that women live longer than men, it is not surprising that in this continuum the 'young' middle class male has most financial resources and the 'old' working class female the least.

In order to understand why old women fare so badly, we need to outline the various sources of income available in old age, and to highlight the causes of variation within and between elderly sub-groups. Most old people are heavily dependent on the state for financial support (Abrams, 1980, p. 48), and this is especially true of women living alone, for whom a majority of their income comes from social security benefits (Age Concern, 1977). The fact that retirement pensions have over the years provided less than the supplementary benefit level accounts for the continued low income of many older people. Only when state benefits are supplemented from other sources – occupational pensions, earnings, savings and other assets – does this picture of poverty begin to change. The situation of older women may also be compounded by poor health; indeed, the most disabled are often the most financially insecure (Townsend, 1979).

State benefits

At present there are a variety of state retirement pensions in operation, and entitlement is partly dependent on the date of pensionable age. The system available for those recently retired consists of a dual pension system introduced in 1978, with both a flat-rate and an earnings-related pension. Although the earnings-related pension is of little or no benefit to the majority of older women currently retired, the introduction of the new pension system attempted to provide a greater degree of equity for women (Social Security Pensions Act 1975). Thus, since 1978 married women in paid employment have been entitled to similar pension rights as men with the same earnings, as well as the right to join universal private pension schemes. A system of 'home responsibilities protection' has also been introduced which credits certain categories of women for time spent at home caring for children and other dependants (Coote and Gill, 1981, p. 134).[7] Yet such concessions may have only limited impact given the structure of women's lives, their predominance in low-paid employment, and irregularity of work history. This becomes more apparent as we examine the conditions of pension entitlement.

The basic pension is available to all those who have reached pensionable age,[8] have retired and have paid national insurance contributions during their 'working lives'.[9] However, many women are unable to qualify for a full pension in their own right. That is especially true of those who have been engaged in the caring roles of looking after children, disabled relatives, elderly spouses and/or parents prior to the introduction of 'home responsibilities protection'.

Under the *basic retirement pension* an unmarried woman claims the single person's pension, albeit at a reduced level. However married and divorced women have the option of either claiming a pension based on their own contributions or, as is often the case, due to a lack of contributions, of claiming as a dependent wife, in which case the pension is based on the husband's or former husband's contribution record. The dependent wife receives 60 per cent of the single person's pension. The expectation then, is that a married couple can live more cheaply than, for example, two siblings. The special treatment of married women was based on the assumption that most would find their main occupation within the home. Thus in the 1940s, when a relatively small percentage of married women were economically active, Beveridge felt justified in making them a special case (Williams, 1982, p. 189; Groves, 1983, p. 44). The pension is therefore awarded in relation to paid employment. Only when widowed and over retirement age is the dependent spouse entitled to the single person's retirement pension. If the widow's husband was not entitled to a retirement pension when he died (e.g. he was too young), then the widow is entitled to a widow's allowance for 26 weeks before receiving the retirement pension. Prior to 1977, the dependent position of married women was encouraged by the fact that they could choose to pay reduced national insurance contributions, and rely on getting a married woman's pension. Since 1977 women cannot choose to opt out of paying full contributions whilst in paid employment. So in future more women will be entitled to the single person's pension in their own right.

The second part of the new dual pension system is an *earnings-related scheme* (SERPS), which is expected to reach maturity by the end of the century. This pension applies *only* to those who have reached pensionable age since April 1978, and again is based on contributions from earnings. Those employers offering a good private occupational pension can 'contract out' of the state scheme. In doing so they have to provide their employees with a guaranteed minimum pension i.e. at least as much as the individual would have received from the state. Being earnings-related, women will continue to receive smaller pensions in their own right because they are clustered in low-paid jobs and have more sporadic work records.

Of course, the majority of old women currently over retirement age do not benefit from the dual pension system. For some their basic retirement pension may be supplemented by a small graduated pension, dependent on contributions paid from 1961 to 1975 when the scheme ended. However, those over 80 years of age (predominantly female) may not qualify for the basic retirement pension, as they have not usually contributed to the scheme. Instead, they can claim a non-contributory retirement pension. Entitlement to this pension is dependent both on certain residence conditions, and that the individual either has no retirement pension or one smaller than the current entitlement. This pension is at a lower rate than the basic retirement pension.

All pensioners with incomes below the supplementary benefit

level are entitled to a means-tested supplementary pension. Therefore given that many old women receive a reduced retirement pension, a great number are entitled to this additional income. In 1978,
Hunt showed that 34 per cent of non-married old women as opposed
to 21 per cent of men were receiving supplementary benefit (Hunt,
1978, p. 28). Yet it has been estimated that some 900,000 elderly
people are failing to claim the supplementary benefit to which they
are entitled. Both the stigma attached to means-testing and the
complexity of procedures appear to contribute to this non take-up of
benefit.

Other sources of income
The poverty of many single women in old age is due to their reliance
on the state pension as the main source of their income; all too few
have additional financial resources (Walker, 1981b; see also Chapter
10). Earnings could form one source, yet only a small percentage of
old people continue to work past pensionable age. Economic activity
rates for male pensioners have declined by 50 per cent since 1945,
and whilst there has been a threefold increase in the employment of
female pensioners during this time (Phillipson, 1982, p. 142), a
majority of this employment is found in the post-retirement years of
60–64 years (OPCS, 1983). Many married women continue to work
as long as their husband is employed, and then the couple retire
together; this has been shown to be particularly true for the wives of
manual rather than non-manual workers (Crawford, 1972). The
reasons for the dramatic decline in employment at pensionable age
are directly related to retirement policies (Walker, 1983c, p.152),
which within a capitalist society favour younger workers at the
expense of the old. Thus to some extent the duration of paid employment is controlled through the operation of both state and private
pension schemes. Whilst older people may defer the take-up of their
state retirement pension until 65 years for a woman and 70 years for
a man, and gain a small increase in pension for doing so, a majority
retire at pensionable age.

For those women currently retired, the percentage receiving income from occupational pensions remains fairly small. In 1975, the
General Household Survey showed that only one-third of elderly
spinsters, 20 per cent of widows and 4 per cent of married women
received an occupational pension (Layard *et al.*, 1978, p. 124). In
1978 Hunt's study showed that 46 per cent of men as opposed to 20
per cent of women received a pension from a former employer or
spouse's employer (Hunt, 1978, p. 28). Part-time women workers
are at a particular disadvantage when it comes to occupational pension schemes. In the survey by Ritchie and Barrowclough (1983), 14
per cent had access to a scheme although had not become members,

while 69 per cent had no company pension scheme available. Finally, old women may improve their financial situation by moving in with family and therefore pooling resources. Although widows appear most resistant to such a move, preferring to remain in separate households (Ermisch, 1982, p. 47), this tendency does increase with advancing age. Some 25 per cent of women 75 years and over live with others, especially their children and children-in-law. Given that those with lower incomes are more likely to move into joint households this can only have a compensatory effect on income maintenance.

Future prospects

In 1982, forecasters predicted that the poverty of elderly women might be abolished by the second quarter of the next century (Joshi and Ermisch, 1982. p. 63). Such optimistic predictions were based on a number of factors, most notably the maturing of the earnings-related pension, and the fact that not only would more women be entitled to the state retirement pension in their own right, but that more would be receiving an occupational pension. Yet although figures for 1977 show that already over 50 per cent of women in full-time paid employment are covered by paid occupational schemes (Fogarty, 1980, p. 62), women in manual occupations do less well, and such figures fail to take account of many of the women in part-time employment. Whilst the law now gives 'equal access' to private pensions schemes for men and women, many still discriminate against women. For example, schemes may exclude certain groups of employees such as part-time workers, or they may fail to preserve pension rights during maternity leave. Such factors work against women obtaining a similar pension status to men (Coote and Gill, 1981, p. 174).

The recent reviews of social security have outlined a number of reforms that will place the financial security of many older women at risk in the future (DHSS, 1985b, 1985d). By reforming the state earnings-related pension and by placing greater responsibility on the individual to obtain an occupational or personal pension, many women will find themselves either with a reduced income from the dual pension system or in receipt of a smaller private pension. The White Paper on social security also states that the state additional pension should be based on lifetime average earnings, rather than the best 20 years of earnings. Given the part-time and sporadic nature of employment for many women, this will actively work against women achieving the maximum additional pension. Also although it is suggested that the position of married women and those caring for disabled relatives will be protected, this will not be through the system of 'home responsibilities protection', but the minimum number of years' earnings since 1978 needed for these groups to get full additional pension, this being calculated on the basis of 20 years (DHSS, 1985d). Without 'home responsibilities protection', meeting a twenty-year rule may still prove difficult for some women.

Proposals are also made that new private schemes should offer equal benefits for equal contributions, thus acknowledging women's longer life expectancy. However, it has also been reported that low-paid workers will not be guaranteed a second pension and employers paying less than the national insurance minimum of £35 a week will not be required to fund a second pension (*Guardian*, June 1985). By placing the responsibility for income maintenance more firmly with the individual and outside the employee/employer relationship, it will prove more difficult to protect the rights of women to equal treatment within the law.

Changes are also suggested in relation to widows' pensions. Here it is the childless widow who loses out, as the proposed lump sum of £1000, instead of the widow's allowance of £150.10 for 26 weeks, means a loss of £300. Other proposals may also lead to greater means-testing for those older women with very low incomes. The current supplementary pension and additional allowances for heating, furniture and dietary payments will be replaced by income support from a new social fund, with pensioners entitled to premium rates to cover all areas of need. The death grant, though inadequate at £30, is also to be abolished, leaving those in need of help with funeral costs to seek a discretional grant from their social security office. Such changes do little to reduce the indignities which many face in old age, and only increase the likelihood that more will slip below the poverty-line.

The pattern of women's dual role, at home and in paid employment, holds the key to their future financial security in old age. Given the current economic situation, the growth of women's paid employment remains uncertain and the increase in the older population may mean that more women have to remain at home to care for elderly people. Yet, even with limited 'home responsibilities protection', many women, especially married women in part-time work, would fail to qualify for a full pension in their own right (David and Land, 1983, p. 147). So although recent concessions in the pension system have taken some account of the caring role of women, the pension system is still fundamentally based upon the contributions of those in full-time paid employment. Until an equitable pension system is developed that takes full account of women's lives, women will still find themselves either economically dependent on their spouse for pension rights in old age or entitled to only a reduced pension based on their own contributions. For the foreseeable future women are still faced with economic dependency and a reduced social status within the social security system, thus leading to financial disadvantage.

Conclusion

For present generations of old women the consequences of their life-long dependent status and domestic role within the family are clearly reflected both in their position with regard to informal and formal social support, and their lack of financial security. Being a woman clearly affects the range and quality of welfare services received in old age. Yet such manifestations of inequality are simply the outward, visible signs of how society treats those who are seen as marginal to its requirements. Leonard has discussed how the marginality of groups such as the elderly, who are no longer engaged in socially necessary labour either through production or reproduction, affects the development of personality and construction of self-identity (Leonard, 1984, p. 180). He argues that, although negative changes in self-identity are not inevitable, there may be a tendency for individuals to view themselves as worthless.

One way of overcoming these feelings is seen through collective action – reinforcing a new definition of self by contact with like others. It is here, then, that the women's movement could play a major role in the lives of older women. Yet a recognition of the situation of older women has been largely ignored. Why should this be? The major concerns of the women's movement have centred on women's rights to equality within education and employment, control over aspects of childbearing and a demand for childcare facilities, self-determination within sexuality and the right to legal and financial independence (Deckard, 1975, p. 331; Wilson, 1977, p. 2). Such demands have reflected the more immediate concerns of younger women, who it appears betray their own ageism, failing to face up to the future prospects of old age and the problems of their mothers' and grandmothers' generations (Lewis and Butler, 1972). Whilst younger feminists have shied away from what may have been seen as the repressive influence of their elders (Rowbotham, 1973, p. 12), so too older women have been made to feel unwelcome within the women's movement (Long 1979, p. 14).

Barbara Macdonald, an American, describes her own painful experiences of being an older woman rejected by younger women:

> All my life in a man's world, I was a problem because I was a woman; now I'm a problem in a woman's world because I'm a sixty-five-years-old woman. Hearing once more that I was not in the right place and thinking, 'If not here, where?' (Macdonald with Rich, 1984, p. 130)

She ascribes this rejection to the fact that the women's liberation movement, as opposed to the earlier suffrage movement, developed within a partriarchally-supported, white middle-class youth culture, which valued both physical as well as political strength, and therefore internalised ageist values (ibid., pp. 33, 37).

A knowledge of the continuity of common experience throughout the lifespan has been lost, due in part to our womanless history and in part to the stigma attached to old age. Only recently have attempts been made to recall and capture the lives and contribution of older women who were founder members of the early women's movement in Britain (Spender, 1983), and as yet little material has been written by older women themselves (Stott, 1981). A recognition of the situation of older women has also been largely ignored by social gerontologists, sociologists and feminist writers concerned with social policy in Britain (see Delamont, 1980). Indeed the invisibility of old women has been amplified by researchers in a wide variety of studies. For although gender is commonly used as a discriminating characteristic in research analysis, in terms of policy formulation old people are commonly seen as a homogeneous 'male' group, and welfare services, however inadequate, usually favour men rather than women.

While Britain has been slow to recognise the unique position of old women, a number of interesting developments have occurred in other countries, most notably in the United States. In the main, such initiatives have been generated through the collective action of older women themselves, pensioners' groups and by intergenerational groups concerned with the abolition of ageism in society, such as the Gray Panthers founded in 1972 under the leardership of Maggie Kuhn. Groups specifically for older women have usually developed alongside established women's groups, and in many respects are reformist in character, for although they recognise the importance of consciousness-raising, they also campaign for change through influencing and enacting legislation.

A good example of such development is seen in the United States. In 1973, Tish Sommers founded the first national Task Force on Older Women within the American National Organisation of Women (founded in 1966), and through her work, and that of other activists, such as Laurie Sheilds, the Displaced Homemakers Movement was launched in 1975. A displaced homemaker is defined as:

> An individual who has, for a substantial number of years, provided unpaid service to her family, has been dependent on her spouse for her income but who loses that income through death, divorce, separation, desertion, or the disablement of her husband. (Sheilds, 1981, p. ix)

Such women are commonly too old for the job market, and are either too young or do not qualify for social security. Their campaign focused on the enactment of new legislation to set up pilot training programmes that would enable homemakers to develop skills that could be transferred to paid employment. After a hard struggle, the Displaced Homemakers Bill was enacted in 1978, and since that time a network of programmes has been set up throughout the United States (Sheilds, 1981), many of which involve other activist groups.

Such initiatives were important in generating an interest in older women within government agencies. As a forerunner of the 1981 White House Conference on Aging (a decennial national conference), a regional conference was convened concerning the needs of older women. It was here that the Older Women's League (OWL) was formed, the first national grassroots membership organisation concerned with mid-life and older women. Current membership has grown to over 10,000 throughout the USA, and major campaign issues have been defined within a national agenda which includes: social security; pension rights; health insurance; caregiver support services; jobs for older women; and the impact of budget cuts. They have increased the recognition of the needs of older women through their literature, meetings and development projects (OWL Gray Papers, 3–8, 1980, 1982). Other action groups included the National Action Forum for Midlife and Older Women, which produces a widely circulated newsletter – Hot Flash, and the Older Women's Caucus of the National Women's Political Caucus (see Porcino, 1983, p. 154).

The enthusiasm and energy demonstrated by such forms of organisation have been reflected during the 1970s and into the 1980s by the growth of conferences (e.g. University of Michigan/Wayne State University, 1975), handbooks (Block *et al.*, 1981; Porcino, 1983) and courses (e.g. Little, 1980), all concerned with the lives of older women, which have made those working with and for old people far more aware of gender-based issues. Interest has also been generated in academic circles, particularly amongst those involved with social gerontology programmes and women's studies courses. Women's studies centres, such as those at George Washington University and at the University of Maryland, have become recognised centres for the study of women and ageing. Examples of recent American academic research include studies of the caring role of women (Brody *et al.*, 1981, 1983) women and retirement (Szinovacs, 1982) and the life-style of older women (Mathews, 1979; Baruch, Barnett and Rivers, 1983).

Of course, examples of growing interest in the status of older women are not all confined to the United States. In West Germany, the Gray Panthers movement has paid special attention to the needs of older women, and in 1975, a European conference organised by CLEIRPPA (a French voluntary organisation concerned with old people) and held as part of International Women's Year, considered the isolation and loneliness of older women (CLEIRPPA, 1975). Recommendations were made concerning income policy, housing, health and social services, but perhaps of more importance was the recognition that only fundamental changes in the lives of all women would result in a better deal for women in old age (CLEIRPPA, 1975, p. 62); a theme reiterated at the 1980 UN World Conference 'Decade for Women – Equality, Development and Peace' held in Copenhagen (Peace, 1980).

To date, interest in the position of older women in Britain has been slow to evolve. However, the first conference concerning 'Women in Later Life' sponsored by the British Society of Gerontology in 1981, was very well attended, and in 1982 the Older Feminists' Network was established following a meeting organised by the magazine *Spare Rib* to find out how they might cater for the needs of older women. Since its formation the Network has held regular meetings in London and now produces a newsletter to keep in touch with over 200 members. Important issues on their agenda include campaigning against the misrepresentation of older women in the media and the formation of an effective lobby over issues such as housing, health, safety, transport, work conditions, pay and pensions (GLC Women's Committee, 1984, p. 21).

In contrast, however, it has been the recognition of a growing frail elderly population and the consequences for women both in terms of their caring and cared-for roles that has forced the issue of age onto both the feminist and gerontological agendas in feminist circles (Finch and Groves, 1983; Evers, 1983). A debate has begun concerning the realities of trying to develop alternative forms of community care which are non-sexist (Finch, 1984). Whereas some favour shared care in the community (Walker, 1981a, 1982b, p. 38; 1983b, p. 168), others believe that a radically new form of residential care may be the only solution (Finch and Groves, 1982, p. 436; Finch, 1984, p. 15). In the final analysis, perhaps neither option really proves adequate, for the problem lies not just in the setting or the organisation, but in the socially constructed inferior and dependent status of both women and old people.

So where does the future lie? Can we predict how the lives of older women may change? As those currently involved in the women's movement age, we must hope that younger women will not deny them the right to participate, that they will confront ageism and sexism together, and that this unity may spread to the wider society. While a majority of women would not admit to being feminists or involved with the women's movement, their lives have been affected by its existence. Future generations of older women will be more likely to have worked outside the home, to be able to control reproduction, to be responsible for their own financial arrangements, to have developed interests outside the home and the workplace and to have lived alone as divorcee, single or widow. Whether or not these factors will help them to develop the degree of self-confidence and personal sense of worth necessary to maintan them in old age is unclear, but the strength of women's position can only be enhanced by a recognition of the value of older women that is more than skin deep.

> Don't think that an old woman has always been old. She is in the process of discovering what 70, 80 and 90 mean. As more and more old women talk and write about the reality of this process, in a world that negates us, we will all discover how revolutionary that is. (Macdonald with Rich, 1984, p. 75 – One of ten suggestions for working on our ageism)

Notes

1. While a majority of carers are female, a sizeable majority of men do care for elderly parents and spouses. In the study by Charlesworth *et al.* (1984) 41 per cent of their sample of carers were men, both husbands and sons.
2. Separate, divorced and widowed women are also excluded from qualifying for the invalid care allowance if they are receiving maintenance allowance or pensions equivalent in value to the ICA.
3. On 1 March 1985, a married woman, Mrs Drake, was awarded ICA for the first time. An appeal tribunal decided that the rule which prevents married women from claiming ICA no longer applies. It has been overruled by an EEC Directive which came into force in December 1984. The Directive states there must be equal opportunities to claim social security benefits and discrimination on the grounds of either sex or marital status must end. The DHSS has appealed against the tribunal decision and the case will now be decided by the European Court of Justice. This decision is still being awaited.
4. Clare Ungerson looks at the implications for the cared-for of the use of the motherhood as a role model for caring/tending. She argues that the motherhood model and its associations with infancy may be inappropriate for other dependent people, and that the tendency to 'mother' may be most acute within the private domain of the family – when mothering is undertaken by strangers she suggests that it may be more acceptable. Motherhood also implies the performance of certain tasks, and by using the examples of (a) removing human excreta and (b) incest taboos, she shows how a set of stereotyped roles become transferred from one group to another.

5. A majority of newly admitted residents (residents less than one year) had formerly been living alone; this was not so true of long-standing residents.

6. The definitions of social class used in these studies make use of standard classifications. It should be acknowledged that definitions of class for women and old people based on either former work history or spouse's former work history, gives a distorted picture of their current position within society.

7. 'Working lives' – i.e. the number of tax years in which you are expected to pay (or are credited with) national insurance contributions i.e. 16–60 years for women; 16–65 years for men.

8. On 26 February 1986 the European Court of Justice ruled that Britain was guilty of sexual discrimination in compelling women to retire five years earlier than men. A test case was brought by Miss Marshall, aged 67, a former dietician who was forced to retire at 60 by Southampton and South West Hampshire Health Authority. On 2 April 1986 the Department of Employment announced that the Sex Discrimination Bill was to be amended to take account of this ruling.

9. Home responsibilities protection (HRP) protects both the widow's and retirement pension rights of someone who cannot work regularly because she/he has to stay at home to look after children or an elderly or disabled relative. The number of years of HRP are deducted from the years of 'working life' in order to calculate qualifying contributions. However, years of HRP cannot reduce years of 'working life' below 20 years. There are also qualifying conditions attached to this new ruling. HRP can only be clamied if you:
   * Look after a child under 16 for whom you get a child benefit.
   * Have been looking after a dependent elderly or disabled relative for at least 35 hours a week and the cared-for receives an attendance allowance.
   * Have been getting supplementary benefit in order to stay at home and care for a dependant.

5 The Development of Social Services for Elderly People: Historical Perspectives

Robin Means

Demographic trends in the United Kingdom have involved a major increase in the 75 and over age group who tend to make heavy demands on social services. A number of the chapters in this book reflect the resultant political debate about the respective roles of the state, the private sector, voluntary organisations and the family in the social and medical care of elderly people. This chapter will attempt to prove this is not a new debate, by looking at arguments throughout the 1950s and 1960s over the most appropriate direction for the limited range of welfare services associated with the National Assistance Act 1948. How did residential care and domiciliary services develop in this period? And to what extent did they reflect changing conceptions of ageing and family care?

Material in this chapter is drawn from research carried out with Randall Smith on the growth of welfare services for elderly people in England and Wales from the outbreak of the Second World War until the reorganisation of the personal social services in the early 1970s (Means and Smith, 1985). Our initial theoretical assumptions stressed how the slow overall growth of such services could only be understood in relation to the lack of utility of frail elderly people in either production or in the reproduction of a new labour force. The 'spin-off' effect of this was to place a large burden upon many women in caring for their elderly relatives. This chapter will attempt to illustrate one reason why this position was amended. The main trends of service development will be described but it will also be emphasised that the continuing debate about hospital care/residential homes/domiciliary services can only be understood in relation to deeply held societal assumptions about family responsibility and the 'natural' caring role of women.

Residential Care and the National Assistance Act 1948

Section 21 of the National Assistance Act 1948 states: 'it shall be the duty of every local authority ... to provide residential accommodation for persons who by reason of age, infirmity or any other circumstances are in need of care and attention which is not otherwise available to them.' Other sections deal with how such residential accommodation was to be managed (Exchequer contributions, charges, etc.), contributions to voluntary organisations, the registration of private old people's homes and the compulsory removal of old people from the community. Local authorities were not given any general power to promote the welfare of old people. Instead section 29 stated this power should only cover those who 'are blind, deaf, or dumb and other persons who are substantially and permanently handicapped by illness, injury, or congenital deformity'. Equally, local authorities were not given further power to provide directly domiciliary services for elderly people. (The National Health Service Act 1946 had given local authorities the power to develop home help services for a range of groups including 'the aged'. As a result, local authorities would not be allowed to develop their own meals-on-wheels services, chiropody facilities, laundry services, visiting schemes or counselling services.)

Few social policy academics have had a kind word to say about the 1948 Act. Brown (1972), Townsend (1964) and Parker (1965) stress the inadequacy of the Act in terms of its 'obsession' with residential care. Parker, for example, summed up the situation in the following way:

> The concern to maintain and foster family life evident in the Children Act was completely lacking in the National Assistance Act. The latter made no attempt to provide any sort of substitute family life for old people who could no longer be supported by their own relatives. Institutional provision was accepted without question. (Parker, 1965 p. 106)

Why did this heavy emphasis upon residential care exist within the Act? What effect did it have upon the subsequent development of welfare services for elderly people?

There seems to have been little if any discussion amongst senior civil servants and politicians about any alternative strategy of state support for elderly people in the 1940s. The 'able-bodied' elderly should live in their own homes on their pension and with support from their family (i.e. daughters or daughters-in-law). The long-term 'sick' should be in hospital. The long-term 'frail' should live with their families or enter a local authority residential home. This lack of imagination about services seems to have reflected the dominant belief that 'frail' elderly people could not manage in their own homes unless living with other members of their family; domiciliary services provided by the state and voluntary organisations could not offer sufficient support for this group. For example, the Nuffield Provincial Hospital Trust founded a meals-on-wheels scheme in Essex in 1947, and the Assistance Board were informed of which groups this was to cover. One of these was 'feeble old people, living alone' but the Trust stressed that 'the ideal solution in such cases will be admission to a residential home, but in view of the lack of such accommodation a mobile meals service would be of value as a preventative measure' (PRO, 1947). Domiciliary services were seen very much as a second-best alternative. The 1947 Nuffield Survey Committee on the problems of ageing and the care of old people were even more firm on this point:

> If sufficient Homes can be provided, and if the homelike atmosphere found in some of them is introduced into all Homes, many old people will prefer no doubt to enter them rather than to continue living in unsatisfactory conditions in private houses. This will lessen the need for extensive plans of home help, home nursing, visiting, and home meals service for old people who would be better off in a Home or Institution. The right sphere for such domiciliary services is in helping able-bodied old people in cases of temporary illness or during convalescence. (Rowntree, 1980, p. 96)

Such attitudes were present in negotiations over the content of the 1948 Act. This Act largely followed the recommendations of the Inter-Departmental Committee on the Break-up of the Poor Law. The committee was chaired by Sir Arthur Rucker (Deputy Secretary, Ministry of Health), and its discussion of local authority services focused on residential care. One section of the Report did deal with 'Special Provision for Certain Handicapped Persons'. This was defined as including the blind, 'cripples' and the 'deaf and dumb'. But the Report went on to warn that:

> If the definition is drawn too wide the class might be held to include all old and infirm people. This will lead to an unnecessary overlap with the Ministry of National Insurance and the Assistance Board and would almost certainly result in local authorities appointing Social Welfare Committees and staff to administer a general welfare service. The outcome would be likely to be not only a duplicated and consequently extravagant system of administration, but also the perpetuation of the Public Assistance Committees and their staffs under a new name. (PRO, 1946)

This quotation underlines how the Rucker Committee perceived the local authorities as having only a limited role in the care of frail elderly people apart from the provision of institutional care. Those left in the community would depend on financial advice from the officers of the Ministry of National Insurance and the Assistance Board unless they could be categorised as suffering from a limited range of physical handicaps.

Another reason for the emphasis upon residential care in this period was that existing institutional provision was extensive and a cause of public controversy. In May 1946, there were 62,957 elderly people (i.e. men over 65 years and women over 60 years) in public assistance institutions and in Homes run by local government bodies in England and Wales (Rowntree, 1980, p. 193). Within this chapter, it is not possible to chart the growth of complaints about the rules and regulations associated with living in large public assistance institutions (PAIs), especially for those not defined as being in need of active medical attention. One example of such criticism was a letter describing 'A Workhouse Visit' which appeared in the *Manchester Guardian* in March 1943. This letter recalled a visit to 'a frail, sensitive, refined old woman' of 84 who was forced to live in the following regime:

> Down each side of the ward were ten beds, facing one another. Between each bed and its neighbour was a small locker and a straight-backed, wooden, uncushioned chair. On each chair sat an old woman in work-house dress, upright, unoccupied. No library books or wireless. Central heating, but no open fire. No easy chairs. No pictures on the walls. . . . There were three exceptions to the upright old women. None was allowed to lie on her bed at any time throughout the day, although breakfast is at 7 a.m., but these three, unable any longer to endure their physical and mental weariness, had crashed forward, face downwards, on to their immaculate bedspreads and were asleep. (Quoted in Samson, 1944, p. 47)

The response to the letter was sufficiently intense and voluminous to encourage an official from the Public Assistance Division of the Ministry of Health to provide an interview on the criticisms to a *Manchester Guardian* reporter. The official asked that all examples of bad conditions should be sent to the Ministry although he admitted that the desired standards were sometimes difficult to achieve in wartime. He stressed that staff shortages during the war had led to an over-emphasis on care rather than the provision of amenities. Old people could wear their own clothes in PAIs as long as they were suitable. Where this was not the case, the clothes provided were not uniforms and they should not be recognisable as workhouse clothes. Overall he emphasised that the war had interrupted the early stages of substantial improvements in the care of old people but that experiments in evacuation hostels had underlined the need to develop small homes with relaxed rules (Means and Smith, 1983). Public assistance institutions were an embarrassment to the Ministry of Health because they were out of step with the ideological consensus being built around the Beveridge Report (1942). They needed to be defused as a potential political issue and this was a central task of the 1948 Act.

The Rucker Report was to accept the need for such 'reforms' in institutional care for elderly people. Such care should remain a local authority responsibility but local authorities would be encouraged to move away from large general institutions and to develop small Homes. The Report also considered payment for residential care. Previously, accommodation in PAIs for reasons other than medical need led to a loss of pension rights. However, the Report argued that 'as a further step towards breaking away from the old association of parish relief and in particular the conception of an institution for "destitute persons", we think that a resident in a local authority's Home should keep charge of whatever income or other resources he may have and pay the authority for his accommodation and maintenance' (PRO, 1946). This 'hotel relationship' would work for most pensioners by their paying the local authority 21 shillings a week from their 26 shillings pension and keeping 5 shillings for pocket-money. The concept of small hotels was enthusiastically taken up by the Minister of Health (Nye Bevan) in the second reading of the National Assistance Bill, when he claimed: 'the whole idea is that welfare authorities should provide them and charge an economic rent for them so that any old people who wish to go may go there in exactly the same way as many well-to-do people have been accustomed to go into residential hotels' (House of Commons, 1947). The implementing circular for the 1948 Act instructed local authorities to concentrate on building Homes for 30–35 residents, and that all Homes should be run 'with a simple code of rules designed for the guidance, comfort and freedom of the residents' (Ministry of Health, 1948).

Residential Homes in the 1950s and 1960s

The 'reform' of residential care in the 1948 Act was greeted with enthusiasm by the bulk of the press, most politicians and many local authority staff (Means and Smith, 1983). One public assistance officer from Middlesex County Council, for example, claimed that:

> The old institutions or workhouses are to go altogether. In their place will be attractive hostels or hotels, each accommodating 25 to 30 old people, who will live there as guests not inmates. Each guest will pay for his accommodation – those with private incomes out of that, those without private incomes out of the payments they get from the National Assistance Board – and nobody need know whether they have private means or not. Thus, the stigma of 'relief' – very real too, and acutely felt by many old people – will vanish at last. (Garland, 1948, p. 36)

By the early 1960s, Peter Townsend, in *The Last Refuge*, was able to prove the extent to which such hopes had proved illusory. He showed that in 1960 former public assistance institutions were still the mainstay of local authority residential provision for handicapped and elderly people. Such accommodation 'accounted for just over half the accommodation used by county and county borough councils, for just under half the residents and for probably over three-fifths of the old people actually admitted in the course of a year' (Townsend, 1964, p. 29). As a result, *The Last Refuge* is often remembered as an attack upon what was often called 'the workhouse legacy' (Ryan, 1966). The research, however, represented an indictment of all forms of local authority residential care including converted properties and new purpose-built Homes. Residents from all three types of Home suffered from a loss of occupation; they felt isolated from family, friends and community; they failed to make new relationships; they experienced a loss of privacy and identity; and there was a collapse of powers of self-determination. Townsend concluded that the long-stay institution failed to give residents 'the advantages of living in a "normal" community' (Townsend, 1964, p. 190) and should be abandoned as an instrument of social policy. The alternative was to improve financial benefits, expand sheltered accommodation and develop preventive medical and domiciliary services.

However, the policy debate about welfare services and elderly people prior to the intervention of Townsend was not couched in such critical, evaluative terms. Three interretated issues dominated the 1950s and early 1960s: first, the capital building programme; secondly, the high cost of hospital care for elderly people; thirdly, the correct definition of in need of 'care and attention'. Godlove and Mann have stressed how the authors of the 1948 Act did not envisage residential homes 'As being adequate for people suffering from incontinence, serious loss of mobility, or abnormal senile dementia. A "Part III home" was to be a home rather than a hospital or a nursing home' (Godlove and Mann, 1980, p. 4). An important aspect of the history of welfare services since 1948 has been the shift of definition of 'care and attention' to include those suffering from the above illnesses and medical conditions. This shift began to occur in the 1950s because of pressure both to restrict local authority capital building programmes and reduce the high cost of hospital care. This chapter does not provide scope for a detailed account of the various twists in the overall building and conversion programme for residential homes. Table 5.1 below is quoted from *The Last Refuge* and underlines the extent of restrictions, especially upon new Homes.

The years immediately after the Second World War have been characterised as an age of austerity in which there were restrictions on many aspects of public expenditure. Britain – and many other parts of the world – was undergoing the strains of moving from a war to a peacetime economy. With respect to capital projects, there was a shortage of labour and building materials and this drastically affected

Table 5.1 Council Homes opened for old and handicapped persons in England and Wales, 1948–60

Year	No. of Homes opened	Of which newly built
1948	97	0
1949	103	0
1950	138	1
1951	112	5
1952	130	5
1953	119	17
1954	99	15
1955	57	13
1956	73	22
1957	72	29
1958	53	26
1959	55	27
1960	76	47
Total	1184	207

Source: Townsend, 1964, p. 22.

plans to build new residential Homes for elderly people. Highest priority was given to what was seen as productive investment (e.g. industrial estates, new towns, housing for families) – the economically active of the present or the future, or to national security. The expansion of the defence programme in 1951 further worsened the situation. The principal regional officers of the Ministry of Health were informed that:

> We are moving into serious difficulties in connection with the Capital Investment Programme for 1951. Though a final decision has not yet been taken it is probable that following the review that has taken place by reason of the accelerated defence programme the amount we shall be authorised to spend in the current year on capital works of adaptation etc. on accommodation provided under the National Assistance Act will be only £600,000 or only two-thirds of what we have been envisaging. (Ministry of Health, 1951)

The annual report of the Ministry of Health confirmed this 'would entail a temporary slowing-up in the construction and bringing into use of new small homes' (Ministry of Health, 1952, p. 314).

This 'temporary slowing-up' proved longer than anticipated by the 1951 Report, and it was not until the early 1960s that the construction of purpose-built residential Homes was accelerated. Many commentators of the period felt this had created a situation in which there was a shortage of residential accommodation and that this required clearer thinking about what was meant by in need of 'care and attention'. This argument was strongly put by Shenfield, who argued that bed shortages meant 'that in the foreseeable future residential homes should only be provided for the really frail and infirm elderly, who must have a substantial degree of care' (Shenfield, 1957, p. 164).

The above quotation brings in the other two key elements of the policy debate about welfare provision for elderly people in the period, namely, concern about the high cost of hospital care and the correct definition of in need of 'care and attention'. Were expensive hospital beds being blocked by the lack of residential accommodation, or were local authorities being swamped by residents in need of constant nursing care? Was there a group not catered for in the existing legislation so that they were 'stranded in the no man's land between the Regional Hospital Board and the local welfare department – not ill enough for one, not well enough for the other?' (Jones, 1952, p. 22). Was there a need for a national system of rest homes or halfway houses that catered for this special group?

The politics of such arguments are difficult to unravel and the self-interest of emerging professional groups (geriatrics, social work, etc.) was a major factor in the ensuing debate about institutional care for 'frail' and sick elderly people which the Minister of Health (Iain Macleod) described in 1953 as 'perhaps the most baffling problem in the whole of the National Health Service' (House of Commons, 1953). At first, there often seemed agreement amongst politicians, civil servants and professionals to expand all types of provision once the problem of limited funds and staff shortages could be overcome. Concern about the 'blocking' of expensive hospital beds soon, however, came to the fore especially from central government. The Phillips Committee (1954), for example, in *The Economic and Financial Problems of the Provision for Old Age* concentrated on pension expenditure but also stressed the high cost of hospital care relative to provision by local authorities. Concern about the cost of the National Health Service was a major political issue in the early 1950s and the Guillebaud Committee was established to investigate this issue (see Chapter 9). Its Report not only stressed the value for money offered by the NHS but described the growth of provision for the 'chronic sick'; it claimed: 'striking results can be achieved by an efficient geriatric unit where there is enthusiasm for the work and determination to see that the three branches of the service are made to work harmoniously and constructively together' (Guillebaud Committee, 1956, p. 218).

However, by this time, the Ministry of Health had decided that a more general review of provision was required. In 1954, C. A.

Boucher (Senior Medical Officer, Ministry of Health) was asked to organise a survey 'of the services available to old people throughout England and Wales in order to obtain a more accurate assessment of the quantity and quality of the hospital and local authority services available to the chronic sick and elderly'. The Boucher Report on *Services Available to the Chronic Sick and Elderly 1954–55* concluded that the main shortage of provision was in local authority residential homes rather than hospital beds.

> The number of beds for the chronic sick in England and Wales is thought to be about sufficient in total if they are properly used and better distributed. The efficient use depends on the strength of the rehabilitation services, the sufficiency of welfare accommodation for the infirm, and the adequacy of the local health services and of the voluntary services. (Boucher Report, 1957, p. 51)

The Boucher Report argued there were 4500 patients in chronic sick wards who no longer needed hospital care and treatment and that the majority would be suitable for welfare accommodation only if more staff were available and more ground floor accommodation, or its equivalent, provided.

Both the Guillebaud and Boucher Reports argued that the respective roles of residential Homes and hospitals could be defined in such a way as to avoid the need for the development of a third form of institution (i.e. halfway houses). Residential Homes had to be developed and designed with the capacity to meet the needs of those labelled as 'infirm' rather than sick. The Guillebaud Report claimed that rest homes or halfway houses 'would only add to the existing confusion by creating yet another category of aged patients and adding to the difficulties of defining borderline cases' (Guillebaud Report, 1956, p. 214). Instead, the Report stressed the value of the criteria used by the Boucher survey to assess whether elderly people were appropriately placed in different types of institution. These guidelines – later issued as Circular 14/57 – stated that local welfare authorities were responsible not only for 'active elderly people' in need of residential care but also for:

(i) Care of the otherwise active resident in a welfare home during minor illness which may well involve a short period in bed;

(ii) care of the infirm (including the senile) who may need help in dressing, toilet, etc., and may need to live on the ground floor because they can not manage stairs, and may spend part of the day in bed (or longer periods in bad weather);

(iii) care of those elderly persons in a welfare home who have to take to bed and are not expected to live more than a few weeks (or exceptionally months).

Hospital authorities were also given a list of responsibilities by this circular and these included the 'chronic bedfast', the convalescent sick and the senile confused. At first glance, 'the partly sick and partly well' were no longer in no man's land. They would increasingly be directed to local authority residential accommodation despite fears this would recreate 'the old "infirmary" ... in modern garb' (Medical Officer, 1954, p. 283.)

And yet Circular 14/57 was provided as 'a working guide'. The paramount consideration was seen as being the interest of the person requiring a service although no guidance was given as to how this 'interest' was to be assessed and interpreted. In reality, such a circular was riddled with problems of interpretation despite the optimistic tone. Could one always decide if a bedfast resident would die in three months or three years? How clear-cut was the distinction between the senile and the senile confused? At what point did spending part of the day in bed justify a resident being labelled as bedfast and thus requiring admittance to a hospital? How could one know if removal to a hospital was inhumane? One suspects that the reality of the situation was that hospitals remained reluctant to accept patients from welfare Homes while local authorities often retained their lack of enthusiasm for providing a nursing service for their most sick clients. Above all, there remained a demand for elderly people for places in residential Homes and hospitals; pressure existed on both hospital and local authorities to persuade the other to accept responsibility for as many elderly people as possible.

The circular could be used in arguments over specific cases, but it did not by itself decide whether elderly people ended up in a welfare Home or a hospital bed. In other words, a bargaining process evolved between staff from hospitals and the personal social services which continues to the present day. One feature of such bargaining was that both sides had to make concessions. More specifically what Davies (1979) calls 'the swop' developed by which many hospitals refused to accept a referral from a residential Home unless that Home (or another in the local authority) would accept a patient from a geriatric unit of the hospital. Elderly people had few rights in this situation and it is likely that many continued to be moved around the various kinds of institutional care, according to the balance of power between the various officials involved. Later circulars would attempt to amplify respective responsibilities further but by the early 1980s the actual placement of elderly people in different types of institution continued to bear little relationship to an 'objective' assessment of their medical and social needs (Wade, Sawyer and Bell, 1983).

The Last Refuge (Townsend, 1964) and other associated work on institutions represented a challenge to dominant conceptions of social and medical need in old age. The primacy of residential

Homes in local authority welfare provision was challenged by Townsend and supported by a number of other authors such as Barton (1959) and Meacher (1972). And yet the theme taken up by state officials in relation to *The Last Refuge* was not the failure of most residential Homes to meet the social needs of most elderly residents but rather the necessity of replacing a limited number of inadequate buildings. In the same year as the publication of *The Last Refuge*, local authorities were asked by the Ministry of Health (1963) to submit ten-year plans for the development of their health and welfare services, for 1963–73. In terms of the proposed capital programme, just over half the money was to be devoted to residential Homes for elderly people (£117 million out of a capital building programme total of £223 million). The stated policy of the Ministry of Health was that local authorities should build new purpose-built residential Homes to replace all unsatisfactory premises whether former public assistance institutions or converted dwellings, and to bring the provision of places in Homes for elderly people by all 146 local authorities up to the national average in ten years' time. Residential provision for elderly people continued to expand – it dominated the capital expenditure of local authorities (Bosanquet, 1978), and provided accommodation for an increasing percentage of the elderly population (Thomson, 1983).

The Department of Health and Social Security conducted a census of residential accommodation on 30 April 1970. This found 2126 local authority Homes for elderly and physically handicapped people with 96,703 places, and 1035 voluntary Homes with 32,486 places (DHSS, 1975). About half the places in the voluntary Homes were sponsored by local authorities. By the 1970s many commentators were beginning to agree with the early critics of residential Homes that they 'have come to loom larger and larger as things that are good in themselves rather than as practical solutions to a pressing difficulty' (Bosanquet, 1978, p. 109).

The second half of this chapter will not attempt an assessment of all the complex factors that encouraged this continuing emphasis upon residential Home provision (e.g. trade union and professional self-interest, the symbolic importance of institutions, concern about hospital costs). The focus will rather be on the reasons why the growth of domiciliary services (home help, meals-on-wheels, laundry facilities, etc.) was so retarded during this period and how this related to conceptions of 'family' (i.e. female) care.

Domiciliary Services and 'Family' Care

In the first part of this chapter we discussed the 1948 National Assistance Act and emphasised the scepticism that was voiced about the capacity of domiciliary services to avoid the need for institutional care for elderly people with high medical and social needs. However, this did not mean that residential care was seen as the preferred alternative for all elderly people to being in their own homes or living with relatives. The optimistic tone of the debate about residential 'hotels' did not survive the pressures discussed in the previous section. By the early 1950s, a consensus had developed amongst state officials, politicians and the professions that elderly people should remain in their own homes for as long as possible for their own happiness and also to reduce financial pressure on the state.

The first of these arguments was put by Townsend in the following way:

> Home was the old armchair by the hearth, the creaky bedstead, the polished lino with its faded pattern, the sideboard with its picture gallery, and the lavatory with its broken latch reached through the rain. It embodied a thousand memories and held promise of a thousand contentments. It was an extension of personality. (Townsend, 1963, p. 38)

The second argument was offered by Sheldon at the International Association of Gerontology Conference in 1954. He stressed the burden of old age dependency on the rest of the community in terms of hospital and residential care provision. This created a need to encourage and support 'their general vigour under natural surroundings and their craving to maintain independence up to and even beyond the best possible moment' (Sheldon, 1955, p. 22).

The Ministry of Health shared such sentiments. The 1953 Annual Report spoke of the 'recognition of the urgency of the task of enabling old people to go on living in their own homes as long as possible' (Ministry of Health, 1959, p. 187). The 1960 Report made an even stronger statement when it claimed that 'the general objective of both health and welfare services, working in co-operation, was to maintain the elderly in the community and to accept admission to hospital or residential care as the right course only where an old person himself accepts the necessity for this and when he has reached a point where the community services are no longer sufficient' (Ministry of Health, 1961, p. 122).

Such views have always been echoed by members of all three main political parties. Throughout the 1950s and 1960s, parliamentary debates about services for elderly people were full of rhetoric about the need to keep the elderly in their own homes. Thompson, for example, argued for this policy in an adjournment debate on the grounds that this 'is what elderly people themselves want' (House of Commons, 1958). Political pamphlets and research reports tended to follow a similar line. Vaughan-Morgan *et al.*, in their pamphlet for the Conservative Political Centre, argued, 'we should devote all our energies to enabling old people to continue being in their own homes', and they went on to justify this in terminology very reminiscent of that employed by Townsend (see above):

> There they are surrounded by the things and people they know and love. There they are required to help themselves in a hundred ways, all calculated to stimulate their physical and mental processes and so maintain their interest in life. At home, insignificant and unimportant possessions and habits, in which the old increasingly find solace, assume positions of great prominence. (Vaughan-Morgan *et al.*, 1952, p. 19)

Thirteen years later, a group within the Labour Party was talking of 'the widely accepted view that the first priority of the welfare state should be to make provision in such a way that old people are enabled to live an independent existence within the community for as long as possible' (The National Labour Women's Advisory Committee, 1965, p. 3). Similar quotations could be provided from the local authority associations, professional bodies and the main voluntary organisations of the period.

Yet this consensus is illusory – there has always been conflict over how to define 'for as long as possible'. This conflict is at the core of the debate about the respective roles of the state, the voluntary sector and the 'family' in the care of dependent elderly people. More specifically, it opens up the question of why the state has proved so reluctant to develop domiciliary services that might delay the point at which institutional care is the only feasible option for many elderly people.

Older people and the family

The true nature of 'family' care for sick and frail elderly people was exposed by Sheldon as early as 1948 in his study of *The Social Medicine of Old Age*. Six hundred elderly people were interviewed in Wolverhampton and the results underlined the fundamental importance of 'tending' from female members of the family during periods of ill-health. The key role in the performance of domestic chores and the management of illness was carried out by wives and daughters. Sheldon found that 'whereas the wives do most of the nursing of the men, the strain when the mother is ill [falls] on the daughter, who may have to stay at home as much to run the household as to nurse her mother' (Sheldon, 1948, p. 164).

Numerous commentators during the 1950s claimed that the creation of the so called 'welfare state' had undermined 'family' responsibility towards a number of groups including elderly people. The medical profession, geriatric social workers, the local authority associations and leading members of the voluntary pressure groups were all willing to express this view at various times. This attitude seemed especially acute within the medical profession because of a belief that hospital beds were being blocked by the refusal of relatives to offer a home to elderly patients. Thompson, for example, was associated with surveys of hospital provision for the elderly sick in the Birmingham area during the late 1940s and he warned:

> It is . . . possible that slackening of the moral fibre of the family and a demand for material comfort and amenity outweighs the charms of mutual affection. . . . The power of the group-maintaining instincts will suffer if the provision of a home, the training of children, and the care of its disabled members are no longer the ambition of a family but the duty of a local or central authority. (Thompson, 1949, p. 230)

Local authority staff and councillors often expressed similar sentiments. The chief welfare officer of the London County Council criticised the weakening of 'filial piety' (Bligh, 1951) as reflected by the abolition in 1948 of section 14 of the Poor Law Act (which required children to relieve and maintain their parents). The Association of Municipal Corporations in their evidence to the Phillips Committee spoke of 'the reluctance of many families to care for their aged relatives' especially after they had entered hospital and that this placed pressure on local authority residential accommodation (Municipal Review Supplements, 1954, p. 108). In 1959 the chief welfare officer for Manchester was lamenting the 'changed attitude towards aged dependents' (*Hospital and Social Services Journal*, 1959, p. 35). And a colleague was warned that 'it would be an administrative nightmare if there was a decline in family responsibility' (*Hospital and Social Services Journal*, 1958, p. 495).

My intention is not to suggest a total consensus on this point. However, it is clear that two questions were frequently posed during this period: did the 'family' still accept its 'responsibilities' towards elderly parents? And did domiciliary services and provision from voluntary organisations support or undermine the 'family' in this respect? Sheldon expressed the dilemma in the following words: 'We must do everything possible to assist the family in the care of its aged dependants without at the same time relieving it of the necessity for still taking an interest in the matter' (Sheldon, 1950, p. 319).

Empirical evidence during this period gave an unequivocal answer to these two questions. Families did 'care' and the bulk of this tending was carried out by wives, daughters and daughters-in-law. The overall message of such research was that the 'belief in the decline in filial care of the elderly is unfounded and an as yet unproven myth' (Lowther and Williamson, 1966, p. 1460). The most influential demolition of this myth is again associated with the work of Peter Townsend.

In 1957, his influential book on *The Family Life of Old People* was first published and this detailed the family system of care that existed in the East End of London in the mid-1950s. A central theme was the extent to which elderly people provided family services as well as received them and that this created an intimate bond between the generations. This case-study approach was later filled out by his major contribution to the cross-national survey of old people over 65 which was carried out in the United States, Denmark and Britain; the results were presented in *The Aged in the Welfare State* (Townsend and Wedderburn, 1965) and *Old People in Three Industrial Societies* (Shanas *et al.*, 1968).

The research results proved that disability in elderly people was more widespread amongst those living in their own homes than those in institutions. However, those in their own homes tended to have more extensive family resources than those in institutional care. Such relatives, and especially female relatives, provided an enormous amount of domestic and nursing care which far outstripped anything provided by the state or voluntary organisations. The minority of elderly people who did receive such services tended to be similar to those in institutional care – they lacked 'family' resources. Such findings led Townsend to conclude:

> The health and welfare services for the aged, as presently developing, are a necessary concomitant of social organisation, and therefore, possibly of economic growth. The services do not undermine self-help, because they are concentrated over-whelmingly among those who have neither the capacities nor the resources to undertake the relevant functions alone. Nor, broadly, do the services conflict with the interest of the family as a social institution, because they tend to reach people who lack a family or whose family resources are slender, or they provide specialised services the family is not equipped or qualified to undertake. (Townsend in Shanas *et al.*, 1968, p. 129)

Rather than being restricted from a fear of undermining the family, domiciliary services needed to be rapidly expanded to support families and help the isolated. Other academics (Meacher, 1970) were able to develop these ideas through their own research and to argue for the development of an overall preventative health and social service strategy that would offer support and guidance to all elderly people rather than the narrow band already seeking institutional care.

Medical and sociological research had consistently answered our two original questions. The 'family' did care and this care was not undermined by services provided by the state and voluntary organisations. However, such research rarely questioned the disparity between the female and male tending of elderly relatives (see Chapter 6). Sheldon had spoken of 'sweated labour' (Sheldon, 1960, p. 1225) but this was to be eased by domiciliary services and the lack of sweat on male brows was not questioned. It was usually assumed that the family ought to care and a failure or refusal to provide physical services (cleaning, shopping, nursing, etc.) was seen as implying a lack of emotional concern. If a woman loved her mother, she would carry out these household tasks rather than expect another agency to do it for her unless she was rich and could afford private domestic help. In the words of Meacher, the 'family structure' was seen as 'the natural care agency' (Meacher, 1972, p. 308). And yet Townsend was aware that such definitions of roles and responsibilities were socially defined rather than just 'natural':

> The answer to the practical question 'does this individual need help?' may depend on a number of hidden assumptions: that the service has to be restricted on grounds of cost or limited manpower to a particular number of people, that the family should normally be expected or obliged to provide care, that with few exceptions individuals should be obliged even in old age, to be self-reliant in at least some respects. These are not just individual value assumptions. More often they are the value assumptions of society or at least certain sections of the population. (Townsend and Wedderburn, 1965, p. 45)

However, the implications of this were not carried through in the research of this period. The intellectual environment did not exist in which to develop a critical view of either the state or the 'family'. At the same time, such research had made a strong case for a major shift of emphasis from residential care to domiciliary services in local authority provision for elderly people. Why did this not occur?

Waiting for the Fiscal Crisis and the Demographic 'Panic'

At first glance, politicians and state officials do seem to have agreed about the need for an expansion of domiciliary services. Voluntary organisations were encouraged to develop such services as visiting schemes and luncheon clubs (Ministry of Health, 1962). The legal obligation of local health authorities to provide chiropody services under the 1946 Health Service Act was confirmed in 1959 (Ministry of Health, 1959). The 1962 amendment to the National Assistance Act 1948 gave local authorities the power to develop their own meals-on-wheels services. The Health Services and Public Health Act 1968 and the Chronically Sick and Disabled Persons Act 1970 both considerably increased the power of local authorities to provide domiciliary support services. However, such lists of legislative developments and exhortation by circular can give the impression of unimpeded incremental progress towards a more 'liberal' policy of social welfare provision for elderly people. However, there is a major difference between legislative intent and service development. Local authority provision remained dominated by residential care throughout the 1960s and early 1970s.

One explanation for this situation is that many welfare 'profes-sionals' refused to accept that domiciliary services could be cost-effective in helping frail and sick elderly people to remain outside institutions. The county welfare officer for Devon, for example, was arguing at an in-house conference in 1967 that:

> I think it is easy to see that the cost of maintaining an old person in the community can be in the region of £10 per week. There may, therefore, be a point at which we must say that the community cannot afford in terms of manpower to provide a home help for more than so many hours per week. This would be because home helps are in limited supply, and because an employee in a residential home would be able to provide a similar service to a number of old people at the same time. (Speed, 1967, p. 65)

The continued belief in the utility of residential care may have retarded the development of domiciliary services. Nevertheless, other commentators made exactly the opposite argument. Residen-tial Homes were expensive; an expansion of domiciliary services would be a cost-effective response to this situation by encouraging relatives to carry on caring for their elderly relatives rather than requesting their admission to a residential Home (Sheldon, 1960).

The interesting question becomes why the first rather than the second argument continued to hold sway despite the large volume of research evidence that pointed in the opposite direction.

Townsend (1981) has pointed to the self-interest of those who work in the residential sector. My own research has underlined that self-interest was equally strong in those voluntary organisations in-volved in domiciliary service provision. These organisations often used pressure-group tactics in a prolonged campaign to restrict the development of local authority powers in relation to meals-on-wheels and related services. Such campaigns took place in an environment whose medical and social work 'professionals' were primarily en-gaged in a debate about the macro restructuring of the NHS and the personal social services rather than the details of service delivery for elderly people (Means and Smith, 1985; Chapters 6 and 7).

However, one other influence upon the continued predominance of residential care will be explored in more detail; welfare services for elderly people only achieve any status on the political agenda during periods of demographic 'panic' and/or fiscal crisis. Argu-ments over the hospital/residential care divide in the 1950s were conducted against a background of concern about the rising elderly population. The demographic projections of the Royal Commission on the Population (1949) had created concern about the future 'burden of dependency' that would have to be carried by the work-ing population; those over 65 would rise by 2 to 3 million over the next 30 years which was defined as problematic because 'the old consume without producing which differentiates them from the active population and makes them a factor reducing the average standard of living of the community' (Royal Commission on Population, 1949, p. 113). This created a climate in which the relative merits of hospital and residential care would be high on the agenda of state officials and politicians. Adjournment debates about services for elderly people were a frequent feature of the House of Commons during the 1950s. The population projections, however, proved inaccurate which led some critics to deride 'the noisy barrage of faulty statistics' (Titmuss, 1955, p. 47). The Guillebaud Report (1956) ensured that the cost of the NHS was no longer defined as a political issue during the late 1950s and 1960s. As a result, the publication of *The Last Refuge* and other research of that period did not encounter a political climate susceptible to a 'moral panic' about the cost and effectiveness of welfare services for elderly people. The state was soon to become far more concerned with race and general urban unrest rather than the possible inappropriateness of traditional residential Homes as a form of state social provision for elderly people. Such attitudes were reflected by staff in social services departments after their formation in April 1971. Phillipson (1982, p. 107) has gone so far as to claim that working with elderly people was seen as a form of professional suicide for aspiring social workers. Numerous research studies have confirmed the lack of enthusiasm of social workers for this client group (Goldberg and Connolly, 1982, pp. 92–3).

Services for elderly people only re-emerged as a major political issue when the fiscal crisis of the state coincided with renewed fears about population trends. The 'burden of dependency' debate was about to be reopened (see Walker, 1980). At first, this situation persuaded central government to agree that domiciliary services needed to be expanded to reduce pressure on residential care. The priorities document of the DHSS (1976) argued that the more domiciliary services can be expanded, the more the pressure on residential accommodation and hospitals can be eased. The government had, therefore, decided to allow for a 2 per cent increase in meals-on-wheels and home help provision although this would be balanced by a cut in the capital programme for residential accommodation and day care.

All of us are now only too aware that a new 'golden age' for domiciliary services was not about to be ushered in. Sophistication in the packaging of such services may have improved through various social work experiments and research projects (DHSS, 1983) but this has occurred against a background of concern from state officials and politicians about the need to restrict the expectations of elderly people and their relatives about the overall availability of domiciliary services. This has been a central message of various government documents such as *A Happier Old Age* (DHSS, 1978), *Growing Older* (DHSS, 1981) and *Care in Action* (1981b), perhaps best summed up in the often quoted statement that 'care in the community must increasingly mean by the community'. Expensive domiciliary services such as home help and meals-on-wheels must only go to those 'in greatest need'.

The definition of 'in greatest need' is, of course, problematic. The author has previously claimed that this concept can be used to exclude elderly people with nearby female relatives (Means, 1981). As Moroney (1976, p. 58) argues: 'Scarce resources are channelled to those with greatest need. In doing so, however, the state is operating on the principle of intervention only when the family cannot or will not provide care.' Moroney is often presented as offering an early radical critique of such resource allocation trends. And yet his theme is exactly the same as Sheldon's in the mid-1950s – how can the state best support the family as the primary care-giver? Moroney makes clear that misjudgements about this partnership will lead to the state being swamped by the expressed needs of dependent elderly people:

> By not offering support, existing social policy might actually force many families to give up this function prematurely, given the evidence of the severe strain many families are experiencing. If this were to happen, the family and the state would not be sharing the responsibility through an interdependent relationship and it is conceivable that eventually the social welfare system would be pressured with demands to provide even greater amounts of care, to become the family for more and more elderly persons. (Moroney, 1976, p. 59)

This message seems to have reached many social services departments which are increasingly keen to encourage qualified social workers to overcome their traditional reluctance to work with elderly people and their relatives. The state may be unwilling to offer sufficient domiciliary services but at least it can 'cool out' the anger and frustration of relatives about this situation. Such counselling can be perceived as a 'low cost input' that helps to ensure the 'family' remains the primary care giver in the majority of cases.

Conclusion
Stacey and Price (1981, p. 8) have argued that:

> Notions of the 'proper place' and 'proper behaviour' are deeply ingrained and emotionally loaded, such that acute discomfort is felt when the norms are violated. For to the actors concerned the norms have come to appear as 'natural', as part of an externally given order without which there could only be chaos.

This surely explains what has been called 'the stunning silence' (Wilson, 1982, p. 46) as to the effect of welfare policies on women during the 1950s, 1960s and 1970s. Women accepted that it was their duty to look after frail and sick elderly parents and in-laws and this view was shared by central government, local government and voluntary organisations. This chapter has underlined the extent to which this attitude was never challenged in the period 1948-71 – the debate was about how best to ensure such responsibilities were carried out.

This consensus has at last begun to break down but this has occurred in a period when social policies seem likely to intensify the exploitation of women. Other chapters in this book address the way forward from the present situation. Can the regimes of residential Homes be amended in such a way as to be more acceptable to elderly people? Can and should 'family' care be developed in such a way as to impose equal obligations upon men and women? Is it feasible to develop a 'community care' policy which is not based on the input of physical care from relatives? Is it possible to argue for more resources for elderly people in a way which does not reinforce stereotypes about the 'burden of dependency' imposed by our ageing population? How can one best balance the interests of frail elderly people and their relatives?

Part II

Ageing and the Welfare State

6 Caring for Elderly People: the Family and the State

Hazel Qureshi and Alan Walker

Social policy is concerned with the collective organisation of welfare provision, both public and private, and therefore tends to concentrate on the activities of the formal bureaucratic social services. The paradox facing social policy with regard to the care of elderly people is that, although they are the major consumers of public social services, the vast bulk of the care they receive does not come from the public sector but from their own families. Within the family it is female kin who are by far and away the main providers of care (Land, 1978; Finch and Groves, 1980; Walker, 1981a, 1982a). Although a sea-change is underway in the official recognition of the role of family and other informal carers (see for example DHSS, 1981; Fowler, 1984) in the past over-emphasis on the public social services, by policy-makers and policy analysts alike, has helped to create a misleading impression of elderly people as welfare dependants and an equally misleading rigidity in the distinction between the formal and the informal sectors. Both of these false constructions are clearly exposed by an examination of the care of elderly people, as is the inadequacy of a social policy analysis based only on the public services. In practice the formal and the informal sectors are interdependent. On the one hand, the formal sector depends on informal carers – if only a small proportion of those with major caring responsibilities for frail elderly people, in excess of 1 million people (Henwood and Wicks, 1984, p. 12), metaphorically downed tools and emotions the personal social services would be swamped. On the other hand, the caring capacity of the informal sector is partly a function of the availability and distribution of social services as well as of the broader social and economic policies of the state (Walker, 1982b).

The main purpose of this chapter is to examine the relationships between the family and the state in the provision of care to elderly people. In doing so we draw on the results of a major survey of elderly people and their principal family carers we carried out recently in

Sheffield (Qureshi and Walker, 1987). We discuss the nature of family care, the impact of state policies, particularly in the personal social services, on the care provided by families, the role of other informal carers, government policies on community care and, finally, an alternative basis for policy which does not exploit the duty felt by families and female kin in particular to provide care for elderly relatives. At the heart of this analysis is the ostensible conflict between elderly people and carers. We show that, in so far as a conflict can be seen to exist, it derives primarily from the failure of the state adequately to meet the needs of *both* elderly people and carers and to strike a balance between these needs. First of all though, we look at the need for care among elderly people.

The Need for Care

We echo the criticisms made in the introduction to this volume of the alarmist and paradoxical character of recent official and public expressions of anxiety about the ageing of the population. The stereotype of elderly people promoted by this sort of exaggerated reaction to population change is at odds completely with the facts of ageing (Walker, 1980). The fundamental fact often overlooked in discussions of the care of the elderly is that, while there is a close association between advanced old age and disability (Townsend, 1979, p. 706), the vast majority of elderly people are able to care for themselves entirely without help, or with only minimal support.

The most recent source of national data on elderly people living in the community (Hunt, 1978, p. 73) showed that the majority are *not* functionally impaired. For example, three-quarters said they could go out of doors on their own without difficulty, 7 per cent only with help, and 6 per cent could not go out. Two-thirds could go upstairs without difficulty, 27 per cent with difficulty, 2 per cent with help, and 4 per cent could not manage to go upstairs. Nearly three-quarters could bath themselves without difficulty, 11 per cent with difficulty, 7 per cent with help, and 8 per cent could not manage to bath themselves.

Mobility and capacity for self-care declines significantly in successively older age groups. For example, the proportion of elderly people who are unable to go out of doors and walk down the road unaided increases tenfold between the 65–69 and the 85 and over age groups. The proportion of those aged 85 and over who are unable to bath, shower or wash all over alone is seven times higher than for those aged 65–69 (OPCS, 1981). Therefore it is among the older age groups that the greatest need and the main demand for social services occurs. For example, those aged 75 and over are six times more likely than those in the 65–74 age group to have a home help (OPCS, 1981, p. 154). Even so, less than one in five of those aged 75 and over receive a home help service.

A similar picture emerges from recent research among elderly people taking part in innovatory home care and neighbourly help schemes and even those in residential care. For instance, 55 per cent of those in the community care schemes and 55 per cent of a sample of old people in residential care, were able to wash without help or with only minimal support. Three-quarters of those in the special schemes and four-fifths of those in residential care are able to dress adequately without supervision (Tinker, 1984, p. 67). This emphasises the fact that, even among those regarded as 'dependent', the vast bulk of care in old age is *self-care*, provided by elderly people themselves.

Having established that the majority of elderly people do not require practical care or 'tending' (Parker, 1981) from other people, we now turn to the significant minority who do need such care. Applying the results of the national survey of elderly people living in the community to the current population of pensioner age suggests that some 590,000 are housebound, 590,000 are unable to climb stairs without help, and 1,477,000 are unable to bath themselves alone. They are concentrated in the older age groups, and it is these that are undergoing the most rapid increase.

There are currently about 3.3 million people aged 75 and over in Great Britain and this total is likely to increase by 500,000 by 1991 and a further 200,000 by 2001, an overall increase of 28 per cent. In 1901 the over 75s comprised one in four of the total population over 65, by 1981 the proportion had risen to two in five and by 2001 it will be one in two (Wicks, 1981). There is likely, therefore, to be an increase in the numbers requiring care over the next two decades and beyond. A rough estimate has been made of some of the increases in the need for care implied by these official population projections (Henwood and Wicks, 1984, p. 16). Between 1981 and 1991 the numbers of people over 65 who are unable to bath themselves might increase by 16 per cent (122,000 persons), those not independently mobile by 17 per cent (183,000), and those living alone by 9 per cent (258,000), although there would be considerable overlap between these groups.

The Supply of Family Care

The need for care on the part of elderly people is increasing. In itself this should not be a cause for alarm, however when coupled with the substantial existing shortfall in formal service provision (Walker, 1982b, pp. 20–1; and below) we believe that expressions of concern about the adequacy of care in the near future are fully justified. Two other factors contribute to the urgency for a radical reappraisal of community care policies: on the one hand, various social and economic changes are resulting in a contraction in the pool of potential carers. On the other hand, there is the continuing unequal gender division in tending and caring. The latter is dealt with in the next section.

There is likely to be a growing 'care gap' between the needs of elderly people and the supply of informal carers (Walker, 1985a, 1985c). In the first place, the decline in fertility during the 1920s and low fertility in the 1930s means that the generation who are now 75 have fewer children than any previous generation. The generation who will become the elderly of the 1990s produced slightly more children but their families were still relatively small (Ermisch, 1983, p. 283). There is no evidence from our survey of family care in Sheffield that the size of the pool of potential family carers has a significant influence on the provision of care; the crucial elements are the presence or absence of daughters and proximity of carers (Qureshi and Walker, 1987). It must be pointed out, however, that Sheffield is an area of traditionally low migration and geographical mobility might increase the importance of the size of the pool of possible carers.

Secondly, family breakdown is likely to have a small impact on the future availability of carers. It is not possible to predict the exact consequences of divorce and family reconstruction on the supply of family care. Obligations towards the care of elderly relatives felt by daughters-in-law compared with daughters are based on marriage and increases in both divorce and cohabitation might weaken the impact of the normative pressure to care.

Thirdly, it is often suggested that the increased involvement of married women in the labour market – in 1983 over half of married women aged 25–35 and two-thirds of those aged 35–54 were economically active – will reduce their commitment to care. There is no firm evidence that this is the case, although in the family care study we found that those in work were less likely to be caring than those not in paid employment. This tendency could become more marked in the longer term. For the time being, what is remarkable is the great lengths that many married women go to – often sustaining three distinct roles at enormous physical and mental cost to themselves – in order to care for elderly relatives and keep them in the community (EOC, 1980; Nissel and Bonnerjea, 1982; Allen, 1983). As a corollary it is sometimes argued that unemployment will enlarge the pool of potential family carers. But this contradicts all that is known about the debilitating, isolating and psychologically damaging effects of unemployment (see for example, Hakim, 1982). Thus, although evidence is scarce, what little there is shows that unemployed men are even *less* likely than those in work to provide care to elderly relatives (Qureshi and Walker, 1987).

None of the available evidence reveals any sign that the family is less willing to care, although it may become less and less *able* to care (a point we return to later). However this does not mean that many carers will experience personal and family crises if present policies continue unchanged.

The Caring Relationship

In the field of social care the terms 'community' and 'family' have for too long masked the fact that it is female kin who carry out the bulk of caring and tending (see Chapter 4). This means that in addition to doing most of the unpaid labour involved in tending or caring for elderly people, women bear the main burden of guilt and worry that usually accompanies the ties of love and affection involved in caring *about* close relatives (Graham, 1983; Ungerson, 1983a and b). A postal survey of carers by the Equal Opportunities Commission (1980, p. 9) found that there were three times as many women carers as men. A recent study of elderly people using short-term residential care found that 85 per cent had female carers (Allen, 1983). A detailed study of a very small group of families caring for severely disabled elderly relatives found that the average time spent on care activities on weekdays was 3 hours 24 minutes, of which 3 hours 11 minutes was spent by wives and 13 minutes by husbands (Nissel and Bonnerjea, 1981, p. 21). Fifteen of the 22 wives spent at least 2 hours a day caring for their elderly relative, but none of the husbands spent this amount of time on caring work. These gender inequalities were even greater with regard to those activities which are the most arduous and difficult and which put the greatest stress on those doing the caring. On average wives spent $1\frac{1}{2}$ hours on these primary care activities and husbands only 8 minutes.

The burden of care falling on women appears to be increasing. In a survey of women's employment Hunt (1968, p. 109) found 5 per cent of women aged 16–64 were responsible for the care of at least one elderly or infirm person in their household and 6 per cent were responsible for at least one person outside of the household. In the recent OPCS survey of women's employment, 13 per cent of all women aged 16–59 were found to have caring responsibilities for sick and elderly dependants, a proportion that rose to 21 per cent among those aged 40–59 (Martin and Roberts, 1984, p. 112).

Caring and tending tasks include physical work, particularly where incontinent relatives are involved, such as lifting, extra washing, cooking, cleaning and shopping. Then there is the mental effort involved in dealing with sometimes confused elderly people. Finally, there is the burden of bearing the total responsibility for the provision of care and medication with little help from other relatives or statutory services (Deeping, 1979). Although many of these caring tasks are similar to ordinary housework it cannot be assumed that they can be performed simultaneously with other tasks. For example, the elderly person may not live with the relative or may require special treatment such as a diet. Moreover all caring and other household tasks may require greater time and effort because of the need to keep an eye on the elderly relative all the time (EOC, 1980, p. 15). Providing care to elderly relatives often has a disruptive impact on family life and on other members of the family. One study of the family care of elderly relatives found that four in every five families were experiencing problems and two in every five severe problems. One-half of the families found that their social life was restricted (Sainsbury and Grad de Alarcon, 1971). This picture of tension between members of the nuclear family was confirmed by Nissel and Bonnerjea (1982) who found that in two-thirds of families there was considerable tension. As well as anxiety, physical and mental stress and interpersonal conflict, the provision of care often results in a lack of privacy and strained relationships with any children because less time can be devoted to them. Moving an elderly relative into the family home in order to care for them can result in cramped accommodation for everyone, lack of privacy and increased tension between family members (EOC, 1980, pp. 32–3).

It is now well documented that for principal carers, women, often married women with children, caring and tending can involve considerable costs. These economic, physical, emotional and psychological costs are discussed in the next chapter (see also Walker, 1982a, pp. 24–5; Parker, 1985, pp. 42–65). But, of course, caring involves a relationship between at least two people. Descriptions of caring from the perspective of the carer tend to concentrate, not surprisingly, on the often considerable burdens that caring entails and sometimes present a picture of the elderly person 'taking over' the household (see for example, Nissel and Bonnerjea, 1981, p. 40). While important advances have been made recently in documenting the previously latent role of carers (Oliver, 1983) we still know very little about caring from the perspective of the elderly person being cared for. This deficiency has been redressed to a considerable extent by the research conducted by the authors in Sheffield (Qureshi and Walker, 1986).

Elderly people do not give up their independence easily; with few exceptions they are reluctant subjects in caring and dependency. Determination often overcomes severe physical handicap (Townsend, 1963, p. 60). Indeed this resilience may itself be the cause of some strain in caring relationships. Elderly people desire more than anything the preservation of their independence, that is, 'intimacy at a distance' with their relatives (Rosenmayer and Kockeis, 1963). Two- or three-generation households require considerable adjustment on the part of elderly people as well as their kin (Williams, 1979, p. 49), especially since it is as likely to be kin who join the elderly person's household as vice versa (Qureshi and Walker, 1987). In addition, the provision of care and tending is not only one-way, towards the elderly people; they are themselves the providers of care for other elderly people. Thus in one study it was found that 30 per cent of the elderly were receiving help from others of their generation (Green, Creese and Kanfort, 1979). Elderly people also provide a great deal of practical help to their children, including child care, shopping, cleaning and cooking (Townsend, 1963; Hunt, 1978; Butcher and Crosbie, 1978). Indeed, reciprocity remains an important feature of the relationship between elderly people and their families and in-ability to reciprocate creates a reluctance to accept help (Townsend, 1963, p. 70).

The dual approach to the analysis of caring we have adopted here suggests that it can be a difficult experience for *both* carers and elderly people. Rather than concentrating on the needs of one group above the other – which can result in inequitable policy proposals (see for example, Finch, 1984) – this sort of analysis indicates that both share a common interest in opposing the current organisation and practice of 'community care' which is instrumental in imposing dependency on carers and elderly people alike (Walker, 1982c).

The failure to provide alternative sources of community-based care or inadequately to support the caring activities of families removes any effective choice for carers and elderly people and increases the likelihood of tension between relatives and breakdown on the part of carers. Elderly people are opposed to residential accommodation, which, not surprisingly, they associate with loss of independence (Tobin and Lieberman, 1976, p. 18). But as long as the whole responsibility for care continues to fall on one person, this prospect is likely to face increasing numbers of elderly people. For their part, women have borne the often considerable physical and mental strain of caring and tending alone for far too long. In order to understand why this unsatisfactory pattern of care has developed it is necessary to examine the role of the state in the care of elderly people and the promotion of family care. As a first step we look at the relationship between the formal sector and the informal sector of care.

The Formal and the Informal Systems of Care
Of the four sectors from which welfare services might be obtained – statutory, voluntary, informal and commercial sectors (Wolfenden, 1978) – the informal sector (the world or relatives, friends and neighbours) is distinguished most sharply from the other sectors, both in terms of principles or organisation, and suitability for fulfilling different types of need. Indeed, Abrams (1978) suggests that

the differences between the formal and informal sectors are so great as to place considerable difficulties in the way of attempts to integrate the two.

First, he points to the differences in the criteria for eligibility for services: informal care is directed towards a particular person on the basis of their social relationships with others: care for a mother, a sister or a friend, for example, whereas formal (statutory or voluntary) care is organised to be delivered to all people in particular, defined categories of need.

Secondly, in the formal sector, acceptable forms of intervention and outcome are prescribed, whereas in the informal sector forms of intervention are more diffuse and less well specified. Of course, this does not imply that there are no 'rules' operating in the world of informal care. On the contrary, it is clear that there are complex sets of social expectations and obligations which influence much of the informal sector activity and which will be considered at more length later. But it is characteristic of the rules of such social exchange that they are not well specified, in particular they are not found in written form, and that although social sanctions may be imposed upon those who do not comply, there are no formal procedures for obtaining redress against those felt to have failed to discharge their obligations.

The disadvantages of formal services are those associated with large bureaucratic organisations: developing rigidity of approach, inflexibility, particularly with atypical cases, difficulties in achieving a quick response and usurpation of power over consumers by professionals. At the same time, of course, the resources and expertise of such organisations are often valued by consumers. Typically within bureaucratic structures there are rules decreeing equal treatment of equal cases, and agents of the organisation, or bureau-professionals, do not enter into direct exchange relationships with clients, nor, strictly, perform additional services for some clients only (Blau, 1964).

The personally directed nature of informal care provides the key to both its advantages and disadvantages in comparison with formal care. Since such care is specifically directed towards certain people, others with similar needs may receive no assistance. So, for example, Abrams (1978, p. 3) suggested that by the standards of the providers of formal sector services the world of informal care is 'something of a disaster' because it does not secure equal provision for all cases in particular categories of need, nor can it adequately meet the needs of all those who do receive its services. However, Abrams (1977, 1978) expounded the theme that care provided by the informal sector is qualitatively different from (and superior to) formal sector care. He argued that because informal care is embedded in pre-existing social relationships, it has a different meaning (from formal care) to recipients. Caring for someone in a practical way is seen as an expression of caring *about* them as an individual. Furthermore, although there may be no obvious difference in the *extrinsic* benefits supplied in a particular caring exchange – commodities such as meals, shopping, cleaning and so on – it is likely that those who receive services will have preferences among the suppliers of such commodities which will depend on the *intrinsic* benefits – such as emotional warmth, affection, interest – expected from potential suppliers.

One implication of this distinction is that, unless no importance at all is attached to consumer preferences, the appropriate relationships between different sectors of welfare provision cannot be determined without taking account of the importance to recipients of intrinsic benefits to be derived from receiving services from one source rather than another. Equally the existence of such intrinsic benefits also places limits upon the applicability of any framework based strictly upon economic exchange. But an ackowledgement of the effects of their existence is essential to an understanding of informal sector provision. In short, the 'mixed economy of welfare' is nowhere near as simple as the economic model its advocates have in mind (Walker, 1984b; Beresford and Croft, 1984).

The Disadvantages of Family Care

As we indicated earlier the assertion of the superiority of family care cannot be accepted without question. In the first place family care entails a grossly unequal gender division in tending and caring activities (a point we return to in the next section).

Secondly, it must be acknowledged that within families it is possible for people to experience the most damaging and emotionally destructive relationships, which can have lasting negative effects upon their lives. The past history of the relationship between an elderly person and their children may not always have been one of mutual exchanges of assistance and affection. Family care can be among the very best or the very worst experiences that human beings can devise for each other.

Thirdly, there is some evidence that elderly recipients of state-provided services see these as an expression of caring *about* them. For example, a study of meals-on-wheels from the point of view of the elderly recipients, concluded that the symbolic function, of demonstrating that people were cared *about*, was the main function being served by the service (Johnson, 1972). It is also the case that agents of the state can provide the intrinsic rewards of affection and interest. The home help service is often mentioned in this respect (Hunt, 1968; Bayley *et al.*, 1983), when accounts were given of the development of personalised commitment to individual clients. This includes such activities as returning to visit after work hours, carrying out errands on the way to or from work, and inviting the elderly person into the worker's own home.

These examples should make clear, however, what appears to be an important distinction between effective rewards and the more instrumental activities that form the basis of the contract between the home help and her employer. It may be that to be recognised as genuine, the affective benefits offered in the caring exchange must be given freely, rather than being coerced or required as part of the job. If warmth or affection are seen to be expressed in the expectation of some promised reward, then this compromises the genuineness of such expressions (Blau, 1964). However it is most likely that the home help behaves in this informal way only with selected clients: she personalises her service to these few only, and thus, only by stepping outside her formal role as an agent of the state (in which all clients should be treated equally), can she offer genuine informal social rewards.

Because the value of intrinsic benefits associated with any caring exchange depends on the meaning attached to such activity by the recipient, and this crucially depends on the perceived motivation of the giver, does it follow that such benefits can only be generated as a by-product of state services and never directly generated by any third party? The belief that this is the case has contributed to arguments against the professionalisation or 'colonisation' of the informal sector (Caplan, 1974; Abrams, 1980; see also Bayley, 1982), on the grounds that to formalise the informal destroys those features which make it so uniquely valuable to recipients. But as we have indicated already, affective benefits are sometimes associated with formal service delivery. Moreover it is not necessary for practical services to be delivered by informal network members in order for such affective benefits to be received. Affective benefits can be delivered independently even though, within a particular caring relationship, the expressive and instrumental aspects of caring may be inextricably mixed. Warmth, affection and interest do not have to come wrapped round practical tasks, nor is the performance of practical tasks necessarily accompanied by such expressions in either the informal or the formal sectors.

The survey of people aged 75 or over and their carers in Sheffield provides a number of examples which illustrate that there is no necessary relationship between the quality of family relationships and the provision of practical assistance. Certainly there were children who helped despite reporting a poor relationship with their parent, both in the present and in the past, although there is evidence (supported by similar results in Levin, Sinclair and Gorbach, 1983) that this was experienced as a particularly stressful situation by the carers, and was more likely to end in the partents' admission to residential care (Gilleard and Gilleard, 1984).

On the other hand, there were also examples where people did not provide help despite feeling that they had a generally good relationship. This might be a consequence of personal incapacity of the carers, or it might simply be the result of differing expectations about the appropriateness of family help with particular tasks. One in three middle-class people over 74 in Sheffield had paid domestic helps, and perhaps felt, as one commented: 'I wouldn't expect my family to provide domestic help. ' Of course, to argue that feelings towards someone, and the provision of practical help *may be* independent, is not to deny that involvement in the process of helping may change the feelings of helpers and helped over a period of time.

The State and Family Care

How can the state influence the provision of tending by families? A variety of direct methods exists, varying from outright coercion – for example, prosecution for neglect of children – through to the provision of incentives, such as tax allowances or additional benefits for those caring for dependants. The state can influence family help less directly by the way it organises and provides services to individuals in need and the assumptions it makes about the nature and availability of such assistance (Moroney, 1976; Land, 1978; Walker, 1981a). Finally, the state's general economic and social policies set the framework of material and social conditions within which individual families find themselves.

It was a recognition of the importance of the social and economic context within which caring relations are reproduced which led one of us to conclude that care *by* the community depends to some extent on care *for* the community (Walker, 1982b).

In the field of the care of the elderly coercion has rarely proved successful. The idea that the state could compel families to offer love and gratitude to their elderly parents was given little credence even by the administrators of the Poor Law. They commented, regretfully, on the fact that even the most obvious needs of elderly people failed to call forth sufficient informal support, despite coercive measures:

> If the deficiencies of parental and filial affection are to be supplied by the parish, and the natural motives to the exercise of those virtues are thus to be withdrawn, it may be proper to endeavour to replace them, however imperfectly, by artificial stimulants, and to make fines, distress warrants, or imprisonment act as substitutes for gratitude and love. The attempt however is hardly ever made. (Checkland, 1974, p. 115)

This emphasises the fact that if informal care is unwillingly given it loses its special qualities and no longer has a claim to be a superior form of care. Indeed, in this situation it can become rapidly destructive of relationships, inducing resentment and guilt in both giver and receiver.

The Impact of Formal Care on Relationships

The state occupies a central role in the maintenance of the present pattern of care which is dominated by the family. Despite the existence of community care policies for the last 30 years, the direct involvement of the state in the caring functions of the family is still relatively small. Social services departments are primarily concerned with crisis intervention, short-term support, and in cases of severe breakdown, long-term residential care. The state is obviously committed to a practice whereby the bulk of support for the disabled elderly is provided by relatives (DHSS, 1978, p. 6). In doing so it tacitly supports the gender division in caring. Without alternative forms of community-based care, and while work and caring roles are still strictly divided by gender, women are effectively coerced into caring, often because of guilt.

From the late sixteenth century to the nineteenth century, the primacy of family responsibility was enshrined in the Poor Laws, and the fear that state help, if too easy to obtain, would undermine family relationships was ever present. The words of an Assistant Poor Law Commissioner in 1834 have a familiar ring today 'social ties . . . [are] now in the course of rapid extinction by the Poor Law'. From his study of the evidence Anderson (1977) reached the opposite conclusion:

> The [legal] obligation to assist was often a source of tension between parents and children throughout the nineteenth century. The 'quality' of relationships was thus clearly worsened in these cases.

Whereas:

> The removal of tension-inducing cash support functions, enables the family to provide effective and idiosyncratic functions which are difficult to bureaucratise.

Most American studies have revealed a preference that long-term financial assistance to the elderly should be provided by the state. However, the concern that 'state interference' may threaten family ties by taking over the functions of the family seem to have persisted even in the area of financial help (see for example, Kreps, 1977). Like the earlier Poor Law fears, this appears to be based on the assumption that intergenerational dependence is essential for the maintenance of family ties. Similar concerns have affected the construction of social policies in Britain: how to strike an appropriate balance between assuming too many responsibilities, and thus weakening family ties, or offering too little help, thus causing the family to collapse under the unrelieved burden of providing care (Land and Parker, 1978). The result is that the organisation and distribution of social services has played a key role in reproducing traditional dependencies within the family based on age and gender.

Community Care and Elderly People
An explicit policy of 'community care' for elderly people with disabilities has been in operation for more than 25 years. In 1958 the Minister of Health stated that the 'underlying principle of our services for the old should be this: that the best place for old people is in their own homes, with help from the home services if need be' (quoted in Townsend, 1962, p. 196). This principle has been reaffirmed by successive ministers and official documents (see for example, Ministry of Health, 1963; DHSS, 1981). In practice, however, this policy was compromised from the outset by the absence of strategic planning to achieve it, the failure to devote sufficient resources to achieve it and the reluctance of the state genuinely to share care with families (Walker, 1982b). Today the allocation of resources within the personal social services is dominated by residential care, which takes over half of the annual budget, compared with the one-fifth spent on community care. DHSS guidelines on community care services (which are themselves below independent estimates of the need for services) are nowhere near being achieved. For example the supply of home helps for those over 65 is only half of the guideline figure of 12 per 1000 population. Provision has increased over the post-war period, but not in line with need: the jam has been spread thinner (Henwood and Wicks, 1984; Walker, 1985a, 1985c). For example, an expansion in the coverage of the home help service has been carried out at the expense of the amount of service received by each elderly person. In the official survey carried out in 1976, 42 per cent of the elderly had home help visits more than weekly compared with 64 per cent in 1962 (Bebbington, 1980).

In 1976, 12 per cent of those elderly people living in the community classified as being in moderate, considerable or severe need were not receiving a home help service, 16 per cent did not receive a visit from a community nurse at least once a fortnight, and 15 per cent did not receive meals-on-wheels at least once a week (Bebbington, 1981, pp. 66–7). Furthermore, the definition of 'need' in this instance included only those living alone and who did not already get help with domestic care and, therefore, excluded all of those elderly people being cared for by relatives and others. The result of these shortfalls in services, the failure to increase resources in line with need, and the assumption that if elderly people are being cared for they do not need statutory services, is that female relatives continue to be the main and usually sole source of care for disabled elderly people.

The state occupies a dual role in relation to community care: it may provide direct support where this is absolutely necessary, but its main concern is to ensure the continuance of the prime responsibility of the family for the support and care of its own members. So, as Moroney (1978, p. 213) has pointed out, by presenting traditional family responsibilities for dependants and the division of labour between the sexes and between generations as 'normal' or 'natural', 'the state supports and sustains these relationships without appearing intrusive, thus preserving the illusion that the family is a private domain'. Thus women and families continue to bear the social costs of dependency and the privatisation of family life protects 'normal' inequalities between family members (Land, 1978, p. 213) and constrains the demand on public social services. In contrast to the constant public debate about expenditure on the social services the privatised costs of caring to the family are rarely discussed publicly.

As well as giving implicit support to the gender division of caring the state operates more openly to sustain it by the differential distribution of social services support (Finch and Groves, 1983). In social security too, the exclusion of domestic tasks from the attendance allowance and married women caring for their husbands from receiving the invalid care allowance reinforces the social division of care and ensures that many carers do not receive any payment for doing so. Two assumptions underlying social policy with regard to the family, as Land (1978, p. 268) has shown, are that men are not expected to look after themselves as much as women are, and that men are not able to look after elderly infirm relatives. This aspect of what has been referred to as the 'naturally negotiated' relationship between the old and young in the family (Johnson, 1973), therefore, takes place within the context of the firm expectation that female relatives will be the principal carers. Underlying the construction of dependency relationships within the family, therefore, is a fundamental conflict between women and men (Walker, 1983a).

Recent developments in community care and other government policies are likely to increase the burden of care that falls on the family while, at the same time, reducing the capacity of families to provide care (for a full account see Walker, 1982b, 1984b). The Conservative government's response to the major expansion in the need for care outlined earlier has been, on the one hand, to reduce the proportion of public expenditure going to the personal social services and so restrict the ability of these services to cope with increasing demand and, on the other hand, to emphasise the traditional role of the family and to encourage the expansion of voluntary and other unpaid help and private formal provision. In the words of the Prime Minister:

But it all really starts in the family, because not only is the family the most important means through which we show our care for others. It's the place where each generation learns its responsibility towards the rest of society.... I think the statutory services can only play their part sucessfully if we don't expect them to do for us things that we could be doing for ourselves. (Thatcher, 1981, pp. 3–5)

This ideology has been translated directly into policy towards the elderly: 'It is the role of public authorities to sustain and, where necessary, develop – but never to displace' informal and voluntary care and support. 'Care *in* the community must increasingly mean care *by* the community' (DHSS, 1981, p. 3). While it is placing a great deal of reliance on the family to provide care to elderly relatives, the government's own economic and social policies are under- mining the ability of families to provide care and reinforcing the gender division in care. In particular the growth of poverty and advent of mass unemployment are putting family ties and relation- ships under enormous strain. The conflict between the family and the state – or more specifically, between elderly people and female kin and the state – is now more explicit than at any previous period in Britain's post-war history.

False Assumptions Underlying Social Policy

Two implicit assumptions underlying the relationship between the family and the state in the provision of care and tending require critical scrutiny. It is assumed that state help, once offered, would inevitably be preferred (at least by those giving help); and, secondly, that the voluntary sector can fill the care gap created by the failure of the personal social services to keep pace with need.

In practice, those elderly people receiving services from their families are *not* anxious to apply for state help instead. In the survey of elderly people and their families in Sheffield, less than 10 per cent of those in receipt of weekly practical assistance from relatives or (in a few cases) neighbours, said that they would prefer such tasks to be performed by a home help. Most people preferred their existing family help even if a home help would have been available. What of those few who would have preferred home help? Most frequently these elderly people did not exactly prefer formal help but wished to relieve a perceived burden upon their family carer. Most elderly people felt (and their carers agreed) that family members were the right people to help them.

Upon what basis are decisions made that informal help is too much trouble for family carers, and so potentially damaging to the quality of relationships? Clearly in each individual case a complex of normative and structural factors are at work. Those factors identified by carers were: the personal capacity of the potential carer, in terms of physical and mental health, and necessary material resources. Secondly, the presence or absence of other prior informal obligations, such as a sick husband, or child or dependent parent (in the case of daughters-in-law). Thirdly, the quality of the relationship with the elderly person. Where there is a choice between family members, decisions about who should help will incorporate normative judgements based on gender-role expectations about the appropriateness of the particular tasks required, and the importance which may be attached to other informal obligations. For example, it may be that a man's obligations to his immediate family are assumed to include remaining in full-time employment, whilst a woman's may not be.

This brief survey should serve to convey the fact that seeking formal help is only the final stage of a dynamic process in which the available sources of informal assistance have all been considered, and the costs associated with them evaluated, *before* any approach is made to statutory services for assistance. (A full account is contained in Qureshi and Walker, 1987.) Moreover, judgements about the quantity of informal help available are made by those with the most detailed and exhaustive knowledge of the informal network, that is, the members themselves.

Current allocation practices in the social services show little respect for, or insight into, these prior processes in the informal sector. We have noted already that statutory services are often delivered, and to some extent rationed, on the assumption that other family members, particularly daughters, should help in preference to agents of the state, especially in tasks where no recognised professional expertise is required. Such services as home help, auxiliaries to assist with bathing, have been denied to, reduced, or withdrawn from elderly people who have local relatives, particularly daughters, available (Hunt, 1978; Qureshi and Walker, 1987). Also it has been clearly shown that elderly people living with relatives are less likely to receive statutory help, no matter what their level of dependency (Charlesworth *et al.*, 1984; Levin *et al.*, 1985).

Although every effort should be made to counter the disadvantages of bureaucratic service delivery, it is important not to lose sight of the fact that the provisions of state services can strengthen family ties. Furthermore, it is important to remember that many statutory services are highly valued by recipients. One example is given in the NISW study of people caring for elderly mentally infirm relatives or neighbours (Levin *et al.*, 1985). Carers who received practical help in the form of home help, day care or community nursing services were *less* likely to suffer strain and *more* likely still to have the elderly person at home, than people who did not receive such assistance. Additionally, it should be noted that the impersonal nature of help delivered through a bureaucratic structure may be seen as an advantage by some of those receiving help. Agents of an outside organisation are detached from past family quarrels or disputes, and have no future expectations of return for services rendered. Equally, from the point of view of carers, there are sometimes situations in which an elderly person behaves less reasonably towards family members than towards agents of the state. A number of carers in the Sheffield study indicated occasions on which their elderly relative 'put on a different face' – generally a more cooperative face – to people from outside agencies. Other evidence (Boyd and Woodman, 1978) suggests that this can be carried to extremes in which an elderly person's capacity for, or willingness to display, independence, drops dramatically as soon as they are returned from hospital or residential Home to the care of their relatives.

We are not suggesting that only relatives promote dependency, whilst statutory services encourage independence. On the contrary, some domiciliary services are delivered in a way which creates dependency and effectively hinders people from functioning independently (Walker, 1981a, 1982c; Paley and Carpenter, 1984). Thus improvement in the quantity and quality of care for elderly people is not simply a matter of increasing the amount of statutory services.

Turning to the second assumption underlying policy, particularly recent developments, it is clear that the potential of the informal sector to take on additional caring responsibilities has been overestimated. Within the family those regarded by both elderly people and carers as the most appropriate persons to provide help are already doing so and often working beyond their normal capacity. Outside of the family, friends, neighbours and volunteers are undoubtedly an important resource for care, but they cannot be regarded as a *substitute* for either family care or formal services. In some close-knit communities the contribution of friends and neighbours to care can be significant, but even in this setting it is secondary to the contribution of the family (Seyd *et al.*, 1984; Wenger, 1984). Other research in more typical locations confirms that neighbours and friends rarely fulfil a principal carer role for disabled elderly people needing considerable daily support (Charlesworth, Wilkin and Duvie, 1983; Tinker, 1984; Qureshi and Walker, 1986). Similarly with volunteers, they are not an adequate substitute for family or formal care and, in fact, formal services are required in order to make the most of voluntary help (Hatch, 1980).

Conclusion: Sharing Care Between Family and State
The recent direction of government economic and social policy has increased the likelihood of female kin being expected more and more to care for elderly relatives in need. At a time when the numbers of

very elderly people requiring care are rising and the pool of family carers shrinking, albeit slowly, the government has reduced the already meagre resources for community-based formal care. In addition to a growth in the coverage of family care the burdens on individual carers are likely to be increased. We are witnessing the heightening of a major conflict between the state and the people. The needs of both elderly people and family carers are not being adequately met by policy. The strains and tensions that exist in a caring relationship, which is imposed on two relatives or which is conducted in an atmosphere of great physical and emotional tribulation, affect *both* sides of the relationship. While the state sustains a casualty-oriented system of care it is effectively supporting the unequal division of labour in care and the detrimental impact this has on carers and elderly people alike.

Policy which seeks to provide an alternative to this unacceptable approach to the care of elderly people by assuming that there is a conflict between elderly people and their relatives and which, therefore, seeks to pursue the interests of one group above the other, is likely to produce unbalanced and equally unacceptable policy options. For example, the proposal that residential care should take the place of care by female kin (Finch, 1984) when all of the available evidence including our own research in Sheffield, shows that overwhelmingly both elderly people and their carers want the disabled elderly person to continue to live in familiar surroundings.

The starting point for an alternative policy which genuinely shares care between family and state, and encourages shared care *within* the family, is a recognition of the fact that 'community care', in the romantic sense used by politicians, probably never occurred and is most unlikely to be realised in advanced capitalist societies (Abrams, 1980).

Secondly, the conditions in which care occurs are determined in large part by state policies in spheres other than the personal social services, especially in employment, health, housing, social security and day care, therefore action in these sectors is a necessary starting point, especially gender equality in the labour market. Equality in family caring roles or parity in their negotiation is only likely to follow from equal access to the labour market. Then income can be provided collectively for home responsibility. The payment of such an allowance without concerted action in the labour market would simply legitimate the inequalities in work and caring roles between the sexes.

Thirdly, as well as sharing care with the family financially there is a need for services which support and substitute for family-based care. These services – including home carers, foster care, home wardens and sheltered accommodation – would be based in the community, would not presuppose that female kin will provide care, and would be oriented towards the needs of carers as well as elderly people. Clearly this pattern of service would require not only a radical transformation of the government's approach to community care but also a similar change in professional attitudes as well.

Finally, bureaucratically organised formal care may not be sufficiently flexible to meet the needs of many carers and elderly people and it is important to encourage quasi-formal and other sources of informal care, providing there is sufficient back-up from the formal services to avoid exploitation of voluntary assistance.

The difficulties of sharing care between family members, friends, neighbours and the state should not be underestimated (Parker, 1981, pp. 22–6). There are some initiatives which provide a few hopeful pointers in the direction proposed here. These include the Kent Community Care Project (Challis and Davies, 1980), the Dinnington project (Seyd *et al.*, 1984) and the Elderly Persons Support Units in Sheffield (MacDonald, Qureshi and Walker, 1984). However, it has yet to be demonstrated by these sorts of schemes that it is possible to provide care to elderly people with disabilities in the community without increasing the burden on female kin. The need to share care more equitably between the state and family and especially between family members has yet to be faced squarely by policy-makers. Some other countries have come closer to this goal and provide some indication of the potential for shared care. For example in Sweden, families rely heavily on community services (Adams and Winston, 1980, p. 247), and Sweden has attempted with some success to coordinate labour market policies with community care policies (Libjestrom, 1978). If a major crisis in the care of elderly people with disabilities – along with the increased dependency of both elderly people and carers – is to be avoided in this country then care must be shared more fairly between the family and the state.

7 Social Work with Old People
Ric Bowl

Social work with old people in the United Kingdom is a relatively recent phenomenon. Its origins can be traced to the 1962 amendment to the National Assistance Act 1948 which empowered local authorities to provide meals and other domiciliary services, with a firm emphasis on keeping old people out of local authority residential care. In fact, concerned with increasing pressure on their residential resources, many local authorities had already begun to employ directly, or by means of grants to voluntary organisations, 'welfare officers' whose duties contained a component of social work with old people (Younghusband, 1959, paras 494–7). These were, however, often people with health and nursing backgrounds and few had social work qualifications. Even in the mid-1960s, when Goldberg *et al.* (1970) started their research on social work and the elderly, most of these workers lacked a professional social work qualification.

The Seebohm Report (1968), which described services for the elderly as 'under-developed, limited and patchy' in many areas, gave a further impetus to the notion of preventive work and placed considerable emphasis on support for relatives caring for the old. The Chronically Sick and Disabled Persons Act 1970 and Health Services and Public Health Act 1970 both extended local authority powers to provide services and encouraged a wider view of a community-based service. However, it was the arrival of the unified social services departments in 1971, with their intended remit of building such a community-based service, that first, potentially at least, brought work with old people into the mainstream of social work activity.

The Impact of Social Work
Despite the legislation of the 1960s and 1970s, considerable evidence exists to suggest that social services departments have maintained hierarchies amongst client groups and that, almost invariably, it is

old people who fall to the bottom of the pile (Rees, 1978; Stevenson and Parsloe, 1978; Goldberg and Warburton, 1979; Howe, 1980).

These and other studies chart a depressingly similar pattern of social work with old people. Black *et al.* emphasise how even in areas where most requests for help involve old people, these receive more superficial attention than those from other client groups. Such work may be characterised as 'routine, unglamorous or even casual' (Black *et al.*, 1983, p. 186) and is often allocated to unqualified social work or ancillary staff. Assessment is frequently scanty and limited to consideration for a particular scarce resource rather than of the all-round needs of the individual, whether it be assessment for aids and adaptations, meals-on-wheels (Means, 1981), residential accommodation or day care (Bowl *et al.*, 1978).

In general, social work for these old people consists of the mobilisation of practical services and any prolonged contact with a social worker is dependent on the time taken to mobilise the resource. Often, there will be no follow-up by the social worker to see if the service being offered is appropriate, or indeed is even being used. More intimate contact may well be sustained by ancillary staff and particularly by home helps, who are often seen as providing psychological support and a flexible range of practical support, going beyond their official remit. The sometimes tenuous organisational links between such staff and social workers and unclear guidance given as to when they should sound the alarm bell, however, undermine the hope that this represents an effective way of monitoring the wider needs of the old people being served.

Marshall (1983) describes the crises likely to be encountered later in life – bereavement, moving house, hospital discharge, the sudden onset of disability, entering residential care; and Rowlings (1981) emphasises potential emotional needs in old age. Yet one study reported that 'it is rare ... for cases to be seen as being significantly complicated by interpersonal and emotional factors' (Black *et al.*, 1983, p. 186). Many clients and their families in this study did not receive the attention they felt they needed. Indeed, many were 'unaware that social workers were equipped to deal with stress and life crises at an emotional or interpersonal level' (ibid.).

The social needs of clients are rarely seen as an issue despite the importance of loneliness amongst the reported problems of old people approaching social services departments. Day care, for example, is often legitimated by reference to its surveillance role, or to the need for physical care; its social role usually being under-emphasised. Needs and difficulties associated with sexuality are also given a low profile (Marshall, 1983).

Marshall and Rowlings relate this pattern to the tendency to stereotype 'the elderly', to see such social and emotional problems as an inevitable part of ageing. They see it as a failure to individualise the client, though it might also be expressed as a failure to view the clients in their own particular social context. There is often very little work directed at building a detailed understanding of the support networks available to an old person, to understanding what friends and relatives do and do not offer, and what strains that might create. Indeed, Black *et al*. report that in Aber, one of the districts they studied, old people living with families received lower levels of service despite higher dependency and considerable evidence of strained relationships with carers. Assessment of such 'community' support is often limited to establishing whether or not a meal is being prepared or shopping done regularly, and assumptions about whether this is appropriate or not rarely questioned. Indeed many formalised assessment procedures rely on simple yes/no responses to such questions (Means, 1981). It is hardly surprising in the circumstances that there is little supportive work carried out with old people with a visible supporting network until the network cracks, often precipitating an ill-considered emergency admission to residential care with little thought for the interests of the old person.

In recent history this concentration on the boundary groups – those most in danger of being admitted into residential care – has intensified. It is advocated in *Care in Action* (1981); and it is these groups that are the subject of innovations such as 'granny fostering' schemes (Greve, 1981; Crowe *et al.*, 1983) and the Kent Community Care Project (Challis and Davies, 1980).

A final characteristic of current practice is that intervention is focused on the individual. Perhaps ironically, in the light of the failure to recognise the individuality of clients, there is little practice directed towards identifying and meeting the collective needs of old people or organising collective solutions. In the areas studied by Black *et al*. (1983) there was very little evidence of sharing of work or information between staff, and therefore little opportunity to collate evidence about the collective needs of any client group, including old people. The workers did, however, have some common perceptions – such as about the difficulties created by restrictions on the telephone budget or the limitations of residential care. None the less, they did not see campaigning for new or more resources to meet the identified shortfalls to be a legitimate part of their role. Further, they rarely addressed themselves to problems of housing and income even though they saw them as underpinning many of the problems of old people. They were seen as the territory of other agencies and therefore outside their own remit.

Nor were the workers able to commit themselves to forms of intervention moving beyond individual casework. The establishment of mutual support groups, of clients or carers, was a relatively underdeveloped area of practice and there was little involvement in community-based attempts to meet needs in relation to informal care networks, voluntary care, etc.

It should not be assumed that such a depressing pattern of work has gone unnoticed, not least by practitioners themselves. There exist many guides to 'good practice with the elderly' (e.g. BASW, 1977; Rowlings, 1981; Mortimer, 1982). Their emphasis is on developing approaches which look beyond the stereotypes of ageing and which recognise the crises which old people face as worthy of intervention, both to provide practical help and emotional support. They also argue for more attention to be given to supporting principal informal carers and for the promotion of genuine choice by old people in the major decisions affecting them. If implemented, such recommendations would greatly enhance the contribution of social work to the lives of many old people.

However, there is little guidance for the hard-pressed social worker on how such innovative and more labour-intensive forms of practice might be achieved. Writers like Mortimer (1982), Brearley (1975) and Rowlings (1981) isolate a number of influences on existing patterns of work. First, the existence within society of ageism with unhelpful stereotypes of the 'problem' elderly. Secondly, insufficient orientation within social work training towards the needs of the elderly – for example, consideration of the social implications of the health, legal and financial difficulties often experienced by old people. Thirdly, the existence within social services departments of priority systems and divisions of labour which disadvantage elderly people. Finally, the lack of preventive work and the inattention to the community development role within social work.

Like the Barclay Report (1982), which chastises social workers for the relative neglect of the elderly in some areas and highlights the inappropriateness of 'rationing by age', these writers offer no real explanation as to why the situation they describe has emerged. Their perspective views social work as a politically neutral activity which offers mainly technical or professional expertise. At the same time, the political influences on both the problems social workers confront and the scope and nature of their interventions are continually minimised (Jordan and Parton, 1983). As a result, the humanistic appeal to do better in social work with old people is unlikely to change deficiences in current practice.

Radical Social Work and Old People

There is, of course, an emergent progressive social work literature now wrestling free of an orthodox Marxist view that social work is simply a softer controlling wing of an oppressive state (Laurie, 1974), and that the only legitimately progressive activity for social workers is as members of their trade union (Goldup, 1976). Within this literature social work is viewed as inevitably a political activity. It recognises the critical role of the capitalist mode of production both in shaping individuals and their social relationships (Leonard, 1984), particularly those situations with which social workers have to deal, and influencing the role and structure of the welfare organisations in which they are employed (Bolger *et al.*, 1981).

The historical development of social work can, for example, be shown to be determined by a series of political decisions and currents strongly tied to the needs of the labour market, though also influenced by the activities of social democratic reformers and pressures from the labour movement (Jones, 1983). In consequence there coexist both concrete benefits for the working class, but also oppressive elements within welfare provision. That the progressive potential of the welfare state is largely unfulfilled is linked to the absence of direct democratic involvement in its administration. It is also argued that the needs of capital and the values of welfare will always remain in tension and that the welfare system can only be truly transformed within the process of building a socialist economy.

In the radical social work literature, however, old people are almost invisible. There is a tendency to see them simply as victims of the class-oppressive nature of social work or people who are almost incidental victims of cuts in the levels of services. There has been some reference to the specific problems of the old (Corrigan and Leonard, 1978), but there is little evidence to suggest that the values of 'radicals' that influence their actions towards old people are any different to those of any other social workers. In part, this might be explained by reference to the concentration of orthodox Marxists on the problems and potential of those engaged in wage labour – an opportunity increasingly denied to old people in our society. Within this framework the betterment of the position of old people is seen as simply integral to, and contingent upon, gains achieved by the industrial working class. However, such an approach fails to recognise the particular forms of disadvantage suffered by old people, or indeed their ability to analyse and strive to change their own situation.

In the last few years, however, we have seen the emergence within the field of social policy of a political analysis of the problems experienced by old people. This has begun to challenge the myth that problems of 'ageing' are neutral, and experienced by everyone in the same way in all societies. Instead, it is argued that the changes that come with age are profoundly affected by socio-economic structures and by the ideologies that accompany them. Problems of ageing are differently experienced according to class, gender and race and are also influenced by continuities in the distribution of material rewards and opportunities for power and personal development earlier in life (see Chapters 2 and 4).

A Political Analysis of Old Age

Material rewards provide one of the clearest examples of the continuities between working life and old age. Walker (1981) has emphasised the links between poverty and social status after retirement with income and occupational status beforehand. However, elimination of such work-based inequalities would be in direct contradiction to the primary capitalist values of the work ethic, monetary incentives and individual independence. Of course, the very material dependence on these unequal pensions and savings is itself a result of the emergence of compulsory retirement, an important element in the experience of poverty in old age (Thane, 1978).

Walker (1981b), Phillipson (1982) and Townsend (1981) also make references to the potential influence of gender in the construction of problems facing old people, a critical issue when a majority are in fact women. Walker (1981b) notes the susceptibility of women to the continuities of income inequalities that he highlights, because of their position in wage labour (often in low-status, poorly paid and boring jobs) and/or engagement in low-status domestic labour. Peace (see Chapter 4, this volume) further demonstrates how state income-support services amplify the relative financial disadvantage experienced by women in old age.

Contrary to the view that age is a great leveller, there is also evidence 'that the situation of the ethnic minority elderly is likely to be a product of the accumulated experiences and problems of a lifetime of membership of a minority group, as well as the current experience of problems associated with age' (Mays, 1983, p. 73). Certainly their own often marginal position in the labour market, or indeed entry into the country as a dependant, means old black people are particularly susceptible to the financial inequalities of old age.

Of course, relative financial disadvantage is only one of the many problems faced by old people. It does, however, underpin or exacerbate a range of conditions in old age. Even the development of health and mobility problems can be linked to the different environments that are made possible by different material standards (Phillipson, 1982). Social structure also creates a series of less direct effects. It shapes the experience and opportunities open to different individuals and, through ideology, places a set of expectations on them. Inevitably this has an influence on the individual's personality development. Leonard (1984) describes it as 'the internalisation of the imperatives of the social order' and identifies the key role of identification and repression in this process. This influence not only contributes to differential personality development that is carried forward into old age but shapes the particular ideological framework which is applied to this period in the life-cycle.

The role of wage labour is critical for it is here that much of man's identity is rooted. The limiting role of more abstract wage labour in individual development has been described elsewhere (Braverman, 1974; Schneider, 1975) but it is also apparent that its sudden absence on retirement leads not only to a fall in material standards but can be experienced as a profound loss. Exactly how retirement is experienced depends on the alternatives to wage labour that are available to individuals, and which they have developed over time. This, in turn, will be shaped by the nature of the working occupation, leading Leonard to suggest that 'only where, as in petit-bourgeois professional occupations, the abstract capacities developed have a use-value after retirement, may the experience be a predominantly positive one' (1984, p. 184). It is, however, the ideological context that conveys the real impact of the absence of labour. Thus, in a society where an individual's worth is closely related to the contribution he makes to the maintenance of the mode of production, retired workers are often viewed as 'unproductive' and 'a burden' (Phillipson, 1982).

The problem of retirement for men is, of course, recognised in the gerontological literature. Ageing, however, is represented as being less problematic for women (Faulkner, 1980). Yet women also carry their experiences into old age. The feminist literature repeatedly draws attention to the powerlessness experienced by women both as wage labourers and in the home, where they are often both emotionally and economically dependent. They may face isolation, passivity and a lack of confidence in their own abilities – all of which may be exaggerated by the specific crises experienced by women in old age, such as a diminishing of their 'physical attractiveness' (Sontag, 1975), widowhood, children leaving home and, for an increasing number, retirement (Beeson, 1975). As with men following retirement, the impact on women of widowhood or losing their parental role, will depend on the extent to which opportunities for other relationships outside the family have been developed (Livson, 1976). For working-class, home-centred women there may have been very few. Ideology is again critical both in sustaining women in a limiting and unfulfilling social role and in casting those no longer able to maintain their role as a 'dependant'. In essence, no matter how limiting it may have been throughout their lives, the dominant ideology now locates old men and old women as falling outside the mainstream of society. They are 'problematic so far as the ideal of the productive and reproductive nuclear family is concerned. Either they are not fulfilling their bread-winning role or they are not performing the normal and healthy functions of parents or children, or they are now a redundant appendage to the active family occupying no role except that of dependent' (Leonard, 1984, p. 189).

Ironically, the specific limiting stereotypes of appropriate behaviour for old people that form part of the dominant ideology, discourage them from engaging in the very mainstream activities that have formerly provided the roots of their identity. Indeed over-commitment to former roles – for example, for women, dedication to their children and home – may even be seen as pathological (Faulkner, 1980).

Old black people experience a further set of complications, though Barker (1984) rightly warns of the dangers of assuming a common experience amongst the many different groups of older blacks. None the less, there are some common threads. Particularly within some Asian cultures there would have been the expectation for men of adopting an 'elder statesman' role within the family. Their experience and knowledge, however, are largely based in another society and have become less valid. In contrast, older Asian women may find their role less transformed as traditional female roles have been less exposed to the influence of the western culture (Mays, 1983). Racism, both overt and institutional, is a further important factor.

Leonard (1984) speculates on the influence on personality of the internalisation of years of experience of both the conscious and unconscious devaluing of black culture – something about which we know too little. It is a process likely to be reinforced when most services available to old black people are not designed to meet their specific needs, when those who do use the mainstream services find they have little experience to share with the white users, and when those white users can be amongst those holding the most negative views of black people (Lalljee, 1983).

Dependency in Old Age

The notion of dependency as a burden is a critical one and has become second nature to us. It may well create increasing depression in many old people. As Leonard remarks: 'In a social order which places so much value on the individual responsibility of adults, dependency is bound to be experienced as failure: "being a nuisance", including being incontinent, often produces guilt and shame in the old person' (1984, p. 191).

The transition to physical dependency may be particularly critical for women for whilst men may experience physical dependency as an extension of past relationships in the family, for women: 'Patient-hood and attendant dependency requires surrender of part or whole of the women's ownership of care work to other women: professional carers' (Evers, quoted in Adams, 1981).

Not only, of course, is the ideological significance of 'dependency' determined by reference to the individual's role within wage labour and domestic labour but so are the resources to combat it; many of the difficulties created by immobility, poor health, isolation, etc.

being alleviated by adequate financial resources (Walker, 1982c). Furthermore, this dependence is directly reinforced by the nature of the services provided. Townsend (1981) asks us to look at how much scope for autonomous action on the part of old people is feasible within institutions and what that must tell them about their status and function in society. Leonard describes the process as infantalising, arguing that 'perhaps because dependency is only fully legitimated in the parent-child hierarchy of the nuclear family, dependency in old age is almost invariably associated with treating the elderly as if they were children' (Leonard, 1984, p. 191).

Townsend also points to the crucial social determinants – lack of family support, suitable housing opportunities, a tendency to bizzare behaviour – which lead many old people going into residential care when their physical needs would not dictate such a decision. The 'choice' as to whether or not to go into residential care is thus constrained by others. For many residents the organisational forms and daily routines of Homes lead to an enforced dependence. With encouragement of the growth of private Homes it is a 'choice' increasingly likely to be faced by the poorer of our elderly, adding further fuel to Townsend's view that the whole process serves 'to regulate and confirm inequality in society, and indeed to regulate deviation from the central social values of self-help, domestic independence, personal thrift, willingness to work, productive effort and family care' (Townsend, 1981, p. 22). 'Community care' shares many of these problems with, for example, regimes in day care often mirroring those in residential Homes (Bowl, 1977; Carter, 1981; Willcocks, 1984).

Old people are rarely involved in managing and running residential Homes or day centres. They have no voice in the planning and administration of overall services and little choice in the critical decisions affecting their future. Community services are an area where the exercise of professional power operates as a further reinforcement of their passive dependent status, a position exacerbated by cuts in resources which reduce the 'choices' workers are able to offer their clients.

So what does such an analysis demonstrate? First, that the problems of ageing are not incidental to the economy of our society: many are determined by relative material disadvantages that stem from the structure of society, others shaped by the ideology that reinforces it. As such they are 'normal' rather than 'pathological', though that is not to say that every individual will experience them in the same way. Not every retired worker internalises the societal evaluation of his or her worthlessness, nor turns in upon himself or herself the anger experienced by that evaluation. Not every woman sees her domestic work as 'not doing very much' or carries the guilt arising from a failure to be able to continue the caring role (see Chapter 4).

Constrained though they may be by the commonalities of class, gender and race, each individual will develop through different experiences, perhaps resisting the roles and images cast for them. This in turn raises the possibility of forging change, exposing, for example, the structural roots of depression or low self-evaluations and directing consequent anger outwards.

Nor indeed would it be right to assume that all existing services, all current practice was dependency-inducing or carried out in ignorance of these structural influences. The analysis simply serves to illustrate the context within which practice is shaped and the barriers to be overcome if a practice is to emerge that better furthers the needs of old people.

Towards a Progressive Practice

Can a progressive social work with old people be constructed? What would it look like? First of all let us examine what it might be in broad terms. My view is that such a progressive social work has to be developed in the context of theory that is sensitive to structural influences in the determination of problems in old age. In contrast, the dominant model in social work teaching, if not in practice, the 'integrated' or 'unitary' model, offers no framework for analysing the systems shaping the problems of clients and rests on the critical assumption that legitimate social work intervention must take place within the social democratic consensus (McLeod and Dominelli, 1982). The analysis described here tries to provide a better understanding of the formation of the problems of the old at both structural and interpersonal levels and to delineate appropriate targets for intervention. Of course, it remains as yet relatively underdeveloped and inadequately described in a chapter of this length. Neither can it lead to a cook-book or recipes for progressive practice with the elderly; nor, in addition, is it about being 'radical' in the space between cases, as one particularly depressing and narrow view has it (Rolston and Smyth, 1982).

Any progressive practice must be tailored to the particular skills and experience of the workers involved and it must be influenced by the organisational setting, both in terms of the resources available and the scope that workers can negotiate for controlling their own practice. Further, many of the individual elements of that practice may well be similar to those of any other social worker. Indeed, such individual elements of practice can rarely be unequivocally 'progressive' and, just as social work overall has both progressive and oppressive potential, radical social work will still reflect that uneasy tension. What this analysis may provide is a framework for making sense of those contradictions, that helps develop an understanding of the barriers to developing progressive practice and that guides those striving towards it. As such it gives rise to a number of important guiding principles.

The first of these is simply to recognise the enormity of the task. The problems of old people are deep-rooted and influenced by many structural forces. Within a capitalist society the notion of the elderly as a burden is, in a bizarre sense, 'real'. Unless they are in paid employment they make no direct contribution to furthering the interests of capital, nor are they likely to do so in the future. Unlike children, they are a poor investment for capital. This is something that will not change until we have an economy organised around social need (Walker, 1982d). It is these fundamental attitudes that are behind the low priority given to services for elderly people and this is certain to be exacerbated in the context of the current transformation of the welfare state.

Many writers have drawn attention to the increasing emphasis given to the control and surveillance functions of the state at the expense of its more caring functions (e.g. Davies, 1980, 1981; Jones, 1983) and there is little doubt that supportive services for old people will come under further pressure. Already, families are being exhorted to take on more and more of the caring role, leading to the exacerbation of a situation in which 'even where family members cannot or will not provide care, the service is refused on the basis that they should do so. [Thus in] practice ... some local authorities are still guided by the principle of family responsibility as enunciated in the Elizabethan Poor Law' (Moroney, quoted in CSE, 1979, p. 101).

Whilst opportunities for developing practice might quite realistically be seen to be limited, it would be wrong to adopt too bleak a view. Small gains have been won for old people, even under recent administrations, and there are examples of progressive changes in social work practice. Indeed, despite all the limitations on their work exposed by our analysis, commentators have continued to emphasise the relative autonomy social workers have over their day-to-day contact with clients (Bolger *et al.*, 1981) and their power to influence the *implementation* of policy at a local level if they act politically (Jordan and Parton, 1983).

The exposure of the structural processes that render the disadvantages suffered by old people in our society as normal rather than pathological suggests a second important organising principle. That is, to break away from the notion that compensatory services should in such circumstances be seen as altruism, a gesture from a benign and generous society for which each old person should be grateful and uncomplaining. This can be best done by viewing old people as a group with a set of rights – to the same income, mobility, housing and physical and mental well-being – as any other member of society. Part of sustaining those rights would be the provision of services to overcome the difficulties created by the handicaps and disadvantages our analysis has exposed. Nor should the price to the old person of sustaining those rights be any loss of independence induced by the nature of the services.

Helping Individuals

Within this broad context, what detailed form might social work practice take? First, we must recognise that part of it must be providing support and guidance in periods of crisis for individual old people and their carers. Radicals ignore at their peril the damaging effects on individuals of structural pressures. As Leonard remarks:

> A radical perspective which ignores or argues away the psychological effects of experience and the need at times to respond to these effects individually, as well as through group, community and organisational action, is in danger of failing to consider others as whole persons, of perpetrating, in another form, a fragmented, dehumanised view of men and women. (Leonard, 1975, p. 51)

There is considerable potential for expanding the contribution of social work in areas such as adjustment to retirement or bereavement; in alleviating the guilt that can arise from anger misdirected at carers or experienced by the frustrated carers themselves; or supporting people during periods of chronic ill-health. Marshall's (1983) study is a sensitive and detailed analysis of how such work might be conducted. In the light of an analysis which sees the impact of later life crises as largely structurally determined, such casework may have as its target building up a shared understanding about the root of the individual's problems, and helping in the rediscovery or re-emphasis of self-worth in the face of an ideology that often devalues the past and the current achievements of old people.

There would be no room in such an approach for scapegoating the daughter who is unwilling or unable to take on the caring role simply because that is society's expectation (see Chapter 6). Instead, part of the task might be to help the older person come to terms with the reasons behind such a clash of expectations (Corrigan and Leonard, 1978). Nor would there be room for the reinforcement of society's devaluation of domestic work. Rediscovery of self-worth might begin by emphasising the ability to handle quite humble tasks (Adams, 1981). For men, the alterations of self-image may include for the first time acceptance of the legitimacy of full participation in domestic labour.

Not all individual work will be of this kind. Mobilising practical services is an important part of the social worker's role. There is also a need to respect people's privacy and not simply casework them for the sake of it. This involves recognition that some needs may be material and some emotional. An important element in individual work, therefore, must be an adequate and open assessment of an individual's all-round needs. It must be an assessment guided by the widest possible understanding of the needs of old people and an awareness of the range of options open in meeting those needs. It must also pay attention to the problems reported and not fit them into predefined and limiting agency categories based on restricted service responses.

The sharing of problems with groups may provide a further source of strength. This can work as part of an activity-oriented group – in my own experience with old people suffering from the effects of a stroke. Worries about dependency and impaired sexuality were raised and discussed alongside more immediate practical problems. Others have experienced similar success with more obviously consciousness-raising groups amongst widows. Adams (1981) focuses attention on the potential benefits of such an approach both with elderly women about to enter Part III residential accommodation, and with groups of longer-term residents, still struggling to come to terms with feelings of powerlessness and lack of confidence and an identity removed by widowhood and the loss of their role caring for children. Carers may also benefit from sharing their frustrations and problems, often gaining strength simply from realising that others feel the same way.

Two important points need to be made about these efforts to alleviate individual suffering. First, I have already discussed the dangers of social work intervention reinforcing notions of dependency. A more critical approach must emphasise equality and democracy in relationships with clients. This has been described as a change in the authority base of the traditional worker-client relationship, 'the social worker much less offering cures, than support in the self-curative process' (Martin, 1984, p. 13). This means being more prepared to listen to the definition of the roots of their problems offered by old people themselves and to work with that accordingly. That is not to accept such a definition as an absolute but to recognise it as a legitimate starting point.

There are particular circumstances in which a less unequal approach is more difficult to establish than in others. Many old people, by the time they come into contact with social services departments, have deteriorated considerably. Some may be demented and may be inclined to tolerate conditions that are hazardous to them. Such circumstances throw into sharp relief the inevitable tensions that exist between a client's right to self-determination and the social worker's role in offering protection.

None the less, within current practice, there is a danger, not just of wrongly diagnosing confusion as dementia (Faulkner, 1980;

Rowlings, 1981), but of underestimating the ability of old people to make judgements about their own situation that may entail a degree of risk. This can be compounded by pressure from principal carers or, more particularly, other professionals for 'something to be done'. For the social worker faced with what might be real physical or emotional risk for the client this may create pressure to take the easy way out, something which is rarely conducive to ensuring the maximum choice for the old person.

The above situation is an example of the growing power over an individual's life that increasing professionalisation has thrust on the social worker (Estes, 1979; Wilding, 1982). For social workers concerned to further client autonomy this presents very real problems. They may be inclined to question the definitions of problems referred to them by other professionals, which often prove to be limited (Rowlings, 1982), but their own professional judgements are inevitably constrained by the fact that they remain individually accountable. This might be altered by more local democratic control, which might institute more 'sharing' of the risk and leave the individual worker less vulnerable. Experience of our current more limited local democracy, however, leaves social workers uncertain and they remain less than enthusiastic about the development of new layers of accountability (Wilding, 1982; Black *et al.*, 1983).

A second concern about efforts to alleviate adjustment to the disadvantages faced in old age is the danger of legitimating the way society restricts the life chances and opportunities of old people – rather in the way Townsend (1981) accuses those researching the problems of old age. Certainly, for social workers sharing the analysis presented here, that would be unacceptable. In their work with individuals and groups they will always be identifying structural constraints that both shape problems and limit their ability to ameliorate them. With its emphasis on consciousness-raising the work offers some prospects of stimulating collective resistance. Work with groups of carers, for example, might not only provide relief but also lead to a shared awareness on their part of the limited resources available to them and a determination to do something about it. It would be inconsistent for the social worker not also to be prepared to confront such issues realistically.

In consequence social workers might see support for and commitment to both local and national campaigns for permanent improvements in income as a legitimate part of their activities, but probably more central is their role in campaigning for local resources. This means tackling the DHSS in those areas where they have elements of discretion such as in fixing additional heating allowances for groups of council tenants. It may involve work to ensure that individuals receive their full welfare entitlements; or campaigns to stimulate awareness of the needs of old people amongst local housing or recreation departments. However, it also means campaigning for resources within social services departments themselves: for example, improved short-term care resources and day care resources needed to support front-line carers; or for the commitment of adequate social work resources to enable the labour-intensive case-work advocated here.

It is not only the fight for material resources that is important. The commonsense ideological assumptions that underpin ageism are also deeply rooted. Yet if old people and others are to be freed from their limiting effect they have to be confronted. It is now perhaps more common for sexist stereotyping and language to be challenged, though it still remains difficult. But how often are we guilty of basing our actions on similarly ageist assumptions, which have inevitable consequences for how we and our colleagues approach work with older people? 'You can't teach an old dog new tricks', 'Old people never change', 'They're simply more conservative', 'They aren't interested, they just want to withdraw', 'They prefer having it done for them' – the list seems endless. Elsewhere these myths are more than adequately debunked (Puner, 1974) but they must be taken on within social work if practice is really to be changed. Of course, as anyone who has ever worked with old people knows, old people can be conservative, they can be racist, they can be disinterested, and they can simply be very awkward; but that is because they are *individuals* who have experienced a particular history not because they are old.

Just as I have advocated a more democratic approach to individual work, it is critical that campaigning work does not reinforce the dependency and powerlessness old people experience. They may not always be their own best advocates – they too may suffer from the stereotypical views of ageing – but there is certainly no reason to suppose that they are any less capable of representing themselves than any other group in society.

This is something that has perhaps been more apparent in the USA with the influential Gray Panthers most prominent. None the less, there has been a growth in the activities of groups such as the British Pensioners Trade Union Action Committee and various regional pensioners groups. Buckingham *et al.* (1979) and Pensioners Link provide some indication of the potential of such groups in influencing health service and local authority policy. Social workers, who often hold knowledge and have access to decisions denied to old people themselves, can be useful allies in these circumstances, encouraging and supporting the identification of mutual problems and possible collective solutions.

Buckingham *et al.*'s (1979) is a realistic and sensitive analysis.

They recognise the sorts of difficulty that can arise in groups of this kind – of unrepresentative activists, of autocratic leadership, etc. – but also show they can be confronted and overcome. Nor should such difficulties be put forward, as they often are, as in some way being a particular problem of old people and therefore a deterrent to efforts to involve them more directly in the administration and running of services.

Such a demonstration would do much to counter the danger of existing provision reinforcing dependency, by extending the opportunities for old people to share the power and responsibility for decisions affecting their lives. Just as old people have demonstrated their abilities to run their own campaigns without the 'leadership' of the professional adopting a position of superior knowledge, so they can, if given the opportunity, contribute to the running of day centres, residential Homes, clubs and other domiciliary services. Such changes will not be easy. It is not ill-will or simply inertia that shapes current practice. In residential and day-care establishments, for example, resource shortages may encourage regimes where staff do everything for the resident or client because in the short run it makes life easier. Nor is such a democratic approach a panacea – many people are not used to that degree of control over their own lives and so it has to be learned by experience. Yet if we are to give old people more meaningful choice it is essential: 'True participation demands that people are given genuine choices at every stage of a process and not just at formalised points within it' (Jordan and Parton, 1983, p. 15). Social workers can and should play a role in encouraging this approach, particularly as there are so many forces pushing in the other direction.

Conclusion: Organisations and Change

The approach advocated here has considerable organisational implications. The emphasis on rights must ideally go hand in hand with breaking down any stigma attached to services and other barriers leading to high levels of *unreported* need (Rowlings, 1982). Higher rates of self-referral might thus be encouraged as part of a greater level of contact with the old people who could both benefit from and/ or contribute to services. If such higher levels of interaction and the encouragement of greater democratic participation, embodied in the approach described here, are to most effectively impact on what is provided, it will also be important that the organisation adopts a flexible approach to the development of services, particularly new services. This would be most easily achieved by adopting a de-centralised mode of organisation, emphasising local control over resources, such as that advocated by Hadley and McGrath (1980). Whether this would be compatible with the organisation of social workers into specialist teams for the elderly, which inevitably serve larger geographical areas, remains an open question. Research has, as yet, been able to tell us little about this, or indeed more generally, about the *effects* of either specialist or patch-based work.

Certainly the limited evidence of Black *et al.* (1983) shows such a specialisation to make no quantitative difference to the social work service offered to old people. None the less, whilst not endorsing the ambivalence of the Barclay Committee on this issue, it is clear that in some local circumstances, such specialism by client group might protect resources for work with old people. Of course, specialisation is a more complex issue than can be addressed here, and it is discussed at great length by a number of commentators (for example, Stevenson, 1981). For social workers striving to adopt the more progressive approach advocated here, it may be an issue of limited relevance. Different organisational forms will create different opportunities and different limitations on their work. They will almost certainly want to try to influence that organisational structure but, to an extent, they also have to work with what they have got.

Irrespective of these organisational constraints they will also run risks. Employers will not always accept the approach advocated here, particularly where there are direct or implied criticisms of their own performance. Workers may find it easier to develop a more progressive practice where there are sympathetic local politicians, though recent history would suggest that even councillors in authorities controlled by Labour's left-wing do not always recognise the legitimacy of a council's workers having a significant voice in shaping an authority's practice.

Protection for individual workers must come principally from working collectively, which will also provide the strength of shared understanding and, at times, constructive comparison of differences in perspective (Hale, 1983). Ideally, one locus of sharing will be the social work team itself – also essential to identifying adequately the shared needs of old people and possible collective solutions, and offering the possibility of a more imaginative division of labour than by the individual case (as others have described in more detail – for example, Bennett, 1980; Bolger *et al.*, 1981; Black *et al.*, 1983).

Other workers in the department and outside – home helps, health visitors, doctors and residential workers – will also need to be involved in developing particular aspects of practice or in sustaining campaigns on particular issues. Although they will not necessarily share the same overall perspective, they may also be further sources of moral support.

The social workers' own trade union will also play a crucial role, particularly where campaigning activities need to include direct criticism of the provision of the department. Trade unions have a legitimate role in questioning the levels of service provided to the public by organisations in which their members work, and some success has been achieved in challenging the nature of services as well as simply protecting jobs (Bolger *et al.*, 1981). Not that gaining the support of your own or other trade unions should be seen as necessarily problem-free. The defence of jobs in the residential sector may be represented as conflicting with efforts to develop community-based alternatives, for example. Also, just as Jones (1983) warns of the need to conquer antagonism amongst some sectors of the working class towards the recipients of welfare generally, the labour movement has at times been as guilty as anyone of reinforcing negative stereotypes of ageing.

Whatever the level of collective support, workers striving towards a more progressive practice have to accept that there will be setbacks, particularly now that welfare expenditure is increasingly being seen as having to come from any surplus the economy can generate. One of their most important allies in sustaining morale will be realism and the setting of limited achievable goals whilst not losing sight of the need for wider change. Furthermore, it is crucial to recognise that social work has only limited potential. Social workers can usefully contribute in the many ways described to the alleviation of the disadvantages old people face. Ultimately, however, many of them are constructed by material and psychological inequalities that develop much earlier in life, and whilst again social workers may have a limited role to play in combating them, those inequalities remain firmly embedded in society's structure, impervious to piecemeal reform, and their elimination awaits more fundamental change in the central principles and institutions that govern our society.

8 Residential Care

Dianne Willcocks

Over the past decade, residential care services for elderly people have come under increasing attack from a number of sources. Critics on the right deplore the inefficiencies of investment in institutional provision and they claim, correctly, that at best it will benefit only a minority of those in need of care. Critics on the left present evidence of the detrimental impact of institutions on the elderly and they argue that old people's Homes have failed to provide a successful challenge to the historical and cultural echoes of the Poor Laws. Accordingly, the best efforts of policy-makers and caring professionals across the political spectrum have focused on the advantages of community care – arguably, to the detriment of residential care. The purpose of this chapter will be to discuss the material circumstances and the ideological commitments that have given rise to this crisis of confidence in residential care for old people. This will provide a base from which to explore future directions for old peoples' Homes.

We begin with an assessment of current provision which stems from the 1948 National Assistance Act. This requires local authorities to provide 'residential accommodation for persons who by reason of age, infirmity or any other circumstances are in need of care and attention which is not otherwise available to them'. There are different attempts to translate this policy into residential practice, but the old age Home has been society's primary way of managing that residual group of elderly people who are deemed to be unable to manage for themselves. We can argue that this represents a form of social control which is designed to limit the demands of older people upon the state, and which serves to emphasise the marginality of the old, the poor, and the women in contemporary capitalist society. But it is also important to ask how much better served are old people living in the community?

The context for this discussion is that growing old is no longer experienced as a novel social event. Substantial numbers of frail and dependent people, aged 75 or over, now come to place their legitimate demands on the state. In response to this, and to criticisms of institutional care, various community alternatives have proliferated in the post-war period and many schemes provide sensitive and imaginative patterns of home care. Yet some 2 per cent of the elderly population continue to occupy residential Homes, for the degree of support that is often assumed to be available to them only in long-term care establishments. Over the years, a series of uncoordinated policy documents on the organisation of residential care (DHSS, 1977a) and the design and location of Homes (MOH, 1962; DHSS, 1973), have advocated particular forms of care. But there has been a marked drift towards separate development for residential and community services, and what is conspicuously absent from all policy statements is the development of a coherent rationale for institutional care.

To understand this, it is necessary to explore the origins of institutional settings and to note the special difficulties of resolving twentieth-century problems with a practical formula inherited from a nineteenth-century philosophy. For this produces a conflict between models of care and control which continues to colour many aspects of policy and practice.

In this chapter, we provide a profile of residential care by looking critically at current provision. A fundamental aim will be to question the future of institutional care. This question will be posed in a contemporary context which contrasts care in the residential setting with living in a 'normal' community in the 1980s. It will be necessary to explore the case against old age Homes as they now exist, and to ask whether we have reneged on our commitment to create caring environments which offer old people security with indepedence. The possibility of constructing an alternative residential model will be explored and this could build upon links between residential Homes and the local community. If there is a future for residential care it must be one which embraces old people actively in the mainstream of progressive social care policies.

The Legacy of Past Care

Not until the birth of the welfare state can we detect a dawning recognition of the elderly experiencing distinct social problems; for the Victorian Poor Law legislation treated the elderly infirm as but one segment of the impotent poor. It is clear that the burgeoning capitalist state deliberately created institutions to punish and stigmatise indigents, and it has been argued that this workhouse model evokes memories which still threaten a potential resident (Townsend, 1981).

In the words of an Assistant Commissioner of the Poor Law,

describing the workhouse: 'our object is to establish therein a discipline so severe and repulsive as to make them a terror to the poor and prevent them from entering' (Townsend, 1981). Thus was the work ethic stimulated; and a range of social deviants which included the elderly poor were punished for transgressing conventional norms. The Poor Law asylums were constructed to provide a harsh regime of custodial care for all of those whom society and medicine had rejected.

The question this raises is: To what extent have social democratic policies of the post-war period successfully challenged this ideological inheritance through the material and organisational form of modern Homes? To what extent have attempts to scale down the gross dimensions of residential environments and to introduce freedom and choice – as proposed, for example, by Townsend (1962) – succeeded? Problems emerge if we examine modern Homes in terms of Goffman's (1961) treatise on the total institution. He describes the routinisation of daily activities plus formal rules and block treatment of clients, based on a rational plan designed to meet the aims of the institution, and not necessarily the needs of elderly clients. This can dehumanise the individual client and may prompt pathological reactions such as a refusal to engage in everyday activities.

Recent studies of care settings suggest that the Victorian legacy may strengthen those barriers which distance the residential Home from the community; in part, through geographical isolation in large buildings which may convey a public institutional image; and, in part, through a social segregation between clients and staff (Peace *et al.*, 1979; Willcocks, *et al.*, 1982). Furthermore, formal language can mark out the Home as an institution (Davis, 1982). Titles such as 'superintendent' or 'officer in charge', together with rule-bound notice boards and distinctive Home names, represent a nomenclature and a series of institutional symbols which become viable and legitimate only in situations where external social controls are imposed to secure institutional goals. Thus we label and give identity to a separate group of people and we construct a boundary which can deter even the most committed and caring outsider from crossing the threshold. These are the real historical legacies which define residential Homes as a separate dimension of care and provide the backcloth for a review of the present situation.

A Current Profile of Residential Care
Recently, there have been significant shifts in the balance between the different sectors of care as a result of the massive growth of private Homes. Best estimates suggest that, at present, 56 per cent of residents live in public sector Homes, 20 per cent in voluntary Homes and 24 per cent in private Homes (Hansard, 1983). Much of

our information about clients, staff and residential life-style is derived from work on local authority Homes (Evans *et al.*, 1981; Allen, 1982; Goldberg and Connolly, 1982). Only recently has interest shifted towards the private sector and research-based data are now appearing (Bird, 1984; Judge, 1984; Weaver *et al.*, 1985a). Current trends have prompted the preparation of a code of practice for residential care (Centre for Policy on Ageing (CPA), 1984) and, for the first time, there is a benchmark against which to judge performance for individual establishments. Here the rights and needs of the individual old person take precedence over the interests of providers or organisations. The text begins:

> Underlying all the recommendations and requirements set out in this code is a conviction that those who live in residential care should do so with dignity, that they should have the respect of those who support them; should live with no reduction of their rights as citizens (except where the law so prescribes); and should be entitled to live as full and active a life as their physical and mental condition will allow. Whether young or old, sound in mind and body, or suffering from disability, residents have a fundamental right to self-determination and individuality. Equally, they have the right to live in a manner and circumstances which correspond as far as is possible, with what is normal for those who remain in their own homes. (CPA, 1984, p. 1)

Design of residential environments
In modern British Homes there have been major environmental changes which promote a less constrained and uniform life-style; over a period of 40 years they have moved away from the workhouse through the post-war sunshine hostel to adapted Homes, large purpose-built Homes, group-unit designs and on to a more individualised, residential flatlet model (Peace, 1983a). Within this progression, the post-war 'social democratic promise' has reformed the living arrangements for old people. Ideals such as 'the family group concept' or 'creation of the homely domestic setting' (DHSS, 1973) are used by policy-makers, who exhibit an obstinate determination to conceive and create an illusion of home within the institution (Kellaher *et al.*, 1983). Research shows that for local authority Homes, over time, there has been a trend towards larger and more complex buildings with fewer storeys, and an increase in private single bedroom space (Peace *et al.*, 1982). The aim has been to integrate public and private living space, to provide residents with greater privacy and a degree of flexibility and choice in daily life. Yet residential life for older people remains predominantly public and collective rather than private and individual. The National Consumer Study of Residential Care provides numerous instances of the way in which organisational structure can negate the legitimate aspirations

of residents (Willcocks *et al.*, 1982). The use of private space and the possibility of retreat from public view is contingent upon staff routine. Meal times structure the 24-hour day, providing the opportunity and rationale for staff surveillance of residents *en masse*. Staff shifts which end at 8 a.m. are responsible for the anxious buzz of dawn activity, designed to hand over a presentable complement of clients who are out of bed, washed and dressed for an early start to the daily round.

Similarly, in group-living homes, staff shifts may be inimicable to the development of the group-worker concept. Both staff and residents express confusion over their respective roles, and life within the small groups may reflect traditional Homes in miniature. What this highlights is the absence of open discussion of conflict between the desire to offer elderly residents a flexible life-style which mirrors the pattern of living in their former home, and the needs of staff as organised labour to achieve balance and structure in their working life.

This in turn raises the difficult question of consumer preference. In response to creative endeavours to stimulate choice in living arrangements (Willcocks, 1984) residents selected those features of Homes which might be classified as normal, unexceptional and non-institutional. They were less attracted to overt technological innovation such as the medi-bath; or artificial social constructions such as group living; their ideas lay in the direction of independence and autonomy.

The client group

Perhaps the single most important characteristic to record about the residential population is its heterogeneity. Each elderly person has a unique personal history and an individual capacity for adjustment and adaptation within the residential environment (Kellaher, 1983).

Yet the prime concern for residential carers is the global question of increasing dependency. One relevant development of recent years is the planned reduction in the number of NHS long-stay geriatric beds which places increased pressure on local authorities to cater for the frail and the confused. This is compounded by a determination by old people and their carers to pursue community living until residential care becomes the only option available to provide the level of support needed.

Certainly, the average age of residents is rising: latest national figures suggest that it is now 85.1 years for women and 83.2 years for men (Willcocks *et al.*, 1982). Staff experience their clients as becoming substantially less fit and they express deep anxiety about the lack of appropriate skills and levels of support required. Yet studies of dependency produce conflicting results: in the National Consumer

Study and similar cross-sectional surveys (Willcocks *et al.*, 1982; Wade *et al.*, 1983) there was some evidence to suggest that the most recent admissions were for a markedly less fit group, but longitudinal work (Wilkin *et al.*, 1978; Charlesworth and Wilkin, 1982; Booth *et al.*, 1983a) has shown that whilst individual Homes experience cyclical shifts, over time there is an overall balancing effect on an area basis, and we may be exaggerating the actual change. The situation is further complicated by the interactive effects of staff routine and physical environment which may possess dependency inducing characteristics (Walker, 1982c; Booth *et al.*, 1983b). Finally, it has been suggested that the problems experienced by staff in dealing with one or two people who are severely behaviourally disturbed may influence adversely the perceptions of staff and residents alike.

A recent study in the private sector (Weaver *et al.*, 1985a) demonstrates dramatically the influence of an impoverished environment on resident dependency. Adapted buildings with poor facilities contributed to a substantial loss of function, and the actions of untrained staff may reinforce dependency rather than counteract it.

The second characteristic of residents that merits special note is the fact that there are more women in care than men on a ratio of 3 to 1; and that for women, going 'into care' and acceptance of the institutional life-style may constitute a qualitatively different kind of experience from that of men (Willcocks, 1983a). Men generally enter residential care at an earlier point in the ageing process, in better health and for different reasons from women; they remain in the Home for slightly longer periods. Furthermore, the acceptance of domestic and physical care by a group of predominantly female staff represents no major threat to men who achieve a relatively high degree of control and satisfaction in residential settings. In contrast, women who enter care are generally older, less fit and have fewer resources to enable them to adjust to the strangeness of receiving care, after accumulated experience of offering care to others. Identity and self-esteem may suffer with removal from the intimate domestic sphere of their former home. It is a substantial indictment of residential care that the life-style is not designed to satisfy the needs of this majority group.

One difficult issue concerning admission is the effect of relocation upon morbidity and mortality, and upon subsequent adjustment to residential life (Hughes and Wilkin, 1980). Leaving home can be a traumatic event and researchers (Lipman, 1967; Tobin and Lieberman, 1979) have charted the deleterious effects of the process of becoming a resident. Efforts have been made by local authorities over recent years to minimise this strangeness and discontinuity by limiting the catchment area for individual Homes and promoting a neighbourhood-based intake. The National Consumer Study revealed that residents who moved less than 2 miles did appear to adjust more readily to residential life, but differences were small and overlaid by other factors. Preparation for the move and an acceptance of its legitimacy appeared to exert some beneficial influence on settling in. Yet, only a minority of one in three residents recalled having any choice of different Homes or indeed, of visiting their final Home before moving in; women appeared to have less choice than men.

The residential staff
Information from the different studies (Allen, 1982; Wade *et al.*, 1983a) confirm that residential staff are predominantly young or middle-aged married women who are highly motivated to work with old people; care staff also seek a job that is convenient. In these studies as in others (Clough, 1981; Evans *et al.*, 1981) there is disturbing evidence of a general ambivalence towards the care task and the role of residential social work. It is lamentable that social work literature has traditionally neglected this area. Social work texts on the elderly tend to focus on skilled social work interventions from field workers, backed up by a sensitive complex of domiciliary support schemes; and residential social work texts tend to focus on services for young people. Sadly, residential social work with old people combines the problem of a less popular client group with the problems of a less popular form of intervention.

So there appears to be a lack of clarity concerning services required for both care staff and senior staff; and there is further uncertainty regarding the appropriate training necessary to equip staff to perform their duties. In the National Consumer Study (Willcocks *et al.*, 1982) there was little evidence of the penetration of Certificate in Social Services (CSS) training, although undoubtedly some improvement will have been achieved more recently. In general, the present situation, which is characterised by differing professional inputs, can produce incoherent outcomes. In particular there appears to be a conflict between social work values and a medical model of care.

Such problems affect staff at all levels. Demands on care staff span domestic chores; offering physical assistance to frail clients; health care tasks; and providing social and emotional support to residents. They are generally graded as manual workers, yet, there is an expectation that they should become involved in social care. This can produce an untenable level of burden which is then associated with frustration and low levels of job satisfaction (Davies and Knapp, 1981).

Residential life-style
Organisational arrangements and the physical attributes of Homes can have a profound influence on daily living arrangements and

levels of social interaction. For example, new friendships tend to occur more frequently in small Homes, group-living Homes and in Homes with a high proportion of single rooms and a close integration between public and private living spaces. Here, where the regime permits, residents can achieve an element of control over the nature and frequency of social meetings and exchange which is conducive to friendship formation and increased levels of social activity (Willcocks *et al.*, 1982).

Small-group living for residents in units of 8 to 12 residents can often improve the social climate of Homes and at the same time make the immediate physical environment more manageable. Yet the complex nature of some purpose-built small-group Homes and the sometimes bizarre arrangements resulting from adapting buildings for group living, can make the overall building less accessible to residents and produce isolation within groups. The reduced scale of a group-living environment can encourage both domestic and recreational activity among residents, but the group design is not a prerequisite for this more positive life-style (Peace, 1983b).

A further complexity of group living is that residents and staff may experience less satisfaction with the Home – both as a living and a working environment. It might be the case that dissatisfaction is associated with greater stimulation and raised expectations in re-organised Homes. However, for some residents, the pressure of small-group living can be intense and they may prefer the relative anonymity of the larger group.

The staff role also appears problematic (Willcocks *et al.*, 1982). Many staff are untrained in the complexities of group work and despite commitment experience increased strain in their working lives as they attempt to adapt to the less institutional model and cope with such problems as group dominance, personality clashes and a series of misunderstandings about the nature of resident self-help.

Current Conflicts in Residential Care Policy: The Case for Reform

This profile exposed certain contradictions contained within the residential world. In the second part of this chapter a number of key issues will be investigated. They relate to conflicts around caring which vex policy-makers and practitioners alike, both at the macro-level of service provision and at the local level of service delivery.

Unit of operation

A major source of dissatisfaction for elderly residents derives from a reluctant recognition that, as individuals, they have ceased to exist. Individuals represent the basic unit of operation around which residential life is constructed yet the organisation of Home life is predicated around a group logic. Over time there has undoubtedly been a reduction in size as establishments have come to accommodate fewer residents (Peace, 1983). Furthermore, the introduction of group living has ostensibly reduced the unit size dramatically to single figures. Yet it remains clear that routinised treatment of residents can persist, despite change, so that an individual old person has difficulty in maintaining personal integrity and self-esteem in the face of what might be experienced as institutionalised oppression.

We might question the logic whereby a group of eight is deemed to be closer to the individual than a group of 40. Throughout their lives, people live as members of families or as individuals; most people do not live within non-familial groups of any size. And where group living operates, the larger establishment can negate any benefit which might be attributed to the organisational strategy of group living. If institutional care is to be retained, a formula must be devised which permits the individual to construct a personalised lifestyle ackowledging basic rights to privacy and independence within a secure setting.

Conflicts around the care task

Residents need to achieve some degree of self-determination or 'mastery' in the ordinary, taken-for-granted activities that constitute daily life (Clough, 1981). Yet under present institutional arrangements there is organisational commitment to a form of task allocation which promotes staff surveillance and the avoidance of risk-taking (Willcocks, *et al.*, 1982). This elimination of the rights to take normal risks threatens the ability of residents to achieve independence and to live a life away from the public gaze (Norman, 1982).

Furthermore, a major part of care staff time is taken up with the performance of physical care tasks and domestic chores. Little time remains for the social needs of residents and, indeed, there is confusion concerning the extent to which staff members could or should allocate time for developing supportive social relationships with residents. An experiment with residential volunteers (Power, 1982) demonstrates common agreement that their contribution would be to strike up new friendships with clients whilst care staff were freed to pursue important duties like physical care and tending. Yet it was more advantageous to the resident when the roles of volunteer and staff member were reversed, for what residents required was the continuity and reliability of real social exchanges with staff who are seen not just for the occasional hour or two every week but across the whole week.

The introduction of a key worker scheme which aimed to restore residents' confidence might thereby create the real possibility of increased resident mastery. Such an approach provides a focus for replacing what might be regarded as disabling practices with a more enabling form of care. Further, this would ease the tension between global surveillance and a more personalised form of support specific to individual need.

Dependency

Residential workers are having to respond to changes elsewhere in the support network at a time when demographic pressures will ensure an increase in overall numbers of frail elderly. First, there has been a dramatic decline in the number of long-stay geriatric beds and District Health Authorities have launched a vigorous campaign against geriatric 'bed-blocking' of the acute wards, aimed at a more efficient use of NHS resources.

Second, the capacity of the community to provide support through informal networks is potentially reduced by the migration of caring family and the increased involvement of women carers in the world of work (see Chapter 5). Third, a *pro rata* decrease in domiciliary support services compounds the difficulty of frail elderly people living alone (Clarke, 1984). One further influence may be exerted by the introduction of private residential Homes into the care network. The fear has been expressed that they may be selective in offering care to a fitter and less demanding sector of the potential clients.

The net result is a complex set of pressures on residential places. This may result in allocation policies which favour the construction of a more dependent clientele for Part III Homes in terms of frailty and confusion. Booth *et al.* (1983c) argue that this change may not be as globally extensive in real terms as earlier writers have claimed, but the question this raises is whether the more dependent old person should be integrated within the normal resident population or whether local authorities should develop specialist Homes.

Some writers demonstrate that good practice can be created in a specialist environment (Pettitt, 1984); but there is another view which has persisted over time which favours integration (Meacher, 1972; Wilkin, 1983). For, where adequate resources are provided, both staff and residents can tolerate a substantial proportion of confused and physically frail residents, with direct benefit to the dependent client group (Evans *et al.*, 1981). And it is argued that the introduction of the specialist Home, as a discrete option along the care continuum (which may extend from maintenance at home in the community to the long-stay psychogeriatric hospital bed) produces one further stage in the discontinuity of care, with elderly people being subjected to a series of disruptive and often unsolicited moves through the system.

To help care staff cope with a mix of dependency levels we should construct a more personalised package of care which protects the 'fit' from the 'unfit' and vice versa whilst securing the interests of both groups individually and reducing conflict between them. For example, the privacy of an individual room permits adaptations around the special needs of the particular client and the creation of personalised environments, thereby assisting the frail or confused to retain and reinforce existing skills and orientation. This can provide an alternative strategy for managing 'difficult' residents. There is increasing evidence to suggest that an excessive use of drug therapy has become the norm in some Homes (Wade *et al.*, 1983b) and this necessitates an urgent response on the part of residential managers to reverse this trend.

Community integration

There is an ever-present danger when considering residential issues of looking at Homes in isolation from the local communities they serve. It is commonplace that elderly people feel hostile towards residential establishments, and there is evidence of particular unease among those people who live near such Homes (Willcocks *et al.*, 1982). These attitudes serve to emphasise the situation of institutions as 'socially marooned' (Townsend, 1981) where neighbours feel intimidated by what can appear as a threatening environment containing a homogeneous group of undistinguished and unidentifiable inhabitants whose apathy and general life-style cause them great anxiety for their own future well-being. Only through a positive reconstruction of the image conveyed by the Home, is it possible to avert this fear of 'contamination' by old age and encourage outsiders to cross the institutional boundary (Willcocks, 1983b).

This raises the issue of what facilities the Home might offer to the community, and how realistic it is to talk about the multi-purpose Home (Wilkin *et al.*, 1982). At a time of economic restraint it may well seem an attractive proposition to exploit the potential of a costly capital asset in order to derive benefit for a wide range of clients. However, this introduces the possibility of different users coming into conflict should their institutional expectations be threatened. It is important to ensure that any territorial rights which residents might wish to establish, by virtue of their assumed occupancy 'contract', are not violated by other Home users. This suggests that a piecemeal approach will not suffice. Establishments should offer a coherent comprehensive package of integrated out-reach care like that of the Elderly Persons Support Unit initiative in Sheffield (MacDonald, Qureshi and Walker, 1984) to offset such difficulties.

Evidence regarding the introduction of day attenders into Homes suggests that the varying demands and expectations of residents and day attenders can have a detrimental effect on social relationships

(Willcocks *et al.*, 1982). Day attenders look at the frailty and apathy of residents and experience real fears for their own future. Meanwhile, residents may perceive demanding day attenders as intruders and resent any encroachment on scarce staffing resources. Similar problems occur when a limited number of short-stay residents are introduced into a long-stay Home, for either assessment purposes or respite care (Allen, 1982). A combined service can create an intolerable burden for staff and a diminishing of quality of life within the Home.

However, there are examples of developments where such an integrated service has succeeded. Moreover it would appear that such initiatives are characterised by a more sensitive approach to community involvement and participatory planning, which aims to secure equivalent status for all users and to locate multi-purpose Homes within a package of care options to serve all old people in the community (Willcocks, 1983b).

The growth of private care

The growth in private care is not an artefact of current political ideology in so far as successive governments have given their support to the mixed economy of social welfare: consultative documents in the 1970s (DHSS, 1976, 1977b) acknowledge the private and voluntary sectors as sources of innovation and cost-effectiveness, and in more recent publications further accolades are given for private initiatives (DHSS, 1981a and b) arguing that 'the increasing needs of increasing numbers of old people simply cannot be met wholly or even predominantly by public authorities or public finance'. Indeed, there is a powerful lobby which claims that the 'rich diversity of welfare pluralism can offer new opportunities for the state of work in partnership with other agencies to promote a more efficient and equitable system of social welfare' (Judge *et al.*, 1983).

But an alternative viewpoint based on experience in the USA voices concern to protect clients from those proprietors who might seek to exploit vulnerable elderly people (Mendelson, 1974). The first detailed study of quality of life inside English private Homes echoes these anxieties, yet demonstrates the difficulties experienced by proprietors in pursuing successfully the dual goals of profit and care (Weaver *et al.*, 1985b). As a means of ensuring good standards in the private sector, and in order to reinforce the framework of accountability, new legislation has been introduced in the Registered Homes Act 1984, along with ministerial regulations and the advisory code of practice (Centre for Policy on Ageing, 1984). This is intended to clarify the role of local authorities and provide the necessary safeguards for those who move into private residential care. However, the adequacy of these measures to promote good practice remains unproven, for the introduction of legislation will not in itself provide universal solutions to the problems posed by the mixed economy of residential care. In the absence of guidelines or resources from the DHSS, social services departments are endeavouring to develop suitable procedures for regulation.

To what extent might the uncontrolled growth of private residential care threaten present initiatives to control levels and forms of institutionalisation or, indeed, to provide alternative models of institutional care? Could it damage programmes which promote an integrated system of community-based and residential care services around local needs through control of relevant resources? There is a possibility that a two-tier system might emerge offering different standards to different client groups. And public expenditure questions arise concerning control and an equitable distribution of benefit for old people when overlapping benefits, allowances and sponsorships are available through different groups of professionals and administrators for selective sub-groups of beneficiaries (Weaver *et al*, 1985a).

Registration processes must render Homes publicly accountable and this may require substantial organisational changes within the local authority to put into practice an effective regulatory system. This may create a problem for registration officers as they seek to achieve parity with other statutory officials and acquire the skills and resources to manage the different managers of private care. It may be unrealistic to expect that 'tools' designed to control the isolated individual Home owner-in-residence (the small businessman) involved in 'cottage caring', will have equivalent force and status in relation to either the locally organised 'professional' groupings of Home owners who attempt to operate a cartel, or the large-scale and diversified enterprises of distant investment companies. One final problem is the way the present system of sporadic private growth, stimulated by central government funding through the board and lodgings allowance, but not directly linked to locally defined needs, may thwart any attempt to democratise welfare services at a local level. It is possible that the downgrading of public sector care could undermine the credibility of the local authority if it fails to meet welfare expectations.

New Directions in Residential Care

An assessment of the need for care suggests that residential services may have a key role to play as part of a flexible mix of support designed to meet the needs, temperament and preferences of different elderly people. Many workers and consumers express satisfaction; many more do not. This should stimulate the search for ways of introducing a radically revitalised residential care service through a substantial re-ordering of the residential environment. First, changes in management policy and organisation would be required to bring Home life into line with the normal expectations and preferences of the elderly. But over and above that it becomes an urgent matter to challenge the social distance which creates a gulf between institutions and their local communities and which generates many negative images. This separation accounts for the strangenesss of residential living in terms of an assumption that elderly people are content to relinquish privacy and personal territory and live out their days in what are predominantly public spaces within Homes.

Willcocks *et al.* (1982) argue that the focus of Home life should switch from public communal space to private personal space; individual needs would take precedence and block treatment would be rendered unacceptable. Change could be introduced through a transformation of spatial arrangements between public and private space; and, concomitantly, a positive development of the relationship between the Old Age Home and the wider community to ensure that such internal changes are reflected in the realignment of Homes with community. The introduction of revitalised care would involve not only organisational change based on staff training programmes but a total reconsideration of the role and working life of staff. The focus for change suggested by the National Consumer Study is the establishment of a facility termed the residential flatlet.

This would be the point of entry and stability within the institution for an individual resident. It would constitute a large, more flexible version of the existing single room; different from sheltered housing in so far as it would remain part of an essentially supportive environment. Yet, the residential flatlet would offer unmistakable personal territory; lockable from the inside and within which the resident would be firmly in control. This flatlet should be large enough to accommodate some personal and large items of furniture such as beds or sideboards which evoke important memories and affirm individual status and identity. Sufficient space would be allowed for residents to sit in comfort, alone or with visitors; and tea-making equipment provided. It is not envisaged that this room would contain elaborate cooking facilities; main catering would be undertaken centrally. But meals could be taken and shared in the flatlets.

Support services could then be built around the flatlet: sanitary services such as a vanitory unit should form part of the flatlet or be located adjacent to it, as with the shower plus wc. Two levels of catering would be necessary to provide centrally prepared and served meals for the most frail, plus self-catering in a kitchenette and dining area to serve a number of residential flatlets. Residents and visitors can then make snacks or light breakfasts. A large lounge must be offered, possibly incorporating part of the entrance hall as an alternative meeting-place. An additional focal point will avoid the potential problem of residents becoming isolated in their rooms. These broad changes in physical design are recommended to stimulate an alternative life-style which permits old people to recreate the essence of their own homes. And it is further argued that change of this kind could provide one means of addressing the issues of care discussed earlier. It is *not* suggested that enhanced design alone will create an improved quality of life. Indeed, this is borne out by a smaller but more recent study (Norman, 1984), but it does provide a model upon which to build. The retention of personal space and life-style based around individual flatlets might allow residents to retrieve dignity and self-esteem and this would change the ethos of a Home, thereby encouraging a more flexible use of the facility, for residents with defensible territory could welcome outsiders, free from anxiety. This 're-modelling', by countering all those aspects of residential life which evoke the total institution, could bring the Home and its people back inside the boundaries of community life – whence it might become possible to mobilise support for the creation of a caring environment which will enhance the experience of old age.

Conclusion

The major thrust of this chapter has been to question the function of residential care and to challenge the continuing isolation and separation from the community and from normal patterns of everyday life – both in ideological and material terms. Furthermore, it is argued that the current status of community care and the apparently high esteem it enjoys are partly predicated upon the deterrent ethos associated with traditional forms of institutional care. Yet the case against residential care is incomplete to the extent that much of our evidence for attacking institutions is based on historical failure. Thus the possibility of creating a better future remains open. The difficulty in evaluating the actual and potential contribution of residential care derives in part from the failure to establish its role and purpose in late capitalist society. Social history shows that the nineteenth-century model for residential care prescribed an institutional form to stimulate the work ethic and punish the feckless. This was functional to the needs of the early industrialists. But, at the same time, changes in family structure, social relations and living arrangements in the community were based on forms that would serve changing methods of production and the shift to urban living. It is only in contrast to the oppressive image of the Victorian institution that we have allowed our sensitivities to be dulled to some of the harsh and exploitative aspects of the prevailing community form.

In the late twentieth century it is less clear how residential Homes operate – except, perhaps as a default option to deal with residual problems of care. And we might speculate that some primitive element of past institutional care remains. At the same time, we might pause to reflect upon the qualities attributed to community living in modern urban society and to ask whether the social and environmental stress associated with the privations of inner-city life might not cause particular hardships to older people. In such circumstances we might question the use of community care as a benchmark against which to measure institutional care. And we should acknowledge that it is unappropriate to judge residential care adversely for failing to achieve levels of happiness that do not necessarily pertain outside the walls of the institution. Residential welfare is here to stay, at least for the time being. It is necessary, therefore, for social policy to provide a basis for the integration into the community of old people's homes and the older people within them.

It is important to develop independent standards, as is the case with *Home Life* (CPA, 1984a), and to locate evaluative criteria with a clear view of an alternative society characterised by greater mutuality and caring among people of different generations. A major thesis is that it should be no more difficult to construct such a way of life in an institutional setting than in the normal community. That is the task for positive and creative social work intervention. At a more pragmatic level it will not be possible in the short term to meet the range of need without recourse to the existing institutional form. In the long term a re-evaluation will be necessary in the light of changes that have taken place within the spectrum of care.

It is argued, then, that something akin to the residential flatlet might provide the acceptable face of institutional security which can be enjoyed by those elderly people who choose it. Such an alternative with appropriate checks and regulation, could be achieved within the public or the private sector.

Such a programme of change would require a series of changes in policy and practice:

(i) Innovation or adaptation to the physical form of Homes to re-establish access to and control over personal territory.

(ii) Changes in social arrangements and management within the Home to redefine individual rights and acceptable risks.

(iii) An alternative management structure for social services departments to integrate service provision and service delivery for old people in the community and in the residential sector.

(iv) Revised training schemes for field and residential management and workers to support an alternative approach to the process of developing institutional care as one option within the community care spectrum.

(v)   Changes in community influence on the running of Homes and involvement in activities within the Homes.

(vi)   In the private sector, the appropriate use of monitoring and regulation procedures to allay anxieties about standards, and to ensure equivalence of service.

In the absence of a critical review of the role and structure of residential care, the best endeavours to obliterate haunting memories of the past are doomed to failure. Minor adjustments will not suffice to shift the balance of institutional control. An alternative response must be designed to acknowledge and compensate for the powerlessness of older people who are obliged to submit to society's caring solutions. Therefore, it becomes necessary to reconstruct a residential environment which captures the traditional essence of home and is represented as but one more option within the spectrum of progressive community care. This would enable us to build a form of social care which acknowledges the fundamental importance of responding to consumer choice, thereby respecting the rights and freedom of individual elderly persons to achieve a happier old age.

9 The Elderly and the Health Services

David Wilkin and Beverley Hughes

The main body of this chapter is concerned with a critical analysis of the development of health services for old people. However, it is important to preface such an analysis with a discussion of some contextual issues. It is impossible to discuss either old age or health without emphasising the social construction of both of these concepts. Ideas about old age and about health are inextricably linked with a complex matrix of powerful social, political and economic constructs. Neither of these concepts is value-free. Each is laden with social values which are always subjective and often emotive. As an essential preliminary to the discussion which follows, we shall briefly discuss the dominant constructions of both old age and health.

The Concept of Old Age

A common assumption, apparent in both social policy and many literary references to old age, is that it is a time of inevitable deterioration in health with consequent problems for the individual and society. Many characteristics are attributed to the elderly as a group, which together have created a powerful negative stereotype of old age. In general, it is seen as a time of decline, loneliness, loss and futility, and old people – in particular the very old – have come to be identified as a major social problem.

The main facets of this negative stereotype of old age and the social, political and economic basis for its existence, have been discussed elsewhere (Walker, 1980, 1981b; Townsend, 1981; Phillipson, 1982). However, there are two features of the stereotype which have been especially important in shaping ideas about, and responses to, the health of old people. First, the identification of the elderly as a separate category has tended to precipitate the view that old people are, by and large, a homogeneous group. Old age is still considered to be the great leveller, and this assumed homogeneity lends support to the view that advanced age itself is a more important determinant of the quality of life than other factors, such as social, economic or environmental circumstances (Owen, 1979). The second feature of the stereotype is that old age is seen as intrinsically a time of deterioration in health, greater physical and/or mental infirmity, and increasing dependency upon others. In terms of the quality of life in general, and of health status in particular, old age has come to be defined as a 'negative situation' (Van der Heuvel, 1976).

Sustained and buttressed by social and political attitudes, the stereotype has persisted despite evidence which appears to contradict it. In relation to the assumed homogeneity of old people, there is evidence that health status in old age is more a product of experiences throughout life, than of age *per se*, and that people from social classes I and II are less likely than those from poorer backgrounds to suffer the most debilitating conditions. An Age Concern survey (1974) found that only 9 per cent of social classes I and II were severely restricted and functionally dependent, compared with 22 per cent of unskilled and semi-skilled manual groups. The view of the elderly as a homogeneous group characterised by inherent and common problems of old age is not one which is supported by even a cursory glance at social statistics (Bosanquet, 1978). Similarly, the extent to which old age is a negative experience, especially in terms of health, has been questioned by the results of several surveys of elderly populations. This point needs careful qualification, since it is clear that for the very old (75 and over) the incidence of illness and disability increases, and that those over 65 years consume about a third of all health and social services expenditure (Phillipson, 1982). Nevertheless, there are many old people who do not suffer ill-health to any marked degree – Hunt (1978) found that 85 per cent of her sample of people over the age of 65 and 46 per cent of those over the age of 85 were usually able to go out without assistance. A large majority of her sample were independent in terms of most of the activities of daily living.

Concepts of Health
Concepts of health – and conversely, ill-health – are complex social constructions. There is no single concept common to all people and appropriate to all situations. Rather, there is a wide variety of alternative and often conflicting definitions. At one extreme is what might be described as an orthodox disease model within which ill-health is defined in terms of the existence of pathologies, and health is seen as the elimination of these pathologies. At the other end of the spectrum, the causes of ill-health and the factors promoting good health are seen in terms of interactions between the individual and his or her environment. The disease model emphasises the role of medical intervention in sustaining good health, whereas the holistic

model tends to view medical intervention as only one among a variety of possible economic, social and psychological measures.

We have identified three broad concepts of health which we feel are relevant to our analysis of the development of health services for the elderly: medical, functional and holistic. The medical conception of health is based on a disease model and is concerned with health as the absence of illness or disease, rather than the promotion of positive health. The focus of interest tends to be not upon the patient but upon the pathological processes affecting particular physiological functions, often limited to a particular part of the patient's body. It is a model derived from nineteenth-century positivist science aspiring to the problem-solving and objectivity of the natural sciences. The role of medical intervention is to identify disease and prescribe appropriate treatment, halting or reversing the pathological processes. The success of treatment is judged in terms of cure, i.e. the absence of pathology.

The functional model is concerned primarily with the ability of the individual to fulfil his or her role obligations. Concern with the presence or absence of identifiable pathology is overlaid with concern over the extent of disability and consequent dependency irrespective of pathology. Disability is defined as the extent to which an illness causes loss of normal functional activity, particularly the ability to undertake the activities of daily living such as self-care or domestic tasks. Dependency is the extent to which illness and/or disability necessitates reliance on others for the performance of functional tasks. The functional conception of health leads to some modification in the role of medical intervention. Medicine is concerned not only with curing illness where this is possible, but also with minimising disability and maximising independence.

A holistic conception of health emphasises that 'the biological and physiological aspects of the human condition are related to social, psychological and cultural aspects' (Wedderburn, 1973). It is a concept based, not on the notion of illness, but rather on well-being, a state which includes freedom from illness and disability but also a degree of personal satisfaction on the part of the individual with his or her physical, mental, environmental and interpersonal circumstances. The holistic model implies a recognition of interdependence and effective health as the bases for the role of health care. Interdependence challenges the basic dichotomy between dependence and independence which is fundamental to the functional conception of health. It explicitly recognises that the patient is not just a passive recipient of care but also an active participant in the transaction (Munnichs and Van der Heuvel, 1976).

The term 'effective health' (e.g. WHO, 1970) is an attempt to view the health of individuals within a broader environmental framework

(Brody, 1977; Williams, 1979). It emphasises the importance of subjective judgements as to how far health problems constitute a problem for living, rather than more traditional and supposedly objective indices such as morbidity, disability or dependence. It requires that professional judgements be synthesised in some way with the views of patients, in order that the health care system can be tailored to individual needs.

Concepts of health in old age

The interaction between concepts of health and stereotypes of old age is extremely important for the development of health services. If old age is regarded negatively and the elderly as a group are assumed to be homogeneous, then the medical model of health produces a tendency to classify all old people as suffering from incurable diseases. Similarly, the functional model tends to emphasise disability and dependence as characteristics of old age. Both models are congruent with the negative stereotype of old age; indeed, it is arguable that the interaction between these concepts of health and the stereotype of old age have been mutually reinforcing. Both medical and functional approaches have tended to see age *per se* as the most significant determinant of health status and have thus consolidated the view of old people as a homogeneous group suffering from inevitable deterioration in health. The holistic model, however, contains a fundamental challenge to existing stereotypes of old age. It is basically antithetical to any stereotype because it emphasises individual participation, both in the definitions of well-being and in the nature of treatment and care. Whilst it does not offer any panacea for the sorts of problem we shall discuss in subsequent sections, it offers some potential for a shift in stereotypes of old age and the pattern of health services.

This discussion of the concepts of old age and health has been necessarily brief, but it provides an important context in which to set the main body of this chapter. We shall argue that the ways in which health services for the elderly have developed are a reflection of the social constructions of health and old age. In charting the development of health services for the elderly we shall be concerned primarily with the post-war growth of hospital and community services under the National Health Service (NHS). However, it is important to recognise that many of the features of modern health services have their roots in nineteenth- and early twentieth-century health and welfare services. Not only the buildings inherited by the NHS, but also much of the ideology and practice of nineteenth-century health care persisted beyond 1948. Some of the problems faced by present-day health services can best be understood through an analysis of their history.

Health Care before the National Health Service

The industrial revolution generated both new health problems and the belief that these could be tackled and overcome through the application of scientific medicine. The rapid growth of towns and cities and the poverty of their inhabitants produced overcrowding, insanitary conditions, malnutrition and, predictably, epidemics of infectious diseases. Although life expectancy gradually improved as standards of living rose and public health measures created a more sanitary environment, it is hardly surprising that 'up until the 1890s there is no evidence of old age having been singled out as a discrete social problem' (McIntyre, 1977).

Despite these poor conditions the basic structure of a modern system of health and welfare services was being established during the nineteenth century in the form of public health measures, Poor Law institutions, voluntary hospitals and private medical practice. For those who could afford it, care was available from general practitioners on a fee for service basis. The voluntary hospitals became the centres of 'scientific' medicine, training doctors and providing treatment for the acutely sick. They were characterised by a disease model of health which sought to establish the causes of ill-health and appropriate measures of treatment. But these institutions had little to offer the aged and chronic sick who were allocated to the residual category of 'incurables', and thus specifically excluded from the voluntary hospitals. The old, unless they were also wealthy, were consigned to the workhouse, or, at best, the Poor Law infirmary.

McIntyre (1977) argues that the period 1890–1910 saw a marked shift in attitude towards the welfare of old people, away from a primary focus on the interests of taxpayers and towards a more humanitarian view of old age. It was increasingly felt that old people should be spared the harshness of the workhouse and the stigma of pauperism. At the same time the provision of health care was undergoing important changes, but not in ways which recognised the needs of old people. Concern was primarily with the health of the fighting and working man, prompted by the poor health of the volunteers for the Boer War (Scrivens, 1982). This, combined with fears of working-class unrest, brought calls for some form of health insurance. The system of state-administered health insurance introduced in 1911 covered lower paid manual workers, but it excluded their dependants. For the elderly this meant continued reliance on the institutions of the Poor Law and slowly developing state hospitals provided by local authorities.

The years to 1939 saw no further fundamental changes in health services for the elderly, but they laid the ground for the post-war formation of the NHS. The creation of a Ministry of Health and various reports prepared during the 1920s and 1930s began to point the way towards a comprehensive health service free at the point of delivery (Briggs, 1978a). In the meantime, the existing structures were under considerable strain, particularly in the hospital sector where there were gross regional inequalities in provision and where the voluntary hospitals were experiencing increasing financial problems. Hospital care for the elderly was mainly provided by the public hospitals where old people were well nursed but often inadequately diagnosed and treated (Brocklehurst, 1975). Following admission for an acute illness episode, patients received scant medical attention and rapidly became bedfast. The elderly remained outside health insurance schemes, unless they had the means to contribute independently to an insurance scheme. At the outbreak of war in 1939, health services for the elderly were perhaps more humane than they had been a century earlier, but old people remained largely outside the scope of medicine. Ill-health continued to be seen as an inevitable corollary of old age. Even diseases which were considered treatable in younger patients were regarded as incurable when the patient was over 60 years of age. The best that could be hoped for was tender loving care – and even this was denied to many.

Establishment of the National Health Service

The outbreak of the war in 1939 prompted the setting up of an emergency medical service designed to meet wartime needs (Means and Smith, 1985). For the first time there was an attempt to bring together the disparate elements of the hospital service into a coordinated whole. Meanwhile, the Beveridge Report (1942) laid the basis for a post-war reconstruction of health and social welfare. The report stimulated enormous public interest, and on the day of its publication a queue a mile long built up outside the government bookshop in central London (Kincaid, 1973). It was widely felt in government that the electorate needed to be persuaded that they were fighting a war to build a new Britain. Forsyth (1966) has commented that the government could not be sure that large sections of the working class were satisfied with the reasons for fighting the war. Thus the creation of a post-war welfare state with the NHS as its centrepiece was less a revolutionary innovation than an attempt to ensure the stability of the existing economic and social order. Doyal (1979) argues that it was a nationalised rather than a socialised service because power remained with the doctors and administrators rather than being transferred to consumers. It remained a part of the existing social and industrial infrastructure rather than becoming a system primarily oriented to the needs of the people it served.

This very brief summary of some of the antecedents of the establishment of the NHS in 1948 is particularly relevant to a consideration of the role of the service in providing health care for the elderly.

Nineteenth- and early twentieth-century concerns with the health of the working class and the need to avert social unrest have their parallels in the creation of the post-war welfare state. Although the NHS introduced universal coverage of free medical care there was concern from the outset over how much such a service would cost. This was particularly apparent in the case of care for the elderly who were seen as being of limited productive value to society. McIntyre (1977) notes that the various official reports produced during the 1940s reflected concern about the elderly as an organisational problem, rather than a humanitarian interest in how best to meet their needs for health care. Thus the Beveridge Report warned of the dangers of being 'lavish to old age' and the 1949 Royal Commission on Population referred to the problem that 'the old consume without producing'.

With the benefit of hindsight, Beveridge's assumption that an improvement in health services would lead to an improvement in health, which would thus limit the cost of the service, was naive. By 1953 the Gillebaud Committee had been set up to inquire into the escalating cost of the service; but the Committee's report tried to alleviate anxieties about the cost of the service (Abel-Smith, 1978). Nevertheless, it went on to advocate domiciliary care for the elderly as a 'genuine economy measure and also a humanitarian measure in enabling old people to lead the sort of life they much prefer' (cited in McIntyre, 1977, p. 54).

Throughout succeeding decades the perceived cost burden of the NHS has continued to exercise the minds of politicians and administrators. Increasing numbers of elderly people have been seen as a drain on resources, often diverting services away from other patient groups. In reality such fears have had little foundation. Indeed it is arguable that, in terms of the ratio between needs and resources, health services have failed to keep pace with the growing number of old people. The professional élite of hospital-based consultants has had a powerful influence in developing the expensive curative services rather than lower cost preventative and caring services. This has resulted in a steady rise in the proportion of total expenditure devoted to hospital services in spite of repeated attempts to give priority to community-based services. The elderly, the mentally ill, the mentally handicapped have suffered resource starvation, reflecting 'not just a lack of medical prestige but also the lack of economic power or productive potential of most of their patients' (Doyal, 1979, p. 197). Nevertheless, the NHS has been unable to ignore the health care needs of an increasingly large section of the population. Both in organisational and humanitarian terms, health care of the elderly has become a major issue. In organisational terms the problems are symbolised by concern over acute hospital beds 'blocked' by elderly patients (Rubin and Davies, 1975; Murphy, 1977), by the workload generated by the elderly in the community (Burns, 1969; Knox *et al.*, 1984) and by concern over the escalating costs of providing for an ageing population (Phillips Committee, 1954; Economist Intelligence Unit, 1973).

Perhaps the most important failing in the establishment of the NHS was the lack of clearly defined objectives for the service. To the extent that objectives were implicit in the service, these were concerned with the provision of a curative service designed to intervene in the course of acute illnesses and return patients to a disease-free state. The NHS has continued the traditions of nineteenth-century medicine by subscribing to a medical model of health. To the extent that elderly people have required the interventions of acute medical care the NHS has provided for them, but it is the treatment and care of those people suffering from a variety of complex physical, mental and social problems which have presented the greatest challenge. It is specialist services for the elderly and the system of primary health care which have been faced with these problems and it is to these services that we now turn our attention.

Hospital Services – The Growth of Specialist Care for the Elderly
Arguably, the single most important contribution of the NHS to the care of the elderly has been to facilitate the development of the speciality of geriatric medicine. Present-day specialists in the field tend to regard Marjorie Warren as the pioneer of modern geriatric medicine (Brocklehurst, 1975). Working in the West Middlesex hospital in the late 1930s, she realised that examination, investigation and treatment could yield considerable benefits for many elderly patients who might formerly have been regarded as incurable. Dr Warren was followed by other pioneers during the early years of the NHS. Demonstration of the success of the energetic application of orthodox medicine led to the development of rehabilitation programmes and a marked increase in the through-put of patients in hospital beds. Such 'hard statistics' convinced the Ministry of Health of the feasibility of geriatric medicine and led to a gradual freeing of resources to build up the speciality. This was not achieved without 'heavy opposition from hospital colleagues in the medical wards who could not see the value of spending time, money, energy and bed space on redundant senior members of society' (Felstein, 1969, p. 15). The fact that such opposition was overcome is demonstrated in the rapid growth in the number of consultant geriatricians, which had reached 391 by 1981.

Before going on to consider the key features of modern geriatric practice and its implications for health care of the elderly, it is important to examine some of the reasons for its growth in the face of strong opposition. This opposition stemmed from the apparent contradiction between the dominant curative ideology of modern medicine and the needs of elderly people for health care which recognises the complex interactions of medical, social and environmental problems. Acute hospital medicine is primarily organ-based and oriented towards brief interventions resulting in cure. The needs of many elderly patients demand a more holistic approach in which complete cure is rare. As the number of elderly patients admitted to acute hospital wards has increased, the problem of 'bed-blocking' by elderly patients who are felt by their doctors no longer to require the services of such wards has also increased. Whatever the views of geriatric medicine held by acute specialists, the wish to free beds occupied by elderly patients created a powerful force for a separate speciality. From the politician's and administrator's perspectives, the evidence that geriatric beds could be provided at lower cost than those in other specialities provided a useful incentive. However, at least as important as these organisational pressures in the growth of geriatric medicine has been the ability of specialists in the field to legitimate the speciality in terms acceptable to their colleagues. This they have done by substituting rehabilitation for cure. Medical intervention in geriatric medicine operates on a continuum between dependence and independence rather than health and illness. The medical model has been shifted in the direction of a functional conception of health. In this way it is possible to achieve success measured in terms of patient through-put, which permits the speciality to claim, if not achieve, parity of status with acute specialities.

It would be impossible in this chapter to offer even a summary of the pattern of care provided by geriatric departments. There are several texts on the organisation and delivery of hospital specialist services for the elderly (Anderson, 1967; Brocklehurst, 1973). However, there are certain distinctive features of these services which are important to this general review.

We have already referred to the philosophy of active intervention designed to return patients to a state of independence. Whilst diagnosis and treatment are important, the outcome of care tends to be judged not by the presence or absence of disease, but by patients' level of functioning, either according to physiological criteria or, more commonly, in terms of 'normal' activities of daily living. Implicit in this approach to health care is the proposition that quality of life can be equated with level of activity (Havighurst, 1968).

Associated with this notion of rehabilitation is a pattern of provision known as progressive patient care, which is designed to facilitate intervention and to achieve the most efficient use of resources. Most geriatric units divide patients between assessment/acute, rehabilitation and continuing care wards. More recently, the establishment of day hospitals has provided a further level of care. Patients are filtered through successive stages, the level of medical intervention becoming progressively less at each stage.

To rehabilitation and progressive patient care can be added a third key feature of geriatric practice, the commitment to multidisciplinary teamwork. The ideology and practice of geriatric rehabilitation and teamwork has been analysed in an important study by Evers (1982), who argues that the dominance of the medical profession has lead to a particular view of the health care needs of the elderly and the role of the health services. The dominance of a model derived from an activity theory of ageing emphasises the capacity of old people to lead independent lives so that continued dependency comes to be regarded as failure, and therefore of little interest to the medical profession. There is little understanding of the importance of interdependence and therefore the potentially positive contributions that disabled people can make in their social relations. Evers argues that although the rhetoric of multidisciplinary teamwork has become central to the provision of geriatric care, it is poorly defined, and its benefits for patients not always apparent. In many instances the mythology of teamwork conceals a traditional hierarchy of social relations of health care in which doctors dominate the team and patients and relatives are usually excluded.

We have concentrated in this section on the growth of geriatric medicine as the example *par excellence* of specialist health care for the elderly. Although we are unable to deal with the more recent, but equally important, growth of psycho-geriatric services (Whitehead, 1978; Jolley and Arie, 1978), most of the general points made for geriatric services are relevant. However, the growth of yet another speciality illustrates a general trend. Evers (1982) notes the trend towards an increasing fragmentation of care tasks within the multidisciplinary team, and Grimley Evans (1977) has pointed to some of the problems encountered in the division of labour in geriatric wards. In addition to these difficulties within specialities, we are now faced with further problems of the divisions *between* specialities. Whilst it is arguable that specialist care is more appropriate care, the increasing fragmentation tends to move health care further and further away from a holistic conception of health. The individual may be cared for as a whole person at any particular point in his or her patient career, but this career is increasingly fragmented as he or she is passed from one mode of care to another as needs change. Such a process certainly achieves the through-put in hospital beds usually associated with active medical intervention, but it may subject elderly people to a grotesque game of 'musical beds'. It also alienates the providers of care from the process and from the people for whom they are caring. The professions subordinated to medicine become part of a production line in which they provide a specialised form of care for patients at only one stage in the process.

Whether or not specialist hospital services have, on balance, proved beneficial to the old people they were intended to serve is at least debatable. Honigsbaum (1979) argues that the position of the elderly in some respects deteriorated after 1948 since they lost their previous (means-tested) right to a bed and could only obtain admission to hospital if a consultant was prepared to accept them. Nevertheless, currently around two-thirds of non-maternity hospital beds are occupied by people aged over 65. Geriatric medicine has certainly established its place within the NHS if not entirely satisfactorily within the medical profession as a whole. But this position has remained tenuous. Geriatric services have always been one of the Cinderella services within the NHS, receiving less than adequate resources, despite repeated attempts to ensure that they were given priority in resource allocation (Allsop, 1984). During a period in which resources for health services as a whole were expanding – or at least not contracting – the outlook for specialist services for the elderly retained a degree of optimism. The new political and economic climate of the 1980s gives cause for serious concerns to which we shall return in the concluding section.

Community Care – The Panacea
The health care needs of most old people are met in the community, frequently without recourse to any form of health services. Ninety-four per cent of all people over the age of 65 live outside of institutions (hospitals, residential Homes, etc.). Where health services are involved in meeting the needs of old people it is usually the members of the primary health care team rather than hospital-based specialists. This situation is hardly new, but recognition of its importance and the desirability of sustaining care in the community is relatively recent.

Although the Guillebaud Committee concluded that the cost of the newly established NHS was not excessive, politicians remained concerned about the potential costs of hospital provisions for the chronically sick. Recognising these fears, the Committee advocated the development of treatment and care of old people in their own homes. McIntyre (1977) argues that the concept of 'community' provided politicians with a means of reconciling their need to deal with the organisational problem of the elderly and their desire to adopt a humanitarian approach. The development of community care and consequent reductions in institutional provision featured in almost all official pronouncements on the health services throughout the 1950s, 1960s and 1970s. It became part of accepted wisdom that community care was cheaper and better than institutional care.

It was not difficult to point to the deficiencies of institutions and there appeared to be strong support for an anti-institution view from respected medical and social scientists (Townsend, 1964; Robb, 1968). However, it became increasingly difficult to disentangle the rhetoric and the reality. Even by 1961, Titmuss was posing the question, 'Community Care: Fact or Fiction?' In this article he described community care as 'that everlasting cottage garden trailer', and urged caution in promoting it. But such reservations did little to contain the enthusiasm of policy-makers. The 1962 *Hospital Plan* (Ministry of Health, 1962a) proposed a reduction in hospital geriatric beds and was followed in 1963 by the document *Health and Welfare: the Development of Community Care* (Ministry of Health, 1963). However, although the hospital plan contained detailed proposals for reductions in the number of beds, the proposals to develop community care failed to provide similar plans for the expansion of community services. Since the 1960s successive governments have clung tenaciously to the view that community care is the best and cheapest form of health care for the elderly. The emphases have shifted slightly but the broad strategy has remained the same.

In practice, the development of primary health care since 1948 owes less to the succession of official reports than to the basic structure of the NHS and, in particular, the division between general practice and hospital medicine. For the first time in 1948, everybody was entitled to register with a general practitioner and receive medical care free of charge. For their part the doctors contracted to provide treatment to all patients on their list up to a maximum of 4000 in return for a fixed annual capitation fee for each patient. Unlike their counterparts in hospital, the GPs did not become salaried employees of the NHS, preferring to retain their freedom as independent contractors. Their separation from the hospitals became complete during the early years of the service, since they were denied access to hospital beds. In the main they provided treatment for illness in response to patient demand. In principle, there was no distinction between different categories of patients, the elderly receiving the same service as all other age groups. For at least the two decades following the establishment of the NHS, general practice remained the poor relation of hospital medicine. Financial rewards were by no means generous, there was no incentive to improve facilities or patterns of care, medical education was controlled by the specialists, and general practice remained at the bottom of the professional status hierarchy.

However, things began to improve in the more favourable economic climate of the 1960s in the context of the pressure to place greater emphasis on community care. The so-called 'Doctors' Charter' of 1965 introduced far-reaching changes, including incentives to improve practice premises and to employ ancillary staff, encouragement of postgraduate education, the development of health centres and additional capitation fees for patients over the age of 65 (BMA, 1965). Since then, general practice has increasingly become the focus for the provision of a comprehensive system of primary health care. Just as teamwork has become an article of faith in geriatric medicine, the primary health care team has established itself as the ideal for health care in the community. The proportion of doctors who had a nurse working in the practice increased from 12 per cent in 1964 to 84 per cent in 1977 and two-thirds had an attached nurse employed by the health authority (Cartwright and Anderson, 1981). Health visitors are less commonly attached to practices and social work attachments remain rare. In health centres the availability of a range of health-care professions, including nurses, social workers, dentists, chiropodists and physiotherapists, seems to offer the opportunity to create a truly community based health care.

However, perhaps the most important feature of primary health care in general and GP care in particular is the variability in facilities, staffing and pattern of care. The status of GPs as independent contractors and the necessary geographical dispersion of the service makes it very difficult to set standards, to ensure that they are adhered to or even to monitor the pattern of care provided. Recent studies carried out in Manchester have described variability in both the structure and process of care (Wood, 1983; Wilkin *et al.*, 1984; Wilkin and Metcalfe, 1984).

Facilities range from the single-handed GP practising from lock-up premises having minimal contact with other health care professions to health centres offering a wide range of facilities and staff. For elderly patients in particular this means that primary health care can depend almost entirely on the GP with whom he or she is registered. Consultation rates for patients over 65 years of age ranged from less than three contacts per patient per year to more than ten. Prescribing rates for the elderly ranged from less than 50 per cent of consultations resulting in a prescription to more than 75 per cent. Although most GPs still visit patients at home, the number of home visits as a proportion of total consultations for the elderly ranged from less than 10 per cent to more than 50 per cent. Lastly, GPs constitute the main point of access to a wide range of other services for old people. Consultant referrals for the elderly ranged from less than 2 per cent of consultations to more than 14 per cent. Almost half of the GPs in the study made no referrals to nurses or health visitors in the course of three weeks' recording, and 65 per cent made no referrals to the social services department.

The system of primary health care in England offers enormous potential to develop a pattern of health care for the elderly which is genuinely responsive to the needs and wishes of the individual and which can be provided in the context of the economic, environmental and social realities of their lives. Unfortunately, this potential remains largely unrealised. Bosanquet (1978) notes that the reality of GP care for the elderly rarely accords with the all too common pious statements about the central role of the family doctor. Williamson's (1964) study of unreported needs among the elderly highlighted the problems long ago, and subsequent calls for screening and more preventative work (Williams, 1979) seem to have gone largely unheeded. Nevertheless, general practice and the primary health care team provide the most promising focus for the development of a pattern of health care for the elderly which goes beyond illness and dependency models of health in old age and begins to develop an approach based on interdependence and effective health.

First and foremost, primary health care deals with definable populations and communities. Many GPs now have age/sex registers which enable them to identify their elderly patients. They provide care not just to the individual but often to a number of generations in the same family and to others in the elderly person's social network. Despite the fact that the method of payment of GPs does nothing to encourage preventative medicine, screening, health education, surveillance, etc., a minority have begun to develop their work in these areas (RCGP, 1972). More generally, the introduction of vocational training and the activities of the Royal College of General Practitioners in tackling issues of quality of care are hopeful signs (Horder and Swift, 1979; Irvine, 1983). There is a new interest, particularly among younger members of the profession, in holistic approaches to medicine and the greater involvement of patients in establishing the objectives of care both at the individual level and at the practice or health centre level (Balint, 1964). These sorts of development, although small in scale, offer some hope of a new direction in health care for the elderly, but they require the provision of incentives through changes in the remuneration of general practitioners and the training and organisation of all members of the primary health care team.

Present and Future Issues in the Development of Health Care

We have tried to show in the preceding discussion of the development of health services for the elderly how present-day provisions have arisen. In doing so we have highlighted the key issues which have influenced the pattern of provision. In this concluding section we want to establish an agenda of those issues which we feel are most important to the future development of health care for the elderly. Such an agenda is necessarily selective and limitations of space mean that there are many important issues which we are unable to discuss.

Nevertheless, we feel that four issues are of particular contemporary significance: resources and control over resources; the growth of the private sector; community versus institutional care; and the role of specialist health services.

These issues should be seen in the context of more general conceptions of health, the role of health care and stereotypes of old age. We have argued that health care has been dominated by a medical or disease model overlaid by stereotypes that treat old age negatively and the elderly as a homogeneous and undifferentiated group. To the extent that the post-war growth of the NHS has resulted in a shift in this model it is towards what we have described as a functional approach, which defines elderly people in terms of their ability to be independent. There is little evidence of a move towards a pattern of health care which recognises the need to see the individual in terms of a relationship to his or her environment and challenges current attitudes to old age. The concepts of interdependency and effective health introduce the need to regard the actors in the situation (i.e. elderly person and significant others) as participants in the process of care whose subjective interpretations of problems and potential solutions should carry more weight than those of the service providers. In considering key issues for the future of health services for the elderly we want to emphasise the need to seek a shift in the conceptions of old age and health which underpin present services.

Resources and control over resources
Perhaps the most fundamental problem facing health services in general and those for the elderly in particular is the level of resources available. As a proportion of gross national product, health expenditure amounted to 6.1 per cent in 1980 in the United Kingdom (Allsop, 1984). This is considerably less than in other European countries and the United States. In recent years attempts have been made to cut the rate of growth of expenditure on the NHS at the same time as the potential demand for care is increasing as a result of demographic change. There is little likelihood of any dramatic change in this pattern in the next decade unless there is a sharp upturn in the economy as a whole. Thus the only prospect for an increase in resources devoted to health care of the elderly is through a redistribution of the resources currently available.

The present government remains committed to the view that improvements in patient care can be achieved through so-called efficiency savings. We consider this extremely unlikely, particularly in the services for the elderly, where the labour-intensive nature of many services makes it virtually impossible to make savings without damaging services to patients. The issue then is one of priorities both in terms of client groups and in terms of the types of service provided.

The policies of successive governments since the late 1950s have included the need to give priority in resource allocation to the Cinderella services and to the development of community-based services. In the most recent period there is some evidence that these priorities have had a limited impact. Thus for the period 1976/77 to 1982/83 gross current expenditure on acute hospital services rose by 1 per cent annually and on inpatient and outpatient services for the elderly and younger disabled by 2.5 per cent. In the same period gross expenditure on health visiting rose 3.6 per cent annually and on district nursing by 4.2 per cent and family practitioner services have 'enjoyed a real volume growth considerably and consistently above that in the NHS as a whole' (House of Commons, 1984a). However, this should be seen in the context of the total budget. Thus, for example, acute inpatient and outpatient services consumed £3726 million in 1982/83 compared to £725 million for geriatric services and £349 million for health visiting and district nursing. Although there has been a marginally faster growth in those services of particular importance to the elderly, this hardly represents a major shift in priorities and has coincided with an increase in demand associated with increasing numbers of people over the age of 75.

The Royal Commission on the NHS (1979) estimated that a growth of approximately 1 per cent per year in total expenditure was necessary merely to allow for demographic change and to make some provision for technological change. Allsop (1984) argues that the government's policy in 'Care in Action' marks a retreat by central government from its responsibilities in caring for dependent groups. Although lip-service is paid to the commitment to community care, the failure to provide any coherent strategy or targets is an abdication of responsibility. It is expected that the informal and voluntary sectors will continue to provide most of the care for elderly people with health problems.

The decentralisation of power over resource allocation which has always characterised the NHS is likely to continue, and indeed may be reinforced. What this means in practice for services for the elderly is that an already weak bargaining position is likely to be further eroded. The need therefore to battle for an adequate share of available resources becomes even more important. However, it is unlikely that any major changes can be achieved without a fundamental shift in the locus of control and a re-examination of objectives. As long as the rules of the game remain the same (i.e. power over resource allocation lying primarily with the medical profession whose priorities emphasise curative medicine), services for the elderly are unlikely to show any dramatic improvement.

There is a need to begin a debate on the objectives of health care for the elderly and thus the sorts of service which might best achieve these. Central to this debate must be elderly people themselves and the health care professions other than medicine. This is not a debate which will take place in the confines of health authorities or even community health councils. The only way in which the balance of power can be altered and services become more responsive to the needs of consumers is through the day-to-day transactions between service providers and consumers.

The women's movement has shown in a limited way how this can be done through questioning existing ideologies and patterns of care both publicly and within the doctor–patient consultation. It will be necessary to build institutions which challenge professional control and which provide the support necessary for individuals to begin to exercise a greater degree of control in their personal transactions within the health-care system. Isolated examples of patient participation groups, carers' organisations and consumer organisations along with the voluntary organisations offer at least a base from which to begin such a process. Such changes will pose challenges to the accepted roles of doctors and will necessitate a review of the content of medical education. The professions, including medicine, are by no means uniformly antithetical to such a process and their support may be extremely important. Clearly, control and a change of direction will not be achieved overnight, but success is much more likely than through a reliance on centralised policy initiatives.

Private health care

A concern to develop services more responsive to the needs of consumers has also been expressed as part of the case to support the growth of a larger private sector in health care. It is argued that the rational sovereign consumer is the best judge of his or her needs and will purchase health care accordingly (Sheldon, 1980). Following the 1980 Health Services Act which relaxed the controls over the private sector, there has been a rapid expansion of the private sector of health care, principally through private health insurance schemes. The present government has suggested as a target an increase in the proportion of the population covered by such schemes from 6.4 per cent in 1981 to 25 per cent (Allsop, 1984).

As far as the elderly are concerned there are two distinct features of the growth of the private sector. First, the general increase in health insurance and private hospitals (mostly acute surgical), and secondly, the increase in private residential and nursing Homes providing long-term care for chronically sick old people.

The general growth of private care will work to the disadvantage of services for the elderly by shifting the balance of resources (not just financial but also skilled personnel) in favour of acute services. Since the insured population consists mainly of younger generations, the needs of the elderly for acute services are neglected by the private sector. Consumer sovereignty in this case means sovereignty for a limited and powerful group of consumers, although even these only have power as individuals to purchase the range of (profitable) services on offer. Control over the range and nature of services provided and the priorities to be given to different sectors remains with the medical profession and those who supply the capital for private health care. It is difficult to see how growth in the private sector could facilitate the review of objectives of health care for the elderly and the shift in control discussed above.

In principle, the growth of private health care for the elderly raises the same issues as the general expansion of private health care. However, it requires special consideration partly because it relies on a different method of finance and partly because it raises more direct questions about priorities within health care for the elderly. Whilst private health care for younger people is being funded largely through insurance schemes, the growth in institutional provision for the elderly is being funded partly through direct payment by elderly people themselves, but increasingly through payments made through the social security system. In this latter case the element of consumer choice is severely restricted by what services the state is prepared to underwrite. Experience so far suggests that these are restricted to institutional provision and that even within that sector the method of review and payment removes any real power from the individual consumer. The combined effect of the profitability of institutional care and the availability of public finance is to pre-empt any rational planning of health services for the elderly, at least in the provision of continuing care. The experience of other countries, in particular the United States (Vladek, 1980), should lead us to be extremely cautious about any expansion of private institutional care whether in nursing Homes or residential Homes.

Community versus institutional care

The growth of private long-term care could well bring to an end the long-running debate about institutional versus community care. We are now faced with a situation in which declared government policy for the NHS remains committed to care in the community, whilst the practical support being given to the private sector stimulates the growth of institutional care. Such a situation only begins to make sense if it is assumed that the humanitarian arguments advanced in favour of community care are merely window-dressing for an abdication of responsibility. The conflict between organisational and humanitarian objectives has always been apparent in the attempts to promote community care, but the contradictions have recently become more obvious. It is important that elderly people themselves, their families and those concerned with services should seek to shift the terms of the debate for the future.

Institutional care and community care should not be seen as alternatives but complementary parts of a comprehensive service. Both at the level of policy and provision and at the level of the individual, people are faced with irrevocable choices between community and institution. In practice they need not be mutually exclusive. The needs of elderly people for care range across a very broad spectrum and change over time. It is the needs of the professions and the service structures rather then the needs and wishes of elderly people, which have led to sharp divisions between different modes of care. Whilst most old people would wish to remain in their own homes for as long as possible this should not mean that the opportunity to enter some form of institutional care should be denied. Equally, the decision to enter a nursing Home or residential Home should not be forced by an absence of any care in the community. What is essential is that the elderly as a group and as individuals have the ability to negotiate patterns of care which best meet their needs.

Role of specialist health services
The issue of the barriers between community and institution also raises in turn the question of specialisation in health services for the elderly. In earlier discussion of the growth of geriatric services we have pointed to the importance of these in fostering a renewed vigour in hospital-based services which had previously largely ignored elderly patients. However, we have also emphasised some of the problems inherent in specialist provisions and the need to develop a holistic conception of health. The history of health services for the elderly, indeed of the National Health Service as a whole, is one of tension between the wish to specialise in order to provide the highest technical standard of care and the need to retain a concept of the whole person in a social context. The separation of general practice and hospital medicine has emphasised the gulf between primary and secondary health care. Within the hospital sector specialisation has provided a route to professional power and prestige through control over a unique knowledge base and resources. Recognition of this fact has led those concerned with care of the elderly to seek the status of independent specialities, first of geriatric medicine, and more recently of psychogeriatric medicine. As these have developed and achieved a command over resources, specialist subdivisions have appeared, so that acute wards, rehabilitation wards, long-stay wards and day hospitals have become separated from each other. The twin processes of specialisation according to

age group and specialisation by mode of care are likely to continue the process of fragmentation of health care of the elderly.

It is necessary in analysing the effects of this process to make a distinction between specialism and separatism. The former may be necessary in certain situations in order to achieve the highest technical standards of care, but the latter must be resisted because it tends to lead to resource starvation, poor quality care, isolation and alienation. Where geriatric services have become separated from the mainstream of hospital activity, they have tended to be housed in inappropriate buildings, deprived of staff, and generally neglected. This has been most obvious in long-stay wards where the quality of care has often fallen far short of acceptable standards. The effects on elderly people condemned to such institutions are obvious and well documented. Less obvious, but also important, are the effects on staff who work in them. They become isolated from their professional colleagues and alienated from the process of care over which they have little effective control. However, specialism does not necessarily lead to separatism. There are examples of hospital-based services for the elderly which have retained their position in the mainstream of secondary health care (Evans, 1977). Nevertheless, there is a basic conflict between the need for integrated health care which treats the whole person in his or her environment and the desire of the professions to create a specialised knowledge base from which to exercise professional power and prestige. Specialist services should be available to elderly people in a setting which provides comprehensive health care capable of meeting a wide range of needs and adapting to changes in needs over time.

It is important to question the objectives of services and to ask why these can only be met in a specialist setting. Specialisation is sometimes advocated on grounds of professional or organisational needs rather than for the welfare of patients. Even where the welfare of patients is cited as the reason, there are often underlying professional and organisational objectives without which the pressure to specialise would be much reduced. Thus, for example, the provision of separate long-stay hospital wards for mentally infirm old people is justified on the grounds of providing a safer environment in which specially trained staff can provide stimulation and a high quality of care. In practice it is not uncommon to find that underlying these proposals is a desire to release beds currently occupied by these patients in order that staff can devote their attention to more 'interesting' and 'rewarding' patients.

However, although the development of separatist health care for the elderly can be resisted within the existing structure of services, the fundamental problem of the balance of power in the system is likely to limit the effectiveness of such resistance. What is required is a shift in conceptions of health and the role of health services, combined with a challenge to social stereotypes of old age. But as we have shown in this chapter, the dominant ideology of health care is based on a medical model reflecting the power of the medical profession. Consumers have little opportunity to challenge medical definitions of and solutions to problems. Fundamental change is only likely to be achieved as part of a wider social and political movement by elderly people which challenges society's attitudes towards old age and seeks to win the power to formulate objectives for health care and manage resources accordingly.

10 Pensions and the Production of Poverty in Old Age

Alan Walker

This chapter has three aims. First, to describe the current financial status of elderly people. The outstanding characteristic revealed by this assessment and, indeed, by all similar ones conducted both officially and independently over the last century, is the widespread experience of poverty and low incomes among elderly people. Yet, despite this weight of evidence, the proposition has begun to be advanced officially that the incomes of elderly people have increased substantially and that they should no longer be regarded as a priority for expenditure. Because of the importance of this argument in determining present and future income-maintenance policy towards the elderly, it is discussed in some detail. Second, to examine the main sources of income in old age and particularly the consequence of the social division between public and private pensions. Third, to augment the analysis of the structured dependency of the elderly in Chapter 2 by examining the specific causes of poverty and inequality in old age. An attempt is made throughout this discussion to review the potential impact of recent government proposals on the incomes of elderly people, but because this chapter was written before the final outcome of the proposals contained in the government's White Paper on the reform of social security this aspect of the analysis is necessarily speculative.

The main theme of the chapter is that a fundamental factor in explaining the persistence of deprivation on a massive scale in old age is not only the failure of social policy to eradicate poverty, but also the crucial role it has played in producing and legitimating the poverty of a substantial proportion of elderly people and the marked inequalities between different groups of them. (For a more detailed account of the approach adopted here see Walker, 1980, 1981b.)

Poverty and Low Incomes in Old Age
Despite the significant political commitment given to pensions in the 1970s, culminating in the introduction of the New Pension Scheme

in 1975 and the series of pledges to uprate pensions in line with earnings or prices, whichever was the greater (Walker, 1985e), which resulted in some improvements in the relative position of elderly people in the income distribution (see below), the principal financial problem faced by the elderly is that of poverty. This is one aspect of the substantial inequalities in income and other resources between the majority of those under and those over retirement age (Townsend, 1979).

Table 10.1 Numbers and percentages of people of different age living at low levels of income (Britain 1975–81) (000s)

Family income in relation to supplementary benefit standard	1975	1977	1981
Adults over pension age			
Below	740	760	1120
Receiving SB	1930	1970	1960
On margins	2870	2860	2810
All on low income	5540	5590	5890
% all pensioners	66.3	65.4	66.8
Adults under pension age			
Below	690	760	1130
Receiving SB	970	1170	1720
On margins	2170	2240	2600
All on low income	3830	4170	5540
% all adults	12.6	13.7	17.3
All under pension age			
Below	1100	1140	1690
Receiving SB	1780	2150	2880
On margins	4120	4110	4540
All on low income	7000	7400	9110
% all adults and children	15.8	16.7	20.4

Source: DHSS (1983c).

While just under one in five (18 per cent) of all persons in Great Britain are over retirement age they comprise two in every five of those living on incomes on or below the supplementary benefit level, the official or social standard of poverty. The risk of experiencing poverty is three times greater for those over retirement age than it is for those below retirement age (see Table 10.1). In 1981 (the most recent information released so far by the government) just over one-third of elderly people were living on incomes at or below the poverty line compared with 10 per cent of those under pension age. In all, two-thirds of elderly people (5.9 million people) live in or on the margins of poverty (i.e. with incomes up to 140 per cent of the appropriate supplementary benefit rates) compared with one-fifth of the non-elderly (DHSS, 1983c).

The elderly person's experience of poverty is an enduring one, without any chance of respite. So, in 1981, the proportion of pensioners in receipt of supplementary benefit for five years or more was more than four times that for younger people (62.6 per cent vs. 14.1 per cent), while the proportion in benefit for ten years or more was nearly seven times greater (40 per cent vs. 5.7 per cent). Furthermore, the proportion of elderly people receiving supplementary pensions for ten years or more had increased by 55 per cent between 1978 and 1981 (DHSS, 1982b, p. 215). The national survey of supplementary benefit claimants carried out by the PSI in 1982 found a similarly large proportion of long-term claimants among pensioners. Also, pensioners were much more likely than other claimants to have been living on unsupplemented social security pensions before claiming supplementary benefit (Berthoud, 1984, p. A5).

Poverty in old age persists despite longstanding social recognition of the problem. The high incidence of poverty among elderly people has been documented in this country in a long tradition of official and independent research studies dating back to the mid-nineteenth century investigations of Mayhew and Chadwick and especially those of Charles Booth (1892, 1894). Subsequent research has confirmed, over and over again, the deep-seated nature of poverty in old age (e.g. Cole with Utting, 1962; Townsend and Wedderburn, 1965; Townsend, 1979). A report from the Ministry of Pensions and National Insurance (1966) was particularly important in establishing officially the acceptance of both widespread poverty among the elderly and also the large proportion eligible for but not drawing supplementary benefit. The Royal Commission on the Distribution of Income and Wealth (1978, p. 234) reported that one in every three elderly families had incomes on or below the poverty line in 1975 and that nearly three in every four lived in or on the margins of poverty.

In order to give a rough indication of income relative to need, the Royal Commission calculated equivalent incomes for different families from equivalence scales related to the supplementary benefit levels (reflecting 'socially' defined needs for families of different composition). Even on this basis the lowest quartile of the income distribution was dominated by elderly people (48 per cent) (Royal Commission on the Distribution of Income and Wealth, 1978, p. 27).

In his national survey of household resources and standards of living, Townsend (1979, p. 788) also found a striking difference in the proportion of elderly and non-elderly people living in poverty:

> Twenty per cent, compared with 7 per cent, were living in poverty; another 44 per cent, compared with 19 per cent, were living on the margins of poverty. At the other end of the income scale, more than twice as many of the non-elderly than of the elderly were living comfortably above the [supplementary benefit] standard. . . . Although the elderly comprised only one sixth of the total population, they comprised one third of those in poverty, and nearly one third on the margins of poverty.

What does living in poverty mean? Again there is a great deal of evidence which demonstrates that social security benefits fail to meet the needs of those, including elderly people, who claim them and that for many life on supplementary benefit is a struggle for existence. The former Supplementary Benefits Commission (1977, p. 28) concluded that supplementary benefit is 'barely adequate' to meet needs. Elderly people living on supplementary benefit were much less likely than those on higher incomes to have various items of household equipment and consumer durables such as a telephone, washing machine, refrigerator, car and central heating. One indication of the inadequacy of supplementary benefit rates is the large proportion of claimants in receipt of discretionary allowances, for example, the PSI survey found that 91 per cent of pensioners received payments for 'additional requirements'. Three-quarters of the elderly people living on supplementary benefit had either no savings or savings under £500. Nearly one in five reported anxiety over money, one-third had debts in the previous year, one in four lacked either a change of shoes or a warm winter coat, and 16 per cent could not afford to buy fuel in cold spells (Berthoud, 1984, pp. A16–32). The latter finding is particularly worrying in view of the susceptibility of older people to hypothermia and the annual toll of deaths due to the cold (Wicks, 1978).

A local study of supplementary benefit claimants in Leeds in 1983 found that one-half of pensioners regarded their income as inadequate. Although non-pensioners, particularly the unemployed, experienced most difficulty managing, two-thirds of pensioners were just 'getting by', two-fifths did not have enough money to spend on food, one-fifth ran out of money regularly, and one-fifth sometimes, before their next pay day (C. Walker, 1984, pp. 17–19). One in eight of the pensioners in this study had sold belongings or cashed in insurance policies prematurely in order to make ends meet. This money was invariably spent on essential items such as food, fuel, clothing and rent. Just under one-half had no savings. When asked what they would do with an extra £5 per week, nearly half of pensioners said they would buy food or other essential items covered by the scale rates (ibid., pp. 23–5).

This picture of penury among the 4.8 million elderly people living on incomes equal to or just above the poverty line and a common struggle to make ends meet is disturbing enough; but there are also 1.1 million living *below* the supplementary benefit poverty line. For several reasons, but primarily because of the stigma associated with claiming (SBC, 1977, p. 29; Townsend, 1979, pp. 879–82), some 800,000 pensioners who are eligible for supplementary benefit do not claim it. Thus the take-up rate of supplementary pensions is only 67 per cent. The average weekly amount unclaimed in 1981 was £5, amounting to £210 million per annum.

Expenditure provides an alternative to income as a measure of living standards. A study carried out by the DHSS, using the data from the 1975 *Family Expenditure Survey*, showed that the expenditure of pensioner households was about one-quarter of the median for non-SB households. In fact the total expenditure of pensioner households on supplementary benefit was less than half that of pensioner households not receiving SB but designated as poor (i.e. in the bottom quintile of the income distribution (Baldwin and Cooke, 1984, p. 44)). Some two-thirds of the budgets of pensioner households receiving supplementary benefit are consumed by food, fuel and clothing. This suggests that in 1984/85 benefit levels a single pensioner would spend about £23.60 out of the scale rate of £35.70 on these items, leaving £12.10 per week to be spent on so-called 'non-essentials'. By comparison, median income level households spend less than half of their budget, which is nearly four times as large on 'essential' items (Baldwin and Cooke, 1984, p. 45).

Official Depreciation of Poverty in Old Age

A considerable body of data could be adduced to show further that there is a significant difference between the incomes and other resources and expenditure of elderly and non-elderly people and that a very large group of old people live in poverty or on its margins (Walker, 1980). Moreover the problem of poverty in old age is not peculiar to Britain, it is endemic among both Western and Eastern advanced industrial societies as well as Third World countries (Hendricks and Hendricks, 1977, p. 236; Maeda, 1978, p. 61; Neysmith and Edwardh, 1984). Yet in recent years the argument has been gaining ground in official circles in Britain that poverty in old age is no longer a serious problem. The ministerial foreword to the Green Paper on elderly people issued by the last Labour government implied that the problem had been solved (DHSS, 1978, p. 4). It was not mentioned at all in the White Paper on the elderly issued by the Conservative government (DHSS, 1981c). This official forbearance turned to antagonism in the mid-1980s when the government and some independent commentators began to question openly the extent of need among the elderly and, either directly or by implication the level of social security expenditure on them. The reviews of social security initiated by the Secretary of State for Social Services, Norman Fowler, were the forums in which the argument against further increases in pensions were most trenchantly expressed (DHSS, 1985a). The present case against raising state pensions rests on two separate propositions.

In the first place, we are told, in effect, that the country cannot afford adequate pensions. That this is a political rather than an economic judgement is demonstrated by the fact the Britain spends relatively less on social security and health as a proportion of its GDP than all other EEC countries except Greece. Furthermore the basic pension is considerably lower relative to earnings than those provided by other EEC countries. Thus, for example, the single man's basic pension was 23 per cent of average earnings in 1980 compared with 41 per cent in the Netherlands, 36 per cent in West Germany and 32 per cent in France (Walker, Lawson and Townsend, 1983). So in comparison with other similar advanced industrial societies, as well as by the evidence of continued widespread poverty among its own elderly people, Britain is not providing adequate retirement pensions. Rather than being based on an assessment of the sufficiency of pension provision the main impetus behind policy is the government's antagonism towards public expenditure.

While all governments have sought to control public expenditure, the Thatcher administration of the 1980s has frequently expressed open hostility towards it. This derives, on the one hand, from an economic argument concerning the use of scarce resources by the state and the necessity for 'high' tax rates to finance expenditure, and on the other, from a more direct ideological aversion to the public sector and the welfare state in particular; although the two influences are fused together in policy, especially the open commitment to roll back the frontiers of the state (Walker, 1982e; Bosanquet, 1983). When searching for public expenditure cuts to reduce the size of the public sector and finance reductions in taxation it is difficult to ignore the largest public expenditure programme: social security, and, in turn, the group which receives by far the largest chunk of that budget: elderly people. Social security expenditure on elderly people was £19,480 million in 1985/86, 49 per cent of the total social security budget. Between 1978/79 and 1985/86 expenditure on the state retirement pension increased by 117 per cent to £16,400 million.

The first signs of the government's fears about the rising cost of pensions appeared in the White Paper *Growing Older* (DHSS, 1981c). This was followed by the leaked report from the Think

Tank, in 1982, which highlighted the cost of pensions as a major factor in the growth of the welfare state budget. Then Norman Fowler announced the inquiry into provision for retirement seven months ahead of setting up his other two reviews – into supplementary benefit and into provision for children and young people. The most ominous warning came in the government's Green Paper on public expenditure and taxation over the next decade:

> The main factor affecting the social security programme is the provision which has to be made for the elderly. . . . The implications of the present state pension scheme and related pensions issues are under study in the Government's Inquiry into Provision for Retirement; they remain the major source of future pressures on social security expenditure. (Treasury, 1984, p. 14)

Both the initial request for evidence and the final report of the Inquiry into Provision for Retirement (published as part of the general review of social security) were obsessed with the rising cost of pensions. The income needs of pensioners were barely considered.

The future of the state earnings-related pension scheme

The primary cause of official concern is the rising long-term cost of the state earnings-related pension scheme (SERPS): 'The certain and emerging cost of the state earnings-related pension scheme should give everyone – of whatever persuasion – pause for thought' (DHSS, 1985a, p. 21). The cost of the basic state retirement pension – by far the largest element in the social security budget – is not set to rise very much over the next 50 years or so, due largely to the de-indexation of the pension from earnings by the Conservative government in 1980. In fact, this change has meant a significant *cut* in the level of pensions: by 1984/85 a pensioner couple had lost £4.80 per week, or 12 per cent of what the pension would have been if the government had not changed the method of uprating. This reduction in the pension will be progressively worsened over the next 50 years unless the government puts into practice its promise to let pensioners share in the rising prosperity elsewhere in the economy. Thus on the government's assumption of 1.5 per cent annual growth, the basic pension will be worth, by 2033/34, about half of what it would have been. Relative to wage-earners, therefore, pensioners' living standards will fall steadily over the next 50 years: the single person's retirement pension will fall from around 21 per cent of average earnings in 1984/85 to around 9 per cent in 2033/34. If the basic pension had kept pace with the projected rate of increase in earnings the cost would have almost trebled in 50 years time (DHSS, 1985b, p. 4). So the government has already effectively restricted the growth in the cost of the basic pension. This leaves the SERPS element of the pension to be tackled. This was one of the main aims behind the Green Paper on the reform of social security, published on 3 June 1985. However the government's objective of abandoning the scheme altogether has had to be modified.

Because SERPS is a relatively new scheme in the process of development to full maturity in 1998 the costs of the scheme do not begin to increase until the turn of the century, then they do so rapidly, contributing to an overall 2300 per cent rise in cost by the year 2025. The government's response to this projected increase in the cost of SERPS was to propose, in the Green Paper, to phase it out over three years for all men aged under 50 and women aged under 45 and replace it with compulsory occupational and personal pensions. For those within 15 years of retirement SERPS was to continue as at present (DHSS, 1985b, p. 5). It was intended to set a minimum level of earnings below which employers would not be required to make pension arrangements for their employees (DHSS, 1985b, p. 6). In other words while the government, on the one hand, had taken steps to reduce the value of the basic pension in relation to earnings, it proposed, on the other hand, to remove from the bulk of future pensioners the right to full earnings-related protection under SERPS and to leave some with no additional pension entitlement at all above the basic pension. This suggests that official pension policy has little or nothing to do with the income needs of present or future pensioners outlined above and has more to do with the government's broader economic and social strategy.

There is further evidence that present policies represent the triumph of ideology over reason, a careful assessment of need and, indeed, common sense. The fact that the main aim of the proposal to abolish SERPS was to shift provision from the public to the private sector was clearly spelt out in the Green Paper:

> The purpose of these proposals is to achieve a steady transition from the present dependence on state provision to a position in which we as individuals are contributing directly to our own additional pensions and in which we can exercise greater choice in the sort of pension provision we make. (DHSS, 1985b, p. 6)

Yet there was no assessment of the inadequacies of the private and occupational pension schemes upon which future pensioners will be required to depend (see below). In addition, the transfer of the cost of one element of pension provision from the public to the private sector would not reduce the overall cost to the nation of pensions and, in view of the duplication of administration, would probably increase the cost.

Much was made in the Green Paper of the increase in the numbers of elderly people and the 'worsening' of the ratio of contributors to pensioners – from 2.3 contributors per pensioner in 1985 to 1.6 in 2035. But, like all such projections of the 'dependency ratio', this is fraught with uncertainty. It rests, for example, on an increase in the fertility rate of 1.7 children per family to 2.1 children, it ignores the impact of a substantial decline in unemployment and it overlooks the fact that government policy itself, in the form of the retirement condition for the receipt of state pensions, is a key determinant of the ratio (see Walker, 1982c). The difficulty is best illustrated by the chief architect of the post-war benefit system. The population projections underlying Beveridge's original national insurance pension scheme predicted that people over pension age would comprise 21 per cent of the population by 1971. That proportion had still not been reached in 1981, when it stood at 18 per cent (Beveridge, 1942, p. 91).

The advice of both the Government Actuary and the Social Security Advisory Committee (SSAC) indicates that the proposal to abolish SERPS was, at best, premature. As the SSAC noted, the contributions necessary to sustain the basic pension and SERPS are not out of line with those being paid currently to meet the costs of exceptionally high unemployment. Even on the most costly of the Government Actuary's assumptions about the movement of earnings, earnings limits and benefits the contribution of employers and employees to the National Insurance Fund would be 16.7 per cent of earnings by 2005/06 compared with 17.65 per cent since 1983. However this did rest on the assumption that unemployment could be reduced to an average 6 per cent between 1985 and 2005. Even the SSAC concluded: 'at this distance of time we do not think these can be solid grounds for altering the scheme now for fear of all the worst outcomes occurring steadily for 40 years' and, furthermore, that 'at this early state in the life of the new pension scheme no case has been made which would justify revision of any of the key features of the scheme established with such care in 1975' (SSAC, 1983, p. 40).

There was evidence, moreover, from public statements by all of the 'independent' members of the Inquiry into Provision for Retirement, including a respresentative of the private pensions industry, that none of them favoured the chosen course of the government.

The weight of influential opinion against abolishing SERPS – including the Confederation of British Industry, the Engineering Employers Federation and particularly the National Association of Pension Funds and insurance companies – and the public outcry which greeted the proposal, caused the government to rethink its plans. Although, when the White Paper on the reform of social security was published in December 1985, there were no doubts as to the government's belief that SERPS represents an unacceptable 'burden' on future generations, the proposals were, with obvious reluctance, for modification rather than abolition:

> The Government believe that the approach put forward in the Green Paper would have achieved the objectives of reform, by which we stand. ... However, the Government recognise the substantial body of opinion which favours modifying SERPS rather than abolishing it. (DHSS, 1985d, p. 12)

The two elements to the government pensions strategy that were present in the Green Paper, but not on an equal footing, emerged more clearly in the White Paper as the twin prongs of policy to reduce the size of the public sector's input. On the one hand, the modification of SERPS in order to reduce its cost and, on the other, the provision of incentives to encourage the spread of private pensions.

There are four main proposals for reducing the cost of SERPS (DHSS, 1985d, p. 13). First, the calculation of SERPS will be based on lifetime earnings, rather than the best 20 years which was considered to be 'over-generous' to those, especially women and working-class groups, with shorter than average periods of employment and non-incremental earnings. Secondly, the occupation sector which is contracted out of the state scheme is to be made responsible for inflation-proofing the guaranteed minimum pension, up to a maximum of 3 per cent, beyond which the state will continue to provide protection. Thirdly, the additional pension will be calculated on the basis of 20 per cent of earnings rather than 25 per cent. Fourthly, the proportion of SERPS that can be inherited by a spouse will be one half rather than the full amount as now. The combined effect of these proposals will be to cut the projected cost of the scheme in half (DHSS, 1985d, p. 15).

While the contribution of the state to direct earnings-related pension provision is to be severely reduced, the private pensions sector is to be encouraged to flourish. Restrictions on those employers contracting out of the state scheme are to be relaxed so that they are no longer liable to provide a guaranteed minimum pension but only a guaranteed minimum level of contributions. Personal pensions will also be allowed to contract out of the state scheme. Extra tax incentives are proposed for all personal pension and occupational schemes that contract out in the five years following the start of the pension changes in 1988: a rebate of 2 per cent more of earnings than the standard rebate of around 5.75 per cent, which will be paid into the occupational scheme or personal pension contributions. This is an extremely generous addition to existing tax incentives clearly intended to give the private pensions industry a major boost that it has been unable, under its own steam, to produce.

All of these proposed changes have been deferred until 1988, that is until after the next election. So, the final shape of SERPS and the public/private mix in pension provision depend on the result of the election. The consensus on which the 1975 earnings-related scheme was based has been abandoned and pensions are once more a political football.

Poverty or affluence in old age?

The second plank in the official case against increasing pensions relative to earnings, as well as against SERPS, is the proposition that the incomes of pensioners have improved recently by comparison with other groups living in poverty (DHSS, 1985a, pp. 12–13). Thus cuts in elderly people's benefits are legitimated by the myth that they are relatively well off, and that Britain may actually be over-providing for old age. This may be seen as one part of the belief in right-wing circles that British society has become too equal in recent times (Abel-Smith and Townsend, 1984, pp. 6–10).

Partly as a result of the growth of mass unemployment and partly as a result of the forceful proselytisation of the ideology of inequality a significant shift has begun to occur in the longstanding consensus about the deprived status of elderly people and, to some extent, about their position as the most deserving of minority groups. Official reports and some independent social scientists have started recently to point to relative improvements in the position of elderly people in the income distribution. The most important of these commentaries was prepared by the DHSS Economic Advisers' Office as a background paper to the Inquiry into Provision for Retirement (DHSS, 1984). This showed that between 1951 and 1984/85 pensioners' share of total disposable income (total income from earnings, savings, investment, pensions and other social security benefits) increased from 7 per cent to 15 per cent (DHSS, 1984, p. 14). The reasons for this improvement include both the growth in numbers of pensioners and their rising incomes. While the former is relatively straightforward (see p. 5) the improvement in the disposable income of pensioners relative to non-pensioners rests on two factors. On the one hand, there has been a slowing-down in the growth of real disposable income among those below pension age, caused mainly by the reduction of the numbers in full-time employment and, on the other, the value of the basic pensions has risen in relation to average earnings (see below). (The main advance in the value of pensions took place in the mid-1970s when, following the encouragement of key trade union leaders occupying powerful positions in Labour's corporate policy-making machinery, the basic pension was index-linked to earnings or prices, whichever rose the faster.)

This official analysis of rising incomes among pensioners was supported by other independent assessments. For example, one recent examination of changes in the distribution of income over the life-cycle showed that whereas 45 per cent of married pensioners were in the bottom quintile of net income in 1971, this had fallen to 28 per cent in 1982. For single pensioners the proportions were 43 per cent in 1971 and 22 per cent in 1982 (Bradshaw and O'Higgins, 1984, p. 30). However, while analyses such as this correctly highlight recent improvements in the relative incomes of pensioners, they have mistakenly been translated into policy proposals which amount to a redistribution of income from the elderly to other groups in poverty.

Three factors should be considered. First, the relative improvement in the value of the basic pension has been modest: from 19 per cent of gross average male manual earnings for a single pensioner in 1948 to 22 per cent in 1983. For a married couple the proportions are 31 per cent in 1948 to 36 per cent in 1983 (DHSS, 1985c, p. 257). Moreover, since the decoupling of pensions from earnings in 1981, the maintenance of the value of the pension established in the mid-1970s has relied on the relatively small growth in average manual earnings. It is likely that this improvement will be undermined once average earnings begin to rise at a faster rate again.

Second, the main improvement in the value of the basic pension has been against some other social security benefits, notably unemployment benefit rather than average earnings. In 1972/73 unemployment benefit and retirement pension were paid at the same rates (and had been for most of the period since 1948), by 1984/85 the latter was worth 26 per cent more than the former. However this increase had as much to do with recent cuts in the value of unemployment benefits as rises in the value of pensions and, therefore, it is partly artificial. Moreover, the decoupling of pensions from earnings has had an immediate impact on the relative value of the retirement pension which fell from a high of 132 per cent of the level of the unemployment benefit in 1981 to 126 per cent in 1984 (DHSS, 1985c, p. 253).

This is *not* a case of special pleading for pensions. The 'advantageous' position of pensioners among the poor has been manufactured by government policies largely outside of the pensions field: the creation of mass unemployment, the abolition of earnings-related supplement, cuts in unemployment benefit, failure to maintain the value of child benefit and encouragement of low wages (Walker, Winyard and Pond, 1983). The outcome of these policies is that there has been a surge of people – particularly families with children

– into the bottom quintile of the income distribution (see Table 10.1) and, because unemployment benefit is set at a lower rate than the pension, the average income of the lowest income group has declined as their numbers have swollen. The answer, of course, is to reverse recent policies and improve the incomes of families with children and especially the unemployed. However, the White Paper on social security does not propose any improvement in social security status of the unemployed. What is more, because of the public expenditure constraints imposed by the government, elderly people are now viewed as the *source* of finance for redistribution to other groups in poverty. The overall effect of this policy will be collective pauperisation, under the euphemism of 'rough justice'. Thus, on the government's own calculations, some 2.2 million pensioners (including 350,000 over 80s) will be worse off as a result of the White Paper's proposals (DHSS, 1985d, Technical Annex).

Third, as the earlier discussion shows, the majority of elderly people still live in poverty in spite of recent improvements in the value of pensions. In so far as elderly people have shifted, or more correctly have been shunted, out of the bottom fifth of the income distribution they have been moved predominantly into the adjacent quintile. In 1971, 74 per cent of single pensioners were in the bottom two-fifths of the income distribution compared with 64 per cent in 1982 (Bradshaw and O'Higgins, 1984, p. 30). The DHSS (1984, p. 17) found that few pensioners are very well off, with only 10 per cent having an income above the average for working families, and that few workers and their families have incomes as low as most pensioners. They concluded that 'although the general position of pensioners has improved considerably in the last 30 years, many pensioners still have relatively low incomes' (DHSS, 1984, p. 17).

In fact, what has been happening, largely due to the influence of occupational pensions, is that incomes among elderly people have been becoming more unequal. This is particularly noticeable between married and single pensioners: 6 per cent of pensioner married couples and 7 per cent of single people were in the top fifth of the income distribution in 1971, by 1982 the figures were 9 per cent and 7 per cent (Bradshaw and O'Higgins, 1984, p. 30). (At the same time it should be noted that 70 per cent of married couples without children where the woman was aged under 35 were in the top quintile.)

Particularly disadvantaged are very elderly (75+) lone women. Forty-three per cent of widows aged 75–79 and 38 per cent of those aged 80 and over were reliant on supplementary benefit in 1982, compared to 28 per cent and 20 per cent of lone men and 17 per cent and 18 per cent of married couples. Even within the same quintile of the income distribution lone women have lower incomes than lone men or married couples. For example in the lowest fifth the average income of married couples was £57 in 1982, compared to £34 for lone men and £32 for lone women (DHSS, 1984, p. 18). Table 10.2 shows the distribution of income according to age, gender and marital status.

Table 10.2 Average disposable income by age, gender and marital status, 1982

Age	Married couples £	Lone men £	Lone women £
60–64	—	—	57
65–69	96	67	49
70–74	86	54	49
75+	78	47	46
All ages	88	55	49

Source: DHSS (1984) p. 18.

One final comment on the position of pensioners' incomes relative to other groups. Acceptance of the official argument for a lower priority for pensioners in social security – including the contraction of SERPS – rests on a denial of poverty as a relative phenomenon, whereby the incomes of the poor are assessed in relation to those in society as a whole rather than according to an absolute standard. It was not surprising to find, therefore, in the Green Paper on social security, that the government attempted to dismiss, albeit unconvincingly, the notion of relative poverty in favour of concentration of the needs of those in the bottom fifth of the income distribution (DHSS, 1985a, pp. 12–13). We have already seen that although there has been, for various reasons, some considerable movement of pensioners out of the bottom fifth of the income distribution in recent years, the proportion living in or on the margins of poverty has remained fairly stable. This is in part attributable to the fact that poverty has been assessed relatively according to the supplementary benefit level and, while pensions have made gains against some other social security benefits, pensioners' incomes have not risen significantly in comparison with incomes in general. This is the problem with a relative standard of poverty as far as the government is concerned: as the living standards of the community as a whole rise so should the minimum incomes of the poor (DHSS, 1985, p. 12). With a government intent on judging the needs of the poor only in relation to other poor or poorer people in society, rather than the better-off, only the very meanest and minimal social security incomes are likely to result.

The official case against better public provision for the elderly – that the country cannot afford to spend more and that pensioners do not need it anyway – has produced a disparaging commentary on need in old age which does not do justice to either the level or the nature of poverty among elderly people. It has proved to be the rationale for a policy which is likely to pauperise further those reliant on the public sector, while at the same time active encouragement has been given to the private sector and those it serves. It is to this social division of income in old age that we now turn.

Sources of Income in Old Age
A description of the main sources of income of elderly people lays the foundation for the explanation of the continuance of poverty in old age.

Table 10.3 Comparison of the components of pensioners' income and total UK household incomes (percentages)

Income component	Pensioners' income, 1984/85	Total household income 1983
Wages and salaries[a]	9	69
Investment and rent	9	6
Private pensions, annuities	22	7
NI retirement pension	49⎫	17
Other social security[b]	11⎭	
Total	100	100

Notes:
a.   Includes self employment.
b.   Mainly supplementary benefit and housing benefit.

Sources: CSO (1985, p. 75); DHSS (1984, p. 16).

Important changes have occurred in the sources of elderly people's income over the last 30 years. In 1951 the proportion of total gross income derived from earnings was three times the current level (17 per cent), while the proportion received from occupational pensions was 15 per cent. The contribution of social security was two-thirds of the current level (42 per cent of total income) largely due to the significant role of earnings (DHSS, 1984, p. 16). These gross income figures hide major differences between different groups of pensioners.

In general, access to private welfare in the form of occupational pensions marks the boundary between the two nations among Britain's elderly that Titmuss originally warned of in 1955 (Titmuss, 1963, p. 74). The NI basic pension is the main source of income in single person pensioner households with gross weekly incomes of less than £80 (in 1982). In fact, the lower the income of this group the greater the proportion provided by the retirement pension: one-half for those with incomes between £50 and £80 and seven-tenths for those on incomes under £50. The proportions of incomes contributed by occupational pensions were 18 per cent and 5 per cent respectively (CSO, 1985, p. 81). Among single pensioner households with weekly incomes of £80 or more only one-quarter was derived from the retirement pension and well over two-fifths from occupational pensions. For two-person households the proportion of income derived from the NI pension nearly halves between those with incomes under £80 and those with £80 or more per week (71 per cent compared to 37 per cent), while the proportion received from occupational pensions increased by nearly five times (7.5 per cent compared to 35 per cent).

In order to explain these substantial inequalities between pensioners in both the sources and, as outlined earlier, the levels of their income, it is necessary to recognise that retirement is not the homogenising experience that popular myth would have us believe. Although the process of retirement has a generally deflating impact on income – resulting in a reduction in income of at least one-half on average – this is by no means universal. The exact extent of this fall in income depends on socioeconomic status prior to retirement, especially occupational class to which we shall return later. For the moment it is important to establish that the state itself – through its social policies – plays the central role in determining the proportion of income derived by elderly people from different sources. One of the clearest ways to demonstrate this is by means of the social division between public or social, fiscal and occupational welfare. As Richard Titmuss first outlined in 1955 this division is not based on 'any fundamental difference in the functions of the three systems . . . or their declared aims. It arises from an organisational division of method, which, in the main, is related to the division of labour in complex, individuated societies' (Titmuss, 1963, p. 42).

The Social Division of Pensions
In total, as Mike Reddin (1984, p. 11) has shown, Britain spends some £50,000 million per annum on retirement income. This comprises all contributions and savings for pension purposes through state, occupational and private insurance. Current state retirement pensions represent less than 30 per cent of this total. This puts both the size and the so-called burden of state pensions into perspective. However, because of the perceived burden of state pensions, as the largest single element in public expenditure, particularly in a climate where most public welfare activities are regarded as damaging, they are constantly under public, political and expert scrutiny, whereas

the cost and effectiveness of the private sector, which consumes the bulk of the national investment in retirement income, is rarely questioned.

Yet the private sector of pensions does not survive unaided, it receives two crucial forms of state subsidy. There is tax relief on employers' and employees' contributions, lump-sum benefits, interest earnings and captial gains, probably amounting to around £5000 million in 1984/85 (Reddin and Pilch, 1985, pp. 23–4; see also Reddin, 1980). Then there is the state guarantee to top up private pensions in order to protect them from inflationary erosion (see below). This reliance of the private sector on fiscal and social welfare is often overlooked in discussions of the merits of private pensions (see for example DHSS, 1985a and b).

The development of pension provision
How did the current system of pension provision arise? The present mixture of public and private welfare, or 'mixed economy' of welfare, in old age has its post-war foundations in the Beveridge Report (1942). Beveridge built on the insurance principle established by the National Insurance Act 1911 and the Widows, Orphans and Old Age Contributory Pensions Act 1925, rather than the non-contributory, means-tested model provided by the Old Age Pensions Act 1908 or another more radical alternative. This meant that pensions were not regarded as a right but were contingent on the establishment of eligibility through the labour market, or 'work-testing' (Shragge, 1984, p. 29). Moreover, pensions and other social security benefits were to provide only the minimum subsistence floor specifically in order to encourage additional private welfare provision (Beveridge, 1942, p. 93). These fundamental principles, which have guided the construction and subsequent operation of the post-war welfare state, are enshrined in the following passage:

> Social security must be achieved by co-operation between the State and the individual. The State should offer security for service and contribution. The State in organising security should not stifle incentive, opportunity, responsibility; in establishing a national minimum it should leave room and encouragement for voluntary action by each individual to provide more than the minimum for himself and his family. (Beveridge, 1942, pp. 6–7)

As well as the contribution condition, a second important condition was proposed by Beveridge and institutionalised by the introduction of the NI pension in 1948: the retirement condition. Those who have built up a right to the state pension by virture of their contributions are only awarded the pension following formal retirement from employment (Beveridge, 1942, p. 95).

The financing of state pensions and particularly the size of the Exchequer contribution has been the overriding political issue in post-war pensions policy. It was dominant too in the preparation of the Beveridge Report. Many of the assumptions that Beveridge brought to his study of social insurance were based not on considerations of social welfare 'but on the prejudices of official economic opinion' and 'the notions of financial soundness which prevailed in Treasury circles' (Kincaid, 1973, pp. 43–4; Walker, 1984c, pp. 53–4). Beveridge and the Treasury officials who scrutinised his proposals had intended that retirement pensions and other social security benefits should be self-financing according to actuarially sound insurance principles. This was to be achieved and a reserve fund established by phasing in the scheme over 21 years.

However the public pressure for retirement pensions was enormous and the National Insurance Act 1946 allowed the claiming of full benefits from the outset of the scheme (Shragge, 1984, p. 48). Thus rather than being based on the insurance principle the NI pension has always been a 'pay-as-you-go' scheme in which those in employment support those drawing pensions. The immediate post-war period also saw a sharp diminution in the Exchequer contribution to social security, from 24 per cent of total receipts in 1950 to 12 per cent in 1953 (George, 1968, p. 62). But it was to rise subsequently in the 1950s as the Beveridge principle of financing pensions began to collapse and the national insurance fund went into deficit.

The response of the government to the rising cost of pensions in the early years of the scheme and worries about the projected increase in the number of pensioners was to set up the Phillips Committee in July 1953, 'to review the economic and financial problems involved in providing for old age, having regard to the prospective increase in the numbers of aged' (Phillips Committee, 1954, p. 1). Like the subsequent inquiry into provision for retirement, set up 30 years later, the Phillips Committee was primarily concerned with the long-term growth in demand for and cost of pensions and the capacity of the working population to finance the scheme. The Committee's report reaffirmed the importance of individual contributions as a measure of 'social discipline' and, among other things, recommended an increase in retirement age to 68 for men and 63 for women. In addition, while not challenging the operation of the 1946 Act, the Committee proposed a limitation of the Exchequer contribution, support for the development of occupational pensions, and a restriction of the Beveridge principle (if not the practice) that NI pensions should provide a subsistence minimum:

A contributions scheme cannot be expected to provide a rate of pension which would enable everybody, whatever his circumstances, to live without other means, such a pension rate would be an extravagant use of national resources. (Phillips Committee, 1954, p.81)

Once older people had worked a full course and fulfilled 'the obligation of service' they were to receive 'an adequate income to maintain them' (Beveridge, 1942, p. 92). In fact this has never been the case. Partly because of the Treasury principle of 'financial sound-ness' accepted by Beveridge, the NI pension was set at a level of bare subsistence rather than adequate maintenance. Beveridge drew on the work of Seebohm Rowntree and, in turn, nutritionists, such as Atwater, on whose work Rowntree's calculations of food needs were based. Furthermore Beveridge allowed only 75 per cent of the scien-tific food value necessary for 'physical efficiency' for old-age pen-sioners, plus 10 per cent for special food needs. The amounts required for clothing and housing were also set lower than those of a person of working age (Shragge, 1984, p. 45).

Thus the definition of need in old age adopted by Beveridge and followed by the 1945 Labour government and all subsequent govern-ments was an extremely conservative, not to say mean, one. Despite longstanding and widespread criticism of the pseudo-scientific basis of the calculations that Beveridge used for his assessment of food and other needs – not least that they bear little resemblance to what people actually spend their money on – they have influenced the levels of pensions and other social security benefits ever since. Not surprisingly, therefore, the single person's basic pension has re-mained at around only one-fifth of average gross earnings over the whole of the post-war period, and today over half of pensioners are eligible for supplementary pensions (though only two-thirds of those eligible actually claim them).

The growth of occupational pensions
The inadequacy of the NI pension in itself created a spur for groups of powerful employees to bargain for additional occupational pen-sions. Moreover some employers were keen to discourage labour mobility in a period of labour shortages. Consequently these schemes grew rapidly in the late 1950s and 1960s. Between 1956 and 1963 the total number of employees with occupational pensions more than doubled, from 4.3 million to 11.1 million (Shragge, 1984, p. 73). Two-thirds were private sector employees. The growth in the coverage of occupational pensions peaked in 1967 at 12.2 million employees and then declined steeply to 11.1 million in 1971 (Govern-ment Actuary, 1978). The decline in occupational pension coverage was in the private sector of employment which fell from 8.1 million in 1967 to 6.8 million in 1971 and subsequently to 5.5 million in 1983 (public sector pensions increased steadily from 4.1 million

members in 1967 to 5.4 million in 1983) and primarily among manual workers. The steepest decline between 1967 and 1971 corresponded to industrial restructuring and rising unemployment. Tax concessions, introduced by the Conservative government in 1970 and 1971, which were designed to encourage occupational pensions, appear to have halted the decline in membership of these schemes. Since then membership has fluctuated from year to year with an average of around 11 million members, where it stood in 1984/85, covering one-half of the employed population (DHSS, 1985b, p. 21). It is the failure of the private sector of pensions to grow further that has led the government to propose new tax incentives.

The provision of occupational pensions is a huge undertaking – in 1982 the total household income derived from such pensions and related benefits exceeded that provided through the state in the form of pensions (James, 1984, p. 3). How effectively does the private sector provide for retirement? What most elderly people require from their pension is a guaranteed assurance to an adequate income that will be secure from inflation.

On the first count – as befits a form of provision introduced originally partly in order to discourage labour mobility – an occupational pension is guaranteed, subject to the vagaries of the market, providing that the employee stays in the same job or the job is in the public sector. If a person changes job, especially in the private sector where transfer is virtually impossible, the pension will suffer. Each year some 6–8 per cent of contributors lose their pension entitlements through job changes. In 1979, 10 per cent of members of occupational schemes withdrew from membership mainly due to job changes. Of these only 7 per cent had their pension rights transferred and only 13 per cent had their pension rights preserved, 60 per cent accepted refunds and one in six got no refund (James, 1984, p. 8). With an average number of job changes in excess of three over a working life and increasing in recession, occupational pension schemes cannot be said to provide a clear guarantee to a retirement income for all of their members.

On the second count, the majority of private sector pension schemes are unable to provide protection against price inflation let alone a higher movement in average earnings. Only one in twenty of members of occupational schemes in 1979 who had been receiving pensions for 12 months or more saw their pensions rise by as much as three-quarters of the rate of inflation. The average increase in occupational pensions between 1979 and 1981 was 24 per cent – half the rate of price inflation (National Association of Pension Funds, 1983). Only one occupational pension scheme member in five belongs to a scheme which specifies an obligation to meet inflation.

Disadvantages of the private sector of pensions

The deficiencies of occupational pensions are highlighted by their failure to meet the needs of those with insecure employment. Very few schemes have any provision for redundancy and as many as 1 million employees have been compelled by job loss to withdraw from their pension schemes (James, 1984, p. 8). Occupational pension schemes are designed by men with male career patterns in mind. Women tend to have lower earnings than men, experience interruptions in earnings due to child-rearing, and are much more likely than men to work part-time. Thus only a quarter of women in the private sector are in such schemes compared with one-half of men, whereas in the public sector the figures are 55 per cent and 90 per cent. Most private pension schemes not only exclude part-time workers but also assume that earnings peak in the final year of employment. This latter assumption not only disavantages women but also many male manual workers as well, which is why the state scheme introduced in 1975 was based on the best 20 years of earnings.

Occupational pensions cement inequalities between different groups in the labour market and ensure that they are carried into retirement.

The higher paid are more likely than the lower paid to benefit from them and from the tax subsidy that goes with them. Because of the greater proportion of manual workers in private pension schemes who leave early or die prematurely there is an effective redistribution of contributions from the less well off to the higher paid. Tax reliefs on pension contributions too are redistributed from the general population to the higher paid.

There is an enormous duplication of administration in the private pensions sector, with 100,000 schemes averaging at one per 120 contributors and 40 pensioners (James, 1984, p. 16). This means that the total cost to the nation of retirement pensions is higher than it would be if administration were unified. Moreover, because pensions rely on returns from investment, which are by their nature uncertain, the management of most schemes will include a margin of error against the event of lower than expected returns. Overall this necessary prudence involves substantial excessive contributions (Reddin, 1984). Government proposals to enlarge the private sector of pensions, therefore, are likely to *increase* the national cost of providing for income in retirement even though the Exchequer cost will be reduced.

One final cause for concern about private pensions: there is no semblance of democratic control over the pension funds, even though they hold in trust the future pensions of some 11 million employees and benefit to a considerable degree from state subsidies. In support of its case for the privatisation of pensions the government argues that 'what is certain is that everybody will be able to rely on the fact that their future pension is their own property' (DHSS, 1985b, p. 9), but occupational pensioners have less control over their pensions than do public sector pensioners. The enormous power of the pension funds and the financial institutions which manage most of them is a relatively unexplored aspect of social policy (one exception is Minns, 1980) but they are likely to come under close scrutiny in any discussion about the restoration of full employment and the need to ensure investment in home-based employment – in short, how to provide tomorrow's pensioners with jobs today.

The reform of state pensions
Because of the continuance of widespread poverty in old age despite the introduction of NI pensions in 1948 several attempts have been made to improve the basic pension. The graduated pension scheme, initiated in 1961, was intended to provide a measure of earnings relation for those not in occupational schemes. At the time it was introduced it would have given an average earner a graduated pension of about half the basic pension. But unfortunately limitation – indeed, the progressive reduction – of the Exchequer contribution of the financing of the scheme was again uppermost in the (Conservative) government's considerations and a clear link was drawn between this and making employees responsible for financing their own retirement (Shragge, 1984, p. 94). As a result the scheme was conceived in cash terms only, with no allowance for inflation, this meant that the pensions were quickly eroded and by the time it was superseded in 1975, the graduated additions were of little consequence to individual pensioners (Bornat, Phillipson and Ward, 1985, p. 26). In order to encourage private pension schemes the option of contracting out of the state pension scheme was allowed for those whose occupational pension schemes met a prescribed minimum standard.

In 1970 a small pension was provided for those over 80 who were too old to join the NI scheme when it began in 1948. In addition, a widow's pension was introduced for women widowed between the ages of 40 and 50 years. In the same year an attendance allowance was introduced for severely disabled people, including those over retirement age, who required attendance. Measures such as these provide small-scale supplementation to retirement income; they were not intended to tamper with the pensions structure established in the immediate post-war period. The only attempt to overhaul that structure, that reached the statute book, was the new pension scheme introduced in 1975 by Barbara Castle.

The Castle plan represented a compromise between the more radical plan prepared by the previous Labour Secretary of State for

Social Services, Dick Crossman, and the Conservative plan prepared by Sir Keith Joseph. The TUC, through the mechanisms of the Social Contract, exerted a considerable influence on the formulation of the Castle plan. One way in which this was demonstrated was the support given to the contributory principle, which was then regarded by trade unionists as a guarantee of protection from government economies (a view that was to change rapidly when the Conservative government started cutting national insurance benefits in 1980). The White Paper, *Better Pensions*, which embodied the Castle plan, identified the main problems with the current system as the inadequacy of the state pension forcing large numbers of pensioners to rely on supplementary pensions, and the failure of occupational pensions to protect widows, those changing jobs and to provide adequate protection from inflation (DHSS, 1974). The government's response to the latter problems was not to legislate for a thoroughgoing reform of occupational pensions but to use the state pension scheme as an example for the private sector and to subsidise the latter's pension provision.

As well as the employment test, the new pension scheme retained earnings-related benefits and earnings-related contributions from the pre-1975 scheme. Where the scheme represented a significant departure from previous practice was in the provision for both state and occupational benefits to be protected against inflation by the state. Pensions are not due to be paid out in full until 1998 after 20 years of contributions have been made. When the full maturity of the scheme is reached – or rather, if it is – an individual's state earnings-related pension (SERP) will be calculated on the basis of the best 20 years of earnings, revalued in line with the growth in earnings generally and averaged, rather than on the final year's earnings basis of most occupational schemes. For the reasons outlined earlier this mechanism offers a better pension to manual workers than the final-year one. An attempt was also made in the new scheme to improve the position of widows and other women. It allows the spouse to inherit the full SERP entitlement of a contributor, provided both are over retirement age and provides for home responsibility credits for the basic pension for those looking after children. This relative 'generosity' to women has been the source of much criticism (Bornat, Phillipson and Ward, 1985, p. 31).

Perhaps the most important aspect of the 1975 new pension scheme was the measure of integration it forged between the public and the private sectors of pensions. Occupational pension schemes are allowed to 'contract out' of the SERPS providing they meet certain minimum standards, for example the pension must have an annual accrual rate of at least 1/80 of pensionable salary for every year in the scheme up to 40 years and the pensions of early leavers with at least five years pensionable service must be transferred or preserved. In return for a rebate on national insurance contributions, contracted-out employers guarantee that employees will receive a pension – the guaranteed minimum pension – at least the size of the one they would have received under SERPS. In addition the government accepted the responsibility for inflation-proofing these occupational pensions once they were being paid, up to a maximum of the same pension as someone in a similar situation under SERPS. In view of the failure of the private pension industry to protect their pensioners from inflation and the closure of many pension funds, particularly in the mid-1970s, this policy must have seemed like a life-line to the pension companies. As Shragge (1984, p. 147) points out, the Labour government was unwilling to take on the powerful pension funds and risk disruption of the economy and, therefore, it had no choice but to 'bail them out at the point of their major weakness – inflation'. Not surprisingly the new pensions scheme was endorsed by both the pension companies and the Conservative party.

Where does this major pension reform leave pensioners in the mid-1980s? The most important point is that the 1975 reforms did not do anything for those already retired and those expecting to retire in the near future. The whole debate then, as now, was centred on what the current generation of younger adults would pay *themselves* when they retired. In short it offered no solution to the problem of poverty among existing pensioners. Meanwhile, with public attention focused on the future cost of pensions the needs of today's pensioners have been completely overlooked. It is assumed that because we are being 'too generous' to ourselves in the future, we are being equally generous to them. While the promise of a basic subsistence pension enhanced by SERPS has been held out to those retiring at the end of the century, many of those already in retirement must rely solely on the subsistence pension and, if they are prepared to claim it, supplementary benefit. The argument that pensions were inadequate was accepted, but only for those retiring in 20 years' time.

Secondly, it provided for the institutionalisation of two nations in old age in the next century, not according to membership of occupational schemes but on the basis of access to earnings-related and inflation-proofed pensions. Three groups of pensioners will be created: those previously employed by a company with an occupational pension who will receive a basic pension, an occupational pension and possibly a SERPS top-up; those contracted into the SERPS who will receive a basic pension and the earnings-related pension; and those with irregular employment records, those who were never employed in pensionable employment including many part-timers and those who provided unwaged domestic labour. Women, people with disabilities, ethnic minorities and others prone to experience disadvantage in the labour market are the most likely to benefit from a pension system based on both an employment test and on the level of earnings achieved in employment. Because pensions are earnings-related, moreover, they will perpetuate earnings inequalities in retirement. Thirdly, instead of addressing the fundamental inequities of the private pension system the new pension provided for the continued survival and possible expansion of occupational pensions. Instead of opting for a universal pension scheme the Labour government chose to maintain the substantial income inequalities between different groups of pensioners and increased the likelihood that the oldest pensioners will continue to be the poorest (Walker, 1981, p. 85).

The future of pensions
What of the future? It can be seen that the Green Paper and White Paper on the reform of social security, issued in June and December 1985, are but the latest in a long line of similar reports which have been consumed with the future cost of state pensions, but oblivious to the needs of present pensioners and the deficiencies of the private sector. Echoing the Phillips Committee both the Green and White Papers are primarily concerned with restricting the public sector of pensions and expanding the private sector. In support of greater individual and private provision for retirement the Green Paper quoted a famous passage from Beveridge in which he argued that state provision should not stifle individual initiative (DHSS, 1985a, p. 2). However, while Beveridge recognised the case for occupational pensions, he argued that 'The existence of this independent provision is not a reason which should lead the State to avoid making comprehensive adequate provision of its own for everybody in old age' (Beveridge, 1942, p. 93). There is no sign in either the White Paper or its Green predecessor that this principle has been accepted by the government. True, commitment is expressed to the basic pension, but steps have already been taken to reduce its value relative to earnings. Moreover it was in response to the failure of the private sector to provide adequate additional cover that the Labour government, with all party support, introduced SERPS in 1975.

It is impossible, of course, to predict the outcome of the debate about SERPS which depends largely on the result of the next election. If the government's proposals are adopted SERPS will be severely reduced in scope and effectiveness. The limited gains made by some manual workers and women under SERPS will be wiped out. Under the 'new partnership' between state provision and occupational and personal provision the inequality between pensioners with and without occupational pensions will be re-established. Again it will be those who are disadvantaged in the labour market who will not benefit from the private sector and the mounting fiscal expenditures which sustain it. If the Conservative government is returned at the next election, the long-term goal of the Green Paper – 'a position in which the state provides a basic pension for all; and everybody also has his [sic] own additional pension for which he has saved through his job' (DHSS, 1985b, p. 5) – would be sought not by the abolition of SERPS but by the purposeful withering of the scheme. This process would leave increasingly large numbers of pensioners with only bare subsistence pensions and many manual workers to the uncertainties and insecurities of the private pensions market. This would seem to be a recipe for private affluence for those with sufficient incomes and security of employment to benefit from the best occupational schemes and public poverty for those who have not.

The Production of Poverty in Old Age
State pensions and other social security benefits have failed to eradicate poverty. Poverty in old age may be seen as one form – usually the most extreme one – of the multifaceted dependent status that most elderly people occupy (Walker, 1981b; 1982c). The inadequacy of explanations of this economic dependency couched in individual terms such as 'disengagement', 'frailty' or 'failing abilities' has been exposed (see Chapter 2; Walker, 1981b). Rather, various social policies have combined to create, enhance or maintain economic dependency and poverty in old age. Thus poverty in old age is primarily a function of low economic and social status prior to retirement and the depressed social status of the retired and secondarily, of the relatively low level of state benefits. In view of the detailed account of this structured dependency provided by Peter Townsend in Chapter 2, it is necessary only to outline the main points. Policies in employment and social security have been particularly influential in the production of poverty in old age.

Retirement policies
The growth of retirement and subsequently, early retirement, has ensured that an increasing proportion of elderly workers have been excluded from the labour force over the course of this century. This social process of exclusion has denied older people access to earnings and the other economic, social and psychological aspects of the workplace. This major social change has progressed rapidly and continues to do so. Between 1931 and 1971 the proportion of men aged 65 and over who were retired increased from under one-half to more than three-quarters, and by 1984 the figure was around 94 per

cent. Thus in a relatively short space of time 'old age' has come to be socially defined as beginning at retirement age and, whether by institutional rule or customary practice, the age at which older workers have to leave the labour force (Parker, 1980, p. 13).

The operation of this social process of exclusion has been closely related to the organisation of production and the demand for labour. Accounts of the emergence of retirement and early retirement suggest that older people have, in fact, been used as a reserve army of labour to be tapped when labour is in short supply, and to be shed when demand falls (Graebner, 1980; Phillipson, 1982; Walker, 1985d). It is *not* that retirement has grown alongside industrialisation – large numbers of older people were economically active in all industrial societies during the first half of this century – but that changes in industrial processes and in the organisation of employment have been developed and managed in ways intended to exlude older workers. Work processes have been reorganised, the division of labour has increased, and the labour process has been rationalised (Braverman, 1976). Various factors have combined to ensure that older workers were the most likely to be affected by these changes. For example, the influential scientific management school of thought in the USA argued that efficiency in the labour process depended on the removal of those with low levels of marginal productivity, which was crudely related to age; the historical tendency of capital to reduce its necessary labour to the minimum; the process of technological innovation and the high birth rate of the early 1960s all provided some impetus for the displacement of older workers and, where necessary, their replacement with younger ones (Walker, 1983c, p. 153). Finally the advent of large-scale unemployment in the 1930s was crucial in the institutionalisation of retirement, and its return in the early 1980s has resulted in the growth of early retirement.

These main factors in the twentieth-century development of British capitalism have combined to reduce the demand for older workers. At the same time, on the supply side, as retirement and early retirement have been encouraged by employers and the state they have been accepted as customary and have become part of trade union bargaining for improved labour conditions. Moreover, many of the changes in production processes, such as the spread of assembly-line production, have reduced the attachment of workers to employment and, together with the failure of employers and the state to improve the working conditions of many, has contributed to a desire to leave work (Phillipson, 1982).

This indicates that, like the experience of employment, attitudes towards retirement and the experience of retirement itself are socially divided. There are those, mainly salaried workers, who are able to choose whether or not to leave work at the retirement age or to leave prematurely or perhaps to work on. The proportion of self-employed people working beyond retirement age is double that of those employed by others (Walker, 1983c, p. 155). Then there are those, predominantly manual workers, who are effectively coerced into retirement and sometimes early retirement by poor working conditions, ill-health, redundancy and unemployment (Palmore, 1978; Olsen and Hansen, 1981; Walker, 1985d). Thus for large numbers of older workers poverty is created *prior* to retirement. In fact sickness and unemployment account for nearly two-thirds of men and one-quarter of women who retire prematurely (Parker, 1980, p. 10). A recent study of 'voluntary' early retirers found that two important factors were health and dissatisfaction with their job (McGoldrick and Cooper, 1980, p. 860). So, for a significant proportion of older workers the retirement age is effectively lowered by unemployment, sickness or injury. As with unemployment itself, semi-skilled and unskilled workers are over-represented among the early retired (Parker, 1980, p. 16).

The policy of disengaging older workers prematurely from the labour force was formalised in Britain in 1977 by the introduction of the Job Release Scheme, which was 'designed to create vacancies for unemployed people by encouraging older workers to leave their jobs' (Department of Employment, 1980). Similar policies have been introduced in other countries, including France and Sweden (Laczko and Walker, 1985). As unemployment has risen in this country so the numbers taking part in job release have increased, to beyond 100,000 in 1984.

Pension policies

The corollary to this social process of exclusion from the labour force is that elderly people are heavily dependent on the state for financial support – around 90 per cent of them receive some form of social security benefit. Elderly people are, in effect, trapped in poverty by their reliance on state benefits, which have already been shown to be inadequate.

The implicit rationale, or social policy, underlying the income differential between those in employment and those dependent on state benefits is the assumption that social benefits are intended to maintain monetary incentives and the work, or rather employment ethic. Thus, paradoxically, even those groups such as the elderly which have worked for a full term are not entitled to non-dependent status, nor freedom from reliance on minimum subsistence income support unless it has been earned through contributions paid to a private pension while in employment. We have seen that retirement has a differential impact on elderly people – depending primarily on prior socioeconomic status and the access it grants to resources which might be carried into retirement – but, in addition, because of the social limitation on the level of state pensions and other benefits for those outside the labour force, retirement imposes a lowered social status on the vast majority of elderly people in relation to younger adults in the labour market (Walker, 1980). Hence the substantial inequalities both among elderly people and between the elderly and the rest of society, which were outlined earlier.

The dependency relationship between elderly people, the state and the labour market was institutionalised by the 'retirement condition', introduced in 1948, whereby state pensions are conditional on retirement rather than age. This has encouraged an end to labour force participation and has established an arbitrary age as the customary retirement age. Ironically, Beveridge had hoped that the retirement condition would encourage workers to defer retirement:

> Making receipt of pension conditional on retirement is not intended to encourage or hasten retirement. On the contrary, the conditions governing pension should be such as to encourage every person who can go on working after reaching pensionable age, to go on working and to postpone retirement and the claiming of pension. (Beveridge, 1942, p. 96)

But, in practice, it has resulted in the adoption of the pension ages as the retirement ages. Together with the high marginal rates of taxation levied on pensioners who take up employment by the notorious earnings rule, it militates against the continuation of work by the elderly. More recently the social security system has been used to further encourage the disengagement of older men from the labour market by awarding the long-term rate of supplementary benefit to those over the age of 60 who are unemployed. Originally this was conditional on them not registering as unemployed.

The social security system is also one of the main mechanisms through which women's dependence on men is enforced both prior to and after retirement (see Chapter 4). Most women still receive pensions as dependants on their husband's contributions and, regardless of their age, have to wait until he reaches 65. Although the Social Security Act 1980 introduced some improvements in the status of women these are only a tentative first step towards 'similar treatment' for women and men rather than equal treatment. Furthermore, until equality between men and women is established in the labour market it is unlikely to be realised in a social security system which is geared to the labour market. Elderly married women are less likely than men to receive a NI retirement pension in their own right and are overwhelmingly less likely to receive a pension from a former employer. Older women are much more likely than men to live in poverty.

This brief review of employment and pension policies is sufficient to indicate that the economic dependency of elderly people – and therefore their poverty – has been socially manufactured partly in order to facilitate the removal of older workers from the labour force. In the interests of narrow financial efficiency and increased profitability mass superannuation has been managed through retirement, early retirement and unemployment among older people. Age-restrictive social policies have been used by the state both to exclude older workers from the labour force and to legitmate that exclusion through retirement. This socially reconstructed relationship between age and the labour market has not only been the primary cause of poverty in old age, but has also formed the basis for the spread of a more general dependency among the elderly, as well as ageism in many aspects of public policy and wider social attitudes.

An Alternative: Effective Social Security in Old Age

Far from eradicating poverty in old age the present system of employment and pensions has contributed to its institutionalisation. An alternative is required to ensure that all pensioners can enjoy a secure old age, free from poverty and deprivation. However one of the prime lessons to be drawn from the analysis of poverty presented here is that genuine social security for elderly people, as opposed to the unfulfilled promise of the Beveridge welfare state, implies major stuctural change rather than reform. Substantial changes will be required in three areas of policy if this goal is to be realised.

Starting with the labour market, as the source of most of the inequities that are carried into retirement, major changes are required in the structure and organisation of work to give older workers access to employment and a genuine choice about retirement. This means a reverse of previous practice, since one of the guiding principles of employment policies over the last 20 years has been the superannuation of older workers. The promotion of full employment throughout the economy is the only realistic way that choice can be restored to older workers. In addition, changes are long overdue in work processes and practices to avoid the creation of ill-health and disability which result in early retirement and early poverty. Then flexible retirement, with a minimum pension age of 60 for both men and women, would provide opportunities for older people to choose when precisely to retire, an option that many older people favour (Walker and Laczko, 1982).

Turning to pensions, it is necessary to begin to plan pensions provision on the basis of the *overall* cost to the nation (Reddin, 1984, p. 14). With an overall contribution of £50,000 million per annum to retirement income, the pensions of all elderly people could, in theory, be trebled and the future cost of SERPS be met without difficulty. This reallocation is not a serious practical proposition but it does indicate that the necessary resources are available if we want to use them to provide security for *all* elderly people. The main issue is really whether or not the government is prepared to ensure that this is achieved through the public sector. The state is demonstrably the most efficient body to transfer resources from the working population to pensioners. It is only the most dogmatic of ideologies that could propose to transfer responsibility for providing a substantial proportion of pensioners' income from the security of SERPS to the uncertainty and insecurity of the private sector. This much was accepted by Beveridge in his damning analysis of voluntary insurance in the inter-war period (Beveridge, 1942, p. 282), but unfortunately this criticism was not translated fully into his recommendations. Subsequent experience of occupational pensions has done little to challenge his conclusions that such private welfare provision is inefficient, wasteful and more costly than state insurance.

In contrast to the focus on what we pay ourselves in the form of future pensions in the debate surrounding the Green and White Papers on social security and, indeed, in most public discussions on pensions since the war, priority should be given to the needs to today's pensioners – their needs are most pressing. In view of the failure of occupational pensions to provide security in old age to all but a few, it is to the state that we must look for social security. The priority is the provision of an adequate flat-rate pension. This is the most straightforward answer to poverty. It would be paid at a level that enables elderly people to participate in the normal life of the community. The depressed aspirations and gratitude of pensioners have been used for too long by politicians to evade the need to increase the basic pension substantially. This is an urgent priority and the pension might then be increased steadily as a proportion of gross average earnings until it reaches a participation standard of probably around two-thirds.

The contribution or employment test which discriminates against substantial numbers of pensioners, especially women, should be abandoned. All pensioners have a need for income *regardless* of whether their previous employment was waged or unwaged.

The role of SERPS or any other earnings-related pension in this social security package is less certain than that of the basic pension. There is no case for the abolition or curtailment of SERPS without redistributing the resources fully to the basic pension. However priority should be given to the basic pension and at least some, if not all, of the money spent on SERPS could be used to improve it. Moreover it is difficult to justify a state earnings-related pension when such a large proportion of pensioners live in abject poverty. SERPS should be modified to end the subsidy to the private sector, in the form of the support it gives to guaranteed minimum pensions, and restricted to a narrowed band of earnings, up to twice average earnings.

These changes could be paid for in large part by the reduction in the coverage of SERPS and ending the concessions and other subsidies to the private sector.

Is there a role for occupational pensions? These appear to have reached a peak in their coverage at half of the workforce, despite the encouragement provided by generous tax subsidies. It remains to be seen whether or not even more generous tax incentives will have the desired effect. However, the very notion of *occupation* as a basis for long-term pension policy must, as Mike Reddin (1985, p. 46) has pointed out, be precarious in view of the unpredictable nature of the availability of current and future employment. Thus the main source of pension provision should be the public sector. There is no need to abolish private pensions but the case for subsidising them from the Exchequer would disappear under the social security system proposed here. However the state could offer to take over the liabilities of employers, although, of course, it is not employers that finance occupational pensions but workers and consumers. Legislation is required to ensure that private pensions provide adequate benefits in return for contributions and allow people to change jobs without loss of pension rights. Moreover, the most efficient basis for portable pensions remains the NI system which already provides a fully portable pension.

Within this pension package the priority needs of some groups of elderly people will need to be recognised. Older people with disabilities are often the most disadvantaged and there is need for an additional disability pension to meet some of the extra costs of disablement. Then there is equality between the sexes. The abolition of the contribution condition would improve the position of women but this must also be linked to disaggregation and the payment of pensions on an individual basis if married women's dependence on their husbands is to be prevented.

Finally, policies are required to ensure that elderly people are able to control their own affairs, including the operation of both public pensions and private pension funds, which are in existence primarily to serve elderly people.

Conclusion

Poverty in old age is one of the major social problems confronting British society. The concentration of poverty and deprivation in old age has persisted despite social recognition for over a century and more than 30 years of welfare state provision. The recurrent issue of pension reform has always been dominated by concern with a narrow conception of cost: direct Exchequer expenditure. Limitations have been placed on this form of public expenditure, while fiscal and occupational costs, which also fall on the whole community, via higher taxes and prices, have been allowed to multiply unchecked. The fact that the needs of elderly people have rarely been central to discussions of pensions reform is a major failing of post-war social policy. Part of the problem is that social policies themselves have been employed to regulate the economy and labour force rather than to meet need. The main lesson from successive pension reforms, including the latest proposal to reduce the scope of SERPS, is that unless there is a fundamental restructuring of the relationship between age and the labour market, on the one hand, and the incomes of pensioners and those in employment, on the other, poverty will persist into the next century and beyond. Resources have been available to provide for social security in old age for at least the last 40 years but the political will has not.

Acknowledgement
Thanks are due to Mike Reddin for his extremely helpful comments on a draft of this chapter.

11 Housing Policy and Elderly People

Rose Wheeler

The need for shelter is universal. Regardless of age, it represents a basic requirement comparable with food or clothing. But housing not only provides people with shelter, it also embodies rights, responsibilities and opportunities distributed differentially across the population as a whole, and over the life-cycle. As a form of provision it is both permanent and expensive. For many elderly people, more than half and sometimes all their waking activities are confined to the home.

Major reliance on the private sector and, related to that, on private lending from building societies to enable people to buy their own homes, has characterised government policy in the UK since the Second World War, regardless of political persuasion. Owner-occupation has taken over from the private rented sector as the major housing tenure, and public responsibility for housing provision has been increasingly restricted to the homeless, the construction and management of housing for those not able or wishing to become owners, and the 'special' housing needs of the disabled and the elderly. The ideological shift of the Thatcher government away from state welfare provision and planning has meant a further boost for home ownership, and severe reductions in government expenditure on housing (Forrest and Murie, 1983).

Within this framework this chapter starts by presenting the housing situation of older people. A picture of extensive deprivation and of unequal opportunity, particularly in relation to younger, better-off households, is portrayed. Next, the policy response to this situation at both central and local government levels is examined. A number of issues are highlighted which spell out the separatist and often negative treatment of older people in the housing arena. So-called 'special' housing needs and problems that are identified largely as age-related, serve to mask the real reasons for housing deprivation in old age – low economic status and the impact of certain social and housing processes. Finally, the chapter examines issues for housing policy that are raised by the growing number of older households and the future direction of housing policy for old age. First, however, let us present a profile of older people's housing and the extent to which it differs from the rest of the population in terms of condition, amenity and warmth.

The Homes of Older People

The vast majority of older people (93 per cent) are to be found in homes of their own in the community. Of these, about 5 per cent live in sheltered accommodation with a warden. The rest live in a wide range of different types, ages and conditions of housing. Just over half of elderly couples, and 38 per cent of older people living alone, are home-owners (OPCS, 1984). Most of these own their homes outright, and this proportion is increasing, both as younger generations with higher levels of home-ownership reach retirement, and as growing numbers of local authority tenants take advantage of the government's commitment to council house sales.

Only 8 per cent of the population now live in private rented accommodation, but this includes a disproportionate number of older people. In the 1982 *General Household Survey*, 15 per cent of lone elderly households and 16 per cent of households headed by someone aged 80 or over, were living in homes rented from a private landlord. In the 1981 Census (Table 11.1), private landlords were providing homes for nearly half a million elderly people aged 75 or over (OPCS, 1983). Nearly half of single elderly households (42 per cent) and just over a third of elderly couples live in local authority housing. The higher proportion of lone elderly people found in this sector reflects the fact that three in every ten live in purpose-built flats or maisonettes (OPCS, 1983b).

Housing conditions

Although most older people live in satisfactory housing, those living in the private sector are much less likely to enjoy the relative comforts and amenities of purpose-built or council dwellings. Their homes are likely to be older, and as a result often tend to be in poorer condition, lacking amenities, and to be cold and difficult to heat. Elderly owner-occupiers, in particular, are much more likely than younger householders to be living in pre-1919 housing (DOE, 1983).

Older housing is more likely to be without basic amenities. In the 1981 Census over half a million elderly people – 6 per cent of all those of pensionable age – were living in homes without exclusive use of a bath or inside toilet, compared to 1 per cent of younger households. The proportion rose to 9 per cent of elderly people aged over 74, and to 11 per cent of lone female householders over that age. Nearly 395,000 people of pensionable age (including 30,000 aged 85 or over) live in homes that have no indoor toilet (OPCS, 1983).

Table 11.1 Tenure and amenity of older people's homes

| | Elderly households | | All households |
	One adult 60 or over	Elderly couple[a]	
	%	%	%
Tenure			
owner-occupied	38	53	55
local authority[b]	42	36	32
private rented	15	9	8
rented from HA[c]	3	1	2
Amenities			
lacking indoor toilet	7	4	2
without central heating	49	46	40
In purpose-built accommodation	30	14	—

Notes:
a. One or both persons aged 60 or over.
b. Includes renting from a New Town Corporation.
c. HA=Housing association.

Sources: OPCS (1984), DOE (1979).

A less easily measured aspect of house condition is its general state of repair. Regular repairs, if neglected, can lead to expensive housing problems; extensive damp resulting from a cracked gutter for example. Many elderly owner-occupiers are burdened with the upkeep of a family house that has now become too big (Tinker, 1981, p. 91). Findings from the 1981 English House Condition Survey illustrate this problem with 41 per cent of elderly owners living in 'poor' or 'unsatisfactory' houses (unfit or needing more than £2500 of repairs), compared to 22 per cent of owner-occupier households with a younger head (DOE, 1983). That survey identified a growing repair problem in the owner-occupied sector which is likely to increase as more and more older people own their own homes. Well over 1 million owner-occupied dwellings were found to need repairs costing £4500 or more (DOE, 1983).

In the private rented sector it may be difficult to get landlords to fulfill their responsibility to look after the fabric of the house, particularly if they themselves are elderly. Yet disrepair and dilapidation, as direct causes of damp, draughty and cold living conditions, can make homes particularly unsatisfactory for those who are at home most of the day or require a warm environment.

Heating and warmth
Warm houses are particularly important for the chronic sick or for those whose mobility is restricted in any way. Yet for a number of

reasons older people's homes may be particularly cold. Homes that are too big may be difficult or expensive to heat. Disrepair – for example, missing roof slates or crumbling pointing – causes draughts and loss of heat. Heating systems are often antiquated or inadequate. About half of elderly households have no central heating (see Table 11.1), and certain groups of people, such as those in private rented housing, are much less likely to have this amenity. The 1976 national survey of the elderly at home found that 30 per cent of those interviewed had no form of heating in the bedroom and a half had no means of heating their kitchen apart from the stove (Hunt, 1978, p. 50). So, although the majority of older people live in homes that are satisfactory, the housing and heating conditions of disproportionate numbers of this group still lag far behind the standard that most of the population in the UK have come to expect. Just how has this situation arisen, and in what ways have policy-makers and practitioners responded to it? We turn now to examine the policy context of housing in old age.

Housing Policies for Old Age

It is important first to distinguish two separate streams of policy that have been concerned with housing and older people. The first is concerned with housing provided specially for elderly people. In the second more recent stream of policy the primary issue has been the condition of the housing stock, with interest in older people a secondary concern. Here, housing policy has begun to develop with particular regard for older people because of their increasingly significant role in the dilapidation of the nation's housing stock.

Consideration of elderly people's housing has developed largely since the Second World War. Circulars and advice from central government have focused, since the 1940s, on the need to maintain independent living in the community; and central government, particularly since the late 1950s, has encouraged local authorities to build grouped accommodation with warden-sheltered housing as it came to be known in pursuit of this policy (Tinker, 1981).

For a variety of reasons sheltered housing was adopted in the 1960s and 1970s (and still by many in the 1980s) by both local authorities and housing associations, with few dissenters, as the panacea for the housing problems of elderly people (Thompson and West, 1984). Although some authorities had in fact provided very little (Social Services Buildings Research Team, 1977), sheltered housing presented those who work for health and welfare services, concerned to protect themselves from the consequences of the elderly at risk, with a solution which encompassed the best of care and accommodation. It provided a manageable and well-defined focus for a dialogue between housing and welfare professionals on housing need in old age and, moreover, it suited the needs of professional groups and politicians for policies capable of permanent and visible display. By the middle of 1983 there were 323,600 units of sheltered accommodation in England and Wales (House of Commons, 1984a, col. 73).

Until recently the belief that sheltered housing was the ideal solution to elderly people's housing needs went unquestioned. At the level of central government, little critical attention was paid to the issue, and there was widespread agreement by health and social services professionals and policy-makers with the sentiment expressed by Jeffreys that 'the single greatest housing need is for more purpose-built sheltered accommodation' (Jeffreys, 1977, p. 12).

From the late 1970s, the provision of sheltered accommodation as the main focus of policy was examined in a number of research projects. The most significant of these, the Leeds University sheltered housing research project (Butler, Oldman and Greve, 1983), was influential in presenting to a wider audience a number of important questions about this emphasis in policy. The main questions raised by the project concerned issues of equity and housing choice, and a central conclusion was that sheltered housing has created an élite whose housing needs differ very little from those of the elderly population in general. Moreover, the researchers questioned the appropriateness of this 'special' provision:

> What is not altogether clear is why somebody living in poor housing conditions should be seen as a candidate for a form of specialized housing, when apparently their requirements could have been met in other ways – either home improvements or a move to better quality housing. (Butler *et al.*, 1983, p. 39)

Growing awareness of both demographic and financial considerations has led also to some doubt as to the feasibility of a more extensive sheltered housing response in the face of escalating demand and costs.

In the political arena, some indication of a broader approach to housing in old age was embodied in a consultation paper in which 'longer-term' measures 'to widen the range of housing for old people' were considered (DOE/DHSS, 1976). The discussion document 'A Happier Old Age', produced by the Labour government in 1978, appeared to take this approach a little further by stating that guidance would shortly be issued to local authorities 'advocating that a wide range of housing options for elderly people should be developed' (DHSS, 1978, p. 29). Such a circular reached the stage of an advanced draft in 1979, but was shelved by the incoming government.

Since 1979, developments have been clearly subordinated to the priority of containing the growth of public expenditure (DHSS,

1981). Local authority housing budgets have been seriously curtailed, with a planned decrease in spending on housing by 1985 of 70 per cent (Murie, 1983e). Yet while financial controls have been more and more tightly implemented, central government has withdrawn from offering policy guidance to local authorities (Meadows, 1981). However, encouraging home-ownership and reducing local authority housing responsibilities to a residual role through financial and man-power constraints has served to focus attention firmly on the housing needs of 'special' groups in the local population. This focus has been a deliberate feature of residual housing policy, in part at least to defend it from its critics:

> We certainly intend to ensure that local authorities are able to build homes for those in greatest need and I have in mind especially the elderly in need of sheltered accommodation and the handicapped. (Michael Heseltine as Secretary of State for the Environment, quoted in Butler *et al.*, 1983, p. 70)

One other factor has served to reinforce this focus of policy. Housing associations, since the Housing Act 1974, have had a brief to house those with 'special needs'. A number of housing associations have specialised in the construction and management of sheltered accommodation and although they only provide one in five sheltered housing units, their focus on this type of housing provision has given them a vested interest in its development. Some housing associations specialising in accommodation for elderly people have begun to develop other initiatives such as the 'Staying Put' scheme to help elderly home owners with repairs and other work. However their main focus remains on sheltered accommodation with some new initiatives based on the extension of this type of housing to the private sector. Some have pioneered sheltered schemes which provide facilities for extra care, blurring increasingly the dividing-line between community and institutional care.

Home improvement policy
But while mainstream housing policy has grouped elderly people together as somehow 'special' in their need for housing, a recent development has instead come to understand elderly people as a 'problem' because of their contribution as home owners to increasing disrepair and dilapidation in the UK housing stock. This concern has led to some recognition of the particular difficulties posed by home ownership in old age, as described in 1983 by the then Minister for Housing and Construction:

> It is already clear that there is a heavy concentration of unimproved properties in a bad state of repair occupied by elderly people with

relatively low incomes. These are exactly the people who stand to derive most benefit from improvement and repair grants but who certainly need most help in taking advantage of them. (Stanley, 1983)

Awareness of the problems of elderly home owners came to light in the mid-1970s in the payment of housing repair costs for recipients of supplementary pension. Meeting such claims within benefit rates raised problems of equity with claimants from other tenure groups, particularly in view of the asset represented by home ownership (SBC, 1978). Moreover, income maintenance policy was not considered to be 'responsible for the standards of the country's housing stock' (SBC, 1980).

Pensioner households in the private sector have, over a period of time, increasingly become trapped in poorer and older housing, without the resources necessary to consider a move or to carry out repairs or improvements. Home improvement policy through the 1970s and early 1980s has failed to recognise the particular difficulties low-income owners have in maintaining or improving their homes. Policy has also achieved little success in securing improvements to housing in the hands of private landlords. Questions of need or equity in policies concerned with the distribution of funds for home improvement are conspicuous by their absence, and rateable value limits to restrict the eligibility of households for grant aid have done little to channel resources to those most in need of them. The 'first come first served' basis of grant distribution in most local authorities has, above all, penalised older people.

That owner-occupiers should be (or are) self-sufficient is the belief that explains central government inaction. Freedom from state intervention also helps to explain why private landlords have been safeguarded from action to improve the housing conditions of their tenants. The impact of these factors has, in time, been compounded by reduced levels of slum clearance in recent years, under-investment in improvement and replacement of housing, and unrealistic expectations about the life of older properties (Kilroy, 1982).

Both the private and voluntary sectors have offered a limited response to this neglect (Wheeler, 1982). In the private sector, building societies, wishing to extend their role beyond the traditional mortgage market, have begun to offer mortgages to older people for home improvement purposes, on which interest only is charged. Capital repayment is deferred until the house is sold or inherited. This is a similar mechanism to the 'maturity loan' used by some local authorities to help recipients of home improvement grants to afford their share of the cost of work.

In the voluntary sector housing associations and other voluntary organisations have grasped the opportunity of the scope for developing housing assistance for older people by setting up 'Staying Put' and 'Care and Repair' experiments which aim to help elderly home owners with repairs, improvements or adaptations to their homes. These initiatives have brought attention to the need for the home improvement process to encompass technical and organisational help (and sometimes social support), but a massive injection of funds would be required if they were to extend beyond their experimental role. A handful of local authorities, similarly, have developed their home improvement grant services, to encompass formal or informal agency help for elderly grant applicants.

In 1982, in a hurried but short-lived attempt by central government to increase local authority housing capital spending, improvement grant levels were increased to 90 per cent and councils were encouraged to spend 'without limit' on this aspect of their housing programme (*The Guardian*, 28 October 1982). It was only after increased expenditure on home improvement grants – their total value rose from £81 million in 1978–79 to £367 million in 1982–83 with estimated expenditure of £650 million in 1983–84 (House of Commons, 1983) – that central government began to consider the problem of home improvement in old age. The Treasury began to question the legitimacy of distributing grant aid on that scale indiscriminately to owner-occupiers (*The Guardian*, 20 October 1983), in the context of awareness of the growing disrepair in the owner-occupied sector and the failure of grant aid to reach those elderly and low-income owners most in need of it (DOE, 1983). Extensive and increasing dilapidation was in evidence in the very sector that 'had been supposed to create self-sufficiency' (Kilroy, 1982). Hurriedly commissioned research to examine the help needed by elderly home owners, and a wide-ranging review in the Department of the Environment of home improvement policy, led up to a Green Paper in 1985. Although likely to produce some welcome assistance with home improvement for these households, this focus has served to divert attention away from more fundamental issues (Wheeler, 1985b). In particular the findings of the English House Condition Survey bring into question the assumed (universal) benefits of owner-occupation, the self-reliance supposedly fostered simply by owning one's own home, and the current distribution of government subsidy to this sector.

The Housing Needs of Older People
Policy developments, therefore, have focused on needs and problems that are assumed to be peculiar to old age. But how far are older people's housing needs distinct or special? And what are the implications of this approach? In this section, it is argued that the policy response that has been based on separate housing solutions for 'old' people has diverted attention away from the diversity of their hous-

ing needs and from the underlying causes of their housing problems, and has prohibited the development of a more comprehensive approach to housing policies for older people. Moreover, a problem oriented approach – keeping old people out of institutional care and responding to the neglect of the housing stock – has largely ignored the housing needs of other groups in the population, for example elderly private tenants, homeless people and ethnic households. And age, like colour or sex, is used to provide explanations for problems that have more to do with social and economic processes and the structure of the society we live in.

The discussion of housing need in old age has developed out of concern expressed by Townsend (1962) and others in the 1960s to reduce the numbers of older people living unnecessarily in institutions. Sheltered housing, as a package of both good housing and additional care and security, was seen to provide a viable alternative which could foster independent living in the community. Thus, the development of sheltered housing provision came in the wake of a backlash against institutional care, with little idea underlying it of the housing need it was intended to meet. 'Need' for sheltered housing was instead defined in terms of target levels of provision for a particular percentage of the elderly population, calculated on the basis of broad indicators of self-care and mobility. Need for the component parts of the package – for age segregation or simply for warm, single-storey, easy-to-manage accommodation – and the possible drawbacks of age-segregated housing, were not considered.

In spite of widespread questioning of policy since the late 1970s, the problem of 'automatically conceptualising the housing needs of older people in terms of "sheltered housing for the elderly" continues to pervade analysis and provision' (Butler *et al.*, 1983, p. 213). In 1982, for example, Heumann and Boldy (1982, p. 25) went to considerable lengths to determine 'that subgroup which would most clearly and obviously benefit from sheltered housing'.

In the home improvement arena, too, the main focus on the lack of improvement activity of older households has served to deflect attention away from the real needs and difficulties experienced in carrying out building work or repairs to their homes. Voluntary organisations, in setting up 'Care and Repair' and 'Staying Put' schemes targeted explicitly at elderly people, have inadvertently reinforced an emerging misconception that the problem is largely age-related.

A critical look at housing need in old age reveals a number of related aspects. The first is need arising from relative deficiencies in house condition and embodying normative expectations of housing standards. Evidence of the relative housing deprivation of many older people, particularly in the private sector, was set out at the beginning of the chapter. Particular illnesses or disabilities, too, have implications for housing if they are not needlessly to become handicapping conditions. Stairs may be difficult to manage, or additional and constant warmth may be necessary. A variety of additional housing requirements are likely to exist for the five out of every ten elderly people aged 75 or over who experience a 'limiting long-standing illness' (OPCS, 1984). Yet if housing in the UK were predominantly single storey, as in Australia; if a wide range of housing types and sizes were available; if flexible provision enabled ease of moving between tenures and different areas; and if high standards of heating and insulation were commonplace, few older people would have housing needs that are distinguishable from those of the rest of the population.

Housing provision that includes an element of care or extra care, security or shared facilities is not a direct response to housing need. Rather it is a response to care or related needs which requires, or is enhanced by, a particular built form or environment. Moreover, the cost of sheltered accommodation would suggest that the proportion of 5 per cent of the elderly population currently housed in it is unlikely to grow substantially (Thompson and West, 1984). A housing policy is required that is directly related to housing need; that recognises the major role of adaptations or alterations to older people's houses, of repairs or improvements, of improved heating and insulation, and of easier transfer between tenures – particularly for home owners – and to different areas and to smaller accommodation. Such a policy would serve to reduce rather than preserve differences in housing status between younger and older households.

The Determinants of Housing Deprivation

How can we explain this single-mindedness and neglect of elderly people in housing policy? It is important to examine the role of professionalism, the contribution of housing processes and, most important, the impact of social and economic inequality throughout working life and in retirement.

The role of professionalism

The story of sheltered housing provision is in many ways an account of the exercise of professional power over the lives of ordinary people (Wilding, 1982). For example, Butler and Oldman (1983, p. 212) identified: 'the way in which the consumers of services, in this case older people, are relatively ignored, whilst the professionals concerned construct an elaborate framework of theory, supposition and myth which shapes their work'.

Health and welfare professionals who work with older people have often come to their own conclusions about where older people should live. Certain political and institutional factors have influenced these conclusions, but ultimately the prescriptive paternalism of professional wisdom has often determined the application of housing solutions for the elderly population. With little consideration of their views, older people have been moved to release their previous larger homes for family use; to make them less isolated and lonely; to reduce the risks associated with living in ordinary homes in the community. In her discussion of civil liberty in old age, Norman (1980, p. 7) describes the way in which this social construction of elderly people's needs compounds an already limited set of opportunities:

> Ordinary people are constrained by work income, housing, and a host of other factors which limit the range of courses open to them. For those who are frail or disabled and living on a pension, what they might like to do and what is physically or financially possible diverge still further. . . . However, there are ways in which society further restricts this narrowing range of choice by imposing on elderly people forms of care and treatment which are the fruit of social perception, social anxiety, convenience, or custom rather than inescapable necessity.

Older people's right to self-determination in housing is thus denied by a mixture of professional paternalism and restricted housing choice, with few real alternatives to sheltered housing on offer. A preoccupation with narrowly defined solutions, coupled with a failure to recognise or respond to disability in old age, has militated against a policy of home alterations and adaptations. Elderly people themselves are thus led to believe that dependency is a fact of life. Regular visits are made by social workers and health visitors to those thought to be at risk from the cold; home helps are relied upon to fill coal buckets; commodes have to be emptied because the toilet is upstairs or outside. The housing needs of older people with disabilities or bronchial, heart and other conditions, are translated into dependency and the need for welfare support (Wheeler, 1983a). House adaptations, though increasing, are still carried out for only a relatively small number of older people. Between 1981 and 1982, for example, social service departments spent £205 million on the home-help service, compared to only £4 million on house adaptations (House of Commons, 1982b). Occupational therapists, whose job it is to pursue measures such as adaptations to encourage independence, are thinly spread; not all local authorities employ them.

Professional decisions are compounded by the fact that, in most local authorities, no single department has overall responsibility for housing provision, and few have amalgamated private sector housing functions with the main housing department of the council. This departmental divide between private and public sector housing provides a further barrier to the development of a comprehensive approach to housing in old age. Moreover, many health and welfare professionals are unaware of the housing assistance and grant aid available for improvements and adaptations to private sector housing. Prescriptions, therefore, are offered within departmental boundaries or within the boundaries of individual professional expertise.

Housing processes and owner-occupation

Not only do private sector housing functions tend to be located separately, they also reflect certain assumptions about owner-occupation which have particular implications for older people. Home owners are viewed predominantly as a homogeneous group of self-reliant individuals, yet routine tasks of property maintenance may present insurmountable problems when income, physical strength, and organisational expertise are lacking. The same assumptions underlie the design of the improvement grant process which requires that applicants are capable and well-versed in dealings with all manner of trades and professions.

Yet in responding now to the under-representation of older home owners in the take-up of grant it is old age and not the grant system itself which receives the blame. The complexity of the grant system has thwarted many younger applicants, but this fact is obscured as elderly home owners become a scapegoat for a system which fails to provide straightforward and positive help with home improvements or repairs.

Although we have witnessed over the last few years the 'discovery' of the poor, elderly owner-occupier, there remains a strong association in many people's minds between owner-occupation and privilege. Life-cycle and class inequalities within tenure groups have been recognised by some writers (Merrett, 1982; Murie, 1983b), but the more usual snapshot picture of tenure differences often obscures the fact that most owner-occupiers, for the last 20 or 30 years of their lives, no longer receive subsidy in the form of mortgage tax relief, yet are likely to be living at lower income levels than younger households. As a significant group of building society investors, older people effectively subsidise younger households with mortgages (BSA, 1983b).

The increased emphasis under the Thatcher government on owner-occupation as the desired form of tenure has encouraged people to believe in the virtues and benefits of home ownership with little awareness of the difficulties and costs it involves. However, it is the elderly owner-occupier rather than any other older person with housing problems who has begun to attract attention, partly because of the preoccupation with this sector, but also because of the scope that exists for solutions by raising mortgage finance.

Social and economic inequality

But although housing processes are important, the roots of housing inequality 'lie deeper within economic and social processes' (Murie, 1983b, p. 225). The housing treatment of older people as a group with special needs or (as owners) representing a particular problem for the housing stock, fails to appreciate the social and economic inequalities that underlie their housing situation. In discussions and analyses concerned with house condition, explanations are often advanced for reluctance to repair or improve housing which emphasise the role of psychological characteristics such as inertia or resistance to change (DOE, 1978, 1983). Yet, in a recent evaluation of a scheme to help elderly owners with repairs or improvements ('Staying Put') we found that financial difficulty was by far the most important single reason for not carrying out improvements or repairs (Wheeler, 1985a). The inflation of building (particularly maintenance) costs makes it increasingly difficult for poorer owners to pay for repairs (Donnison and Ungerson, 1982, p. 196).

The starting point for an explanation of (housing) disadvantage lies in the social and economic institutions and processes which distribute resources prior to retirement (Walker, 1981b, p. 75). Inequalities thus created, Walker (1980, 1981b) argues, are compounded in old age by low resource levels that are 'socially determined', and which in turn further restrict housing comfort and choice. As Donnison and Ungerson (1982, p. 235) point out: 'some of the most intractable housing problems are not principally housing problems at all. Bad housing conditions are a product of poverty. If we retain a very unequal distribution of income and wealth, we shall not easily achieve a more equal distribution of housing'.

In owner-occupation, the house itself can be used to create additional resources by 'trading up' or, more commonly in retirement, by 'trading down' to a smaller property. But as we have seen, for an increasing number, home ownership represents disadvantage rather than opportunity. As builders have produced cheaper housing to attract lower and lower income purchasers, so many householders who can least afford it are burdened with the repair costs of poor construction. The building boom for owner-occupation in the 1930s, the sale of housing to sitting tenants when private landlordism has become unattractive, and the sale of council housing in the 1970s and 1980s, have all served to bring housing, not always in the best condition, within the reach of households on lower incomes (Ball, 1984).

In 1982, 336,000 pensioner owner-occupier households were in receipt of supplementary benefit (DHSS, 1983), with an additional weekly sum of only £1.80 (up to November 1985) to cover the cost of regular maintenance and the insurance of the property. Many more owner-occupiers in old age live at income levels only marginally above that of supplementary benefit. In 1975, 17 per cent of all households were living at incomes below 140 per cent of supplementary benefit level compared to 63 per cent of single pensioner owner-occupiers (Murie, 1983b, p. 121). In the English House Condition Survey: 'Of those owner-occupiers who would need to borrow three or more times their income [to carry out necessary renovation] . . . 77 per cent were headed by a person of retirement age and over half had an annual income below £1820' (DOE, 1983, p. 11).

The position of women living alone is likely to be particularly disadvantaged (Walker, 1981b, p. 87). As home owners, women are likely to experience additional problems with the finance and organisation of repairs, and they may be less familiar with the responsibilities of home maintenance, in many cases dealt with previously by their husbands. Similarly, as tenants lone elderly women may be less likely to identify housing defects to their landlords.

In housing, therefore, and particularly in the private sector, economic status, together with certain social and housing processes, underlies the disadvantages experienced by many older people.

Towards an Alternative Housing Policy
Housing need in old age has implications not only for policy for older people but for housing policy generally. There have been few housing studies that have focused on housing in old age and most have been concerned with a particular group rather than the population at large (Karn, 1977; Butler *et al.*, 1983). The wider implications for housing policy of an ageing society and the real challenge for the development of housing provision have been neglected. The main focus of housing policy and discussion has been on the point of entry and has shown much less interest in the (lengthening) tail end of people's housing careers. Some of the issues (and anomalies) raised when viewing housing policy from the perspective of later life are discussed below. The implications for housing finance, and for the wider spectrum of social policies concerned with the care of older people in the community, are considered briefly.

A look at housing finance from the perspective of old age raises a number of issues. In terms of subsidy, equity between different tenure groups becomes more complex when life-cycle considerations are taken into account. Most elderly owner-occupiers, for example, are outright owners and therefore no longer in receipt of mortgage tax relief. In a different setting, the housing and building control legislation, by favouring length of residence, increases considerably the subsidy available for older people to take out a mortgage to buy their home from the local authority (Murie, 1984). A 60 per cent discount on the purchase price for those resident for 30 years or more serves to enhance (with age) the incentive to buy. Research on council house sales has already shown this new group of owner-occupiers to be much older and with lower incomes than other first-time buyers (BSA, 1983a; OPCS, 1984). The current government's emphasis on owner-occupation and its merits are also given weight in policies which aim to make entry to home ownership easier. Young households are encouraged to pursue schemes to reduce or defer costs in the early years of a mortgage. There has been little consideration, however, of later stages in the life-cycle when the costs of owner-occupation may be equally hard to bear.

A growing interest in the use made by owner-occupiers of the equity 'stored' in their homes throws up further anomalies in policy. Mortgages are becoming freely available for older people on an interest only basis, for improving, repairing or adapting their homes. Mortgage annuity schemes, or home income plans as they are sometimes called, enable people over the age of about 75 to take out a more substantial mortgage on their homes (usually around 75 per cent) with which to purchase an annuity from an insurance company to provide income. Government policy encourages these schemes by making them eligible for option mortgage subsidy (now MIRAS) yet property repairs and maintenance are not eligible for this subsidy.

Encouraging the use of home equity in this way (Fogarty, 1981; Wheeler, 1986) raises some important questions for policy. A conflict may exist between policies which seek to develop the potential of pensioners' own homes to provide income, and policies which aim to encourage home equity to be reinvested in housing and its up-keep. More important perhaps is the question of the relationship between private and public funding. What criteria should be used to decide the balance between private (home equity) and public funding for improvements or adaptations to elderly owners' homes? How far should elderly owner-occupiers be expected to release home equity for other purposes, such as care, to reduce the call on public resources? Remortgaging in old age has received little critical attention as a development in policy (Wheeler, 1983b). Yet its impact and benefits will stem directly from the value of the properties involved, reflecting considerable regional and income inequalities.

The second issue for housing policy concerns the contribution of warm, easy-to-manage housing in policies concerned with the well-being of older people. The role of housing has been recognised in the narrow context of 'special' provision, but the right of older people living in their own homes in the community to warm and suitable living conditions has not appeared on the political agenda. Provision remains piecemeal and disjointed, militating against local housing policies that can recognise the importance of warm and suitable housing in the lives of older people.

A multidisciplinary (and inter-departmental) approach to housing provision for older people is required which encompasses a range of health, welfare and housing interests. In this way packaged solutions which include enhanced levels of care and security may become simply one housing option among many. Securing a similar standard and choice of housing for the rest of the local elderly population – by encouraging heating and other improvements, or adaptations to their homes, by making convenient new housing available, and by flexible arrangements to switch tenure or location as required – should become the central focus of policy. Warmer and more suitable housing for older people will contribute significantly to community care policies in helping to maximise independence in the home.

Conclusion

The justification for a comprehensive and multidisciplinary approach to housing policy in old age is twofold. To tackle the inequalities that result in substantial numbers of older people living in cold and dilapidated housing and, secondly, to develop housing policies that no longer serve to widen, but to narrow, the differences in housing status between older and younger better-off households. In continuing to support the belief that more sheltered housing is required, a housing policy for old age that fails to address questions of inequality and disadvantage is inadvertently endorsed.

The costs of home ownership for many older people are clearly very high. Real choice of tenure, with opportunities available throughout the life-cycle to switch from owning to renting, should be one aim of future policy.

A radically different approach to housing provision for older people, focusing flexibly on occupants and their needs, regardless of tenure, is required. The improvement (and adaptations) programme required will represent a massive call on public resources until beyond the end of the century (Kilroy, 1982, p. 130). Policies are needed to secure the upkeep of owner-occupied property, and the maintenance of homes after major repairs or improvement work has been carried out (Labour Housing Group, 1984, p. 63).

Complete replacement of some housing stock, and new building to include a choice of tenure and house type, including small, single-storey homes, will be important features of any strategy. New building, in turn, provides an opportunity for house design to become more flexible and geared to producing homes that are easy to maintain and manage, and easy and efficient to heat.

Mixed estates, and the use of infill sites for single-storey accommodation, will help to stem the creation of elderly ghettoes, or age-segregated accommodation. Housing for elderly people which is grouped together may contribute to an unnecessarily negative image of old age.

Above all, older people simply have a right to enjoy housing which is comfortable and which suits their individual requirements. This is no more and no less than expected by the majority of younger, better-off households in the population.

Acknowledgement
I would like to thank Ken Wright, Paul Wilding and Alan Murie for their helpful comments on an earlier draft of this chapter.

Part III

Alternative Policy Developments

12 Social Policy on Ageing in the United States

Jon Hendricks and Toni Calasanti

Understanding policy developments on ageing in America is a complex task, requiring a greater amount of theoretical sophistication than is often encountered in discussions of social policy. First and most importantly, we need to be aware that we are dealing not with a series of disjointed service strategies but rather with a multiformity of socially constructed decisions which serve both to define and to delimit the day-to-day experiences of the elderly in the United States. Investigation of social policy requires bearing in mind a number of considerations with regard to their formulation, their purpose and function, and their place in the larger culture of which they are a part.

In discussing American ageing policies we must be aware of two important arguments. First, the situation of the elderly cannot be understood apart from the political economy which created the institutional arrangements characteristic of free-market economies. Implicit is the view that the lives of older people depend in large measure on factors outside their personal influence and control. Secondly, we maintain that both state and private intervention policies designed for an older population replicate the status hierarchy and structural arrangements of the private sector in the later years. In either case it is a question of politics as well as demography in the determination of who is old, who gets what, and how it is to be distributed (Myles, 1984a and b; Estes, 1984). Two early proponents of the kind of political economy perspective utilised here – Estes (1984) and Dowd (1980) – suggest there is little in the current lives of the elderly or even in the pathways by which they attained their present standing that is not the result of factors operating during the early and middle years of their working lives. Until the real and present impact of these infrastructural arrangements are recognised, problems addressed by one generation will recur as equally pressing in subsequent generations. Whatever else social policy formulated to aid older people may do, it does *not* alter pre-retirement distributions of money, health or psychological well-being. In short, policies for older people take as given the conditions imposed by lifelong involvement in the social and productive system (Walker, 1980, 1981b).

Obviously, social policies must be discussed in relation to macro-level population changes as these underlie the distribution of both public services and values in any given society. As populations age – that is, when older cohorts grow disproportionately compared to younger cohorts – we might expect to see an increase in the so-called societal burden. It must also be borne in mind, however, that this ageing of the population means there is a decline in the numbers of the recently born and hence there is a decrease in the burden imposed by those at the other end of the age continuum. As a consequence, net public expenditures and related burdens may not be altered to any great extent. For the foreseeable future, the size of birth cohorts will be far more influential in the allocation of finite resources than what happens among older cohorts – unless, of course, some cataclysmic change strikes all older members of a society. So long as births remain at or below zero population growth levels, the United States will not experience a net growth in the number of 'dependent' persons before the middle of the next century.

In the light of these considerations, the present discussion seeks to fulfil two major functions: first, to provide an overview of the social policies on ageing in America; secondly, to set these policies within the context of the political economy which gave rise to them. We shall begin by reviewing economic, health and social policies designed for elderly people in the United States. We shall discuss how these policies came into existence, and explore their relationship with components of the national culture. This task necessarily involves an examination of the state, which legislates and administers public programmes, as well as its interrelationship with modern capitalism. Finally, we turn to the future. Here we are concerned not with an attempt at prediction but with an effort to highlight areas for further inquiry and, perhaps, intervention.

Financial Security for the Elderly in the United States
In the United States the advent of publicly supported old age assistance programmes came later than in most European countries. Faced with the poverty of the Depression era, declines in productivity, and what was viewed as a stagnating labour force, the first legislation was enacted in 1935. This was a turning-point in state support for the elderly. With its passage, social security set in place a new and dynamic relationship between public, private and individual welfare (Achenbaum, 1983). Individuals were provided with a goal towards which they could dedicate their working lives,

one which was felt to be their right by entitlement. At the same time, employers were relieved of corporate level complicity in the economic well-being of workers released on account of age. At a time when the United States had more workers than jobs, when industry was in major need of development capital as well as a stable labour force, no more optimal solution could have been found than to shift the responsibility to the public sector and dress it in the guise of altruism.

But the impact of the Depression (by the late 1930s over 50 per cent of elderly Americans were unemployed), demanded some type of intervention. With the 1935 Social Security Act, the United States joined other Western European states in legislating the right of needy individuals to minimal public support for their subsistence. As always, political compromises altered the intent of the original Bill, and the version of the initial Title I, which provided old age assistance, left it to individual states to set amounts and conditions of coverage rather than providing a national code. So strong were the feelings of states' rights that seven states declined to affiliate for a few years, preferring to retain their own Poor Law provisions in the determination of appropriate relief. Even the so-called social insurance movement prior to 1935 had realised the political realities of local administration and drawn up their charters to reflect regional proprietary interests. On the other side, the industrialists who served on Roosevelt's Advisory Council on Economic Security which helped draft the cumulative Bill, fought for as much federal control as possible in order to keep circumvention, competition and economic gain among employers from getting out of hand (Quadagno, 1984).

Not surprisingly, not all workers benefited from social security. In the early years it is estimated that only 60 per cent of the workforce was employed in occupations and industries included under the coverage. Even today, there are certain categories of workers who remain excluded or are insured under alternative federal civil service or state plans. Nearly all those who worked in occupations which were less industrialised or those marked by seasonal employment found themselves excluded from the benefit package. As Achenbaum (1983) notes, the same people who were subject to racial and other forms of discrimination in life as well as in the workplace found themselves on the outside looking in.

By 1939 the insularity of the adequacy and equity provisions of Titles I and II had begun to cause problems. Leaving it to the states to determine what was an adequate retirement benefit led to a tenfold disparity in benefits across the various states. As amended in 1939, social security sought to bring about a closer correspondence of adequacy and equity while assuring dependants of retired workers that coverage would be continued in the event of the wage earner's death. It also 'blanketed in' many workers who would not otherwise have qualified and set the system on a pay-as-you-go basis, thus avoiding having to build a sizeable trust fund. During the war years further amendments were proposed but in all cases met with little positive response. Acknowledging a debt to agriculture for its part in the war effort, the Wagner–Murray–Dingell Bill sought to include domestic workers and farmers, and provide a measure of health insurance to all recipients. The war economy seemed to be doing the job, however, by improving employment prospects for everyone; thus no expansion was deemed necessary or appropriate at that time.

Between the end of the Second World War and the mid-1960s, social security was amended on five occasions. With each revision additional occupations were incorporated, and cost-contributing formulas were rewritten. Disability benefits were added in 1956. Finally, the relative importance of Titles I and II shifted as more and more aged began to draw transfer payments under the latter while fewer sought welfare assistance under the former. With dramatic increases in the number of workers contributing, the modest appreciation in the numbers claiming benefits did not appear to be cause for alarm. Employers were also content as there was acceptance of their claim that their contributed portion was actually a workers' fringe benefit, and could be utilised to reduce taxable revenues. Concern over the adequacy of coverage or the importance of a retirement wage (Myles, 1984b) were seldom discussed as the economy continued to expand.

If there have been any glory years in the recognition of the needs of older Americans they came in the decade between the mid-1960s and the 1970s. During this period legislation for the elderly underwent major revision. Benefits were tied to the consumer price index, medical care was recognised as a necessary plank if the well-being of the elderly were to be placed on a sound footing, and a number of social service benefits were developed. However, no sooner were these various reforms implemented than a crisis was declared. The decade leading up to the present time has seen major retrenchments in federal policies or accusations against the elderly themselves for either not saving for a rainy day or an over-reliance upon mandated services. The policy – if it can be called that – since the 1973 publication of long-range deficits in the social security budget (Freeman and Adams, 1982), has amounted to little more than brinkmanship. Short-range or long, real or not, the perceived crisis in the provision of basic support to the elderly in the United States has promulgated a recessionist attitude, one which has had a substantial impact on social policies.

In general terms, there has been a politicisation of policies in relation to the elderly. In 1965, a number of reforms were enacted affecting older people. Not only was the social security programme itself amended, but passage of the Older Americans Act brought medical insurance and a number of other benefits to the elderly for the first time. As we shall see, besides increasing benefits for the elderly themselves, these changes also shifted the discussion of issues concerning America's older citizens into the political arena where they have been buffeted by the maelstrom of politics. And that is the bad news. It is not that benefit packages for any particular group should be sheltered from the political agenda, only that rhetoric does not necessarily lead to true consideration of alternatives, an examination of the larger economy lying behind the proclaimed crises or a rewriting of the original formulation. For example, in the initial drafts of the Social Security Bill, there was consideration of making the system self-supporting from payroll taxes. Late in the negotiations, however, President Roosevelt, mindful of the need to mend his political fences, added the self-financing stipulation. Further, the political debate of late has not looked to the dramatic swings in the American economy and their effect on payroll taxes. The language of politics draws attention to the most visible target, and is limited in taking much else into its focus. Before examining the political climate further, let us first bring the discussion of economic security up to date.

The decade after 1965 saw significant changes. First, benefits were increased by Acts of Congress and finally indexed to the consumer price index, thus maintaining replacement rates. Secondly, the original old age assistance programme was replaced with a supplemental security income (SSI) plan in 1974. The hope was that putting disposable income into the hands of the poor would, as the old Keynesian principles advocated, prime the pumps of private enterprise through public expenditure. SSI now has two components: a basic federal payment and an optional state supplement. To qualify, a person must either be over retirement age, or be blind or otherwise disabled. In addition, income must fall below specified parameters, as must other assets, and the recipient must meet standard residency requirements. For those who qualify and are not otherwise supported, the 1985 benefit level was $325 a month. Social security itself (technically, old age, survivors and disability insurance) is financed out of payroll withholdings. OASDI is withheld from pay cheques at a 1985 rate of 7.05 per cent (up to $39,600 annual earnings) and matched by an equal amount from employers. To be eligible, a retiree must have worked in covered employment (approximately 90 per cent of all occupations are included) for 40 quarters. Benefit levels are geared to earnings and may be received in full upon reaching 65 years. Earlier benefits may be claimed after reaching 62, but doing so results in a lifetime reduction of monthly payments. Should a worker elect to continue working after 65 years, benefits may still be earned but are subject to a 1985 means test of $7320 until age 70. Other sources of income after 65 years are not included in this proviso so those who have private pensions or unearned income may draw their benefits regardless of other income. For those who draw social security only, replacement rates are presently slightly over one-half of income received in the years immediately prior to retirement. As a general rule, single people, women and ethnic minorities receive slightly less, and males, whites and couples receive slightly more than the average income for older US citizens.

The latest round of amendments to the Social Security Act came in 1983. They were designed to insure solvency over the next 75 years by reducing benefits, raising the rate and ceiling of taxation, and enlarging the number of covered occupations. In addition, after the year 2000 retirement age will be raised to 67. Together with demographic shifts – the low birth rates of the late 1920s and the 1930s will mean fewer retirees in the 1990s – these changes will ensure that adequate finance is available to the system as a whole as worker/retiree ratios are stabilised. Of course, none of these calculations considers the fact that lower birth rates reduce the number of dependants at the other end of the age continuum. If the system is left as it is, the real crunch will come when the 'baby boom' cohort begins to retire. Again, however, a more important aspect of the system's well-being is future trends in national productivity (affecting employment rates) and fertility rates (Munnell, 1984).

At the time of writing, the prospect of a cost of living adjustment freeze is a real possibility. With 1985 poverty thresholds of approximately $5000 for a single person and $6300 for a family headed by a person over age 65, the threat of poverty level subsistence is real for an additional half million older Americans, most of whom are women. If such a move is realised, it is estimated that 2.3 million more elderly will be living at or below the poverty line by 1990. In essence, this is a misguided attempt by the Reagan administration to reduce the federal deficit. Not only does it ignore the benefits paid to a variety of non-aged (but still deserving) groups who are now included in the categorical benefit package designed for the elderly, but it also ignores the complexity of the struggle behind a mass of statistics.

A huge number of private pensions are also available to American workers, but historically they have seen poor returns. For those who do receive a private annuity in addition to their social security payment, pensions are between 60 and 75 per cent of prior earnings. To ensure payment from private sources the Employee Retirement Income Security Act (ERISA) was passed in 1974 and a Pension

Benefit Guarantee Corporation created to guarantee payments. By mid-1984 private pension plans were the single largest pool of capital in the United States, having reached over $900 billion. The federal government, recognising that less than one-half of all workers were covered by private pension arrangements, has been concerned not to set policing and monitoring requirements too stringently to avoid discouraging the setting-up of new plans. The fact that half of the workers covered were not vested and thus at risk either by changing jobs or from poor performance of their pension funds does not appear to have been as significant an issue. How funds are invested and what interest rates are returned to the pension account is a hotly debated issue and many problems still remain. Between 1980 and 1982 private pension funds were abandoned at a record rate, placing an inordinate burden on federal insurance protection. For those funds that perform too well, a quirk in the law permits windfall profits to go to the pension company and not to individual beneficiaries. At present such surpluses total $1.1 billion, a share of which needs to find its way to those who may draw a pension (Keller, 1984).

Individual retirement accounts (IRAs) are another way to increase post-retirement income. They enable individuals to invest up to $2500 annually in banks, stocks and bonds and a variety of other sources, thereby reducing taxable annual income by an equal amount. This money may then be withdrawn upon reaching retirement age and is taxed at that time. From the early 1980s investment opportunities have been liberalised for individuals seeking deferred income through IRAs, and a similar broadening of interpretations under the ERISA regulations. It is quite likely that Congress will soon act to expand IRAs since they have proved to be popular among the electorate. At the same time, money invested in either of these two privately controlled locations is being used to promote capital investment by the vendors directly or via loans to other private enterprises.

Health Care Policies for the Elderly
Payment for medical costs incurred by the elderly was introduced in 1965. This was the culmination of a long period of debate within political and medical circles. Such assistance was first proposed by Teddy Roosevelt in 1908 as part of a plan for national health insurance. In various guises, similar legislation was proposed and defeated by those with a vested interest in keeping federal government out of medicine, and the structure of the medical professions. In 1957, however, a concerted push was made for coverage for beneficiaries of social security. Finally, in July 1965, a Bill which had undergone 80 revisions passed both Houses of Congress. Not only did the legislation

do nothing to change the health care delivery system but doctors and hospitals were permitted to select their own fiscal intermediaries to monitor payments. Politics, having made itself felt in the provision of medical attention, has left the elderly paying over half their own medical expenses and twice as much as the rest of the population for just the kind of care the Bill was intended to provide. That the focus of the insurance is on short-term, acute illnesses should not be regarded as mere chance. The American Medical Association did not mistakenly spend over $50 million lobbying against a Bill (Tiberi, Schwartz and Albert, 1977) which covered more than hospital expenses to acute care in its compulsory part and only added physician and limited outpatient services in the voluntary sector (Estes *et al.*, 1984).

Part A of Medicare provides basic hospital care to all who qualify for social security or railroad pensions, selected others who pay a premium, and to their dependants under stipulated conditions. Having paid a (1985) deduction of $400, beneficiaries receive insurance for 60 days' hospitalisation. After that time they may receive an additional 30 days provided they pay the first $100 a day; additional coverage is drawn against a lifetime reserve of 60 days and carries a deduction of $200 a day. If, after being in the hospital for three days, the attending physician prescribes treatment in an extended care facility, patients receive 20 days of care without charge and can then obtain an additional 80 days of care provided they are able to pay a daily deduction of $50.00. Since the Bill is constantly being amended, items that are allowable at one point in time may not be covered in subsequent hospitalisations.

Part B of Medicare is available for a monthly premium of $15.50 (in early 1985). Once an annual deduction is paid, the Health Care Financing Administration pays 80 per cent of approved charges. Principally, these are doctors' fees, office drugs or supplies, emergency room services, some house calls, prescribed treatments and services, and chiropractic care. A wide and confusing range of ancillary services are not covered and payment formulas are based on whether the doctor or patient submits the bill. As a result of the convolutions of the coverage, older patients are finding their health care expenses increasing twice as fast as their pension incomes.

A complementary Act, Medicaid, was passed as Title XIX of the Social Security Act. It provides medical welfare for the needy and is based on means-tested criteria. For those aged over 65 receiving supplemental security income, Medicaid provides basic coverage without voluntary contributions. The programme is funded jointly by federal and state governments and is, therefore, subject to state-determined eligibility regulations based either on categorical income determinations or on medical need – designed for those whose incomes may be above the threshold but who are otherwise unable to meet the expense of their treatment. Benefits under Medicaid generally correspond to those of Medicare. While Medicaid patients in theory are free to choose their physician and hospital, in practice it is increasingly the case that they are refused treatment or find local state proscriptions against many benefits. Since fee scales are set by the regulating bureaucracy and filing procedures are often complicated, doctors are often unwilling to treat the medically indigent.

A number of proposals are currently being made to limit medical coverage. In 1984, payment schedules were changed drastically. Hospitals are now reimbursed according to a formula of diagnostic-related groupings and not on the basis of actual costs incurred. If hospitals release patients before the stipulated cut-off period, the savings go directly to the institution on a *pro rata* basis. If care extends beyond the mandated cut-off point, no additional costs are reimbursed by the government. In a further effort to limit reimbursements, sweeping changes are being proposed in types of service, deductions and family responsibilities. For Medicaid alone, a fiscal year cutback of $1 billion was proposed for 1986. Limitations to Medicare are equally drastic, though there is little evidence to suggest the kinds of constraint being considered will result in significant net savings. According to many critics, the policies being proposed as cost-cutting measures are based more on the ideological positions of the decision-makers than on demonstrated savings potential. Though the cutbacks are defended on the basis of the proportion of the federal budget earmarked for the elderly, the US Senate Special Committee on Aging estimated that once programmes which are largely self-funded are set aside, the remainder actually account for only 4 per cent of the budget (Navarro, 1983; Estes *et al.*, 1983; Storey, 1983).

Social Provisions for the Elderly

The Older Americans Act 1965 provided for the development of policies relating to assistance, senior centres and social services. In addition, housing and travel subsidies are available under other federal laws and appropriations procedures. The Older Americans Act has become a target of deep budget cuts and changing domestic priorities under the Reagan administration. While provision for community services was originally deemed an important illustration of the government's recognition that unmet needs lie beyond the extension of economic and health insurance, those same services are now seen as liberal and inefficient, not speaking to or enabling the elderly and their families to provide for their own welfare.

Nutrition programmes have been subjected to major retrenchments and have now been reduced to nearly half their budgets of only a few years ago. The Food Stamp Programme, designed to ensure adequate nutrition to all poor, including the elderly, has similarly been severely cut. Since much of the financial assistance is in the form of grants to states for the provision of local services, it is not readily apparent just which client group will be most severely hit. What is known is that the current decisions made by the government undermine 20 years' effort to develop a coordinated service delivery system. Shifting the onus to individuals and families will result in a fragmenting of responsibility, and if the history of such moves is any indication, it may well sound their death knell as well.

Cost-containment strategies have also made deep cuts into housing subsidies. Before the present crisis, liberal subsidies were available both for construction and rent for elderly persons' housing. New proposals will raise the eligibility for rent subsidy to a level that will reduce the pool of eligible older persons by at least one-third (Storey, 1983). A related move will eliminate construction assistance and replace it with a voucher system which the elderly will use to acquire housing in the private market. If an administration proposal to count food-stamp assistance as income is approved, an even smaller number of elderly persons will be eligible. At present (1985), a two-year freeze on housing subsidies is in effect and it remains to be seen if the programme will be revived.

As might be expected, decentralisation of the actual operation of such social provisions means implementation is left to local administrative agencies. While the services that are provided are better than none at all, the ideological implications are significant. Local determination of adequate nutrition, social programmes and activities results in a multitude of delivery plans covering the whole continuum of effectiveness. It is at the discretion of local agencies to set ceilings on amounts, eligibility periods and scope of services, and whether or not to use the private sector in many instances.

As is the case in a number of welfare states, social programmes look better on paper than they are in fact: in the United States they look unsatisfactory even on paper. The reality, however, is even more disturbing. Criticism is easy, solutions are not. Regardless of the pitfalls of central control, delegation of authority to local and private agencies does not strike us as a way to enhance service delivery. As Estes and Newcomer (1983) point out, personal ideologies enter into the decision-making process. Cutting the pie into smaller slices is going to multiply the ideologies shaping implementation. The new federalism (as the decentralisation drive is commonly called in the United States) leaves most decisions in the hands of service providers, thereby eroding both quality and client input. The battle for reform must now be waged in the many jurisdictions where services operate, rather than in a central forum. At the local level, private interest groups are, if anything, more powerful than at the national level. Programme development and cost-containment strategies intermingle more when they are combined at the lower levels of the delivery network where private market considerations are more likely to hold sway. In short, social services are being decided at a level and by the type of bureaucracy that is more easily politicised, than influenced by corporate and private vested interests (Estes and Newcomer, 1983).

The Political Economy of Ageing Policy

Discussion of social policy and the aged has focused primarily on the plight of the elderly. In recent years, however, this trend has been reversed in a new strand of theorising. A number of North American analysts (e.g. Kutza, 1981; Crystal, 1982) have stressed the enormous expenditure on the elderly which has enhanced the quality of life for the majority while leaving a small proportion of the aged in virtually the same underprivileged position. Both argue – albeit from different vantage points – that allocations for the aged are sufficient, and point to either irrational or ineffective policy formation. Essentially, they take the various programmes outlined above as given, neither exploring the roots of the apparent lack of cohesion nor questioning the intent of these policies. Indeed, it is assumed that the reason why the elderly have been the recipients of numerous programmes is due to their 'political legitimacy' (i.e. society views the elderly positively as a 'deserving' group) as well as their 'political utility' – they represent a large number of potential votes (Meenaghan and Washington, 1980, p. 227). This group, more than others who also depend on state support, can therefore demand and receive more and higher benefit levels.

Missing in this formulation, however, are two crucial realities. First, the elderly actually played a very minor role in the initial development of policies designed to benefit them (Myles, 1983, p. 20); further, while the Social Security Act 1935 was intended to be age-based (Quadagno, 1984), the Act, together with other more recent policies are actually differentially distributed according to designations of 'deserving' versus 'undeserving' elderly. These designations approximate previous class membership, and serve to maintain inequality throughout the life-cycle (Estes, 1983). The consistency with which income maintenance, health care, and housing programmes perpetuate this pattern belies a simple notion of irrationality or inefficiency in policy formation as the underlying cause.

While research into the constitutive elements of social programmes for the elderly is still in its infancy, a number of attempts have recently appeared. On the one hand, there are descriptions of

the political and/or bureaucratic processes that led to the enactment
of one or more policies; the focus is either on small policy-making
groups, agencies, actions of federal officials, or some combination of
these. Meenaghan and Washington (1980), for example, do this in a
cursory fashion, while Derthick (1979) takes an in-depth look at the
development of social security from a similar perspective, describing
the workings of officials in the social security administration in a
rather autonomous fashion. Another approach involves an evaluation of the socioeconomic resources of governments as they shape
the nature and scope of pension programmes (Dye, 1979). As instructive as these endeavours might be, they leave a number of
questions unresolved. The structural constraints, above and beyond
those implied by socioeconomic level, within which interest groups
in the policy-making process operate, are not elucidated, nor are the
limitations that public officials face (Myles, 1983). Essentially, we
need to move beyond the notion of social welfare policy as a response
to various social problems (Meenaghan and Washington, 1980), to
an analysis of both the social construction of these problems as well
as the political economic structure in which struggles for welfare
policy take place. While we have alluded to various aspects of these
tensions throughout the previous discussion, we have not yet provided a theoretical overview from which policy trends can be examined. To do so we focus primarily on the state. As the state is
ultimately responsible for the enactment and functioning of welfare
programmes for the aged, we must investigate the nature of political
arrangements and their relation to other spheres of society.

The State, Modern Capitalism, and Welfare: A Theoretical Perspective

There can be no doubt that the state has increasingly intruded into
the social fabric of modern capitalist societies. It intervenes in the
economic sphere through a variety of policies, deals in multiple
services that both 'protect' and aid the public (Himmelstrand *et al.*,
1981), and is itself a major employer. As a result, research interest
in the state has increased significantly (Giddens, 1982, pp. 77–8).
While there are a number of competing paradigms, for our purposes
we follow Poulantzas in viewing the state as a relation – as a dynamic
process both reflecting and redefining the class struggle (Carnoy,
1984). A more static version of this approach views the dominant,
capitalist class as a unified group, which uses the state as a tool for its
own enhancement (Giddens, 1982, p. 80); such a position is ex-
emplified in the approach by policy analysts who view welfare as a
social control mechanism. Social programmes are seen as a means to
pacify less powerful groups who do not fare well under the particular
institutional framework of society, to keep them from aggressively

seeking change (Meenaghan and Washington, 1980, pp. 9–10). The classic statement of this perspective is found in the work of Piven and Cloward (1971), who maintain that welfare expands and contracts in relation to downturns and upswings in the economic cycle. More recent formulations point to three different social control responses: segregation of the deviant from the rest of society; containment of such isolated groups via benefit levels that discourage challenging their position; and resocialisation, through such processes as education, therapy and the like (Meenaghan and Washington, 1980).

This instrumentalist view of the nature of the state has obvious shortcomings (Giddens, 1982) – the questionable premise that there is in fact a unified, dominant group; or the obvious exceptions to the notion that all other groups are powerless. The working class has often, in fact, been seen as an agent of change (Gough, 1979; Navarro, 1984). Myles' (1984a) analysis of the pension reforms in Canada in 1965, in which the working class did play a role, is one such example. Further, it is impossible to distinguish 'a' ruling class; rather there are actual and potential divisions within the dominant group (Giddens, 1982), such as bankers, those involved in health care provision, an insurance élite, and so on. At various junctures the interests of one or more of these factions may be served to the detriment of another; a state-imposed freeze on medical costs will cut the profits of one group while aiding in the accumulation process of those involved in providing insurance coverage. Obviously this cannot be explained by pointing to the state merely as an instrument of the élite. A more dynamic view of the state is necessary.

An analysis of the state in modern capitalism and its relation to welfare necessarily involves consideration of four interrelated themes: the relative autonomy of the state; the contradiction between accumulation and legitimation; the displacement of economic struggles into the political sphere; and the tension between commodification and decommodification. Each of these is discussed briefly as they reflect and shape class struggles and the nature of welfare. This perspective will then be used to examine selected old age policies in the United States, and inform the debate on the future of these programmes given the present political and economic climate.

The notion of the relative autonomy of the state stands diametrically opposed to the instrumentalist view. While a theoretical basis for both of these positions can be found in the works of Karl Marx (Giddens, 1982), theorists such as Offe, while recognising the power of capitalists, do not view the state as a tool of the élite (Carnoy, 1984, p. 15). Rather the state is 'a specific *relation* between classes. . . . This becomes, in effect, the rule of the ruling class only while it is dominant in that struggle; and it is a dominance which cannot be assumed, but must be renewed and re-asserted continually' (van Krieken, 1980, p. 25). Further, this dominant class is itself fragmented (Carnoy, 1984), with different sub-groups combining or dividing to exert pressure in different historical contexts. There can be no doubt that the state also enacts legislation that is a boon to those with traditionally less power (e.g. the provision of free education). Accordingly, it is possible to see that the state is a relatively independent agent.

The contradictions in the relative autonomy of the state, however, are apparent when we examine its two main interests in modern capitalism: accumulation and legitimation. Its survival is predicated on its ability to generate revenue, which in turn is dependent upon a prospering economy (van Krieken, 1980). Yet the state does not have direct control over its operation. In a sense it is dependent upon capitalists to generate profit and at the same time must undertake policies which will help them do so. By the same token, the state must be receptive to the needs of the working class: legitimation is equally based on its support. Overall, it must provide services for both select populations (like welfare, price supports, etc.) as well as for the community as a whole (such as road maintenance). Consequently, a constant tension is generated, as the more dominant will resist attempts to generate revenues for projects which do not benefit them (Giddens, 1982, pp. 84–6). Clearly, the state is caught between the need to enhance accumulation while justifying its existence to society as a whole.

Offe (1972a) pursues this analysis further in his depiction of the strain between commodification and decommodification. For capitalist society to run smoothly, from the perspective of the dominant class and the state (which is ultimately dependent upon the economy), everything should be a commodity (i.e. bought and sold in the marketplace) in order for accumulation to proceed unfettered. However, two problems arise: first, not everything can be turned into a commodity form. For example, some labour will not be bought (this is represented in unemployment figures) and some material goods which are produced will not be sold. More importantly, throughout history the working class has sought to decommodify certain goods (e.g. welfare and education), and obtain them without payment. Whilst this process is contradictory to the movement towards commodification, the state has often been in the position where it must accede to these demands, not only to maintain legitimacy, but in response to the power of the working class. Through this analysis it becomes clear that the state is not merely a 'mediator' but is actually a *part* of the struggle. Indeed, Poulantzas and others have argued that the class struggle, which is predicated on economic grounds, has been displaced into the political sphere (Carnoy, 1984, p. 126). Such notions as 'democracy', in which everyone has an equal say, often masks this dynamic and confines it to the political arena (Giddens, 1982).

The relevance of these arguments for the investigation of policy for the aged is readily apparent. Contemporary debates are often couched in terms of an 'intergenerational struggle', in which younger members of society are said to resent the increasing burden that support for the elderly entails. Without adopting a purely instrumentalist view, it can be seen that the creation of policies such as national pensions was intimately related to the needs of the economic structure which is disguised by the eventual formation of age-based programmes (Graebner, 1980; Quadagno, 1984).

Once this 'deferred wage' begins to be a drain on both the state and capitalists (Myles, 1983, 1984a and b), the arguments are set up to justify ideologically attempts to curtail such programmes. For example, much current controversy has revolved around the so-called 'age/dependency ratio' which 'reveals' an ageing population perceived to be a burden on society. Yet, these ratios are often segmented – that is, they do not take account of the relative decline in the younger population in their calculation – thus presenting a highly skewed picture. Indeed, it was just this potentially inflammatory figure that was utilised by the US President's Commission on Pension Policy in 1980 (Friedmann and Adamchak, 1983). Similarly, dependency ratios do not reflect the large increase in female labour force participation (Myles, 1984b). Computation and projection of dependency measures to the year 2050 which include the smaller numbers of children and actual figures of employed women present quite a different view. Not only is overall societal dependency not increasing, but it does not reach the levels seen in the 1960s (Friedmann and Adamchak, 1983). A wide range of class-based reasons may account for such distortion (Calasanti, 1985); in all likelihood it revolves in part around the fact that the US government is only now facing the realities of the increase in deferred wages won in 1969–72, while corporations are also confronted with the loss of a percentage of future profits (Myles, 1984a). Moving the struggle for pensions from the economic sphere into the political arena effectively shifts the struggle into the heart of the state itself, while hiding its class basis.

The State and the Development of Selected Age Policies in the United States

By necessity the following discussion will be brief. A full exposition of the processes by which programmes for the aged developed in America requires more than a single chapter; nevertheless the political economic bases of such policies have only recently been the focus of scholarly attention. While some authors have examined medical and/or housing policies from this perspective (Estes, 1979; Olson, 1982), the majority have focused on income maintenance. This, then, will be the thrust of our discussion.

In order to examine the state dynamics involved in the creation of the national pension system in the United States, it is first necessary to describe the underlying political and economic context. To do so involves a recognition that neither the state nor capitalism are static; changes in the mode of production and in the class struggle are reflected in and shaped by the state (Poulantzas, in Charnoy, 1984, p. 126). Fine and Harris (1979) point to three stages of capitalism, each of which calls forth a different dynamic in the political sphere: competitive capitalism, simple monopoly capitalism, and state monopoly capitalism. Carnoy (1984, p. 110) makes a similar but two-pronged distinction: in competitive capitalism, the state is simply involved in promoting the reproduction of the mode of production. Within the monopoly form, however, this task becomes far more complex: it must not only mediate between the political and ideological sphere (the conditions of production) and the economic sphere, but also play a direct role within the relations of production.

While the transition to monopoly capitalism in the United States in the early part of the twentieth century does not explain the nationalisation of retirement, it does lend some insight into the issues involved. For example, during this period, the federal government played a very minor role in welfare; most such programmes were the province of charity organisations (Meenaghan and Washington, 1980). Indeed, the image of the elderly that resulted from the contact of workers within these institutions may well have played an important part in the development of the belief that to be old is to be dependent (Haber, 1978) – the ideological foundation for subsequent legislation for the aged. The formation of monopoly capitalism was well underway by 1920 (Edwards *et al.*, 1975), however, which suggests a change in class relationships and hence in the nature of the state. As this form of capitalism grows, so too does the class struggle within the political sphere.

In a pioneering study, Graebner (1980) points to a variety of interrelated processes which led to the creation of a nationalised pension scheme. A push for rationality and efficiency in production (backed by the scientific management principles associated with Taylorism) contributed to employers' desire to allow the retirement of older workers. At the same time, increased labour power in the form of trade unions played a significant role. The campaign for a shorter working day, however, was met with management demands that productivity be maintained. In effect, this meant speeding up machinery, which put older workers at a disadvantage and made them appear more inefficient. Similarly, the drive for seniority was met with the demand that retirement be introduced to keep labour costs down. In addition, while many establishments did introduce pension policies, control of them was firmly in the hands of management who could revoke them at will. The result was that such programmes were often used to prevent strikes, settle labour disputes, or inhibit unionisation altogether. Not surprisingly, then, unions desired a national policy which would reduce the labour control impact of private pension schemes.

In many ways, the depression was the spur which brought these factors to a head. Graebner indicates that the Social Security Act was passed because it served two timely functions: it artificially decreased unemployment by relabelling a portion of the unemployed 'retired', and also stimulated consumption by giving the new retirees money to spend in the marketplace. Both these measures were designed to contribute to economic recovery.

While Graebner's work is highly suggestive, it leaves a number of issues unanswered. For example, while it implies that unions had a stake in nationalising pensions, the unions played only a very minor role in the drafting of the Social Security Act (Myles, 1983). Further, many employers were strongly opposed to any such legislation (Quadagno, 1984). In addition, the transition to monopoly capitalism led to different techniques of labour control in core and peripheral firms (Gordon *et al.*, 1982). Thus to regard the nationalisation of retirement as a tool of such dominance does not speak to the important disparities in the organisation of work in these diverse industrial spheres.

Olson's (1982) political and economic inquiry into policies for the aged also presents a sound argument for the ways in which these programmes actually work to the benefit of the capitalist class. However, she too implies a unified dominant group and therefore a rather static conception of the state.

Quadagno's (1984) work in this area offers additional perspectives. She effectively identifies the different groups of capitalists involved (core and peripheral employers, southern aristocracy, and so on) and their struggle within the political sphere, as well as pressures from the elderly in the Townsend movement and the constraints on state managers. For example, it appears that monopoly capitalists had interests which were often at variance with those of peripheral employers. These differential goals were intimately related to their disparate positions within the capitalist system as a whole. Further, each of these groups had unique political channels at their disposal. Monopoly capitalists had access to national political leaders, whereas the power of the periphery was felt via local congressional leaders who were more attuned to the needs of their regions. Thus both groups exerted influence, in different ways, and to varying degrees. While she treats the state as a mediator – a neutral entity – rather than as a relation, Quadagno's work is instructive none the less.

As we have seen, since its inception in 1935, social security has undergone a number of revisions. The changes at the end of the 1960s and early 1970s, coming as they did at a time of economic boom, cannot be explained by easy allusion to the situation in the 1930s. Again, monopoly capitalism – and hence the nature of class struggle embodied in the state – had significantly changed. Thus the forces and processes leading to reforms must be examined from a different perspective. The alterations in pension policy in the USA must be viewed in relation to the structure and organisation of the class struggle between capital and labour for wages in general, as apparent within the state, to get behind the dynamics of the development of increases in 'deferred wages' (Myles, 1983, 1984a).

In several works, John Myles (1983, 1984a and b) has looked at some of the dynamics involved in recent pension policies in both the United States and Canada. His arguments demonstrate the need to place the state within the context of a particular historical form of capitalism to understand the nature of the struggle for programmes for the aged.

The initial income maintenance programmes for the elderly in North America were based on a principle of equity, geared toward the needy. Prior to the Second World War, in both the United States and Canada benefits were a form of social insurance, based on a notion of subsistence. Their universal character represented a more dramatic plunge in income for middle-class workers. Being a more powerful group than manual workers, they were able to organise for change as a part of their contracts of employment ensuring a system of occupational pensions. This effectively divided retirees into two groups: the poor, living on social security, on the one hand; and those who received social security in addition to their occupational pensions. Not only did such a policy promote inequality, it also spelled an important danger for the continuation of the welfare system. Since the middle-class elderly had access to occupational pensions, they were in effect removed from the political struggle to improve the state pension. At the same time the support of this group was important for the maintenance of the federal system. As noted before, the state is the seat of struggle for different groups to vie for specialised services. The endorsement of the majority of the working population, especially those with the most power, is vital to fight the mounting opposition of others who would prefer to have the funds spent for their own interests (Myles, 1984a).

In contrast to the implementation of the Social Security Act 1935, in which unions played a minor role (Quadagno, 1984), the AFL–CIO was actively involved in the pension reforms of 1969–72 (Myles, 1983, p. 31). Similarly, the Canadian Congress of Labour began a campaign for changes in 1953 which were finally enacted in 1965. While labour was vital in the process, they were not necessarily the most important group (or reason) for reforms. Rather, Myles terms the move to a 'substitutive principle' an 'institutional response to the problems generated by a new phase in the development of modern capitalism' (Myles, 1984a, p. 24).

While most increases in national pensions come in election years, the argument that these improvements were a result of voter–politician interaction belies the struggle between various capitalist groups and workers within the state under 'full employment capitalism'. After the war, and until the beginning of the economic crises of the 1970s, capitalism in North America was booming and unemployment relatively low. This was inimical to capitalist interests, in so far as the smaller reserve labour pool coupled with the booming economy placed greater power in the hands of workers to command higher wages. During the war, when the war effort also led to low unemployment, a system of 'deferred wages' or a 'retirement wage' was instituted. Workers agreed to accept smaller increases in present wages in exchange for a programme of pensions to be reaped in the future. Not only did such a programme decrease cash outlay for capitalists at the time, it also channelled money back into the market (Myles, 1984a, pp. 24–35).

This strategy was the eventual basis for the pensions revisions enacted in Canada. When the struggle for reform began in 1953, the substitutive principle was opposed by capitalists, since it reduced the labour-control aspect inherent in the flat-benefit system which kept receipts below minimum wage levels (see Quadagno (1984) for further elucidation of this mechanism). However, the enactment of the present funded system in Canada was quite attractive, in so far as it allowed the provinces to finance their debts by borrowing from the surplus. While pension reform was a potential blow to the private sector, and in particular to insurance and trust companies, the legislation was enacted through the alliance of two power blocs with very different motivations: the provinces, who saw the pooled system as a financial boom to offset debts, and labour (Myles, 1984a, pp. 15–16, 35–7). In the United States, where the pay-as-you-go system prevails, the Nixon administration simply adopted the strategy used by industry during the Second World War. The pressure on wages and squeeze on profits were alleviated by the use of wage controls, while social security was reformed to pacify labour and the electorate (Myles, 1984a, p. 37).

The effects of the changes in pension structures in North America are not as straightforward as at first they may seem. While Myles has aptly documented a shift in power from capital to labour during this period of full employment, for the observer to conclude that workers 'won' and capitalists 'lost' is to take a rather static and simplified view of the process. In the United States, for example, while capitalists were curtailed in the sense that their contributions to pension plans led to higher costs, they were also able to keep the covered wage base low and block further reforms (Myles, 1984a). In addition, it would be a grave error to depict the contemporary situation as a 'victory' for workers. The movement beyond the ideology of 'equity' in which all citizens have a right to something (what Myles (1984b) refers to as a 'citizen's wage') has taken us to a class-based system which perpetuates the inequality experienced throughout the lives of various workers. The gains do not accrue to all workers in the same way.

The class nature of benefits

Because the processes described above occurred within the constraints of a class-based system – a form of monopoly capitalism – the outcome reflects the inequities of this structure. In the United States, income ceilings which had restricted coverage were lifted while benefit levels were increased (Myles, 1984a). Again, the primary recipients of these reforms are middle-class workers.

Olson (1982) has stressed the importance of viewing policies for the aged from the standpoint of inequality, for it reveals not only the differential distribution of resources, but also the disparate funding methods which are disproportionately paid by those least able to do so. In terms of the former, Nelson (1982) has distinguished three different groups of elderly in relation to social policy. The *marginal elderly* are predominantly minority group members and women who have experienced low incomes throughout their lifetimes and remain poor despite income transfers. Increased social expenditure on behalf of the aged population continues to benefit this group – the neediest – the least. Even analysts of the most optimistic persuasion admit that blacks and women are 'less positively affected' by the attempt to alleviate poverty through national income-maintenance programmes (Meenaghan and Washington, 1980). The majority of elderly are *downwardly mobile*, have few private resources, and experience a decline close to the poverty level upon retirement. The largest benefits accruing from a combination of various old age policies go to the *integrated elderly* who initially had the highest incomes.

Recent policy innovations, such as individual retirement accounts (IRAs) in the United States perform in a similar manner. Presented as a programme designed to 'promote independence' and 'help the elderly help themselves' by providing tax shelters and savings for the future. IRAs, like many tax loopholes, presuppose enough present income to take advantage of the policy. Only the higher income groups can afford to participate in the programme; thus it serves to distinguish classes of elderly even more. The exclusion of private pensions or unearned income from means testing further allows elderly who are better off to reap full benefits while penalising the aged poor who try to supplement meagre social security payments by working.

Table 12.1 Coverage of occupational pensions and health insurance (USA, 1981)

Percentage of employees with present pension coverage by industry[a]

Core		Periphery	
Mining	57.0	Agriculture, forestry, fisheries	10.4
Construction	36.1	Wholesale trade[b]	42.7
Manufacturing[b]	58.9	Retail trade	10.3
Transportation, public utilities[b]	65.1	Business services	27.0
Finance, real estate, insurance[b]	47.7	Personal services	9.6
Professional and related[b]	50.8	Entertainment and recreation	16.5
Public administration	76.4		
Total	57.15	Total	25.59
Total employees with pension	44.3		

Percentage group health plans, by industry

Core		Periphery	
Mining	84.1	Agriculture, forestry, fisheries	24.1
Construction	58.9	Wholesale trade[b]	71.4
Manufacturing[b]	82.0	Retail trade	38.9
Transportation, public utilities[b]	81.0	Business services	52.2
Finance, real estate, insurance[b]	70.0	Personal services	20.4
Professional and related[b]	61.5	Entertainment and recreation	31.8
Public administration	76.8		
Total	73.51	Total	46.29
Total employees with pension	62.0		

Notes:
a. Based on scheme developed by Tolbert, Horan, and Beck (1980).
b. Since many industries are lumped together in this classification scheme, it was necessary to designate sectoral location on the basis of best fit. Therefore, these industrial groups are predominantly core or predominantly peripheral.

Source: US Bureau of the Census, 1983. Statistical Abstract of the United States: 1984 (104th edn; Washington, D.C.: US Government Printing Office, p. 436).

The continuation of class divisions into old age is even more apparent when we look at additional pension coverage outside that provided by the state. While national plans have already been shown to be distributed along class lines, it is evident that this only reinforces the inequities that exist in private schemes. If we acknowledge that monopoly capitalism describes a system whereby the economy is divided into core (monopoly) and peripheral (competitive) sectors, it can be seen that former core employees not only have an edge in income received while in the workforce, but also upon departure (Hendricks and McAllister, 1983). This is graphically demonstrated in Table 12.1 which shows the extent of private pension coverage in the United States by industrial sector.

Core and peripheral divisions play an important role in the eligibility for public pensions as well. Social security in the United States requires 39 years of covered employment to reap full benefit (Myles, 1984b). Peripheral workers, however, subject as they are to structurally-induced, unstable work histories (Hendricks and McAllister, 1983) are extremely unlikely to be able to meet these eligibility criteria. This is the same group which has a low likelihood of having access to, and/or collecting, private occupational pensions.

Olson's second point, alluded to above, regarding the inequity of the burden of support for social policies for the aged has been echoed by other researchers who note that while transfer payments in the United States have obviously increased, social security has served to redistribute income among the lower-middle and lower-class workers rather than between the well-to-do and this group (Fano, 1982). Estes (1983, p. 178) combines these notions in her work, examining income maintenance, medical and other social programmes for the elderly. The fact that the social security tax is regressive, and is only paid on income up to a certain point ($39,600 at present) means that the lower and lower-middle classes pay a relatively larger share into the system. Further, the upper-class elderly are more likely to have private pensions and participate in IRAs and private health insurance plans. Government expenditure for Medicare is larger for this group, as they are better able to pay deductions and co-payments. The poorer elderly, while they have paid relatively more into the system, face means tests for supplemental security income and Medicaid, receive the minimum in social security benefits, have less access to private pensions and medical services, cannot afford private health insurance, and are not the recipients of federally mandated priorities in either social services block grants or the Older Americans Act. Obviously, increased social assistance to the elderly cannot be regarded as aid to the aged *per se*; policy enactments which grow out of struggles within the state have retained their class bias.

The Future of Ageing Policy in North America: The Struggle Continues

Even if we were to view the revisions in ageing policies as 'victories' for workers, despite the inequalities, one fact remains: nothing is assured. The 'win' is itself dynamic; federal support promised to the elderly is contingent upon the ability and/or desire of the state to honour its promises. Even indexing retirement benefits to the cost of living is subject to this proviso; while this obviously is a gain for the elderly, the terms of the contract can always be changed.

Predicting the future of North American ageing policy is thus problematic in so far as it involves, to some extent, identifying groups which will come to play a part in the state struggle within a context that is not yet known. However this attempt need not proceed wholly in the dark if we can extrapolate from past tensions and present contradictions. While we cannot know what will happen, we can point to some trends.

Since the majority of social assistance programmes are earmarked for the aged, the contemporary system is often viewed as a welfare state for the elderly (Myles, 1984c). This in turn leads to dire predictions about the ability of the state to provide for an increasing number of aged. However, sheer numbers of persons of a certain age do not necessarily lead to an increase in political power, especially given the heterogeneity of classes represented by this group. As recent scholars have aptly demonstrated, 'the relationship between population aging and old age entitlements is an historically contingent relationship, not a necessary one' (Myles, 1984a, p. 21). As we have already shown, societal dependence is not expected to increase dramatically in the future; however, the composition of the dependent group is changing, with an emphasis on older, rather than younger, cohorts (Myles, 1984c).

While Walker (1982c) has provided an excellent discussion of reasons why dependence in the young is more tolerated than among the aged, we would like to go beyond his analysis to suggest that at the present time the demographic argument has become an important tool in policy struggles in the state. Poulantzas (1979) has argued that the state can legitimate itself to the working class not only materially (through economic rewards, like pensions) but also ideologically. This means that a population can sometimes be swayed to give up certain rewards through the use of ideology – religion, or in the case of recent US strategies, in the name of 'patriotism' – in order to maintain national security, freedom, financial solvency, and so on. Viewed from this perspective, the use of segmented dependency ratios takes on an added dimension. While there is still strong public support for social policies for the aged (Myles, 1984c), it is apparent that the ideological framework is also being laid to justify cutbacks, or at least freezes. Growth in the over 65 age group has already been used as an argument to curtail entitlements (Myles, 1984a, p. 21), as can be seen in recent legislation in the area of health care in the United States.

What underpins such ideological arguments? What are the pressures apparent in the state in contemporary capitalism? Again, the work of Offe (1972a) can be used to shed some light. The struggle between commodification and decommodification within the state is a dynamic process; that is, once a product, such as health care, becomes decommodified (becomes part of welare), there is no inherent reason why it must retain that status. In other words, there is also a constant tension to re-commodify those things which have been taken out of the marketplace. Gilbert (1983) has documented the trend toward profit-making in welfare, pointing not only to the 'nursing home "industry"' but to amendments in social policies which allow more and more services to be contracted out to enterprises that are geared towards profit-making. Similarly, the replacement of housing construction assistance with the voucher system places the monies spent on shelter firmly in the marketplace, where it can again be used for profit. Olson (1982) indicates several other areas in her examination of who benefits from various social policies. A glance at the policies we have outlined suggests many more. Undoubtedly, this group of capitalists will play an important role in future discussions of cut-backs in welfare for the elderly, since they stand to lose in the process. A rather odd alliance between these business interests and selected groups of elderly is possible.

On the other side of the coin, there are a number of capitalists who are now being confronted with the reality of the 'deferred wages' they granted during the 1950s and 1970s. Essentially, they have given a portion of their future profits away before these have already been reaped; the notion of variable capital has thus been changed, as some of it has effectively been frozen. These capitalists, then, have a stake in eliminating or decreasing these plans as much as possible (Myles, 1984a). At the same time, union strength is declining (New York Times News Service, 1985), making workers even more vulnerable.

Finally, the state is in a position to desire cutbacks in policy for the aged. In Canada, promises to pay pensions are based on future profits, thus taking away flexibility in the use of any such surplus. In the United States, a number of policy changes which take money away from the elderly have already been noted. That the defence budget and a number of tax shelters for the well-to-do have drastically increased under the present administration is obvious; while some of the interest groups involved in these instances are apparent on the surface, the medical professions do not appear to play a direct role, and would thus be overlooked without deeper probing. It should also be clear that re-commodification can occur indirectly: for example, cutbacks in medical service provisions effectively force people back into the private sector – they have no choice if they desire health care.

The move towards re-commodification is readily apparent (Giddens, 1982, p. 86–7). How far this will go, and the effects it has on old age policy is unclear. As we have already seen, the private pension industry in North America is an extremely lucrative one, and cutbacks in federal programmes may work to keep this business booming – an important consideration, given the amount of investment (and development) capital involved. By the same token, the Canadian provinces have a financial interest in keeping the funded system solvent, given the utility of this programme for their continued growth. Re-commodification in this instance may be difficult to achieve, especially since legitimation may spell the need to restrict the flexibility of private pension plans, making them more accountable to those who pay into them. The contradictions inherent in the process are multiple; whatever the direction taken, the elderly poor will ultimately bear the brunt of the fall-out from the struggle.

While the profession most involved with welfare administration on the practical level – social service workers – is seemingly aware of the structural issues involved in policy formation, the majority appear to see the goal of effecting change in this process as beyond their purview, as 'unrealistic' (Meenaghan and Washington, 1980). Unless this changes, it cannot be assumed that this group will play a significant role. At the same time, there are other professional and advocacy groups who define their existence in terms of providing services to the elderly (Kearl *et al.*, 1982) and who might be expected to put up resistance to many proposed changes. Much thus depends on the strength of these and various other groups involved in the struggle – capitalists who make a profit from welfare; those who have portions of their variable capital frozen; labour; different classes of elderly; and perhaps others who have not yet made their voice heard. On an ideological level this tension can be seen in the contradiction inherent in the notion of the coexistence of citizenship and class rights (Myles, 1984b). The displacement of the struggle in the economic sphere into the political arena neither negates the economic tensions nor destroys the contradictions created through such relocation. What is even more uncertain is how the form of the economy will shape and reflect this struggle. At the present time we have an admixture of a 'recovering' economy with still high levels of unemployment, a situation quite different from that prevalent either during the inception or the revisions of income maintenance programmes in North America. New coalitions, based on this particular type of capitalism, will have to be formed to shape ageing policy.

Finally, we must bear in mind the fact that the state is under pressure not only to provide services for the elderly, but for other groups as well. While this is obvious, too often our debates on the future of ageing policies focus exclusively on struggles over provisions for that group alone. We forget that the conflict exists not only between the elderly and other so-called dependent populations, but also between these groups and the recipients of the majority of 'welfare' – capitalists. Offe (1972b) puts it succinctly in his comment on welfare: 'Rather than "creeping socialism", it is the most generous underwriter of large business enterprises in capitalism's short but glorious history.' The need to shore up, defend or otherwise aid this 'other' welfare system has already bled much of the available federal revenues dry; whether this will call forth a new surge of power in retaliation is uncertain at this time.

Myles (1984c) presents three possible scenarios for the future. The two which seem most likely are, first, the further subjection of entitlements which are based on citizenship rights to the inequities of the marketplace. The second suggests a victory of democracy over the rights of class membership; that is, increased democratic control of the economy. While he points to this possibility in Sweden, the more socialist make-up of that country appears to make it more amenable to such a path. Given the present conservative mood in North America, such an outcome may never be realised.

13 Social Policy and Ageing in France

Anne-Marie Guillemard

Although the proportion of older people in the population was significant as early as the late eighteenth century, France did not develop a public policy towards this age group before other countries. In 1790, 8 per cent of the population was over 60 years of age whereas in Great Britain this percentage was not reached until 1910. For a long time, the French population was one of the most aged in the world. Since 1968 however, the populations of other industrialised European countries have been growing older than that of France where today, 13 per cent of the population (7.5 million) are 65 and over. None the less, according to the EEC's social budget, France has devoted a smaller share of its national income to this age group than neighbouring countries. In 1970 for instance, France had about the same percentage of elderly people as Great Britain but spent only 8.5 per cent of its national income on benefits and services for them, whereas Britain spent 9.4 per cent. This comparison suggests that the adoption of public policies towards the elderly can never be taken to be simply a rational, mechanical reaction by governments to new problems and demands.

This chapter presents a sociological interpretation of the dynamics behind the adoption and development of such policies in France. To this end, the history of public interventions in this field during the last 40 years is discussed. This is followed by an examination of the main forces that have generated the official management of old age in France. In the conclusion, the current situation and prospects are discussed. But first, the general framework employed in this analysis of old age policies calls for some introductory remarks.

The Nature of Old Age Policies

The purpose of this analysis, unlike that in many other studies about social policies, is not limited to reconstituting the decision-making process behind a specific public measure. Instead of a restricted or fragmentary approach, a full account is given of the interactions between the ways that French society has provided for the elderly and the manner in which the reality of old age has been reconstructed. This comprehensive approach has been adopted not merely because of its exhaustiveness. It also follows a fundamental principle of analysis: how can the patterns of social relations which underlie decisions in social policy be interpreted without analysing, over time, the relevant interests and intentions of the major actors involved? This condition must be met in order, on the one hand, to observe how the focus of disputes about policy has shifted and, on the other, to reconstitute the arguments between actors, all of whom have attempted to impose their own definitions of old age policy and to shift the issues in accordance with their own interests and rationale. Once this condition is met the way is open to understanding the social dynamics behind the making of public policy.

'Old age policy' has, therefore, been defined broadly. It refers to *all public interventions that shape the relations between the elderly and society*. This definition reflects a refusal to lay down an *a priori* definition of old age and, at the same time, a desire to study the processes that construct and reconstruct the social reality of old age.

Secondly, this broad definition encompasses each of the three major axes, or issues, around which the state has organised its interventions in the relations between society and the elderly and which, in turn, have shaped arguments about how old age should be managed. The first is the establishment and extension of the right to retirement. The second is concerned with the definition of a 'way of life' for the elderly. This includes the various arguments about the needs of this group and the ways to satisfy them. Out of this debate have come measures for improving the quality of life by setting up health facilities, opening old people's homes and providing the services that help the elderly to continue living in their own home. The third issue has to do with whether or not ageing workers should participate in the labour force. This is often at the centre of disputes and negotiations about employment policies.

Thirdly, this analysis pursues two lines of inquiry. The one leads to asking how social policies are determined by the structure of antagonistic class relations. The other, closer to the sociology of organisations, sees within such policies the workings of the state as an organisation. It raises questions about the relationship between state and society, and about the degree to which various branches – legislative, executive, administrative – of the former merge or diverge. (For further discussion of these issues see Guillemard, 1980.)

This approach to old age policies attempts to separate clearly two poles – state and society – in order to discern the precise ways in which public policies are related to each of them. This effort is, in my opinion, the only means for improving our understanding of the degree – fluctuating as it does from one historical period to another – to which the state is independent of or dependent on civil society. The underlying hypothesis is that interventions by the government in society reflect the interconnections, continuously subject to strain and to change, between the state and social forces. These interventions are rooted in social relations, but they are also impelled by the dynamics of the state itself in so far as it is more or less independent of those individuals who represent social classes. This interpretation of the dynamics behind the adoption and development of old age policies in France is based on empirical research over a period of nearly eight years (Guillemard, 1984).

Three Periods in the Public Management of Old Age

It is possible to distinguish three successive ways in which old age has been managed by the French state in the post-war period. Each of these is characterised by the kinds of intervention and priority assigned to them by the state according to the previously mentioned axes – retirement, employment and way of life.

The first period: retirement was the predominant concern

Until the early 1960s, the government mainly intervened in the sphere of old age through retirement policy. Measures for improving the quality of life and living conditions of the elderly were limited to public assistance, which offered relief from shortcomings in the system of retirement that was then being set up. Such measures sought to satisfy the most acute needs by providing lodgings or by dispensing assistance in cash or in kind. Among such programmes were the establishment of a 'social card' for underprivileged elderly persons (1949); allocations for covering the cost of rent increases (1951); and special provisions for those who were not part of any retirement pension scheme. These measures, however, were subordinated to retirement policy. Likewise, there were no publicly adopted measures concerning older workers apart from the conditions laid down for retirement. Although labour was scarce and remained so till 1948, no public policy encouraged these workers to stay in the labour force. Only the pension plan indirectly affected employment in as much as it offered incentives for postponing retirement.

There were two distinct phases within this period. Shortly after Liberation, public authorities set up social security (1945) which instituted a universal right to a pension upon retirement. This brief but intense phase of public involvement was followed by a less active one during which most of the state's interventions still occurred along the same axis though with less commitment. Old age insurance under social security was not extended to fulfil the intentions of the 1945 Act. Instead, it provided only minimal coverage. As officially estimated during the debate, in 1956, about setting up a national solidarity fund (NSF) that would provide supplementary allowances to the poorest elderly persons, the percentage of older people whose incomes fell under the very low NSF threshold was more than 80 per cent. This statistic gives some idea of what minimal coverage under social security meant. Meanwhile, the issue of retirement was being shifted further and further from the public domain to the bargaining tables around which labour and management sat. The principle of universal, national solidarity – of coverage against the 'old age risk' for all working people – tended to be reduced to the right to what we might call a 'minimum wage pension'.

Special funds were proliferating and, consequently, 'fragmenting' the right to retirement income. Although old age insurance under social security should have been, in compliance with the 1945 founding principles, extended to all workers, in fact it covered only those on wages or salaries but not even all of them. In certain branches (mines, railways, electricity and gas), separate retirement funds had been maintained; and for self-employed professionals, others were created. Moreover, 'supplementary' pension funds were set up at first for white-collar workers (in 1947) and later for other occupational groups. They offered benefits above the basic rate under social security. The universal right to retirement and retirement benefit was split up into as many pieces as there were funds.

The second period: public policy shifts to the way of life issue
Starting in the early 1960s, the state once again became involved in the management of old age by intervening in the living conditions of the elderly. For the first time, measures concerned with 'way of life' did more than stretch out a safety net to provide relief to those persons who were not sustained by pensions. They, in fact, constituted a plan for reintegrating the elderly within society, for helping them to lead, as long as possible, normal and autonomous lives, instead of hastening along the time when they had to be taken into the care of institutions. This called for the construction of appropriate housing and for the extension of the home or neighbourhood facilities and services that this group of citizens needed in order to remain in their own homes. Thus social policy towards the elderly was reorganised around the way of life issue. That was the meaning of the phrase 'old age policy' newly coined by the Study Commission

on Old Age, set up by the Prime Minister in 1960, which reported in 1962.

During this period, which lasted approximately from 1960 to 1975, the public management of old age completely changed focus. Policies about the retirement and employment of the elderly as well as the provision of pensions were subordinated to and had to contribute towards, achieving the major intention of public interventions: the provision of an integrated way of life for senior citizens. This resulted, in particular, in the setting up of facilities and services aimed at helping the elderly remain in their own homes. For instance, there were very few 'home helps' assigned to the elderly in 1960, but by 1978, about 250,000 elderly persons were benefiting from their assistance. Furthermore, clubs for the elderly have mushroomed from a few hundred before 1970 to more than 30,000 today; and the number of community centres offering meals to the elderly rose from 538 in 1969 to more than 2000 in 1976.

The third period: towards bipolarity
Since 1975, the management of old age has tended to be polarised along two of the three policy axes.

Along the way of life axis, public action in favour of integrating the elderly is clearly being reduced to a programme for keeping them out of institutions and at home. This home maintenance programme symbolised the state's first financial commitment to a policy of integration when it was adopted as part of the Sixth National Plan (1970–75). But the very same programme was included in the Seventh Plan (1976–80) and has, since then, been affected by the prevailing ideas according to which the social services should be cut during the economic recession. Government appropriations for this programme have still been as small and experimental as under the Sixth Plan (Guillemard, 1980, pp. 99–131, 217–25). In many respects, priority has been given to measures which are rich in symbolic value but easily controllable in terms of costs. For instance, among the facilities and services that were most developed under the Seventh Plan were clubs and intergenerational activities, whereas those more expensive formal services that were indispensable for helping the elderly remain living at home were not extended at all. In the whole of France in 1980, only 2000 elderly people were provided with health care at home. The importance of the way of life issue in shaping public old age policies has been dwindling.

On the other hand, the importance of managing the labour force participation of ageing workers has been increasing, as a result of the recession and of worsening unemployment. Since 1977, new measures for covering unemployed older persons allow them to stop working at the age of 60, whether they resign or are dismissed, and to receive adequate compensation. People in these two categories were guaranteed, under unemployment compensation, an income equal to 70 per cent of their gross pay until the age of 65 when they would transfer to regular retirement pensions. These measures have encouraged companies, usually after some negotiations with potential beneficiaries, to shed ageing employees at a time when jobs are becoming scarce. As a consequence, the number of beneficiaries between 60 and 65 years of age rocketed from 91,000 in 1977 to 303,805 in 1981.

Recently, such measures have been extended to the 55–59 age group and now cover more than 700,000 individuals. More than a quarter in the private sector were on pre-retirement at the end of 1983. The government has gradually given up defending the right of older workers to have jobs and has accepted – even encouraged – early retirement under the system of unemployment compensation. The degree of change in public policy can be seen by contrasting the government's clear-cut decision, in 1971, to keep older workers in the labour force with the recommendation, in March 1981, by the Minister of Labour that employers and employees should extend early retirement schemes to other age groups and with the decision in 1982 to sign, with companies, 'early retirement solidarity contracts' that would allow workers 55 years and over to retire (Guillemard, 1983). Policies about employment of the elderly are no longer subordinate to the way of life policy. On the contrary, they have come into direct conflict with it.

The state's management of old age can be seen to have split into two contradictory sets of policies. Aiming as they do at expelling ageing workers from the labour force, early retirement schemes have been superimposed upon measures for integrating the elderly within society. The government is torn between two policies. The first calls for retiring ageing workers in order to allocate work according to the criterion of age; hence, the right of such workers to stay in the labour force has to be restricted. The second is a continuation of former programmes that have sought to improve the living conditions of the elderly and to promote integration. Policies about the labour force participation of the elderly have been counteracting the way of life policy that was being implemented at the same time. Public authorities have been forced to waste their energy as they use the way of life policy to fight against the exclusion and segregation that the 'unemployment', or early retirement, policy has been producing and aggravating. The contradiction between these two poles of public involvement has plunged old age policy into a crisis. Furthermore, these early retirement schemes based upon redundancy payments have distorted traditional retirement policy because the right to a pension has been transformed into the obligation to withdraw from the labour force. Work has been forbidden, and the right to rest has become compulsory leisure.

The Two Systems of Action Behind Old Age Policies
After this outline of the successive ways in which old age has been publicly managed, we need to look at the systems of action that have generated policies. The empirical analysis of the social determinants that make and change these policies has brought to light two fundamentally different systems of action.

Social policy as compromises in disputes between labour and management
The one system of action is organised around the confrontation between the major forces in industrial society: management and labour. It is deeply implicated in the shaping of policies about retirement as well as about the labour force participation of ageing workers. Here, measures are adopted as a result both of the complex relations – disputes, negotiations and compromises – between these two opposing forces and of the regulation and formulation of these relations by the state.

These representatives of different social classes have their own versions of old age policy which they attempt to impose upon each other. As the organisers of production, employers seek to subordinate this policy area to manpower requirements, which vary with the business cycle. Their aim is to reduce management of the last phase of life to one of the factors that can be adjusted in order to manage the labour force according to the necessities of the production process, for example, in regulating the mobility, stability and skills of labour. In contrast, the unions try to win acceptance of their version of old age policy, which focuses upon the retirement issue. Their constant, almost exclusive, goal has been to consolidate and broaden the right of workers to rest and not to be alienated in the later years of life. Within this system of action, the state's role is to formulate compromises between these two opposing forces. The nature of these compromises depends upon the degree to which, at any time, the state is receptive to one or the other of these forces.

Retirement policy prevailed as the means of managing old age during the first historical period because, between 1945 and 1947, the unions were powerful and the government was responsive to their interests. Just after the Second World War employers as a group tended to be kept out of party politics. Meanwhile the state had to be reconstructed; its authority restored; and national unity re-established. Because its autonomy was reduced, the state could not act independently but had to rely upon the predominant social forces in politics and in society itself, particularly upon the working class as organised through the unions and political parties. The interests of this class amply permeated the state through the three-party system, which dominated the Constituent Assemblies and held the reins of government.

However the creation of a general retirement fund under social security in 1945 did not just enact this class's interests. It resulted from a compromise according to which, in exchange for the constitution of a welfare state that would ensure a measure of redistribution of wealth, the bonds among members of the nation, as well as between them and their government, were renewed. Accordingly, all were to help in reconstructing the nation. Throughout this period, the fluctuations of public retirement policy mostly came from the balance of power between management and unions and from the ability of these forces to sway the state. Thus, the right to retirement, as part of labour law, advanced when the unions were powerful or active. But when their influence on society or the state declined, no advances were made in extending this right, and retirement policy tended to be fragmented, as during the second phase of this first period. Starting in 1947, working-class power was ebbing, and a multitude of interests were being expressed by groups that belonged to the new and traditional middle classes. So dependent upon the political system and its parties under the Fourth Republic, the government, pressured by these groups, split the universal right to retirement into different programmes, as we have seen.

The same system of action has come into play during the adoption of employment policies concerning older workers. However these policies result from a balance of power in favour of employers, who have been able to win over society and the state to their version of old age policy. The patterns of social relations underlying the third of the previously mentioned periods can be analysed in a similar way so as to cast light on the combination of forces that have steered the public management of old age towards the employment axis.

Social policy as the outcome of the dialectical relations between the state's administration and society
The second, entirely different system of action has shaped policies related to the way of life of the elderly. Its dynamic has to do not with the opposition between forces representing social classes but rather with the dialectical relationship between the state's administration – the civil service – and society. It centres on the intermediate groups that stand between the administration and society. These groups form what Gremion (1976) has called 'peribureaucratic links'. The prevalence of way of life policies during the second

historical period can be explained by the predominance of this system of action.

Such policies seem to reflect not class struggle but the state's ability to act upon society. As stated in the 1962 programme advocated by the Prime Minister's Study Commission the proposal for reshaping the relationship between the elderly and society represented a new claim by the state upon society. The state claimed to be able to act upon and reshape society in conformity with collective objectives. The sudden appearance of this new proposal for reorganising public interventions into an innovative way of life policy, which aimed at the social integration of the elderly, is to be understood in terms of changes in the relations between the state and society. These changes occurred with the establishment of the Fifth Republic and the construction of a Gaullist state in which powers were more concentrated. The new institutions made the state freer from political parties and interest groups. It had greater autonomy because the civil service and the government were, in effect, combined (Birnbaum, 1977). The adoption of this innovative old age policy can be related to the state's new freedom of action. The state itself redefined the basic issue in this policy area and thus also redefined its role in the management of the relations between the elderly and society.

This new public programme shifted the focus of debate from retirement to integration. It pinpointed new ways in which the state could be more directly involved. Public actions were no longer confined to the economic sphere, to the transfer of income through pensions; they could take place outside retirement policy and beyond the influence of the forces behind it. These measures did more than just regulate economic relations; they became social and political in nature and justified direct involvement by the state in society. By supporting such a policy, the state bestowed a new citizenship upon the elderly who were no longer treated like underprivileged persons (to be helped through relief programmes) or former workers (to be paid through retirement funds) but like senior citizens with recognised rights to integration. In turn, the state attained broader representativeness and greater legitimacy. None the less, this new programme would not have succeeded had it not attracted and unified a set of disparate individuals and groups who found, therein, a means both of becoming representative, either locally or nationally, and of extending their influence.

A complicated, limited system of fragile alliances backed this innovative way of life policy and provided a new social basis for public interventions. Among the major actors who entered this alliance were elected city officials and professionals in the medical and social fields – the doctors and social workers who through this definition of old age as senior citizenship, obtained the means of enhancing and opening up their professional activities. Various social service associations hooked up to this alliance as they sought to renew their clienteles and reach out beyond the recipients of public relief. Many of the supplementary retirement funds also joined this alliance. Their competition had led them to foresee the new demands that were being formulated in the captive market which their beneficiaries represented. Furthermore, they wanted to underscore differences with the social security retirement funds. These peripheral innovators soon became the intermediaries between the state's administration and its environment. The modernising coalition that was developing within the state chose them as its representatives. They played a dual role: as intercessors who helped the elderly attain recognition and as the supporters of the administration's activities. This joining of forces from the administration and from society cast doubt on the legitimacy of the traditional intermediaries, such as public assistance offices and charitable organisations, through whom relief came. The elderly way of life policy was related to the greater autonomy of the state's administration and to the support for this administration in the rest of society. This new policy for integrating the elderly resulted from the complex interactions between an innovative, technocratic plan conceived by an activist state that sought the means for directly intervening in old age, and several local and professional groups, who, for various reasons, had a common interest in advocating an alternative way to manage old age.

The resurgence of class actors

During the most recent of the three previously mentioned periods, the policy – which has rapidly developed since 1975 – of retiring older workers has come into conflict with the way of life policy. Although the latter has been extended, it is no longer the moving force that it used to be. It is being reduced to a single aspect, namely, maintaining the elderly in their homes through the provision of community-based services and facilities. The new way in which old age is being managed is related to the resurgence, in public decision-making, of the role of those representing social classes.

The increasing importance attached to the employment axis for the management of old age reflects changes in the relations among social forces. These changes have favoured employers and enabled them to win the state and society over to their version of old age policy, which thus becomes a means for managing the labour force. The creation and extension of early retirement schemes make these points quite clear.

Signed in March 1972 by employer and employee organisations, the first agreement for guaranteeing the income of elderly unemployed persons can be viewed as a successful counter-attack by management. It aimed at countering the strong union movement, which had been growing since 1970, in favour of lowering the age of retirement, a priority in labour disputes at that time (Guillemard, 1983). The extension of measures of the sort contained in this agreement has, since then, quite literally resulted in the large-scale retiring of older workers. A major step in this direction was the 13 June 1977 management–union agreement which granted pre-retirement not only to workers of 60 years or older who were dismissed but also to those who resigned.

The extension of such measures and the polarisation of public interventions along two contradictory axes should not be taken as merely the mechanical result of worsened conditions in the labour market. The underlying factors are much more complicated. They are of two sorts.

In the first place, as the presidency passed from Gaullists to Giscard d'Estaing, the state's freedom of action was lessened. There was a trend towards a neo-liberalist state, which would not intervene as often or as systematically in economic or social affairs. The state handed some of its duties over to business, whose initiatives it intended to support or complete. As a consequence, the way of life policy lost impetus. Public authorities also left the question of ageing workers to the bargaining process between employers and employees and, thereby, approved the extension of measures that eliminated these workers from the labour force.

Secondly, the recession has affected social relations in two ways that have reinforced the resurgence of class divisions. On the one hand, management of the economy has been emphasised to the detriment of social transformations, such as the integration of the elderly. This shift of priorities has given more weight, in debates about old age policy, to the arguments of business forces and of employers as the organisers of production. They have been able to win acceptance of their policy about older workers. This policy consists of reducing the number of persons on wages or salary in a controlled but flexible way, namely through arrangements that are negotiated following the usual procedures but that can be revised and adjusted according to the necessities of the production process.

On the other hand, the recession has simplified the issues in dispute between the social classes. The unions have given up their offensive on retirement and are making a defensive stand on employment. In unfavourable circumstances, they have chosen the lesser evil: to support employment for young people and accept the retirement of older workers. The 1971 union slogans for lowering the age of retirement ('retirement in an easy-chair, not in a casket') have been replaced by remarks such as 'It's better to be retired than unemployed'. The times have changed, and the unions have accepted restrictions on the right of the elderly to work. As a result of this simplification of issues, employers and unions have reached something approaching an agreement on pushing older workers out of the labour force. This policy has been extended rapidly. In the meantime, the way of life policy has been watered down but prolonged because of its support among the French people and in the state's administration. Public old age policy is coming apart, splitting along two axes.

Towards a conceptualisation of the social determinants of public policies
Attention must be drawn to the theoretical implications of this discovery of the simultaneous presence of these two systems of action within the decision-making process behind public old age policy.

This analysis shows that there are a number of factors comprising the social determinants of public policies. Such policies never merely reflect the class struggle, nor can their meaning be reduced to the autonomous operations of a bureaucratic machine above and beyond class relations. Public policies never completely coincide with the realities of the state or of social relations. Instead, they continuously reflect the kind of linkage, which is always subject to strain and to change, between these two realities. Observations in the field of old age policy tend to prove that the state has no essence. In other words, the state's actions can be analysed neither as the autonomous dynamics of a machine nor as a simple means of social domination. From one period to another, as shown, the state's major interventions successively reflected the interests of the working class (in 1945 with the creation of social security), the interests of economic power-holders (early retirement schemes) and the degree of autonomy of an administrative machine and its technocracy (the adoption of a new way of life policy).

This research draws attention to the ever-changing, complicated nature of relations between state and society. It casts doubt on any analysis that conceives of these relations in terms of total independence or of total fusion. On the contrary, they should be analysed in terms of on-going *inter*actions. Trends in public policies are a function of the systems of mediations through which social forces manage to influence the state.

The Crisis of French Old Age Policies: The Current Situation and Prospects
In as much as public interventions along the three axes of old age policy have reflected the balance of power and debates among various social groups, such measures tend to be fragmentary rather

than coherent. In this sense, there is no coherent old age policy. The only attempt to make one occurred during the 1960s; but since it did not receive the support it needed within French society, its implementation ended in the application of a new programme for helping the elderly to remain in their homes. This programme was added on top of other programmes rather than being used to link them into a coherent whole.

The foregoing analysis pinpoints the origins of incoherences in public interventions. These origins do not only lie in the poor functioning of the administrative machine; they also reside in the social dynamics through which interventions are generated. Rather than being part of an overall plan, old age policies result from compromises between social forces. They ensue from logics that are distinct, even incompatible (as during the third period). The crisis of old age policy is, in the first place, a crisis of the rationale behind public interventions. This latter crisis has been putting an ever-heavier financial overload upon the state, which is wasting its energy as it tries to repair the damage that other public measures have been producing later in the life-span. The crisis goes along with a crisis of legitimacy since retirement itself is being called in question. This system of protection is no longer thought to be a source of well-being and progress; it is also seen as a cause of rigidities and as a restriction on freedom of choice since it is being forced upon rather than accepted by persons who are less and less old.

Moreover, the contradictory nature of public interventions has blurred the very meaning of old age. Owing in particular to the early retirement schemes, the number of phases in the later years of life is being thoughtlessly increased. The successive conceptions of old age, which correspond to the changing ways in which it has been managed, are being confused. The identity of this age group is less and less clearly defined by society. These persons are not really unemployed, not really retired. More and more often, they refuse the label 'senior citizen'. The boundaries of old age are becoming blurred, and there is a strained contrast between the images that these persons have of themselves and the images that society offers them. In agreement with Habermas (1975) we can conclude that the rationale crisis (owing to which the administrative system has been unable to reconcile diverse socioeconomic exigencies) is being shifted towards the cultural system in what he has called a 'motivation crisis'.

The socialist period: contradictions become embedded in the state
Has the change of government in May 1981 affected these contradictory trends in public interventions, which have resulted in both inflated costs and confused policies? Has the creation of a Ministry of

National Solidarity and the establishment of a State Secretariat for the Elderly impelled old age policy in another direction? Have recent measures corrected the tendencies of earlier policies, which have been making more people at younger ages into outcasts and a financial burden? A close look at public interventions in recent years does not justify an optimistic conclusion that the contradictions have been resolved. Instead, the policies introduced by the Left seem both to have further fragmented the decision-making process and also to have further incorporated the resulting contradictions into the state.

The principal decision made by the Socialist government as soon as it came to power was to breathe new life into the welfare state model. Rather than undertaking long and risky negotiations with the aim of establishing new kinds of solidarity that would lessen age segregation, the government took new initiatives along the retirement axis by proposing to reform the age of retirement. Decisions were made as though the damage wreaked by the recession would disappear if a new impulse were given to the existing system of social protection. By advocating equal protection through broadening the right to retirement, the government ignored two facts: that the procedures for making social transfers had been unable to reduce inequality and that the recession was producing new kinds of 'social rejects'. Given these facts, the return to a unified retirement programme could only increase the load on the welfare state but could not reshape society because it did not reach far enough down to the origins of the divisions that mark modern French society.

These new initiatives along the retirement axis confirm the model of public decision-making that has been described above. The power of this model to explain current trends is also demonstrated. Since pro-union political forces have – after such a long time – come to power, the extension of the right to retire has been taken into consideration. Retirement policy is now on a footing with employment policy. Employer-inspired schemes for guaranteeing, under the unemployment compensation system, the wages of workers over 60 years old who have taken early retirement are now lapsing but have been incorporated into the unions' proposal for the right of everyone to retire at 60. Does this mean that job measures are being absorbed into retirement policy so that ageing workers be given back their basic rights, notably the right to decide at what age they will leave the labour force? The reform of the retirement age is more equitable than the previous early retirement schemes. In particular, it has put an end to the precarious conditions under which these schemes guaranteed income. Furthermore, it has extended to certain categories excluded from these schemes the chance to stop working at 60. None the less, it has not re-established the workers' right to choose. To achieve this end, the right of ageing workers to continue working would have to be respected.

In the current situation, the major issue is jobs, and various pressure groups have tacitly agreed that these are to be distributed according to age. Therefore, pressure is being put on older workers to resign. The measures for lowering the retirement age (which include regulations about working while on retirement) hinder the extension of the right to work. The same can be said about the 'solidarity contracts' and the fast-growing 'early retirement/ resignation' scheme that allows persons over 55 to leave the labour force. Unlike the 'pre-retirement' schemes that parties had worked out within the established bargaining framework (UNEDIC), the solidarity contracts are signed by companies *and* by the government, which takes on part of the costs. The principal innovation lies in the fact that the state has become directly involved in the policy of retiring ageing workers. Hence, the earlier pre-retirement schemes have not really been eliminated through the reform of the retirement age; instead they have been shifted towards a younger age group where the impact upon unemployment is more effective. The number of early retirees has swollen, and the specialisation of age groups (young people in training programmes, 'adults' in the labour force and ageing people in the inactive population) is deepening under the fictitious label of 'intergenerational solidarity', which hides the unequal competition between young and old in the labour market.

The Socialist government has advanced the right to retire as a way of both proving its commitment to and of reviving the principles of solidarity, laid down in 1945, that have always been backed by organised labour. However, this reform seems to be out of phase both with the social demands generated by the recession and with the major concerns of unions. In the meantime, the government has not resisted the temptation to go on using retirement (or rather pre-retirement) as a means of both letting companies lay off employees and of socially insuring unemployment. How could it resist when the unions have been pressuring it to yield?

The way of life policy has also been given new impetus (Ministère des Affairs Sociales, 1982). The range of social services and facilities offered to the elderly (for example, home helps and the provision of health care at home) has been improved. The means of local co-ordination including coordinators and departmental gerontological plans have been developed. In addition, departmental and national committees of pensioners and of elderly persons have been set up. This renewed concern for the way of life issue only affects what is happening downstream in the lives of older people. This sphere of action corresponds to the jurisdiction of the State Secretariat for the Elderly.

Quite significantly, this newly created Secretariat was involved neither in the reform of the retirement age (a reform steered through the legislative process by the Minister of National Solidarity) nor in measures concerning ageing workers (which were drawn up in the Prime Minister's office as part of a jobs programme). In spite of its assigned duties, this executive body has had few means of strongly affecting the roles of the elderly in society, nor of concretely defining the solidarity between generations, for instance, through the solidarity contracts or the earlier retirement age. These measures have caused more and more people at younger ages to become outcasts in and a financial burden upon society. They have worsened the age segregation that the Secretariat endeavours to reduce by providing medical as well as social services and facilities.

Measures about the way of life issue, because they do not have any effect upon the mechanisms that have transformed these persons into a socially unproductive group who live on transfers from the wages of working adults, can only increase the consumption of social services. As a result, people socially defined as being old, as they become more and more dependent upon specific channels of consumption, are not given the right to decide about their way of life, their living conditions, their participation in the labour force or their involvement in society.

Under these circumstances, the efforts – whether to provide services and facilities or to reform retirement – by Pierre Mauroy's first government amounted to an attempt at reviving the welfare state and the mechanisms for redistributing wealth. The additional social protection has not taken the elderly out of the vicious circle that makes them into a financial burden. It has created no new forms of solidarity, nor of citizenship. Instead, it makes social expenditures spiral ever upwards. In a swing of the pendulum, the austerity measures adopted since the summer of 1982 attempt to limit these costs.

Conclusion

The change of government in May 1981 has not fundamentally transformed the state's interventions in old age. Decisions are still made on an *ad hoc* basis and are contradictory. Made in reaction to diverse problems (employment, retirement, social services), they are not part of an overall plan. At best, old age policy is a set of dispersed, circumstantial actions. The centres within the state where these decisions are made have increased in number, but they are separated from each other. A state Secretariat has been set up but not given the power to manage retirement or to deal with questions about the jobs of older workers. Its interventions have been reduced to a 'policy for old people' that, though providing tangible benefits, is unable to solve the major problems of this age group. These problems are generated at previous stages in the life-span. Their source lies in the policies on occupational training and jobs, in the definition of social solidarity and in the organisation of work and of leisure throughout the life-span. The lowering of the retirement age to 60 and the shifting of early retirement schemes to 55 exacerbates age segregation and worsens the old age crisis.

Since May 1981, new actions – lacking coordination and often diverging – have been undertaken along all three axes of old age policy. The state has given new impetus to the way of life policy, extended the right to retirement and become more directly involved in employment policy. As a consequence, the contradictions in old age policy have not only held firm but have become embedded in the state.

Will the contradictions in French old age policy along these three axes persist together with the resulting age segregation? Or will a new political awareness, closely related to the expectations and actions of various social forces, 'despecialise' the activities of all age groups so that work, education and leisure become available to all? In spite of the present-day crisis of old age policies, is there not some hope in that the social meaning of old age is becoming less and less clear? Will these trends open the way to managing the relations between the elderly and society differently? As the boundaries of this 'target group' blur, is it possible to hope that not old age but the whole life-span be managed publicly; that a policy on old age be replaced by a policy on ageing? The latter would not have as a consequence the formation of an ever-growing group of elderly persons who are a financial burden and social rejects. On the contrary, it would aim at enabling everyone, through all phases of life, to be autonomous, to decide freely about their future and to contribute to society.

Acknowledgement
My thanks to the Fondation Nationale de Gérontologie, Paris, for their support, and to Noal Mellott, CNRS, Paris, for translating this chapter from French.

14 Conclusion: Alternative Forms of Policy and Practice

Chris Phillipson and Alan Walker

In this chapter we focus on the work which must begin among those involved with older people, to resolve some of the issues raised by the various essays in this volume. We concentrate, in this chapter, on changes at the level of professional practice and organisation, suggesting innovations for workers in the health and social services. Before doing this, however, there is a brief summary of a major theme running through many of the contributions.

A number of the contributors to this volume have highlighted the role of economic, political and social policy in influencing ideas and beliefs about old age. It is possible to see, in fact, from the various historical arguments, and from the contemporary illustrations provided, that state policy plays a crucial role in the social construction of old age. We can see this in at least two senses. First, age boundaries move according to labour market and demographic pressures. In the 1980s, for example, we find a relocation of old age towards the middle point of the life-cycle. This is promoted through policies which exclude older workers from the labour market; the right to employment being removed as a means of reducing manpower in the economy (Phillipson, 1982). This process can, however, be contrasted to the early 1950s where the state – faced with labour *shortages* – actively discouraged retirement and attempted to push back the starting point of this traditional (if imprecise) marker of old age.

Secondly, in addition to redefinitions of the onset of old age, policies also influence the life-styles and social relationships through which old age is constructed (Walker, 1983c). A major factor here (as identified by Walker and Peace) is the impact of poverty, with just over one in four of people over retirement age coping with incomes equal to or below the supplementary benefit 'poverty line'. At the same time, social divisions in retirement are also important: some people can *choose* to retire; others (perhaps the majority of working-class retirers) find the point at which they leave work and the amount of money they have to live on, are elements largely outside their control. These divisions are being reinforced by the state given the erosion in the value of the flat-rate state pension. This pension is worth, in 1985, 21 per cent of average earnings; by 2033/34 its value will have fallen to 9 per cent of average earnings.

Economic and social policies are therefore central in the creation of the 'structured dependency of the elderly' (Townsend, 1981). But the effect of these policies has been exacerbated by those acting as paid carers. Dependency arises, in fact, from the pressure of economic deprivation and exclusion, and through the power of professional carers. The former has been documented in some detail in this book (see, in particular, Chapters 3, 10 and 12). The latter has been identified and discussed by Bowl and Means, but some additional points need to be made before outlining some proposals for reform.

Professional Workers and Older People

A range of policies have been analysed or proposed in this book in relation to such fields as housing, family care, health provision, pensions and the labour market. All of these areas are, however, the concern of various professional groups, and it is their influence (in addition to that of the state) which can seriously affect whether old age is a time of dependency or freedom to choose a range of life-styles, safe from the threat or reality of financial hardship.

Unfortunately, care for older people has suffered from a number of defects. Most of the caring professions (e.g. district nurses, health visitors and social workers) had their origins in work with children and young families, the elderly forming a very small proportion of the worker's caseload. Virtually all responded on an *ad hoc* basis to the increased demands from an ageing population. Their involvement was rarely guided by specialist training; short- and medium-term objectives were often confused and contradictory. With limited resources at a local level, there was a tendency to 'ghettoise' work with the old, often placing it in the hands of the lowest paid and least trained.

This process was additionally complicated by the professionalisation of social work and related groups. Professionalisation occurred in the absence of any close understanding about the needs of older people. Yet it was characteristic of professionals to assume that they were in touch both with the emotional and material needs of their clients, and that they possessed adequate 'theoretical' knowledge about the social and biological construction of old age.

It is possible to see, in fact, two conflicting trends in the post-war period. On the one hand, an older population attempting to establish new life-styles in the face of diminishing possibilities within the labour market (see Chapter 2). On the other hand, the growth of new professions (and the consolidation of old ones) who sought to interpret and channel these demands into acceptable and conventional forms. Professionals have, in fact, often functioned as 'moral overseers' shaping and manipulating the behaviour of older people (and other client groups) in areas such as sexuality, politics and education (Wilding, 1982; Offe, 1984). The process is often seen at its worst in the authoritarian regimes inside many older people's Homes, but other contexts (sheltered housing schemes, long-stay hospital wards, day centres, etc.) have suffered a similar fate (Fennell *et al.*, 1981; Townsend, 1981).

Criticism of the work of the health and social service professions can be traced at least to the 1960s. Illich's study *Medical Nemesis* (1974) introduced the notion of iatrogenesis – doctor-induced diseases. But the debate has since widened to include problems which arise through the activities of a range of professional groups. Carroll Estes, in her study *The Aging Enterprise* (1979), highlighted the inequalities inherent in the relationship between the expert and client. She argued that:

> Publicly funded social services are more than systems for distributing services; they are systems of *social relationships* that reflect and bolster power inequalities between experts and lay persons, as well as between providers and recipients of service. . . . Services strategies in general, and those for the aged in particular, tend to stigmatize their clients as recipients in need, creating the impression that they have somehow failed to assume responsibility for their lives. The needs of older persons are reconceptualized as deficiencies by the professionals charged with treating them, regardless of whether the origins of these needs lie in social conditions over which the individual has little or no control, in the failings of the individual, or in some policy-maker's decision that a need exists. (Estes, 1979, p. 235)

The process described by Estes has been influential in shaping images and attitudes towards ageing. Many people have low expectations about life in old age (and about their rights to health and social support). Indeed, such feelings may be reinforced both by the activities of the state and via encounters with professional carers (Phillipson and Strang, 1984).

The impact of professional care has been additionally important in, first, rationing the access of older individuals to skills relating to medical and counselling needs (Savo, 1984); and secondly, controlling knowledge about the health and welfare system. The combined effect has been to reduce the individual's confidence in being able to control and influence his or her own ageing. Understanding and controlling old age is increasingly viewed as the responsibility of 'experts' and 'professionals', though ironically, as we have noted, many of these will have experienced only limited training in work with older people.

It seems unfortunate that the issues surrounding self-care should have been narrowly defined in terms of *more* individual and family activity and *less* support from statutory services. An alternative view is that self-care could actually entail both more support from formal carers (as people become more conscious of their rights) and greater control by older people of skills and knowledge to assist them through the period of old age (Phillipson and Strang, 1984). Such a perspective entails a challenge to professionals, since it suggests the idea of them losing at least some of their skills (and their power); and a renegotiation of the boundaries dividing the expert from the client (Savo, 1984; Glendenning, 1985a).

These are difficult times to argue for 'de-professionalisation' or the transfer of skills. Professions are inevitably on the defensive in a context where the resources for care are being cut back and where numbers of staff are also being reduced. But it is possible to argue both for an expansion in community and hospital-based staff and a qualitative change in their relationship with older people (Walker, 1985c). Indeed, the latter will come onto the agenda regardless of the actions of practitioners and policy-makers. Older people, as is being shown in America and by some groups in Britain, will be disinclined to continue in the role of passive consumers of health and social services; they will, increasingly, demand a voice in the development, organisation and staffing of neighbourhood-based services. But the question to be resolved is how to change the relationship which has developed between older people and workers in the community and in institutions. In the short and medium term we would propose a number of areas for action: first, training and education; secondly, activity within the community; thirdly, organisational changes; and finally, supporting a new politics for old age.

Teaching Gerontology
The problems arising from professionalisation have been reinforced by weakness in the teaching of gerontology and the basic and continuing education of aid carers. We need to recognise, in particular, the division between geriatrics and gerontology: the former addressing problems relating to malfunctioning in the older adult; the latter identifying (through, for example, longitudinal studies) the characteristics of normal ageing. The perspective of geriatrics has dominated teaching about older people for groups such as health visitors and district nurses (Phillipson and Strang, 1986). However, it has also been applied to groups such as social workers and students of social policy. For these groups, the bias in teaching has been towards the social pathology of ageing, with emphasis on the impact of events

such as bereavement, chronic illness, loneliness and family break-down. By contrast, areas relating to developmental growth in later life and the learning abilities of older people are virtually ignored (Johnston and Phillipson, 1983).

The imbalance in teaching, together with its medical orientation, has created a number of problems. First, it may lead the student to identify growing old with different forms of medical or social ab-normality, most of which are only open to partial relief; few being preventable by earlier or more effective interventions. Thus, the idea of old age being, in certain crucial respects, socially constructed (Walker, 1980, 1981b; Phillipson, 1982) is only slowly being accepted on social work and related courses.

Without this perspective, workers have selected a limited range of strategies when working with older people. Carroll Estes (1980), for example, distinguishes between accommodative (the majority) and restorative approaches. She sees the former as actively discouraging people from becoming independent, with emphasis given to alleviat-ing problems, often only temporarily, rather than eliminating them. This approach suggests a stereotype of the older person as one whose independence or improvement is unlikely; maintaining the status quo is the most that can be achieved. In contrast, a restorative approach focuses upon assisting the older person in helping himself or herself to fulfil their potential in old age.

Clearly, the two approaches imply different teaching perspectives, as well as different strategies for work in the community. The implications of the latter will be explored later in this chapter.

A second problem arising from conventional teaching about older people, is the stress on the benevolent character of welfare legisla-tion. This perspective underplays the social control element in sup-port for older people (the contrast between the critical social policy relating to children and women is striking in this regard). Because of the recency of ageing as a *mass experience*, the welfare state has been a powerful force in influencing beliefs about old age. Indeed, for many people their view of ageing is formed almost exclusively around the philosophy and standard of support arising from pension and welfare legislation. However, to view this subject purely in terms of its material benefits would be mistaken; it must also be seen as an ideological force through which ideas about growing old are pro-jected and around which people's lives are controlled and managed: the social control elements in passive forms of community and residential care are illustrative of this theme (Townsend, 1981).

The failure to explore and identify these issues in teaching pro-grammes creates problems for practitioners when they are attempt-ing – as many do – to develop an alternative practice when working with older people. Clearly, what is needed is a reorientation in teaching which looks at the social as well as biological construction of old age, and which identifies the impact of discrimination and stereotyping of older people in the shaping of health and welfare services.

The immediate need is to develop courses and modules which elaborate the following themes:

(1) Examining stereotypes of old age.
(2) Understanding normal ageing.
(3) Avoiding client dependency.
(4) Identifying components of a 'healthy old age'.
(5) Reviewing social, biological and psychological theories of ageing.
(6) Cross-cultural variations in ageing.
(7) Confronting low self-esteem.
(8) Understanding transitions in later life.
(9) Reviewing concepts of 'growth' and 'deterioration' in old age.
(10) Developing skills for assisting self-health care (i.e. individual activities) and self-help care (group activity) amongst older people.
(11) Transferring counselling skills to older people.
(12) Developing skills to assist social and political organisation amongst older people.

Such themes need to be inserted into the full range of vocational and continuing education programmes received by paid carers, and should be maintained as part of a commitment to the theory and practice of educational gerontology (Glendenning, 1985b).

Activity Within the Community
New forms of training will go some way to meeting current problems, but we must also look to a new type of interaction between the workers and the older client, one which is founded on challenging myths and stereotypes about old age. This will involve a process of 'unlearning' and 'relearning' about ageing, in settings where older people can meet paid carers (both professional and non-professional) on equal terms. A number of settings exist where this might be developed. Well woman/man clinics, focusing on preventative care, provide a forum whereby older people can realise greater control over the quality of their health in later life. In their most radical form they offer the possibility of 'de-professionalising' areas of health care to which older people have been denied access (e.g. skills needed to treat chronic illness; diagnostic skills which the individual could use in making an estimate of their health status).

Pre-retirement courses have, hitherto, been a minority interest, and regarded as a palliative by many people. However, they can be used to introduce a debate about diversifying life-styles in retirement, and challenging the dependency often experienced in the transition from work (Phillipson and Strang, 1983). At present, most courses are run immediately before retirement and are largely concerned with 'teaching' workers how to cope with a lower income and potential ill-health. An alternative approach would be for community-based programmes to be provided around the ages of 45 to 50, focusing both on long-term planning for retirement and short-term mid-life changes. The former might focus upon political strategies which individuals might need to develop (in concert with others) to promote the necessary financial and social changes for retirement; the latter might consider changes at a more personal level (e.g. examining the household division of labour or relationships with elderly parents). In general terms, the focus of pre-retirement work would be to assist individuals and groups in identifying how they can *control* the process of social ageing; and how they can become more resilient to the ideologies and divisions fostered by the state.

This activity might be complemented by discussion and education groups in the community, comprising young as well as old, and professional as well as non-professional carers. These groups might examine, from a critical perspective, the social construction of childhood, youth and old age, and the forms of discrimination and oppression associated with each phase of the life-cycle. Groups could suggest and experiment with new ideas about ageing, and the implication these might have, for example, for professional practice. They might also help formal and informal carers identify ageist beliefs and attitudes which may be present in caring work.

In the various settings described above, the worker must encourage styles of practice whereby the older woman seeking health advice, or the older worker knowledge for their retirement, becomes their own advocate. But this objective, desirable though it may be, has its limitations. For people in their eighties and nineties living alone, suffering, perhaps, from a chronic illness, articulating their own individual needs may be difficult; particularly if they are aware of social pressures defining them as a burden. The role of the paid carer in these situations must be that of someone who goes beyond merely fitting individuals into an existing pattern of resources; instead, they must take on the role of community activist, pressuring their nurse or area social services manager for a reassessment of local priorities. Moreover, they may have to develop and refine their groupwork skills, helping groups of carers (or older people themselves) to campaign for improvements in health and social care.

Organisational Changes

Organisational changes to health and social care must also be part of the process of challenging professional power, and the dependency it creates. Here we shall make just two suggestions: one which is currently in operation; and another which exists in outline form in a limited number of areas.

Elderly persons support units

The elderly persons support units (EPSUs) innovation in Sheffield indicates one way forward in the reorganisation of social services provisions for the elderly. If the radical potential of this initiative is realised it should represent a significant departure from the traditional approach to elderly people as passive, dependent recipients of social services towards one where elderly people have much more control over their own lives, including the services they receive.

EPSUs are a major innovation not only in the care of elderly people but also in the organisation of social services. Sheffield's Family and Community Service Department are replacing the traditionally divided structure of service – domiciliary, day care and residential care – and the assumption that goes with them that when the domiciliary and day care services can no longer cope with a person then admission to a residential Home or geriatric hospital is the only alternative. In the place of that rigid structure geared to different levels of disability, EPSUs are intended to provide an integrated and flexible deployment of resources, including social service workers. It is hoped that the provision of EPSU-based services will prevent the growth of dependency among elderly people and remove or substantially reduce the need for admission to residential care (for a full account, see MacDonald, Qureshi and Walker, 1984).

The units are locally based and are staffed by people occupying a specially created social services post: community support worker. The objective is to provide the whole range of services required by elderly people in their own homes, from routine domiciliary assistance through to comprehensive care of the same level as that available in a residential setting. Units will provide 24-hour, seven-day a week cover if necessary. One unit opened in October 1984 and others are in the process of planning and construction.

The EPSU innovation is an exciting and potentially radical development for the personal social services. It represents a rejection of the government's assumptions that families can be left to cope with caring alone or with only minimal support and, instead, a desire to create genuinely non-exploitative forms of collaboration with the informal sector. In this way the social services will begin to operate less as a casualty service and more as a preventative one. Other initiatives and experiments in the care of elderly people, born out of the search for alternatives to residential care, have concentrated on mobilising and organising the informal sector of carers, primarily female kin. The structure, organisation and delivery of formal social services have changed very little and, as a result, they have often ended up exploiting the female carers. Moreover, there have been very few attempts to provide a full substitute for residential care.

Of course, big questions remain, particularly about how far this radical promise will be carried into practice and how, if at all, social workers will alter their traditional attitude to elderly people in response to this development. A major evaluation of the EPSU initiative is being conducted at Sheffield University. On the outcome of this must rest conclusions about the quality and effectiveness of the care provided by EPSUs. So far it has demonstrated that at least one local authority is prepared to devote substantial extra resources to the care of elderly people in the community rather than seeking to save money by increasing the burden on female kin, to reorganise the delivery of social services, and abolish divisions between staff by function and actively to oppose the common ageist assumptions which dominate society including the social services.

The EPSU initiative has at least two elements which need to be generalised throughout the health and social services. First, it raises the issue of closer collaboration between services, and between formal and informal carers; secondly, central to the approach is an attempt to use services as means of confronting rather than creating dependency. However, for these objectives to have any hope of long-term success, there must be a more systematic approach to the organisation of services for older people.

Community gerontology teams

In this context, we would advocate the information of *community gerontology teams*, to work on a 'patch' or neighbourhood basis. These teams might consist of formal and informal carers, together with representatives from pensioner action groups, who meet regularly to discuss issues affecting older people. More specifically, they might develop three functions: first, influencing local and national planning affecting older people; secondly, advising carers working with older people; thirdly, developing experimental projects and initiatives concerned with devolving power over health and social issues to elderly consumers.

The teams might also divide into those concentrating on people in the pre-retirement phase; and those entering the period of late old age (75–80 and over). Projects for the former might be:

* Setting neighbourhood targets in relation to reducing levels of coronary heart disease.
* Expanding facilities for mid-life counselling and pre-retirement education.
* Identifying the health and social needs of carers of older people.

* Changing the division of labour in neighbourhood care for older people (i.e. broadening the range of care work undertaken by men).

For those in late old age, some possible projects might be:

* Improving self-care skills in the management of chronic illness.
* Promoting the participation of frail elderly people in the planning of services.
* Developing innovatory projects to tackle issues such as hypothermia or the problems arising from disability in old age.
* Developing reforms in areas such as town planning, with the creation of a built environment more suitable for very elderly people.

Conclusion: A New Politics for Old Age

The various arguments and examples presented above underline the need for a new politics of ageing. Groups of older people must start building their own organisations and stimulate their own national as well as local political structures. Of course, much *is* already being done. Pensioners are now holding well-publicised and well-attended national days of action. They also have their own papers (*Grey Power*, *Senior Citizen* and *Pensioner's Voice*, to name but three). And they have their own action groups (e.g. The British Pensioners' and Trade Union Action Association and National Federation of Old Age Pensioners Associations). But it must be admitted that only a minority of older people are active in these groups. The reasons for this are not difficult to understand. First, inequality amongst pensioners widened during the 1970s. The resulting social divisions meant a fragile base upon which to build a political constituency to fight public expenditure cuts in the 1980s. Secondly, because of the unattractive stereotypes attached to old age, older people may resist identification with senior citizens' groups. Thirdly, the timespan needed for the achievement of political and economic goals must also be reckoned with. A man aged 70 can expect a further nine years of life, after 80 just five years. Where such goals seem remote, people's awareness about the possibility of their death (or serious illness) may cause them to feel that involvement in political life is futile.

These points indicate that successful political organisation amongst older people will require inter-generational support, support from the feminist and labour movement, *and* support from professional workers. The latter can provide many simple but vital forms of help: giving access to photocopying facilities, providing rooms for meetings or occasional secretarial assistance. Community work support may also be important in the early stages of the life of a group, to provide the necessary confidence that local and national campaigns can be developed. (The work of the London-based organisation Pensioners Link has been particularly useful in this regard.) But support of another kind, from a variety of groups, is also necessary. This must involve challenging the ideology of old age as a 'cost' and 'burden'; it entails the construction of an alternative vision for old age; and it involves rejecting the subordination of social to economic policy, and the view that expenditure on social and health policy is wasteful and burdensome. All these elements help to marginalise old age. In the 1980s, this marginalisation created a climate which focused on the need to restrict the scope of state pensions. It also created a climate where old age became synonymous with frailty and dependency.

In social policy terms, the task over the next ten years is to break the link between growing old and becoming dependent. This will involve action on both political and economic fronts; but it will also involve, as we have seen, a challenge to our work as carers – in both formal and informal settings. Crucially, it will demand that older people become centrally involved in the planning and administration of services; in the running, in other words, of *their* welfare state. We need a social policy that demonstrates that this *is* possible, and which helps to suggest ways in which it can be achieved. We hope that this book of critical readings will represent a contribution to this task.

Bibliography

Abel-Smith, B. (1978) *The National Health Service: The First Thirty Years*, London, HMSO.

Abel-Smith, B. and Townsend P. (1984) 'Introduction: Challenging Government Assumptions', in Fabian Society (ed.), pp. 2–11.

Abrams, M. (1978) *Beyond Three Score and Ten*, Age Concern, England.

Abrams, M. (1980) *Beyond Three Score and Ten: a Second Report on a Survey of the Elderly*, Mitcham, Age Concern.

Abrams, P. (1977) 'Community Care', *Policy and Politics*, vol. 6, no. 2.

Abrams, P. (1978a) *Neighbourhood Care and Social Policy*, Berkhamsted, Volunteer Centre.

Abrams, P. (1978b) *Work, Urbanism and Inequality*, London, Weidenfeld and Nicolson.

Achenbaum, W.A. (1983) *Shades of Gray: Old Age, American Values and Federal Policies Since 1920*, Boston, Little, Brown.

Adams, C.T. and Winston, K.T. (1980) *Mothers at Work*, London, Longman.

Adams, L. (1981) *Old Women – The Experience of Ageing and Implications for a Feminist Social Work Practice*, unpublished M.A. dissertation, University of Warwick.

Age Concern (1974), *The Attitudes of the Retired and Elderly*, London, Age Concern.

Age Concern (1977) *Profiles of the Elderly*, vol. 4, Mitcham, Age Concern.

Allen, I. (1983) *Short-Stay Residential Care for the Elderly*, London, PSI.

Allsop, J. (1984) *Health Policy and the National Health Service*, London, Longman.

Altmann, R. (1981) 'Incomes of the Early Retired', *Journal of Social Policy*, vol. 11, pp. 355–64.

Anderson, M. (1977) 'The Impact on the Family Relationships of the Elderly of Changes Since Victorian Times in Governmental Income Maintenance', in E. Shanas and M. Sussman (eds), *Family, Bureaucracy and the Elderly*, Duke University Press, Durham, N.C.

Anderson, W. Ferguson (1967) *Practical Management of the Elderly*, Oxford & Edinburgh, Blackwell.

Anderson, W. Ferguson and Judge, T.G. (eds) (1974) *Geriatric Medicine*, London, Academic Press.

Apte, R.Z. (1968) *Halfway Houses*, London, Occasional Papers in Social Administration.

Atchley, R. (1977) *The Social Forces in Later Life: An Introduction to Social Gerontology*, 2nd edition, Belmont, Calif., Wadsworth.

Avon Social Services Department (1981) *Third Dependency Census: November 1980*, December, Bristol.

Avon Social Services Department (1983) *Homes for the Elderly: Dependency Census (November 1982)*, Report of the Director of Social Services, 8 June, Bristol.

Babic, A. (1984) 'Flexible Retirement: An International Survey of Public Policies', *Ageing and Work*, vol. 7, Part 1, pp. 21–36.

Baldwin, S. and Cooke, K. (1984) *How much is Enough?*, London, Family Policy Studies Centre.

Balint, M. (1964) *The Doctor, His Patient and the Illness*, London, Pitman Medical.

Ball, M. (1983) *Housing Policy and Economic Power: the Political Economy of Owner Occupation*, London, Methuen.

Barber, J.H. and Wallis, J.B. (1976) 'Assessment of the Elderly in General Practice', *Journal of the Royal College of General Practitioners*, vol. 26, pp. 106–14.

Barclay Committee (1982) *Social Workers: Their Role and Tasks*, for NISW by Bedford Square Press/NCVO.

Barker, J. (1984) *Black and Asian Old People in Britain: First Report of a Research Study*, Mitcham, Age Concern Research Unit.

Barton, R. (1959) *Institutional Neurosis*, London, John Wright and Sons.

Barton, R. (1966) *Institutional Neurosis* (2nd edn), Bristol, John Wright & Sons.

Baruch, G., Barnett, R. and River, C. (1983) *Lifeprints: New Patterns of Love and Work for Today's Women*, New York, McGraw-Hill.

Bayley, M. (1982) 'Helping Care to Happen in the Community', in A. Walker (ed.), pp. 179–216.

Bebbington, A.C. (1980) 'Changes in the Provision of Social Services to the Elderly in the Community Over Fourteen Years', *Social Policy and Administration*, vol. 13, no. 2, pp. 114–23.

Bebbington, A.C. (1981) 'Appendix', in E.M. Goldberg and S. Hatch (eds).

Bebbington, A. and Tong, M. (1983) 'Trends and changes in old people's homes: provision over 20 years', in DHSS (1983b).

Beck, S. (1984) 'Retirement Preparation Programmes: Differentials in Opportunity and Use', *Journal of Gerontology*, vol. 39, no. 5.

Beeson, D. (1975) 'Women in Studies of Ageing: A Critique and Suggestion', *Social Problems*, vol. 23, pp. 52–9.

Belbin, R.M. (1965) *Training Methods for Older Workers*, Paris, OECD.

Benedict, R.C. (1978) 'Trends in the Development of Service for the Ageing Under the Older Americans Act', in B.R. Herzog (ed.), *Ageing and Income*, New York, Human Sciences Press, pp. 280–306.

Bennett, B. (1980) 'The Sub-Office: a Team Approach to Local Authority Fieldwork Practice', in M. Brake and R. Bailey (eds), *Radical Social Work and Practice*, London, Arnold, pp. 155–81.

Beresford, P. and Croft, S. (1984) 'Welfare Pluralism: the New Face of Fabianism', *Critical Social Policy*, Issue 9, Spring, pp. 19–39.

Berthoud, R. (1984) *The Reform of Supplementary Benefit*, Working Papers, London, PSI.

Beveridge, W. (1942) *Social Insurance and Allied Services*, Cmnd. 6404, London, HMSO.

Bird, N. (1984) *The Private Provision of Residential Care for the Elderly*, Social Work Today Monograph, University of East Anglia.

Black, J. *et al.* (1983) *Social Work in Context*, London, Tavistock.

Bland, R. and Bland, R.E. (1983), 'Recent research in old people's homes: a review of the literature', *Research, Policy and Planning* 1(1).

Blau, P. (1964) *Exchange and Power in Social Life*, New York, Wiley & Sons.

Bligh, E. (1951) 'Welfare of the Aged', *Journal of the Royal Sanitary Institute*, vol. LXXI, no. 1, pp. 45–7.

Block, M.R., Davidson, J.L. and Grambs, J.D. (1984) *Women over Forty: Visions and Realities*, New York, Springer Publishing Co.

Blyton, P. (1984) 'Partial Retirement: Some Insights from the Swedish Partial Pension Scheme', *Ageing and Society*, vol. 4, Part 1, pp. 69–84.

BMA (1965) *A Charter for the Family Doctor Service*, London, BMA.

Bolger, S., Corrigan, P., Docking, J. and Frost, N. (1981) *Towards Socialist Welfare Work*, London, Macmillan.

Bolling Manard, B., Kart, C.S. and Van Giles, D.W.L. (1975) *Old Age Institutions*, Lexington, Mass., Lexington Books.

Bolling Manard, B., Woehle, R.E. and Heilman, J.M. (1977) *Better Homes for the Old*, Lexington, Mass., Lexington Books, pp. xiv, 31, 135.

Bond, J. (1976) 'Dependency and the Elderly: Problems of Conceptualisation and Measurement', in Munnichs, J.M.A. and Van der Heuvel, W.J.A., *Dependency or Interdependency in Old Age*, The Hague, Nijhoff.

Bond, J. and Carstairs, V. (1982) *Services for the Elderly*, Scottish Health Service Studies, 42, Edinburgh, Scottish Home and Health Department.

Booth, C. (1892) *Pauperism: A Picture; and the Endowment of Old Age: An Argument*, London, Macmillan.

Booth, C. (1894) *The Aged Poor: Condition*, London, Macmillan.

Booth, C. (1899) *Old Age Pensions and the Aged Poor*, London, Macmillan.

Booth, T. (1978) *Finding Alternatives to Residential Care – The Problems of Innovation in the Personal Social Services*, Local Government Studies.

Booth, T. (1985) *Home Truths*, Aldershot, Gower.

Booth, T. and Phillips, D. with Barritt, A., Berry, S., Martin, D. and Melotte, C. (1983a) 'A Follow-up Study of Trends in Dependency in Local Authority Homes For the Elderly (1980–82)', *Research, Policy and Planning*, vol. 1, no. 1(2), pp. 1–9.

Booth, T., Barritt, A., Berry, S., Martin, D. and Melotte, C. (1983b) 'Dependency in Residential Homes For the Elderly', *Social Policy and Administration*, vol. 17(1), pp. 46–62.

Booth, T., Phillips, D., Barritt, A., Berry, S., Martin, D. and Melotte, C. (1983c) 'Patterns of Mortality in Homes For the Elderly', *Age and Ageing*, vol. 12, pp. 240–4.

294   Ageing and Social Policy

Bornat, J., Phillipson, C., and Ward, S. (1985) *A Manifesto for Old Age*, London, Pluto Press.

Bosanquet, N. (1978) *A Future for Old Age*, London, Temple Smith.

Bosanquet, N. (1983) *After the New Right*, London, Heinemann.

Boswell, D., and Clarke, J. (eds) *Social Policy and Social Welfare*, Milton Keynes, Open University.

Boucher Report (1957) *Survey of Services Available to the Chronic Sick and Elderly, 1954–1955*, Reports on Public Health and Medical Subjects, no. 98, London, HMSO.

Bowl, R. *et al.* (1978) *Day Care for the Elderly in Birmingham*, University of Birmingham, Social Services Unit.

Bradshaw, J. and O'Higgins, M. (1984) 'Equity, Income Inequality and the Life Cycle: An Analysis for 1971, 1976 and 1982', University of York, mimeo.

Braverman, H. (1974) *Labor and Monopoly Capital: The Degradation of Work in the Twentieth Century*, New York, Monthly Review Press.

Brearley, C.P. (1975) *Social Work, Ageing and Society*, London, Routledge & Kegan Paul.

Briggs, A. (1978a) 'Making Health Every Citizen's Birthright: The Road to 1946', *New Society*, 16 November, 383–6.

Briggs, A. (1978b) 'The Achievements, Failures and Aspirations of The NHS', *New Society*, 23 November, pp. 448–51.

Briggs, A. (1983) *Who Cares?*, Chatham, Kent, The Association of Carers.

British Association of Social Workers (1977) *Social Work with the Elderly: BASW Guidelines*, Birmingham, BASW Publications.

Brocklehurst, J.C. (ed.) (1975) *Geriatric Care in Advanced Societies*, Lancaster, MTP.

Brocklehurst, J.C. (1983) *Textbook of Geriatric Medicine*, 2nd edition, Edinburgh, Churchill Livingstone.

Brody, E.M. (1977) 'Environmental Factors in Dependency', in A.N. Exton-Smith and J. Grimley Evans (eds).

Brody, E.M. (1981) 'Women in the Middle' and 'Family Help to Older People', *The Gerontologist*, vol. 21, no. 5, pp. 471–9.

Brody, E.M., Johnsen, P.T. and Fulcommer, M.C. (1984) 'What Should Adult Children do for Elderly Parents?: Opinions and Preferences of Three Generations of Women', *Journal of Gerontology*, vol. 39, no. 6, pp. 736–46.

Brown, J. (1950) 'The Role of Industry in Relation to the Older Workers', in *The Aged and Society*, New York, Industrial Relations Research Association.

Brown, M. (1972) *The Development of Local Authority Welfare Services From 1948–1965 Under Part III of the National Assistance Act 1948*, Manchester, PhD. Thesis.

Brown, R.A. (1957) 'Age and "Paced" Work', *Occupational Psychology*, vol. 31, no. 1, pp. 11–20.

Bruegel, I. (1979) 'Women as a Reserve Army: A Note on Recent British Experience', *Feminist Review*, vol. 3, pp. 12–23.

Buckingham, G. *et al.* (1979) *Beyond Tea, Bingo and Condescension: The*

Work of Task Force with Community Groups of Pensioners, Stoke-on-Trent, Beth Johnson Foundation.

Building Societies Association (1983a) 'Building Societies and Council House Sales in 1982', *BSA Bulletin*, no. 34, pp. 29–31.

Building Societies Association (1983b) *Building Societies and the Savings Market*, London, BSA.

Burnbaum, P. (1977) *Les Summets de l'Etat*, Paris, Le Seuil.

Burrage, M. and Phillips, D. (eds) (1973) *Nine Old People's Homes in a London Borough*, London School of Economics.

Butcher, H. and Crosbie, D. (1978) *Pensioned Off*, York, University of York/Cumbria CDP.

Butler, A., Oldman, C. and Greve, J. (1983) *Sheltered Housing for the Elderly*, London, George Allen & Unwin.

Calasanti, T. (1985) 'The Social Creation of Dependence, Dependency Ratios, and the Elderly in the United States', Paper presented to the Midwest Sociological Society, St Louis, April.

Canter, M.H. (1983) 'Strain Among Caregivers: a Study of Experience in the United States', *Gerontologist*, vol. 23, pp. 597–604.

Carnoy, M. (1984) *The State and Political Theory*, Princeton, Princeton University Press.

Carpenter, M. and Paley, J. (1984a) 'Getting What They Ask For', *Community Care*, 1 March.

Carpenter, M. and Paley, J. (1984b) 'A Culture of Passivity', *Community Care*, 8 March.

Carstairs, V. and Morrison, M. (1971) *The Elderly in Residential Care*, Scottish Health Service Studies, no. 19.

Carter, J. (1981) *Day Services for Adults: Somewhere to go*, London, Allen & Unwin.

Cartwright, A. and Anderson, R. (1981) *General Practice Revisited*, London, Tavistock.

Casey, B. and Bruche, G. (1953) *Work or Retirement*, London, Gower.

Census, 1971 (1975) *Non-Private Households*, London, HMSO.

Centre for Policy on Ageing (1984) *Home Life: A Code of Practice for Residential Care*, Report of a working party sponsored by the DHSS, under the chairmanship of Lady Kina Avebury.

Challis, D. and Davies, B. (1980) 'A New Approach to Community Care for the Elderly', *British Journal of Social Work*, vol. 10, no. 1, pp. 1–18.

Charlesworth, A. (1983) *Gender and Caring: Service Support for Male and Female Carers*, Paper presented at the 1983 Annual Conference of the British Society of Gerontology, University of Liverpool.

Charlesworth, A. and Wilkin, D. (1982) *Dependency Among Old People in Geriatric Wards, Psychogeriatric Wards and Residential Homes 1977–81*, Research Report no. 6, University of Manchester, Department of Psychiatry and Community Medicine.

Charlesworth, A., Wilkin, D. and Durie, A. (1984) *Carers and Services: A Comparison of Men and Women Caring for Dependent Elderly People*, Manchester, EOC.

Clark, R., Kreps, J. and Spengler, J. (1978) 'Economics of Ageing: A Survey', *Journal of Economic Literature*, vol. XVI, September.

Clark, R. and Spengler, J. (1980) *The Economics of Individual and Population Ageing*, London, Cambridge University Press.

Clarke, L. (1984) *Domiciliary Services for the Elderly*, London, Croom Helm.

Clayton, S. (1984) 'Elderly Women and the Challenges of Inequality', in D.B. Bromley (ed.), *Gerontology: Social and Behavioural Perspectives*, London, Croom Helm, pp. 185–91.

CLEIRPPA (1975) *Isolation and Loneliness of the Aged Women*, Paris, CLEIRPPA.

Clough, R. (1982) *Old Age Homes*, London, National Institute Social Services Library no. 42.

Cole, D. with Utting, J. (1962) *The Economic Circumstances of Old People*, Welwyn, Codicote Press.

Coleman, A. (1982) *Preparation for Retirement in England and Wales*, ed. Joy Groombridge, Leicester, NIAE.

Conference of Socialist Economists (1979) *Struggle over the State: Cuts and Restructuring in Contemporary Britain*, London, CSE Books.

Coote, A. and Gill, T. (1981) *Women's Rights: a Practical Guide*, Harmondsworth, Penguin Books.

Corrigan, P. and Leonard, P. (1978) *Social Work Practice Under Capitalism*, London, Macmillan.

Crawford, M. (1972) 'Retirement and Role Playing', *Sociology*, vol. 6, pp. 217–36.

Crossman, L., London, C. and Barry, C. (1981) 'Older Women Caring for Disabled Spouses: a Model for Supportive Services', *The Gerontologist*, vol. 21, no. 5, pp. 464–70.

Crowe, D. *et al.* (1983) 'Home from Home: An Assisted Lodgings Scheme for Elderly in Birmingham', *Clearing House for Social Services Research*, vol. 12, no. 7, pp. 1–42.

Crystal, S. (1982) *American's Old Age Crisis: Public Policy and the Two Worlds of Ageing*, New York, Basic Books.

CSO (1982) *Social Trends 13*, London, HMSO.

CSO (1983) *Social Trends 14*, London, HMSO.

CSO (1985) *Social Trends 15*, London, HMSO.

Cuming, E. and Henry, W.E. (1961) *Growing Old*, New York, Basic Books.

Cuming, E. (1963) *Further Thoughts on the Theory of Disengagement*, International Social Science Journal, XV, 3.

Daniel, W.W. (1982) *Whatever Happened to the Workers of Woolwich?*, London, PEP.

Davies, B. (1980) 'Policies and Priorities in Youth and Community Work: A Review of Two Decades', in F. Booth and A. Dearling (eds), *The 1980s and Beyond*, Leicester, National Youth Bureau, pp. 5–17.

Davies, B. (1981) *The State We're In*, Leicester, National Youth Bureau.

Davies, B. and Knapp, M. (1978) 'Hotel and Dependency Costs of Residents in Old People's Homes', *Journal of Social Policy*, 1, pp. 1–22.

Davies, B. and Knapp, M. (1981) *Old People's Homes and the Production of*

Welfare, London, Routledge & Kegan Paul.

Davies, M. (1979) 'Swapping the Old Around', *Community Care*, 18 October, pp. 16–17.

Davies, M. and Land, H. (1983) 'Sex and Social Policy', in H. Glennerster (ed.), *The Future of the Welfare State: Remaking Social Policy*, London, Heinemann Educational Books, pp. 138–56.

Davis, L. (1982) *Residential Care: A Community Resource*, London, Heinemann Educational Books.

Deckard, B. (1975) *The Women's Movement: Political, Socioeconomic and Psychological Issues*, New York, Harper & Row Publications.

Deeping, E. (1979) *Caring for Elderly Parents*, London, Constable.

Delamont, S. (1980) *The Sociology of Women: an Introduction*, London, George Allen & Unwin.

Department of Employment (1970) *Ryhope: A Pit Closes*, London, HMSO.

Department of Employment (1980) *Job Release Schemes*, London, Department of Employment.

Department of Employment (1982) *Family Expenditure Survey 1980*, London, HMSO.

Derthick, M. (1979) *Policy-Making for Social Security*, Washington, D.C., Brookings Institution.

Devon County Council (1979) *Residential Accommodation for the Elderly 1978–79*, Social Services Department, Research and Training Section.

Dex, S. (1984) *Women's Work Histories: An Analysis of the Women and Employment Survey*, London, Department of Employment Research Paper no. 46.

Dex, S. and Perry, S.M. (1984) 'Women's Employment Changes in the 1970's', *Employment Gazette*, vol. 92, no. 4.

DHSS (1973) *Local Authority Building Note 2: Residential Accommodation for Elderly People*, London, DHSS.

DHSS (1974) *Better Pensions: Fully Protected Against Inflation*, Cmnd. 5713, London, HMSO.

DHSS (1975a) *Social Security Pensions Act*, London, HMSO.

DHSS (1975b) *The Census of Residential Accommodation 1970: 1 – Residential Accommodation for the Elderly and for the Younger Physically Handicapped*, London, HMSO.

DHSS (1976a) *Priorities in the Health and Personal Social Services*, Consultative Document, London, HMSO.

DHSS (Social Work Service) (1976b) *Some Aspects of Residential Care*, Social Work Service 10 (July), pp. 3–17.

DHSS (1977a) *Residential Homes For the Elderly: Arrangements for Health Care. A memorandum for guidance*, July, London, DHSS.

DHSS (1977b) *The Way Forward*, London, HMSO.

DHSS (1978) *A Happier Old Age*, London, DHSS.

DHSS (1979a) *Report of the Royal Commission on the National Health Services*, Cmnd. 7615, London, HMSO.

DHSS (Social Work Service) (1979b) *Residential Care for the Elderly in London*.

DHSS (1981a) *Care in Action: A Handbook of Policies and Priorities for the Health and Personal Social Services in England*, London, HMSO.

DHSS (1981b) *Care in the Community*, London, DHSS.

DHSS (1981c) *Growing Older*, Cmnd. 8173, London, HMSO.

DHSS (1982a) *Health and Personal Social Services for England 1982*, Government Statistical Service, London, HMSO.

DHSS (1982b) *Social Security Statistics 1982*, London, HMSO.

DHSS (1983a) *Elderly People in the Community: Their Service Needs*, London, HMSO.

DHSS (1983b) *Seminar on Residential Care for Elderly People (Wednesday 19 October 1983): Background Papers and Synopses of Research*, London, DHSS.

DHSS (1983c) *Social Security Statistics 1983*, London, HMSO.

DHSS (1983d) *Tables on Families with Low Incomes – 1981*, London, DHSS.

DHSS (1984) *Population, Pension Costs and Pensioners' Incomes*, London, HMSO.

DHSS (1985a) *Reform of Social Security*, Cmnd. 9517, London, HMSO.

DHSS (1985b) *Reform of Social Security – Programme for Change*, Cmnd. 9518, London, HMSO.

DHSS (1985c) *Social Security Statistics 1984*, London, HMSO.

DHSS (1985d) *Reform of Social Security: Programme for Action*, Cmnd. 9691, London, HMSO.

DOE (1978) *Adaptations of Housing for People Who are Physically Handicapped*, Circular 59/78, London, DOE.

DOE (1979) *English House Condition Survey 1981*, Part 2, London, HMSO.

DOE/DHSS (1976) *Housing for Old People*, a consultation paper.

Donahue, W. and Tibbitts, C. (1957) *The New Frontiers of Ageing*, Ann Arbor, University of Michigan Press.

Donnison, D. and Ungerson, C. (1982) *Housing Policy*, Harmondsworth, Penguin Books.

Dowd, J. (1980) *Stratification Among the Aged*, Monterey, Calif., Brooks/Cole.

Doyal, L. (1979) *The Political Economy of Health*, London, Pluto Press.

Economist Intelligence Unit (1973) *Care with Dignity: An Analysis of the Costs of Care for the Disabled*, London, National Fund for Research into Crippling Diseases.

Edwards, R., Reich, M. and Gordon, D. (eds) (1975) *Labour Market Segmentation*, Lexington, Mass., D.C. Heath.

Elias, P. and Main, B. (1982) *Women's Working Lives: Evidence from the National Training Survey*, Institute for Employment Research, University of Warwick.

EOC (1980) *The Experience of Caring for Elderly and Handicapped Dependants*, Manchester, EOC.

EOC (1982a) *Caring for the Elderly and Handicapped: Community Care Policies and Women's Lives*, Manchester, EOC.

EOC (1982b) *Who Cares for the Carers?: Opportunities for Those Caring for the Elderly and Handicapped*, Manchester, EOC.

EOC (1984) *Eighth Annual Report 1983*, Manchester, EOC.

Ermisch, J. (1982) 'Resources of the Elderly: Impact of Present Commitments and Established Trends', in M. Fogerty (ed.) *Retirement Policy: the Next Fifty Years*, London, Heinemann Educational Books, pp. 41–61.

Ermisch, J. (1983) *The Political Economy of Demographic Change*, London, Heinemann.

Estes, C.L. (1979) *The Ageing Enterprise*, San Francisco, Josey-Bass.

Estes, C.L. (1980) 'Constructions of Reality', *Journal of Social Issues*, vol. 36, no. 2.

Estes, C.L., Swan, J. and Gerard, L. (1982) 'Dominant and Competing Paradigms in Gerontology: Towards a Political Economy of Ageing', *Ageing and Society*, vol 2, no. 2, pp. 151–64.

Estes, C.L. (1983) 'Austerity and Ageing in the United States: 1980 and Beyond', in A.M. Guillemard (ed.), pp. 169–85.

Estes, C.L. (1984) 'Austerity and Aging: 1980 and Beyond', in M. Minkler and C.L. Estes (eds), pp. 241–53.

Estes, C.L., Gerard, L.E., Zones, J.S. and Swan, J.H. (1984) *Political Economy, Health and Ageing*, Boston, Little, Brown.

Estes, C.L., Newcomer, R.J. and Associates (1983) *Fiscal Austerity and Ageing*, Beverly Hills, Calif., Sage.

Evans, G., Hughes, B., Wilkin, D. with Jolley, D. (1981) *The Management of Mental and Physical Impairment in Non-Specialist Residential Homes for the Elderly*, Research Report no. 4, University of Manchester, Departments of Psychiatry and Community Medicine.

Evans, J. Grimley (1977) 'Current Issues in the United Kingdom', in A.N. Exton Smith and J. Grimley Evans (eds), pp. 128–46.

Evans, J. Grimley (1983) 'Integration of Geriatric with General Medical Services in Newcastle', *The Lancet*, 25 June, pp. 1430–33.

Evers, H. (1981) 'Care or Custody? The Experience of Women Patients in Long-Stay Geriatric Wards', in B. Hutter and G. Williams (eds), *Controlling Women: the Normal and the Deviant*, London, Croom Helm, pp. 108–30.

Evers, H. (1982) 'Professional Practice and Patient Care: Multi-disciplinary Teamwork in Geriatric Wards', *Ageing and Society*, vol. 2, no. 1, pp. 57–76.

Evers, H. (1983) 'Elderly Women and Disadvantage: Perceptions of Daily and Support Relationships', in D. Jerrome (ed.), *Ageing in Modern Society*, London, Croom Helm, pp. 25–44.

Exton-Smith, A.N and Evans, J. Grimley (eds) (1977) *Care of the Elderly*, London, Academic Press.

Fabian Society (ed.) (1984) *Social Security: the Real Agenda*, London, Fabian Society.

Faulkner, A. (1980) 'Ageing and Old Age: The Last Sexist Rip-Off', in E. Norman and A. Mancuso (eds), *Women's Issues and Social Work Practice*, Itasca, Illinois, Peacock, pp. 57–89.

Feldman, J.J. (1983) 'Work Ability of the Aged Under Conditions of Improving Mortality', *Health and Society*, vol. 61, no. 3, pp. 431–43.

Felstein, I. (1969) *Later Life: Geriatrics Today and Tomorrow*, London, Routledge & Kegan Paul.

Fengler, A. and Goodrich, N. (1979) 'Wives of Disabled Men: the Hidden Patients', *The Gerontologist*, vol. 19, pp. 175–83.

Fennell, G. *et al.* (1981) *Day Centres for the Elderly in East Anglia*, Centre for East Anglian Studies, University of East Anglia.

Finch, J. (1984) 'Community Care: Developing Non-Sexist Alternatives', *Critical Social Policy*, no. 9, pp. 6–18.

Finch, J. and Groves, D. (1980) 'Community Care and the Family: A Case for Equal Opportunities?', *Journal of Social Policy*, vol. 9, no. 4, pp. 487–514.

Finch, J. and Groves, D. (1982) 'By Women for Women: Caring for the Frail Elderly', *Women's Studies International Forum*, vol. 5, no. 5, pp. 427–38.

Finch, J. and Groves, D. (eds) (1983) *A Labour of Love: Women, Work and Caring*, London, Routledge & Kegan Paul.

Fine, B. and Harris, L. (1979) *Re-reading Capital*, London, Macmillan.

Fogarty, M. (1975) *40 to 60: How We Waste the Middle Aged*, London, Centre for Studies in Social Policy/Bedford Square Press.

Fogarty, M. (1980) *Retirement Age and Retirement Costs*, London, Policy Studies Institute, Report no. 592.

Fogarty, M. (ed.) (1982) *Retirement Policy – The Next Fifty Years*, London, Heinemann Education Books.

Forrest, R. and Murie, A. (1983) 'Residualization and Council Housing: Aspects of the Changing Social Relations of Housing Tenure', *Journal of Social Policy*, vol. 12, no. 4, pp. 453–68.

Forsyth, G. (1966) *Doctors and State Medicine*, London, Pitman Medical.

Fowler, N. (1984) Speech to the Joint Social Services Annual Conference, Thursday, 27 September.

Freeman, G. and Adams, P. (1982) 'The Politics of Social Security: Expansion, Retrenchment, and Rationalization', in A. Stone and E.J. Harpham (eds), *The Political Economy of Public Money*, Beverly Hills, Calif., Sage, pp. 241–61.

Friedmann, E.A. and Adamachak, D.J. (1983) 'Societal Ageing and Generational Dependency Relationship: Problems of Measurement and Conceptualization', *Research on Aging*, vol. 53, no. 3, pp. 319–38.

Garland, R. (1948) 'End of the Poor Law – and a New Era Dawns in British Social Welfare', *Social Welfare*, vol. 11, no. 2, pp. 36–7.

George, V. (1968) *Social Security: Beveridge and After*, London, Routledge & Kegan Paul.

Giddens, A. (1982) *Sociology: a Brief But Critical Introduction*, New York, Harcourt Brace Jovanovich.

Gilbert, N. (1983) *Capitalism and the Welfare State: Dilemmas of Social Benevolence*, New Haven, Yale University Press.

Gilleard, C.J., Belford, H., Gilleard, E., Whittick, J.E. and Gledhill, K. (1984) 'Emotional Distress Amongst the Supporters of the Elderly Mentally Infirm', *British Journal of Psychiatry*, no. 145, pp. 172–7.

Glendenning, F. (ed.) (1985a) *New Initiatives in Self-Health Care for Older People*, Staffs, Beth Johnson Foundation Publication in association with Keele University Adult Education and the Health Education Council.

Glendenning, F. (ed.) (1985b) *Educational Gerontology: International Perspectives*, London, Croom Helm.

Godlove, C. and Mann, A. (1980) 'Thirty Years of the Welfare State: Current Issues in British Social Policy for the Aged', *Aged Care and Services Review*, vol. 2, no. 1, pp. 1–12.

Goffman, E. (1968) *Asylums*, Harmondsworth, Penguin.

Goldberg, E. and Connelly, N. (1982) *The Effectiveness of Social Care for the Elderly*, London, Heinemann.

Goldberg, E.M. *et al.* (1970) *Helping the Aged*, London, Allen & Unwin.

Goldberg, E.M. and Warburton, W.M. (1979) *Ends and Means in Social Work: The Development and Outcome of a Case Review System*, London, Allen and Unwin.

Goldup, J. (1976) 'It's the Same Old Song', *Case Con*, no. 22.

Gordon, D., Edwards, R. and Reich, M. (1982) *Segmented Work, Divided Workers*, Cambridge, Cambridge University Press.

Gough, I. (1979) *The Political Economy of the Welfare State*, London, Macmillan.

Government Actuary (1978) *Report of the Committee on the Economic and Financial Problems of the Provision of Old Age*, Cmnd. 9333, London, HMSO.

Graebner, W. (1980) *A History of Retirement*, New Haven, Conn., Yale University Press.

Graham, H. (1983) 'Caring: A Labour of Love', in J. Finch and D. Groves (eds), pp. 13–30.

Greater London Council Women's Committee (1984) *Bulletin*, Special Older Women's Issue, issue 20, October, London, GLC.

Green, S., Creese, A. and Kanfert, J. (1979) 'Social Support and Government Policy on Services for the Elderly', *Social Policy and Administration*, vol. 13, no. 3.

Gremion, P. (1976) *Le Pouvoir Periphérique*, Paris, Le Seuil.

Greve, J. (1981) *Assisted Lodgings for the Elderly*, Summary Report, University of Leeds, Department of Social Policy and Administration.

Griew, S. (1964) *Job Re-design*, Paris, OECD.

Griffith, G.W. (1958) Speech given at the Royal Society of Health Annual Congress, *Hospital and Social Services Journal*, 9 May, p. 495.

Groves, D. (1983) 'Members and Survivors: Women and Retirement Pensions Legislation', in J. Lewis (ed.), *Women's Welfare Women's Rights*, London, Croom Helm, pp. 38–63.

Groves, D. and Finch, J. (1983) 'Natural Selection: Perspectives on Entitlement to the Invalid Care Allowance', in J. Finch and D. Groves (eds).

Guillebaud Report (1956) *Report of the Committee of Enquiry into the Cost of the National Health Service*, Cmnd. 9663, London, HMSO.

Guillemard, A.-M. (1980) *La Vieillesse et l'Etat*, Paris, Presses Universitaires de France.

Guillemard, A.-M. (1983a) 'La Dynamique Sociale des Cessations Anticipées d'Activité', *Travail et Emploi*, no. 15, March, pp. 15–32.

Guillemard, A.-M. (ed.) (1983b) *Old Age and the Welfare State*, London, Sage.

Guillemard, A.-M. (1984) *Dynamique et Crise des Politiques de la Vieillesse*, *Contribution à une Sociologie des Politiques Sociales*, Thèse d'Etat, Paris, Ecole des Hautes Etudes en Sciences Sociales.

Haber, C. (1978) 'Mandatory Retirement in Nineteenth-Century America: the Conceptual Basis for a New Work Cycle', *Journal of Social History*, vol. 12, no. 1, pp. 77–96.

Habermas, J. (1975) *Legitimation Crisis*, Boston, Beacon Press.

Hadley, R. and McGrath, M. (eds) (1981) *Going Local: Neighbourhood Social Services*, London, National Council for Voluntary Organisations/ Bedford Square Press.

Hale, J. (1983) 'Feminism and Social Work Practice', in B. Jordan and N. Parton (eds), pp. 167–87.

Hare, E.J. (1977) *Three Score Years and Then?: A Study of Practical Alternatives to Residential Care*, Norfolk County Council.

Harris, A. (1971) *Handicapped and Impaired in Great Britain*, London, HMSO.

Harris, A.I. (1968) *Social Welfare for the Elderly*, Government Social Survey, vol. 1, London, HMSO.

Harris, A.I. *et al.* (1972) *Income and Entitlement to Supplementary Benefit of Impaired People in Great Britain*, London, HMSO.

Hatch, S. (1980) *Outside the State*, London, Croom Helm.

Hatherley, R. (1983) 'Senile Dementia: Who Suffers Most?', *New Age*, no. 23, Autumn, pp. 12–13.

Havinghurst, R.J. (1968) 'Personality and Patterns of Ageing', *The Gerontologist*, vol. 8, pp. 20–3.

Health Advisory Service (1983) *The Rising Tide*, London, DHSS.

Hendricks, J. and Hendricks, C.D. (1977) *Ageing in Mass Society*, Cambridge, Mass., Winthrop.

Hendricks, J. and McAllister, C.E. (1983) 'An Alternative Perspective on Retirement: a Dual Economic Approach', *Ageing and Society*, vol. 3, no. 3, pp. 279–99.

Henretta, J.C. and Campbell, R.T. (1976) 'Status Attainment and Status Maintenance: A Study of Stratification in Old Age', *American Sociological Review*, vol. 41.

Henry, J. (1965) *Culture Against Man*, New York, Random House.

Henwood, M. and Wicks, M. (1984) *The Forgotten Army: Family Care and Elderly People*, London, Family Policy Studies Centre.

Heron, A. (1962) 'Preparation for Retirement: A New Phase in Occupational Development', *Occupational Psychology*, nos 1 and 2, pp. 1–9.

Heron, A. and Chown, S.M. (1960) 'Semi-skilled and Over Forty', *Occupational Psychology*, no. 4, pp. 263–74.

Heron, A. and Chown, S.M. (1967) *Age and Function*, London, Churchill.

Heumann, L. and Boldby, D. (1982) *Housing for the Elderly: Planning and*

Policy Formation in Western Europe and North America, London, Croom Helm.

Himmelstrand, U., Ahrne, G., Lundberg, L. and Lundberg, L. (1981) *Beyond Welfare Capitalism*, London, Heinemann.

Honigsbaum, F. (1979) *The Division in British Medicine: a History of the Separation of General Practice from Hospital Care, 1911–1968*, London, Kogan Page.

Horder, J.P. (1983) 'General Practice in 2000: Alma Ata Declaration', *British Medical Journal*, vol. 1, p. 191.

Horder, J.P. and Swift, G. (1979) 'The History of Vocational Training for General Practice', *Journal of the Royal College of General Practitioners*, vol. 29, pp. 24–32.

Hospital and Social Services Journal (1959) 'Present-Day Problems of the Welfare Services', 9 January, p. 35.

House of Commons (1947) *Hansard*, vol. 444, 24 November, col. 1609.

House of Commons (1953) *Hansard*, vol. 522, 14 December, col. 167.

House of Commons (1958) *Hansard*, vol. 582, 12 February, col. 535.

House of Commons (1981) *Hansard*, vol. 998, London, HMSO.

House of Commons (1982) *Hansard*, vol. 34, 16 December, col. 253.

House of Commons (1983) *Hansard*, vol. 48, no. 49, 15 November.

House of Commons (1984a) *Fourth Report from the Social Services Committee Session 1983–84*, London, HMSO.

House of Commons (1984b) *Hansard*, vol. 57, no. 130, 26 March, col. 74.

House of Commons (1984c) *Hansard*, vol. 57, no. 133, 3 April.

Howe, D. (1980) 'Division of Labour in the Area Teams of Social Services Departments', *Social Policy and Administration*, vol. 14, no. 2, pp. 133–50.

Hughes, B. and Wilkin, D. (1980) *Residential Care of the Elderly: A Review of the Literature*, Research Report no. 4, University of Manchester, Departments of Psychiatry and Community Medicine.

Hunt, A. (1968) *Women's Employment*, vol. 1, London, HMSO.

Hunt, A. (1970) *The Home Help Service in England and Wales*, London, HMSO.

Hunt, A. (1978) *The Elderly at Home*, London, HMSO.

Hunter, G.M. (1981) 'Improving Geriatric Care in General Practice', *Geriatric Medicine*, January, pp. 60–3.

Illich, I. (1975) *Medical Nemesis*, London, Calder and Boyars.

Institute of Gerontology (1975) *No Longer Young: the Older Woman in America*, Proceedings of the 26th Annual Conference on Aging, University of Michigan/Wayne State University.

Irvine, D. (1983) 'Quality of Care in General Practice: Our Outstanding Problem', *Journal of the Royal College of General Practitioners*, vol. 33, pp. 521–3.

Isaacs, B., Livingstone, M. and Neville, Y. (1972) *Survival of the Unfittest*, London, Routledge & Kegan Paul.

Itzin, C. (1984) 'The Double Jeopardy of Ageism and Sexism: Media Images of Women', in D.B. Bromely (ed.), *Gerontology: Social and Behavioural Perspectives*, London, Croom Helm, pp. 170–84.

Jackson, M. (1984) 'Early Retirement: Recent Trends and Implications', *Industrial Relations Journal*, vol. 15, no. 3, pp. 21–8.

James, C. (1984) *Occupational Pensions: The Failure of Private Welfare*, London, Fabian Society.

Jeffreys, M. (1977) 'The Elderly in the United Kingdom', in A.N. Exton-Smith and J.G. Evans (eds), *Care of the Elderly: Meeting the Challenge of Dependency*, London, Academic Press.

Johnson, M.L. (1973) 'Old and Young in the Family: a Negotiated Arrangement', Paper given at the British Society for Social and Behavioural Gerontology Conference.

Johnson, M.L. (1981) 'Community Care for Elderly People: A Case Study in Symbolic Social Policy', *Policy Studies* vol. 2, Part 2.

Johnson, P. (1985) *The Economics of Old Age in Britain: A Long-Run View 1881–1981*, Discussion Paper no. 47, Centre for Economic Policy Research.

Johnston, S. and Phillipson, C. (1983) *Older Learners: The Challenge to Adult Education*, London, Bedford Square Press.

Jolley, D.J. and Arie, T. (1978) 'Organisation of Psychogeriatric Services', *British Journal of Psychiatry*, Vol. 132, pp. 1–11.

Jones, C. (1983) *State Social Work and the Working Class*, London, Macmillan.

Jones, D.A. and Vetter, N.J. (1984) 'A Survey of Those Who Care for the Elderly at Home: Their Problems and Their Needs', *Social Science and Medicine*, vol. 19, no. 5, pp. 511–14.

Jones, R. Huws (1952) 'Old People's Welfare – Successes and Failures', *Social Service Quarterly*, vol. 26, no. 1, pp. 19–22.

Jordan, B. and Parton, N. (1983) *The Political Dimensions of Social Work*, Oxford, Blackwell.

Joshi, H.E. (1962) 'Secondary Workers in the Cycle', *Economica*, vol. 48.

Joshi, H. and Ermisch, J. (1982) 'The Trend to Increased Female Labour Force Participation and Women's Pension Rights in the Transition to Maturity', in M. Fogarty (ed.), *Retirement Policy: the Next Fifty Years*, London, Heinemann Educational Books, pp. 62–5.

Jowell, R. and Airey, C. (1984) *British Social Attitudes: The 1984 Report*, Aldershot, Gower.

Judge, K. (1984) *Residential Care for the Elderly: Purposes and Resources*, University of Kent, Personal Social Services Research Unit.

Judge, K., Knapp, M. and Smith, J. (1983) 'The Comparative Costs of Public and Private Residential Homes for the Elderly', DHSS Seminar Papers on Residential Research, October.

Kamerman, S.B. and Kahn, A.J. (eds) (1978) *Family Policy: Government and Families in Fourteen Countries*, New York, Columbia University Press.

Karn, V. (1977) *Retiring to the Seaside*, London, Routledge & Kegan Paul.

Kearl, M.C., Moore, K. and Osberg, J.S. (1982) 'Political Implications of the "New Ageism"', *International Journal of Aging and Human Development*, vol. 15, no. 3, pp. 167–83.

Kellaher, L., Peace, S. and Willcocks, D. (1983) *The Essence of Home*, London, Centre of Environments for the Handicapped.

Keller, B. (1984) 'Another Stab at Pension Reform', *The New York Times*, 15 July.

Kidd, C.B. (1962) 'Misplacement of the Elderly in Hospital', *British Medical Journal*, 2.

Kilroy, B. (1982) 'Public Expenditure on Housing', in A. Walker (ed.), *Public Expenditure and Social Policy*, London, Heinemann Educational Books.

Kimbell, A., Townsend, J. and Bird, M. (1974) 'Elderly Persons' Homes: A Study of Various Aspects of Regime and Activities ... and their Effects Upon the Residents', Cheshire Social Services Department Research Section.

Kincaid, J.C. (1973) *Poverty and Equality in Britain*, Harmondsworth, Penguin.

King, R.D., Raynes, N.V. and Tizard, J. (1971) *Patterns of Residential Care*, London, Routledge & Kegan Paul.

Knox, J.D.E., Anderson, R.A., Jacob, A. and Campion, P.D. (1984) 'General Practitioners' Care of the Elderly: Studies of Aspects of Workload', *Journal of the Royal College of General Practitioners*, vol. 34, pp. 194–8.

Kreps, J. (1977) 'Intergenerational Transfers and the Bureaucracy', in E. Shanas and M. Sussman (eds).

Kutza, E.A. (1981) *The Benefits of Old Age: Social Welfare Policy for the Elderly*, Chicago, University of Chicago Press.

Labour Housing Group (1984) *Right to a Home*, Nottingham, Spokesman Books.

Laczko, F. and Walker, A. (1985) 'Excluding Older Workers from the Labour Force: Early Retirement Policies in Britain, France and Sweden', in M. Brenton and C. Jones (eds), *Year Book of Social Policy in Britain 1984*, London, Routledge & Kegan Paul.

Lalljee, R. (1983) *Black Elders: A Discussion Paper*, Nottingham, Social Services Department Research Section.

Laming, H., *et al.* (1984) *Residential Care for the Elderly: Present Problems and Future Issues*, London, PSI.

Land, H. (1978) 'Who Cares for the Family?', *Journal of Social Policy*, vol. 7, no. 3, pp. 357–84.

Lang, A. and Brody, E.M. (1983) 'Characteristics of Middle-Aged Daughters and Help to Their Elderly Mothers', *Journal of Marriage and the Family*, no. 45, pp. 193–202.

Laurie, P. (1974) 'The Real Police', in *Meet Your Friendly Social System*, London, Arrow.

Layard, R., Paichaud, D. and Stewart, M. (1978) *The Causes of Poverty*, Royal Commission on the Distribution of Income and Wealth, Background Paper no. 5, London, HMSO.

Le Gros Clark, F. (1966) *Work, Age and Leisure*, London, Michael Joseph.

Leonard, P. (1975) *Personality and Ideology: Towards a Materialist Understanding of the Individual*, London, Macmillan.

Leonard, P. (1975) 'Towards a Paradigm for Radical Practice', in R. Bailey and M. Brake (eds), *Radical Social Work*, London, Arnold, pp. 46–61.

Levin, E., Sinclair, I. and Gorbach, P. (1983) *Supporters of Confused Elderly Persons at Home*, NISW Report (publication by Allen and Unwin pending).

Lewis, M.I. and Butler, R.N. (1982) 'Why is Women's Lib Ignoring Old Women?', *International Journal of Aging and Human Development*, vol. 3, pp. 223–31.

Libjestrom, R. (1978) 'Sweden', in S.B. Kamerman and A.J. Kahn (eds), pp. 19–48.

Lipman, A. and Slater, R. (1977) 'Status and Spatial Appropriation in Eight Homes for Old People', *The Gerontologist*, vol. 17, no. 3, pp. 250–5.

Little, V. (ed.) (1980) *The Older Woman*, A collection of papers written in conjunction with a new course, Career training in aging, School of Social Work, University of Connecticut, Spring.

Livson, F.B. (1976) 'Patterns of Personality Development in Middle-Aged Women: a longitudinal study', *International Journal of Ageing and Human Development*, vol. 7, no. 2, pp. 107–15.

Long, P. (1979) 'Speaking Out on Age', *Spare Rib*, no. 82, May, pp. 14–17.

Lowther, C. and Williamson, J. (1966) 'Old People and Their Relatives', *The Lancet*, 21 March, p. 1460.

Lowy, L. (1980) *Social Policies and Programs on Ageing*, Lexington, Mass., Lexington Books.

Luker, K.A. (1982) 'Screening of the Well Elderly in General Practice', *Midwife, Health Visitor and Community Nurse*, vol. 18, p. 6.

Macdonald, B. with Rich, C. (1984) *Look Me in the Eye: Old Women, Ageing and Ageism*, London, The Women's Press.

MacDonald, R., Qureshi, H. and Walker, A. (1984) 'Sheffield Shows the Way', *Community Care*, 18 October, pp. 28–30.

McGoldrick, A. and Cooper, C. (1980) 'Voluntary Early Retirement – Taking the Decision', *Employment Gazette*, August, pp. 859–64.

McIntyre, S. (1977) 'Old Age as a Social Problem', in R. Dingwall, C. Heath, M. Reid and M. Stacey (eds), *Health Care and Health Knowledge*, London, Croom Helm, pp. 41–63.

Mackay, D.I. (1973) 'Redundancy and Re-engagement: A Study of Car Workers', *Manchester School*, September.

Mckenzie, H. (1980) *You Alone Care*, London, SPCK.

McLeod, E. and Dominelli, L. (1982) 'The Personal and the Apolitical: Feminism and Moving Beyond the Integrated Methods of Approach', in R. Bailey and P. Lee (eds), *Theory and Practice in Social Work*, Oxford, Blackwell, pp. 112–27.

Maeda, D. (1978) 'Ageing in Eastern Society', in D. Hobman (ed.), *The Social Challenge of Ageing*, London, Croom Helm.

Makeham, P. (1980) *Economic Aspects of the Employment of Older Workers*, Research Paper no. 14, London, Department of Employment.

Marshall, M. (1983) *Social Work with Old People*, London, Macmillan.

Martin, G. (1984) 'Transforming Our Love into Deed', *Social Work Today*, 4 June, pp. 12–14.

Martin, J. and Roberts, C. (1984) *Women and Employment: A Lifetime Perspective*, London, HMSO.

Masterton, G., *et al.* (1981) 'Role of Local Authority Homes in the Care of the Dependent Elderly: A Prospective Study', *British Medical Journal*, 283, 22 August.

Mathews, S. (1979) *The Social World of Old Women*, Beverly Hills, Sage Publications.

Mathieson, G. (ed.) (1957) *Flexible Retirement: Economic Policies and Programs for Industry and Later*, New York, Putnam.

Mays, N. (1983) 'Elderly South Asians in Britain: A Survey of Relevant Literature and Themes for Future Research', *Ageing and Society*, vol. 3, pp. 71–97.

Meacher, M. (1970) 'The Old: the Future of Community Care', in P. Townsend (ed.), *The Fifth Social Service: A Critical Analysis of the Seebohm Proposals*, London, Fabian Society.

Meacher, M. (1972) *Taken For a Ride*, London, Longman.

Meadows, W.J. (1981) 'Local Government', in P.M. Jackson (ed.), *Government Policy Initiatives 1797–80*, London, Royal Institute of Public Administration.

Means, R. (1981) *Community Care and Meals on Wheels*, University of Bristol, School for Advanced Urban Studies (Working Paper no. 21).

Means, R. and Smith, R. (1983) 'From Public Assistance Institutions to "Sunshine Hotels": Changing State Perceptions About Residential Care for Elderly People', *Ageing and Society*, vol. 3, Part 2, pp. 157–81.

Means, R. and Smith, R. (1985) *The Development of Welfare Services for the Elderly*, London, Croom Helm.

Medical Officer (1954) 'Institutions for Ailing and Frail Old People', 3 December, p. 283.

Meenagham, T.M. and Washington, R.O. (1980) *Social Policy and Social Welfare: Structure and Applications*, New York, The Free Press.

Men and Women (1953) *First Report*, Cmnd. 8963, London, HMSO.

Mendelson, M. (1974) *A Tender Loving Greed*, New York, Knopf.

Merrett, S. (1982) *Owner Occupation in Britain*, London, Routledge & Kegan Paul.

Mezey, A.G., Hodkinson, H.M. and Evans G.J. (1968) 'The Elderly in the Wrong Unit', *British Medical Journal*, 3.

Miller, E.J. and Gwynne, G.V. (1972) *A Life Apart*, London, Tavistock.

Ministère des Affairs Sociales et de la Solidarité Nationale (1982) 'Retraites et Personnes Agées, Politique Sociale et la Solidarité Nationale', *Journal Officiel*, 8 June.

Ministry of Health (1948) 'National Assistance Act 1948', *Circular 87/48*, 7 June.

Ministry of Health (1951) 'National Assistance – Welfare Services: Capital Investment Programmes', *File 94020/1/112 Part A*. This file is still at the DHSS and has not yet been processed for the Public Records Office.

Ministry of Health (1952) *Report of the Ministry of Health covering the period 1st April 1950 to 31st December 1951*, Cmnd. 8655, London, HMSO.

Ministry of Health (1954) *Report of the Ministry of Health for the year ending 31st December 1953*, Cmnd. 8321, London, HMSO.

Ministry of Health (1957) 'Local Authority Services for the Chronic Sick and Infirm', *Circular 14/57*, 7 October.

Ministry of Health (1959) 'National Health Service Act, 1946, Section 98: Chiropody Services', *Circular 11/59*, 21 April.

Ministry of Health (1961) *Report of the Ministry of Health for the year ended 31st December 1960*, Cmnd. 1418, London, HMSO.

Ministry of Health (1962a) *A Hospital Plan for England and Wales*, Cmnd. 1604, London, HMSO.

Ministry of Health (1962b) *Local Authority Building Note No. 1: Residential Accommodation for Elderly People*, London, HMSO.

Ministry of Health (1962c) 'Development of Health and Welfare Services: Co-operation with Voluntary Organisations', *Circular 7/62*, 12 April.

Ministry of Health (1963) *Health and Welfare: the Development of Community Care*, Cmnd. 1973, London, HMSO.

Ministry of Labour and National Service (1959) *Annual Report for 1958*, Cmnd. 745, London, HMSO.

Ministry of Pensions (1954) *Report of the Committee on the Economic and Financial Problems of the Provision for Old Age* (Chairman: Sir J. Phillips), London, HMSO.

Ministry of Pensions and National Insurance (1966) *Financial and Other Circumstances of Retirement Pensioners*, London, HMSO.

Minkler, M. and Estes, C.L. (eds) (1984) *Readings in the Political Economy of Ageing*, New York, Baywood.

Minns, R. (1980) *Pension Funds and British Capitalism*, London, Heinemann.

Moroney, R.M. (1976) *The Family and the State*, London, Longman.

Morris, J. (1983) 'Social Security: the Phoney Crisis', *Monthly Review*, vol. 34, no. 9, pp. 1–16.

Mortimer, E. (1982) *Working with the Elderly*, London, Heinemann.

Municipal Review Supplement (1954) 'Evidence of AMC to the Phillips Committee', June, p. 108.

Munnell, A.H. (1984) 'Navigating a Few Rough Spots Ahead: the Social Security Solution, cont.', *The New York Times*, 12 August.

Munnichs, J. and Van der Heuval, W. (eds) (1976) *Dependence and Interdependence in Old Age*, The Hague, Nijhoff.

Murie, A. (1983a) 'Housing: a Thoroughly Residual Policy', in D. Bull and P. Wilding (eds), *Thatcherism and the Poor*, Poverty pamphlet 59, London, Child Poverty Action Group.

Murie, A. (1983b) *Housing Inequality and Deprivation*, London, Heinemann Educational Books.

Murie, A. (1984) 'The Right to Buy: Emerging Issues', *Housing Review*, vol. 33, no. 4, pp. 132–3.

Murphy, F.W. (1977) 'Blocked Beds', *British Medical Journal*, vol. 1, pp. 1395–96.

Murrell, K.F.H. (1959) 'Major Problems of Industrial Gerontology', *Journal of Gerontology*, vol. 14, p. 216.

Myles, J. (1983) 'Comparative Public Policies for the Elderly: Frameworks and Resources for Analysis', in A.M. Guillemard (ed.), pp. 19–44.

Myles, J. (1984a) 'Does Class Matter? Explaining America's Modern Welfare State', Paper presented to the Conference on 'Theoretical Approaches to American Social Politics' sponsored by the Center for the Study of Industrial Societies, University of Chicago, November.

Myles, J. (1984b) *Old Age in the Welfare State: the Political Economy of Public Pensions*, Boston, Little, Brown.

Myles, J. (1984c) 'Conflict, Crisis, and the Future of Old Age Security', in V. Minkler and C. Estes (eds), pp. 168–76.

National Advisory Committee on the Employment of Older Men and Women (1955) *Second Report*, Cmnd. 9262, London, HMSO.

National Association of Pension Funds (1983) *Survey of Occupational Pensions Schemes*, London, NAPF.

National Labour Women's Advisory Committee (1965) *Survey into Care of the Elderly: Second Interim and Final Report*, London, Labour Party.

Navarro, V. (1983) 'The Administration's Health Policies: Four Myths', *Social Policy*, vol. 14, no. 2, pp. 20–2.

Navarro, V. (1984) 'The Political Economy of Government Cuts for the Elderly', in M. Minkler and C. Estes (eds), pp. 37–47.

Nelson, G.M. (1982) 'Social Class and Public Policy for the Elderly', in B. Neugarten (ed.), *Age or Need? Public Policies for Older People*, Beverly Hills, Sage, pp. 101–29.

New York Times News Service (1985) 'Federal Survey Finds Union Membership Still Dropping', February.

Neysmith, S.M. and Edwardh, J. (1984) 'Economic Dependency in the 1980's: Its Impact on Third World Elderly', *Ageing and Society*, vol. 4, Part 1, pp.21–44.

Nissel, M. and Bonnerjea, L. (1982) *Family Care of the Handicapped Elderly: Who Pays?*, London, PSI.

Norman, A. (1982) *Rights and Risks*, London, Centre for Policy on Ageing.

Norman, A. (1984) *Bricks and Mortar*, London, Centre for Policy on Ageing.

O'Connor, J. (1973) *The Fiscal Crisis of the State*, New York, St Martin's Press.

Offe, C. (1972a) *Structural Problems of the Capitalist State*, London, Macmillan.

Offe, C. (1972b) 'Advanced Capitalism and the Welfare State', *Politics and Society*, vol. 2 (Summer), pp. 479–88.

Offe, C. (1984) *Contradictions of the Welfare State*, London, Hutchinson.

Older Women's League (1980a) *Older Women and Health Care: Strategy for Survival*, Gray paper no. 3, Washington, D.C., Older Women's League.

Older Women's League (1980b) *Welfare: End of the Line for Women*, Gray Paper no. 4, Washington, D.C., Older Women's League.

Older Women's League (1982a) *The Disillusionment of Divorce for Older Women*, Gray Paper no. 6, Washington, D.C., Older Women's League.

Older Women's League (1982b) *Till Death do us Part: Caregivers of Severely Disabled Husbands*, Gray Paper no. 7, Washington, D.C., Older Women's League.

Older Women's League (1982c) *Not Even for Dogcatcher: Employment, Discrimination and Older Women*, Gray Paper no. 8, Washington, D.C., Older Women's League.

Oliver, J. (1983) 'The Caring Wife', in J. Finch and D. Groves (eds), pp. 72–85.

Olsen, H. and Hansen, G. (1981) *Living Conditions of the Aged 1977*, Copenhagen, National Institute of Social Research.

Olson, L.K. (1982) *The Political Economy of Ageing: the State, Private Power, and Social Welfare*, New York, Columbia University Press.

OPCS (1981) *General Household Survey 1980*, London, HMSO.

OPCS (1982) *General Household Survey 1981*, London, HMSO.

OPCS (1983a) *Census 1981, National Report Great Britain*, part I, CEN 81 NR (I), London, HMSO.

OPCS (1983b) *Census 1981: Persons of Pensionable Age*, London, HMSO.

OPCS (1984a) *General Household Survey 1982*, London, HMSO.

OPCS (1984b) 'General Household Survey, Preliminary Results for 1983', *OPCS Monitor*, July.

Orloff, M.R. and Skocpol, T. (1984) 'Why Not Equal Protection? Explaining the Politics of Public Spending in Britain, 1900–1911 and the United States 1880s–1920', *American Sociological Review*, vol. 49, no. 6, pp. 726–50.

Owen, F. (1979) 'The Health of the Old', *New Society*, 15 September.

Palmore, E.B. (1976) 'Compulsory versus Flexible Retirement: Issues and Facts', in V. Carver and P. Liddieard (eds), *An Ageing Population*, Sevenoaks, Hodder and Stoughton, pp. 87–93.

Parker, G. (1985) *With Due Care and Attention*, London, Family Policy Studies Centre.

Parker, J. (1965) *Local Health and Welfare Services*, London, George Allen & Unwin.

Parker, R. (1981) 'Tending and Social Policy', in E.M. Goldberg and S. Hatch (eds), *A New Look at the Personal Social Services*, London, PSI, pp. 17–32.

Parker, S. (1980) *Older Workers and Retirement*, London, OPCS.

Parsons, T. (1942) 'Age and Sex in the Social Structure of the United States', *American Sociological Review*, 1, 604–16.

Parsons, T. (1964) *Social Structure and Personality*, New York, Free Press of Glencoe.

Pattie, A.H. and Gilleard, C.J. (1979) *Manual of Clifton Assessment Procedures for the Elderly*, Sevenoaks, Hodder and Stoughton.

Peace, S. (1980) *An International Perspective on the Status of Older Women*, Washington, D.C., International Federation on Ageing.

Peace, S. (1983a) 'The Design of Residential Homes – An Historical Perspective', DHSS Seminar Papers in Residential Research, October.

Peace, S. (1983b) 'A Pleasure to Live In?', *Community Care*, no. 455, 24 March.

Peace, S., Hall, J. and Hamblin, G. (1979) *The Quality of Life of Elderly People in Residential Care*, Research Report, Polytechnic of North London, Department of Applied Social Studies.

Peace, S., Kellaher, L. and Willcocks, D. (1982) *A Balanced Life: Phillips Committee (1954) Report of the Committee on the Authority Homes*, Polytechnic of North London, Department of Applied Social Studies.

Pensioners Link (1983) *Pensioners Link*, Task Force Annual Report 1982–83, London, Task Force.

Personal Social Services Council (1977) *Residential Care Reviewed*, London.

Pettitt, D. (1984) 'Residential Home for the Elderly Mentally Infirm', in B. Isaacs and H. Evers, *Innovation in the care of the Elderly*, Beckenham, Croom Helm.

Phillips Report (1954) *Report of the Committee on the Economic and Financial Problems of the Provision for Old Age*, Cmnd. 933, London, HMSO.

Phillipson, C. (1981) 'Women in Later Life', in B. Hutter and G. Williams (eds), *Controlling Women: the Normal and the Deviant*, London, Croom Helm, pp. 185–202.

Phillipson, C. (1982) *Capitalism and the Construction of Old Age*, London, Macmillan.

Phillipson, C. and Strang, P. (1983) *The Impact of Pre-retirement Education: A Longitudinal Evaluation*, Stoke-on-Trent, Department of Adult Education, University of Keele.

Phillipson, C. and Strang, P. (1985) *Health Education and Older People: The Role of Paid Carers*, Stoke-on-Trent, Health Education Council in association with the Department of Adult Education, University of Keele.

Phillipson, C. and Strang, P. (1986) *Training and Education for an Ageing Society: New Perspectives for the Health and Social Sciences*, Stoke-on-Trent, Health Education Council in association with the Department of Adult and Continuing Education, University of Keele.

Pinker, R.A. (1974) 'Social Policy and Social Justice', *Journal of Social Policy*, vol. 3, no. 1, pp. 1–19.

Piven, F.F. and Cloward, R.A. (1971) *Regulating the Poor: the Functions of Public Welfare*, New York, Vintage Books.

Plank, D. (1978) *Caring for the Elderly: Report of a study of various means of caring for dependent elderly people in eight London boroughs*, Research Memorandum, Greater London Council.

Porchino, J. (1983) *Growing Older, Getting Better: a Handbook for Women in the Second Half of Life*, Massachusetts, Addison-Wesley.

Poulantzas, N. (1979) 'The Political Crisis and the Crisis of the State', in J.W. Frieberg (ed.), *Critical Sociology*, New York, Irvington, pp. 357–93.

Power M., Clough, R., Gibson, P. and Kelly, S. (1983) *Helping Lively Minds: Volunteer Support in Residential Homes*, University of Bristol, School of Applied Social Studies.

Preston, C.E. (1975) 'An Old Bag: the Stereotypes of the Older Woman', in *No Longer Young: the Older Woman in America*, Proceedings of the 26th Annual Conference on Aging, The Institute of Gerontology, University of Michigan/Wayne State University, pp. 41–5.

PRO (1946) 'Mobile Meals and Allied Services', File *AST 7/851*.

PRO (1947) File *CAB 134/698*. A copy of the Rucker Report is attached to the minutes of the seventh meeting of the social services committee.

Puner, M. (1978) *To the Good Long Life*, London, Macmillan.

Quadagno, J.S. (1984) 'Welfare Capitalism and the Social Security Act of 1935', *American Sociological Review*, vol. 49, no. 5, pp. 632–47.

Qureshi, H. and Walker, A. (1986) *The Caring Relationship*.

Reddin, M. (1980) 'Taxation and Pensions', in C. Sandford, C. and R. Walker (eds) *Taxation and Social Policy*, London, Heinemann, pp. 115–34.

Reddin, M. (1984) 'Cost and Portability', in Fabian Society (ed.) pp. 11–14.

Reddin, M. and Pilch, M. (1985) *Can We Afford Our Future?*, Mitcham, Age Concern.

Rees, S. (1978) *Social Work Face to Face*, London, Arnold.

Rimmer, L. (1983) 'The Economics of Work and Caring', in J. Finch and D. Groves (eds), pp. 131–47.

Ritchie, J. and Barrowclough, R. (1983) *Paying for Equalisation: a Survey of Pension Age Preferences and Their Costs*, Manchester, EOC and SCPR.

Robb, B. (1968) *Sans Everything: A Case to Answer*, London, Nelson.

Roberts, C. (1981) 'Women's Unemployment'. Paper presented to SSRC Workshop on Employment and Unemployment', October.

Rolston, B. and Smyth, M. (1982) 'The Spaces between Cases: Radical Social Work in Northern Ireland', in R. Bailey and P. Lee (eds), *Theory and Practice in Social Work*, Oxford, Blackwell, pp. 201–28.

Rosen, S. (1982) 'United States', in J.J. Rosa (ed.), *World Crisis in Social Security*, Paris, Fondation Nationale d'Economie Politique, pp. 150–80.

Rosenmayer, L. and Kockeis, E. (1963) 'Propositions for a Sociological Theory of Ageing and the Family', *International Social Service Journal*, vol. 15, no. 3, pp. 410–26.

Roth, J.A. and Eddy, E.M. (1967) *Rehabilitation for the Unwanted*, New York, Atherton.

Rowbotham, S. (1973) *Woman's Consciousness, Man's World*, Harmondsworth, Penguin Books.

Rowlings, C. (1981) *Social Work with Elderly People*, London, Allen & Unwin.

Rowlings, C. (1982) 'Practice in Field Care', *Research Highlights*, no. 3, pp. 146–57.

Rowntree, B.S. (1980 edn) *Old People: Report of a Survey Committee on the Problems of Ageing and the Care of Old People*, New York, Arno Press.

Royal College of General Practitioners (1972) *The Future General Practitioner*, London, RCGP.

Royal Commission on the Distribution of Income and Wealth (1978), *Lower Incomes*, Report no. 6, London, HMSO.

Royal Commission on the NHS (1979) *Report*, Cmnd. 7615, London, HMSO.

Rubin, S.G. and Davies, G.H. (1975) 'Bed Blocking by Elderly Patients in General Hospital Wards', *Age and Ageing*, vol. 4, pp. 142–7.

Ryan, T. (1966) 'The Workhouse Legacy', *The Medical Officer*, 11 November, pp. 270–1.

Sainsbury, P. and Grad de Alarcon, J. (1971) 'The Psychiatrist and the Geriatric Patient', *Journal of Geriatric Psychiatry*, vol. 4, no. 1, pp. 23–41.

Samson, E. (1944) *Old Age in the Modern World*, London, Pilot Press.

Sanford, J. (1975) 'Tolerance of Debility in Elderly Dependants by Supporters at Home: its Significance for Hospital Practice', *British Medical Journal*, vol. 3, pp. 471–3.

Savo, C. (1984) *Self-Care and Self-Help Programmes for Older Adults in the United States*, Working Papers on the Health of Older People no. 1, Health Education Council in association with the Department of Adult Education, University of Keele.

Schiphorst, B. (1979) 'Development of a functional rating chart for the elderly: application in Cleveland and Sunderland social services departments', *Social Work Service*, 19, March.

Schneider, M. (1975) *Neurosis and Civilization*, New York, Seabury.

Scrivens, E. (1982), 'The National Health Service: Origins and Issues', in D.L. Patrick and G. Scambler (eds), *Sociology as Applied to Medicine*, London, Ballière Tindall, pp. 195–212.

Seebohm Committee (1968) *Report of the Committee on Local Authority and Allied Personal Social Services*, London, HMSO.

Seyd, R., Tennant, A. and Bayley, M. (1983) *The Home Help Service*, Working Paper no. 6, The Dinnington Project, Department of Sociological Studies, University of Sheffield.

Shanas, E. (1979) 'Social Myth as Hypothesis: the Case of the Family Relations of Old People', *The Gerontologist*, vol. 19, pp. 3–9.

Shanas, E. and Sussman, M.B. (eds) (1977) *Family, Bureaucracy and the Elderly*, Durham N.C., Duke University Press.

Shanas, E., Townsend, P., Wedderburn, D., Henning, F., Milhøf, P. and Stehouwer, J. (1968) *Old People in three Industrialised Societies*, London, Routledge & Kegan Paul.

Shaw, L.B. (1984) 'Retirement Plans of Middle-Aged Married Women', *The Gerontologist*, vol. 24, no. 2.

Sheldon, A. (ed.) (1980) *The Litmuss Papers*, London, Centre for Policy Studies.

Sheldon, J. (1948) *The Social Medicine of Old Age*, London, Oxford University Press.

Sheldon, J. (1955) 'The Social Philosophy of Old Age', in *Old Age in the Modern World*, Report of the Third Congress of the International Association of Gerontology, Edinburgh, Livingstone, pp. 15–26.

Sheldon, J. (1960) 'Problems of an Ageing Population', *British Medical Journal*, 23 April, p. 1225.

Shenfield, B. (1957) *Social Policies for Old Age*, London, Routledge & Kegan Paul.

Shields, L. (1981) *Displaced Homemakers: Organising for a New Life*, New York, McGraw-Hill.

Shragge, E. (1984) *Pensions Policy in Britain*, London, Routledge & Kegan Paul.

Sinclair, I., Crosbie, D., O'Connor, P., Stanforth, L. and Vickery, A.

(1984) *Networks Project: A study of informal care, services and social work for elderly clients living alone*, National Institute for Social Work Research Unit.

Smelser, N.J. (1959) *Social Change in the Industrial Revolution*, Chicago, University of Chicago Press.

Social Security Administration (1984) *Social Security Programs Throughout the World – 1983*, Research Report no. 59, Washington, D.C., US Government Printing Office.

Social Services Buildings Research Team (1977) *Local Authority Housing for Elderly People*, Oxford, Oxford Polytechnic.

Sontag, S. (1972) 'The Double Standard of Ageing', *Saturday Review*, vol. 55, 23 September, pp. 29–38.

Sontag, S. (1975) 'The Double Standard of Ageing', *No Longer Young: The Older Woman in America*, The Institute of Gerontology, University of Michigan/Wayne State University.

Speed, M. (1967) 'The Future Development of Welfare Services for the Aged', in Report of a conference on *Prospects for the Elderly*, Devon County Council, mimeo, pp. 63–7.

Spender, D. (1983) *There's Always Been A Women's Movement this Century*, London, Pandora Press.

SSAC (1983) *Second Report 1982/83*, London, HMSO.

Stacey, M. and Price, M. (1981) *Women, Power and Politics*, London, Tavistock.

Stanley, J. (1983) 'The Building Societies and Home Improvement', in Building Societies Association (ed.), *Rehabilitation of Owner-Occupied Homes*, London, BSA, pp. 21–7.

Stearns, P. (1975) *Lives of Labour*, London, Croom Helm.

Stearns, P. (1977) *Old Age in European Society*, London, Croom Helm.

Stevenson, O. (1981) *Specialisation in Social Services Teams*, London, Allen & Unwin.

Stevenson, O. and Parsloe, P. (1978) *Social Services Teams: The Practitioners' View*, London, HMSO.

Storey, J.R. (1983) *Older Americans in the Reagan Era: Impacts of Federal Policy Changes*, Washington, C.S., The Urban Institute Press.

Stott, M. (1981) *Ageing for Beginners*, Oxford, Basil Blackwell.

Supplementary Benefits Commission (1977) *Low Incomes*, London, HMSO.

Supplementary Benefits Commission (1978) *Annual Report 1977*, London, HMSO.

Supplementary Benefits Commission (1980) *Annual Report 1979*, Cmnd. 8033, London, HMSO.

Szinovacz, M. (ed.) (1982) *Women's Retirement: Policy Implications of Recent Research*, Sage yearbooks in women's policy studies, vol. 6, Beverly Hills, Sage Publications.

Talmon, Y. (1961) 'Ageing in Israel, A Planned Society', *American Journal of Sociology*, vol. LXVII, no. 3.

Talmon, Y. (1963) *Dimensions of Disengagement: Ageing in Collective Settle-*

ments, Paper given at research seminar on social gerontology, Markaryd, Sweden.

Talmon, Y. (1972) *Family and Community in the Kibbutz*, Cambridge, Mass., Harvard University Press.

Taylor, G.F., Eddy, T.P. and Scott, D.L. (1971) 'A Survey of 216 Elderly Men and Women in General Practice', *Journal of the Royal College of General Practitioners*, vol. 21, pp. 267–75.

Taylor, R. and Ford, G. (1983) 'Inequalities in Old Age: an Examination of Age, Sex and Class Differences in a Sample of Community Elderly', *Ageing and Society*, vol. 3, no. 2, pp. 183–208.

Thane, P. (1978) 'The Muddled History of Retiring at 60 and 65', *New Society*, 3 August, pp. 234–6.

Thatcher, M. (1981) Speech to WRVS National Conference 'Facing the New Challenge', Monday, 19 January.

Thomson, D. (1981) *Provision for the Elderly in England 1830–1908*, University of Cambridge, PhD, 1981.

Thomson, D. (1983) 'Workhouse to Nursing Home: Residential Care of Elderly People in England Since 1840', *Ageing and Society*, vol. 3, part 1, pp. 43–70.

Thompson, A. (1949) 'Problems of Ageing and Chronic Sickness', *British Medical Journal*, 30 July, pp. 250–1.

Thompson, C. and West, P. (1984) 'The Public Appeal of Sheltered Housing', *Ageing and Society*, vol. 4, Part 3, pp. 305–26.

Tibbitts, C. (1960) *Handbook of Social Gerontology*, Chicago, University of Chicago Press.

Tiberi, D.M., Schwartz, A.N. and Albert, W.C. (1977) 'Envy versus Greed: Proposed Modifications of Medicare Policy', *Long-Term Care and Health Services Administration Quarterly*, pp. 275–83.

Tinker, A. (1981) *The Elderly in Modern Society*, London, Longman.

Tinker, A. (1984) *Staying at Home: Helping Elderly People*, London, HMSO.

Titmuss, R.M. (1955) 'Age and Society: Some Fundamental Assumptions', in *Old Age in the Modern World*, Report of the Third Congress of International Association of Gerontology, Edinburgh, Livingstone, pp. 46–9.

Titmuss, R.M. (1963) *Essays on the Welfare State*, 2nd edition, London, Allen & Unwin.

Titmuss, R.M. (1968a) *Commitment to Welfare*, London, Allen & Unwin.

Titmuss, R.M. (1968b) 'Community Care: Fact or Fiction?' in *idem.*, *Commitment to Welfare*, London, George Allen & Unwin, pp. 104–9.

Tobin, S.S. and Leiberman, M.A. (1976) *Last Home for the Aged*, London, Jossey-Bass.

Tolbert, C., Horan, P.M. and Beck, E.M. (1980) 'The Structure of Economic Segmentation: A Dual Economy Approach', *American Journal of Sociology*, vol. 85, no. 5, pp. 1095–116.

Townsend, P. (1962) *The Last Refuge*, London, Routledge & Kegan Paul.

Townsend, P. (1963) *The Family Life of Old People*, Harmondsworth, Penguin.

Townsend, P. (1972) 'The Needs of the Elderly and Planning of Hospitals', in Canvin, R.W. and Pearson, N.G. (eds), *Needs of the Elderly for Health and Welfare Services*, University of Exeter.

Townsend, P. (1979) *Poverty in the United Kingdom*, Harmondsworth, Pelican Books.

Townsend, P. (1981) 'The Structured Dependency of the Elderly: The Creation of Social Policy in the Twentieth Century', *Ageing and Society*, vol. 1, no. 1, pp. 5–28.

Townsend, P. and Davidson, N. (1982) *Inequalities in Health*, London, Pelican.

Townsend, P. and Wedderburn, D. (1965) *The Aged in The Welfare State*, London, Bell.

Treasury (1978) *The Government's Expenditure Plans 1979/80 to 1982/3*, Cmnd. 7439, London, HMSO.

Treasury (1984) *The Next Ten Years: Public Expenditure and Taxation into the 1990s*, Cmnd. 9189, London, HMSO.

Tulloch, A.J. and Moore, V.A. (1979) 'A Randomised Controlled Trial of Geriatric Screening and Surveillance in General Practice', *Journal of the Royal College of General Practitioners*, vol. 29, pp. 733–42.

Ungerson, C. (1983a) 'Why Do Women Care?', in J. Finch and D. Groves (eds), pp. 31–50.

Ungerson, C. (1983b) 'Women and Caring: Skills, Tasks and Toboos', in E. Gamarinkow, D. Morgan, J. Purvis and D. Taylorson (eds), *The Public and the Private*, London, Heinemann, pp. 62–77.

US Bureau of the Census (1983) *Statistical Abstract of the United States: 1984*, (104th edn), Washington, D.C., US Government Printing Office.

Van Krieken, R. (1980) 'The Capitalist State and the Organisation of Welfare: an Introduction', *The Australian and New England Journal of Sociology*, vol. 16, no. 3, pp. 23–35.

Vaswani, N., Parker, C. and Mitchell, K. (1978) *OR study of the Care of the Elderly in Calderdale: report of the operational research service of the DHSS*, ORS Note 41/77, March.

Vaughan-Morgan, J. *et al.*, (1952) *The Care of Old People*, London, Conservative Political Centre.

Verbrugge, L.M. (1984) 'Longer Life But Worsening Health? Trends in Health and Mortality of Middle-Aged and Older Persons', *Milbank Memorial Fund Quarterly*, vol. 62, no. 3, pp. 516–19.

Vladek, B.C. (1980) *Unloving Care: The Nursing Home Tragedy*, New York, Basic Books.

Wade, B. and Finlayson, J. (1983) 'Drugs and the Elderly', *Nursing Mirror*, 4 May, pp. 17–21.

Wade, B., Sawyer, L. and Bell, J. (1983) *Dependency with Dignity*, London, Bedford Square Press.

Walker, A. (1976) *Living Standards in Crisis*, London, Disability Alliance.

Walker, A. (1980) 'The Social Creation of Poverty and Dependency in Old Age', *Journal of Social Policy*, vol. 9, no. 1, pp. 45–75.

Walker, A. (1981a) 'Community Care and the Elderly in Great Britain: Theory and Practice', *International Journal of Health Services*, vol. 11, no. 4, pp. 541–57.

Walker, A. (1981b) 'Towards a Political Economy of Old Age', *Ageing and Society*, vol. 1, no. 1, pp. 73–94.

Walker, A. (1981c) 'Social Policy, Social Administration and the Social Construction of Welfare', *Sociology*, vol. 15, no. 2, pp. 225–50.

Walker, A. (ed.) (1982a) *Community Care: The Family, The State and Social Policy*, Oxford, Basil Blackwell & Martin Robertson.

Walker, A. (1982b) 'The Meaning and Social Division of Community Care', in A. Walker (ed.), pp. 13–39.

Walker, A. (1982c) 'Dependency and Old Age', *Social Policy and Administration*, vol. 16, no. 2, pp. 115–35.

Walker, A. (1982d) 'Why We Need a Social Strategy', *Marxism Today*, September, pp. 26–31.

Walker, A. (1982e) 'The Social Consequences of Early Retirement', *The Political Quarterly*, vol. 53, no. 1, pp. 61–72.

Walker, A. (ed.) (1982f) *Public Expenditure and Social Policy*, London, Heinemann.

Walker, A. (1983a) 'Care for Elderly People: a Conflict Between Women and the State', in J. Finch and D. Groves (eds), pp. 106–28.

Walker, A. (1983b) 'A Caring Community', in H. Glennerster (ed.), *The Future of the Welfare State: Remaking Social Policy*, London, Heinemann Educational Books, pp. 157–72.

Walker, A. (1983c) 'Social Policy and Elderly People in Great Britain: the Construction of Dependent Social and Economic Status in Old Age', in A. Guillemard (ed.) *Old Age and the Welfare State*, Beverly Hills, Sage Publications, pp. 143–67.

Walker, A. (1984a) 'Conscription on the Cheap: Old Workers and the State', *Critical Social Policy*, Issue no. 11, Winter, pp. 103–110.

Walker, A. (1984b) 'The Political Economy of Privatisation', in J. Le Grand and R. Robinson (eds), *Privatisation and the Welfare State*, London, Allen & Unwin, pp. 19–44.

Walker, A. (1984c) *Social Planning*, Oxford, Martin Robertson/Basil Blackwell.

Walker, A. (1985a) 'Care of Elderly People', in R. Berthoud (ed.), *Challenges to Social Policy*, London, Gower.

Walker, A. (1985b) 'From Welfare State to Caring Society? The promise of informal support networks', in J.A. Yoder, J.M.L. Jonker and R.A.B. Leaper (eds), *Support Networks in a Caring Community*, Dordrecht, Martinus Nijhoff, pp. 41–58.

Walker, A. (1985c) *The Care Gap: How can local authorities meet the needs of the elderly?*, London, Local Government Information Unit.

Walker, A. (1985d) 'Early Retirement: Release or Refuge from the Labour Market?', *The Quarterly Journal of Social Affairs*, vol. 1, no. 3, pp. 211–29.

Walker, A. (1985e) 'Making the Elderly Pay', *New Society*, 18 April, pp. 76–8.

Walker, A. and Laczko, F. (1982) 'Early Retirement and Flexible Retirement', in House of Commons Social Services Committee, *Age of Retirement*, HC 26–II, London, HMSO, pp. 211–29.

Walker, A., Winyard, S. and Pond, C. (1983) 'Conservative Economic Policy: the Social Consequences', in D. Bull and P. Wilding (eds), *Thatcherism and the Poor*, London, CPAG, pp. 13–26.

Walker, C. (1984) *The Reform of the Supplementary Benefit Scheme*, Leeds University, Department of Social Policy and Health Services Studies.

Walker, R., Lawson, R. and Townsend, P. (1984) *Responses to Poverty: Lessons from Abroad*, London, Heinemann.

Ward, R.A. (1984) *The Ageing Experience: An Introduction to Social Gerontology*, 2nd edn, New York, Harper and Row.

Weaver, T., Willcocks, D.M. and Kellaher, L.A. (1985a) *The Business of Care: A Study of Private Residential Homes for Old People*, Polytechnic of North London, Centre for Environmental and Social Studies in Ageing.

Weaver, T., Willcocks, D.M. and Kellaher, L.A. (1985b) *The Pursuit of Profit and Care: Patterns and Processes in Private Residential Homes for Old People*, Polytechnic of North London, Centre for Environmental and Social Studies in Ageing.

Webb, S. and Webb, B. (1929) *English Poor Law History. Part II: The Last Hundred Years*, vol. I, private subscription.

Wedderburn, D. (1973) 'The Aged and Society', in J.C. Brocklehurst (ed.), *Textbook of Geriatric Medicine and Gerontology*, Edinburgh, Churchill Livingstone, pp. 692–717.

Welford, A.T. (1958) *Ageing and Human Skill*, London, Oxford University Press for the Nuffield Foundation.

Welford, A.T. (1976) 'Thirty Years of Psychological Research on Age and Work', *Journal of Occupational Psychology*, vol. 49, pp. 129–38.

Wenger, C. (1984) *The Supportive Network*, London, Allen & Unwin.

Wheeler, R. (1982) 'Staying Put: a New Development in Policy?', *Ageing and Society*, vol. 2, Part 33, pp. 299–329.

Wheeler, R. (1983a) 'Staying Put in Old Age: the Contribution of House Adaptations', *Design for Special Needs*, no. 30, pp. 16–18.

Wheeler, R. (1985a) 'Don't Move: We've Got You Covered', Institute of Housing, London.

Wheeler, R. (1985b) 'Missing the Target', *Roof*, September to October, pp. 25–7.

Wheeler, R. (1986) 'Home Equity Conversion: Development, Policy and Issues', *Housing Review*, vol. 35, no. 1, pp. 5–9.

Whitehead, T. (1978) *In the Service of Old Age: The Welfare of Psychogeriatric Patients*, Aylesbury, HM & M.

Wicks, M. (1978) *Old and Cold*, London, Heinemann.

Wicks, M. (1982) 'Community Care and Elderly People', in A. Walker (ed.), pp. 97–117.

Wilding, P. (1982) *Professional Power and Social Welfare*, London, Routledge & Kegan Paul.

Wilding, P. (1983) 'The Evolution of Social Administration', in P. Bean and S. MacPherson (eds), *Aproaches to Welfare*, London, Routledge & Kegan Paul, pp. 1–15.

Wilkin, D. (1983) 'The Mix of Lucid and Confused Residents', DHSS Seminar Papers in Residential Research, October.

Wilkin, D., Hughes, B. and Evans, G. (1982) 'Better Homes for the Elderly', *Community Care*, 6 May.

Wilkin, D. and Jolley, D.J. (1979) *Behavioural Problems Among Old People in Geriatric Wards, Psychogeriatric Wards and Residential Homes, 1976–1978*, Research Section, Research Report no. 1.

Wilkin, D., Mashiah, T. and Jolley, D.J. (1978) 'Changes in Behavioural Characteristics of Elderly Populations of Local Authority Homes and Long-stay Hospital Wards (1967–77)', *British Medical Journal*, vol. 44, pp. 1274–6.

Wilkin, D. and Metcalfe, D.H.H. (1984) 'List Size and Patient Contact in General Medical Practice', *British Medical Journal*, vol. 50, pp. 1501–5.

Wilkin, D., Metcalfe, D.H.H., Hallam, L., Cooke, M. and Hodgkin, P.K. (1984) 'Area Variations in the Process of Care in Urban General Practice', *British Medical Journal*, vol. 289, pp. 229–32.

Willcocks, D.M. (1983a) *Gender and the Care of Elderly People in Part III Accommodation*, Paper presented at the British Society of Gerontology Annual Conference at the University of Liverpool, September.

Willcocks, D. (1983b) *Gender Differences in Part III*, Conference paper given to International and Cross-Cultural Studies in Ageing Conference, Dubrovnik, May.

Willcocks, D. (1983c) *Residential Homes as Community Care: A Future Place For Old People's Homes in the Community They Serve*, DHSS Seminar Papers on Residential Research, October.

Willcocks, D. (1984a) 'Changing the Face of Day Care', Paper presented to Harlow Local Authority Day Conference on Day Care, 19 October.

Willcocks, D. (1984b) 'Consumer Research in Old People's Homes', *Research Policy and Planning*, vol. 2, no. 1.

Willcocks, D.M., Peace, S.M., Kellaher, L.A. with Ring, A.J. (1982) *The Residential Life of Old People: a Study of 100 Local Authority Homes*, Research report no. 12, Survey Research Unit, Polytechnic of North London.

Williams, D.W. (1982) *Social Security Taxation*, London, Sweet & Maxwell.

Williams, I. (1979) *The Care of the Elderly in the Community*, London, Croom Helm.

Williamson, J. *et al.* (1964) 'Old People at Home: Their Unreported Needs', *The Lancet*, no. 1, pp. 1117–20.

Wilson, E. (1973) 'Caring for an Ageing Population: the Problems for Society', *Nursing Times*, vol. 69, no. 14, pp. 486–8.

Wilson, E. (1977a) *Women and the Welfare State*, London, Tavistock Publications.

Wilson, E. (1977b) 'Women in the Community', in M. Mayo (ed.) *Women in the Community*, London, Routledge & Kegan Paul, pp. 1–11.

Wilson, E. (1982) 'Women, the "community" and the "family"', in A. Walker (ed.), pp. 40–55.

Wirz, H. 'Sheltered Housing', in Lishman, J. (ed.) (n.d.) Developing

Services for the Elderly: Research Highlights no. 3, Aberdeen University.

Wood, J. (1983) 'Are the Problems of Primary Care in Inner Cities Fact or Fiction?', *British Medical Journal*, vol. 286, pp. 1109–12.

World Health Organisation (1970) *The Social Sciences in Medical Education*, Copenhagen, WHO Regional Office for Europe.

Wright, F. (1983) 'Single Carers: Employment, Housework and Caring', in J. Finch and D. Groves (eds), pp. 89–105.

Wright, K.G., Cairns, J.A. and Snell, M.C. (1981) *Costing Care*, Social Service Monographs: Research in Practice, Sheffield University.

Younghusband Working Party (1959) *Report of the Working Party on Social Workers in the Local Authority Health and Welfare Services*, London, HMSO.

Zabalza, A., Pissarides, C. and Barton, M. (1980) 'Social Security and the Choice between Full-time and Part-time Work and Retirement', *Journal of Public Economics*, vol. 14, pp. 245–76.

Index